REQUIEM FOR A COLLEGE

Jonathan Nichols

ISBN 9798825403311

Dedication

For my beautiful wife, Debbie and our beloved dogs, Chewie and Butterscotch. You are why I survived this.

For my wonderful parents, John and Connie Nichols. You are *how* my family survived this. God bless and love you.

For Bob Neville and Mark Nestor. Your guidance, wisdom, and insight made this possible.

For Justin, Jose, Alex, Stephen, and Nate. Young men who had every reason to move on, but chose to stay and fight instead. Freedom Fighters!

For every former faculty member uprooted from home and moved to another city or state, for every former professor forced to adjunct, for every former employee still struggling financially, for every former student who had to switch schools, for every former student who did a fifth year of college because not all credits transferred, and for every former student who dropped out of college because they could not afford a fifth or sixth year…this is for you.

Cover photography by Fr. Tim McFarland.

Special thanks to: Colby Alexis and Brienne Hooker.

Table of Contents

Works Cited

"When you want to know how things really work, study them when they're coming apart."

--William Gibson

Dramatis Personae

SAINT JOSEPH'S COLLEGE

FACULTY

Brian Capouch Professor Emeritus, Computer Science

Dr. Anne Gull Professor of Chemistry

Jordan Leising Assistant Professor of Political Science

Dr. Michael Nichols Associate Professor of Philosophy

Dr. Michael Steinhour Assistant Professor of Sociology

Dr. April Toadvine Associate Professor of English

Chad Turner Assistant Professor of History

Dr. Bill White Professor of History

STUDENTS

Jose Arteaga Senior communications and political science major

Justin Hays Senior psychology major

Alexander McCormick Senior chemistry major and senior class president.

Stephen Nickell Senior political science major

Jared Smith Senior philosophy major and Student Body President

Nate Wade Senior political science major

ADMINISTRATION

Dr. Robert Pastoor President

Dr. Chad Pulver Vice-President for Academic Affairs

Spencer Conroy Vice-President for Business Affairs

Dr. Tom Ryan Associate Vice-President for Academic Affairs

Kris Sakelaris

Carol Wood

ALUMNI

Jackie Bradway Director of Communication for Alumni Association

"THE GANG OF FOUR"

Doug Monforton CEO of Michigan Chemical Products

Paul Muller CEO of OA Finance

Mark Nestor President of ICRMS Management Consulting

Bob Neville President of The Neville Group

FACULTY AND STUDENTS FROM OTHER COLLEGES

Dr. John Ashbrook Professor of History, Sweet Briar College

Dr. Camilla Smith Barnes Professor of Mathematics, Sweet Briar College

Justin Carlson Student, Dowling College

Milt Heinrich Professor of Art, Dana College

Jeanne Kay Student and activist, Antioch College

Dr. Hassan Rahmanian Professor of Economics, Antioch College

FAMILY

Debbie Carnahan-Nichols Wife

Connie Nichols Mother

Dr. John Nichols Father

Dr. Michael Nichols Brother

CHAPTER ONE: Playing cards while the bomb ticks

HELL IS REAL.

At least that's what the billboard says. It's a pitch-black affair with those three words painted white in giant, block lettering. The sign faces southbound traffic on Interstate 65 just west of Hebron, Indiana. The rural octogenarian who sponsored the ad asserts that she did not intend it to cause trouble, but only to bring the word of Jesus to travelers.[1] Upon encountering the billboard…and you really can't miss it…motorists might well wonder about Indiana. I used to see the billboard at the beginning and the end of every week, unaware of what its message would mean to me in early 2017.

On the cold morning of Monday, January 9th, 2017, I pried myself out of bed before dawn in my suburban Chicago home. It was a routine. I would leave my wife, Debbie, and our two dogs, and I would return late the following Friday. She would remain at home for she needed to care for family in the suburbs. Not an ideal situation to say the least. It took both an important job and an important place to take me away from them each week.

That place was Saint Joseph's College. That job was professor.

As a dim sun rose, painting the icy sky in fluorescent hues, I passed the "Hell" sign. That meant my drive of just over 100 miles neared its end. There was not much to see on the drive. The surrounding land is quite flat, allowing for wide, expansive vistas of corn and soybean fields, small herds of cattle plus the occasional horse, and a whole lot of green trees. That January morning, all such foliage long since fell away for the winter and the fields all laid empty.

I took the northernmost Rensselaer exit off of I-65 and turned left onto Highway 114, heading east. After passing the rows of fast food establishments that tend to spring up near interstates, I once again drove between farmers' fields. Mud littered the road in places, fallen from large, tractor tires after the melt of a recent snowfall. That morning, however, the clumps were frozen after overnight temperatures plummeted. Even through rolled up windows I smelled the dirt. Sometimes you can also smell manure or rotting cornstalks, all depending on season.

Soon I approached the Jasper County Sheriff's station and county jail on my left and I checked my speed. I might arouse suspicion, speeding while sporting plates from Illinois (pronounced "Ill-e-noise" by many locals.) A neon green poster board caught my eye to the right, stapled to a telephone pole and bearing a message handwritten in black magic marker: "FAST INTERNET" and then a phone number. Houses appeared fast and grew denser in clusters. Most of them were ranches but the deeper into town, the two-story and the split-level home became more common. I followed the green sign for Saint Joseph's College and turned right, headed down College Avenue, one of the small town's "main drags" of stores and eateries.

I arrived at the college campus, greeted first by its many trees, all looking that January morning as mammoth, dead sticks stuck in the ground by playful kids. In warmer months they would explode in green, along with the rolling, manicured lawns punctuated by marble statues of clergy and holy figures. There is also the omnipresent red on campus, no matter the climate. Most every campus building has a red brick exterior. During warmer months, ivy grows on a few of these bricks, completing an almost stereotypical collegiate milieu. In the fall, the setting sun falling on the walls gives the bricks an auburn glow.

As I passed the sleeping black oaks lining College Avenue, I could see the football field and the Hanson Recreation Center and Scharf Field House complex for athletics, the word "PUMAS" emblazoned in purple on the awning of the fieldhouse front entrance. The "Puma" was the mascot of Saint Joseph's College, a moniker held by no other college in the United States at the time. It became the official Saint Joe mascot in 1939 as rumors flew that an actual puma stalked the environs of Rensselaer.[2]

That puma never seemed to materialize. No matter. The rumor of a beastly cat on the loose came to be associated with the College anyway and the "Pumas" nickname was thereafter applied to all sports teams, students, alumni, or really anyone connected to the College. In 1962, a student named Joe Daleiden ran a campaign for junior class treasurer, promising to bring a real live puma to campus for homecoming. He delivered. The three-month old puma cub Daleiden acquired was "friendly enough," but found gleeful enjoyment in shredding both clothing and skin with its claws. The College did not allow the puma to be kept into adulthood, but that is perhaps unfortunate. Passing through the campus gates, one could almost imagine a full-grown puma stalking between the many trees, living as the institution's spirit animal and protector.[3]

I turned right and drove onto campus, dodging a deep crack in the college pavement grown worse from the elements and neglect. The weaving maneuver allowed for a quick admiring of both the frozen reflecting pond and the Chapel on the left. The term "chapel" might seem a misnomer as it conjures images of a tiny church or a room-sized place of worship tucked into a hospital or army base. Such notions belie the grandeur of the Romanesque, twin-spired, cathedral-like structure that forms the visual centerpiece of Saint Joseph's College. Across from the Chapel sat the three-story Science Building. In August, the open lawn in front of the building would be striped with white lines and serve as a practice field for the marching band.

The Banet Core Educational Center, or "the Core Building" as most of us called it, was my true destination as it housed both my office and my classrooms for the day. I parked in the building's lot, my car's nose pointed towards the Halleck Student Center. Most every Puma came to Halleck as that is where the cafeteria, or "the caf," is. Complaining about the food is an old Saint Joe pastime, but that never seemed to stop a line from snaking up the Halleck steps on "chicken nugget day." A couple hundred students would wait and wind their way into the caf, trying to get the nuggets while hot and slather them with precious barbecue or honey mustard sauce.

You could always recognize the students. Being a student body of 60% athletes, they wore their own Puma "uniform" of sorts, regardless of gender: sweats, burgundy Puma starter jackets, and bouncy-soled Nike or Adidas flip flops with thick sports socks…the footwear of choice even in the snow and chill of winter.

And I can assure you, winters do get cold in Indiana.

A frigid wind swept across the parking lot. I noticed I just parked next to my colleague, Chad Turner.[4]

Chad wrapped a scarf around his neck and adjusted his black-framed glasses. Peeking out from beneath his coat I could see his usual bow tie and jacket. A friendly young guy, he came to Saint Joe in 2015 after doing graduate work in New York City. As a fellow lover of New York, I would often check in on how he was doing with the transition from the nation's largest city to a few of the nation's remotest cornfields and cow pastures. He would chuckle and say something to the effect of, "if it doesn't kill you, it makes you stronger."

But both Chad and his wife Jess grew up in the Midwest. In fact, Jess and her family hailed from Mishawaka, Indiana, just to the north. As their parents aged and as milestone events in the lives of siblings, nieces, and nephews passed by, both Chad and Jess yearned to go home.

"26-year-old single Chad loved New York, but 34-year-old married Chad was ready to get out of the city. Jess also really wanted to get out of her corporate job and start a handmade party goods business." he told me.

As fortune would have it, he spotted an ad for the position of Assistant Professor of History at a small college in Indiana. In April of 2015, Jess and Chad went to stay with family in Mishawaka and Chad made the drive to Saint Joseph's College for the interview. The drive down from Mishawaka is about an hour and 45 minutes, and most of it is very rural.

"I remember thinking, 'Wow, this place is in the middle of nowhere!'" Chad said. "I pulled onto campus on this unseasonably chilly May morning and parked by the Halleck Center. I didn't really know where I was going so I went in to ask."

The first person he met was Saint Joe's head of security.

"He was very friendly and helpful and I remember that, as I was leaving, he wished me good luck and said that he hoped I got the job," Chad said.

As is often the case in academics, the interview process took the entire day. Chad didn't mind, however. Saint Joe already started to grow on him.

"I think what I liked is that it felt like they were all trying to sell me on the school being a good fit for me as much as I was trying to sell them on me being a good fit," he said.

On Monday, May 18th, Chad and Jess were back in New York City. Chad's cellphone rang and caller ID showed a number with a 219 area code.

"I knew exactly, who it was," Chad said.

Nervous, he answered the call. Saint Joseph's College made him an offer to be full-time faculty. He accepted.

"Jess and I went to a local restaurant for dinner and had a bucket of beers to celebrate," Chad said. "I was so excited. I had beaten the odds in a terrible job market. We would be living an hour and forty five minutes from Jess's family and two and a half hours from mine. Close enough, but not too close, you know?"

Despite coming from a large public university, he took to the tight-knit group of faculty at the small private college with relative ease.

"People who were so patient and helpful as I peppered them with questions," Chad said. "Every walk down the hall resulted in stopping to have conversations with folks along the way. I quickly felt like I had found a place where I fit well," he said. "I really felt connected to my fellow faculty and with my students in a way that I did not feel at other institutions. Very early on, people began to tap me for my knowledge of medieval history, and started preparing me to take over a leadership role."

The faculty comradery, the active support the administration gave in helping him buy a home in Rensselaer, it all motivated Chad to contribute all he could to the College. He walked with me into the Core Building that first day of the semester eager to get to work.

Elsewhere, Brian Capouch[5] remained fast asleep that same Monday morning in his house out amid the rural vastness of Indiana. Something of Saint Joe's own version of Henry David Thoreau, Brian often extolled the virtues of nature, independent thought, and simple living. In something of a contrast, he devoted his academic study to computer science, becoming an expert on most forms of programming languages. In fact, he stayed up all through the previous night working on a new software project. He hit the bed around 4am.

--

“I get my best stuff done in the middle of the night,” Brian often said.

And he could afford to do that. Brian retired from Saint Joe in 2016, ending a career as a professor that spanned nearly 30 years. Wiry and with a head of thinning hair, his unquenchable drive to stay busy made going gentle into the good night of retirement, let alone getting more than four hours of sleep per night, anathema. He bought and restored several buildings in Monon and in his hometown of Medaryville, renting to tenants and tussling with town councils over ordinances from time to time. This led him to become an impromptu expert on the law, perhaps even enough to pass the bar. But that’s Brian. Once he becomes interested in a subject, he absorbs it like a sponge and can then give anyone a “memory dump” if asked even the slightest question. Renovating 100-year-old houses spurred him to research genealogy and thereby become a bona fide expert on local history. A lifelong passion for cooking led him to develop what may be Indiana’s largest private collection of restaurant-grade kitchen appliances.

Confirming such a claim would be difficult as precious few receive entry to Brian's bachelor pad situated deep in the country. He admits without hesitation to a scant amount of space with which to entertain guests, due to the fact of his ever-increasing collections of…everything. From those kitchen appliances to lawn mowers to stacks of newspapers going back decades.

"I have a narrow walkway," he once said, stressing those last two words with typical Capouch vigor. "If I turn sideways, I can slink past my newspaper stacks and reach my bedroom. But if I'm off just one fraction of an inch, I could knock everything over and find myself in the middle of one heinous mess."

He has a story for every occasion. So many stories in fact that friends and colleagues have often pressed him to write his memoirs. One such anecdote involved his acquisition of an ice blue 1968 Pontiac Bonneville. The vehicle's only detriment was that the speakers were inoperable. Undeterred, Brian took a genuine fighter pilot helmet he found at a surplus store and rigged cable from the Bonneville's console to the helmet's built-in radio system. Whenever he wanted to listen to music while driving, he donned the helmet. Ingenious though the contraption might have been, Brian later thought it better to trade in the Bonneville for 27 Muscovy ducks.

"And if you've ever seen a pair of them fuck, it is the ultimate animal copulatory act," Brian said.

It might have been just as well to have the waterfowl. The Bonneville no doubt would have joined the other vehicles that dotted Brian's property, including two Saturn coupes, three Saabs, a 1991 Chevy S-10, a 1970 Chevy C10, a 1985 Ford school bus modded out to be a portable tool room, and an old sedan that he let students paint over with all manner of graffiti in 1990. He called this car "The Emotional Rescue Mobile" after his favorite Rolling Stones album. The kids loved it.

Brian missed teaching with the ache of an open wound. In all honesty, he also missed faculty meetings. He could always be counted on to "speak truth to power," asking pointed and tough questions of administrators no matter who was holding the office. He made brutal inquiries about the soundness of college finances, the direction of strategic goals, and a demand for shared governance with the faculty. Part of this grilling represented a quest for honesty and transparency. Part of it was just the good old-fashioned fun of jabbing "the man" in the side from time to time.

Somehow, the brightest students on campus tended to gravitate to Brian. Once a week he would return to the cafeteria and have dinner with them, discussing issues of the day and learning of the students' recent exploits while telling stories of his own. Brian assured the students that despite retirement; he never stopped learning or being active in his chosen discipline. That January, Brian was preparing to present at OSCON—the O'Reilly Open Source CONvention—in May in Austin, Texas. Brian did 100% of his teaching with open source software tools. At OSCON he would demonstrate the uses of Electron, a project from GitHub that allows native applications to be developed using web development technologies.[6]

Justin Hays[7] emerged from his campus apartment that January morning, wearing his runner's leggings and his Patagonia hat as he crossed the intramural field. He kept stopping to chat with friends in impromptu, after break catch ups. One reminded him of a basketball game coming up soon. Justin wasn't on the team, but he would be there in the fieldhouse stands. Another mentioned rehearsals for an upcoming winter play. Justin was no actor, but he would be in the theater for one of the three shows. That's what Pumas do.

Justin is an "All-American Boy." That is a criminal act of cliché, but it really does sum him up. The tall, blond, and clean-shaven psychology student from Brownsburg, Indiana towed an extensive list of college accolades behind him. These included being twice named Division II Cross Country Academic All-American, three appearances on the Dean's List, the Department of Psychology's Academic Excellence Award, and more track and field trophies and records than there is room to mention. The previous month, he earned admittance to the prestigious Maurer School of Law at Indiana University. As exciting as that was, it left Justin with bittersweet feelings. In but a few short months he would graduate and leave Saint Joseph's College. It was hard for him to imagine time could have gone by so fast.

He felt an instant connection with the campus during his first visit as senior in high school. As he walked between the red brick buildings and the lush green trees, he knew he would be a Puma. Later, he would reflect that it was all about community. He vowed that even after graduating, he would never forget the memories made and "all of the friends who have become my brothers."

Once a Puma, a student gets woven into a fabric comprised of thousands of individuals bonded by a common experience. This experience is not a mere sharing of four years together in the same location, but also becoming part of a hundred years of joint service and participation combined with an education emphasizing moral reasoning and a responsibility to improve the human condition. To be a Puma is to be part of a family. Like most families, the constituent parts don't always get along that well, thus dispelling any unwarranted notions of Saint Joe's as a paradisiacal commune. But like many families, Pumas remain together, united over what matters to them and remaining "Involved for Life" as the College's publication tagline read.

Justin intended to live up to that slogan, but first he would enjoy every moment remaining in his time at the College.

“I was eager to make it memorable,” he said. “Savor every day, every night, and every weekend.”

He acquired senior housing that year in the campus apartments. Such real estate, as campus legend had it, would go a long way in creating “memorable” weekends with friends. Nevertheless, Justin would in no way allow good times to dull his performance in the classroom. He would remain a dedicated learner, assessing information with keen insight and offering his responses in his trademark calm, confident, and articulate manner.

I know this because Justin was one of my students.

This story is my story. It might even be one of the most unique tales in all of American higher education.

My first dim memories of life are of me by that reflecting pond I mentioned. I, along with my brother, grew up both in Rensselaer and on the campus of Saint Joseph’s College. We were there because of my father.

Dr. John Nichols came with his wife Connie to Rensselaer, Indiana in 1968 to teach philosophy at Saint Joseph’s

College. At the small Catholic college, he found an opportunity to help establish the kind of humanities curriculum he always wanted. It would be a liberal education program that would serve as a sort of "grand unified theory" of the academic disciplines. A Saint Joseph's student would not take individual, "cafeteria style" general education classes, but instead, through a continuous cycle of reading, discussing and writing, come to see literature, philosophy, history, politics, and other fields of academics as interconnected subjects making up the common human story.

It would be called the Core program. Through my father's work and the teamwork of many talented professors, it became Saint Joseph's College's crown jewel.

While I'm not quite as impressive, I was born about two years into the Core program's existence. My brother Michael arrived seven years later and both of us grew up in the public-school system of Rensselaer. As a professor's son, I turned out to be a skinny kid who loved books, computers, and *Star Trek* in a town where football and basketball were their own religions. Looking back, I'd probably have to put the blame for any bullying from the young Rensselaereans at 50/50. Besides being a geek with a capital "G," by high school I'd adopted a fashion sense based solely on emulating the members of Duran Duran.

I swore I would leave Rensselaer after high school and never come back.

I sure was wrong.

It is said that familiarity breeds contempt, but that did not happen with me and Saint Joseph's College. Something inside me recognized what the College could do for me and I knew I needed to be there. So, I confounded all my friends by choosing Saint Joe for my undergraduate degree. It was one of my smartest decisions, for I had many of my best years there, during which I met life-long friends and was exposed to the many ideas of the world. Not long after I graduated, my brother Michael followed the family path and attended Saint Joseph's. He met his wife Jeanette during his time there and married her in the Chapel. To further this unlikely story, each of us returned to our beloved College to teach. Older and possibly wiser, we considered our positions at Saint Joseph's to be dream jobs, and, through adult eyes, we even saw the appeal of Rensselaer. The town was clean, quiet, and safe, no small considerations for Michael, a father of two boys.

In the field of English studies, we call this “irony.”

I did smirk to myself with that very thought in my mind on the morning of January 9th, but I knew the College was a part of me and I was a part of it. I knew Michael felt much the same and somehow there we were, sharing with fellow faculty the responsibility of caring for and growing something our father helped build.

We, all the faculty, were building something…a college and a curriculum that would stretch well into the future.

Before the holiday break, the English Department met and discussed exciting new strategies to at last carry the department into the 21st Century. Michael became Dean of Core at the dawn of the academic year and just before that I took on the role of Director of Core One, our first semester program for freshmen. I was also directing Extended Core, a freshmen bridge program for students needing an extra academic boost before starting their college careers. New possibilities beckoned and through collaborative work with tremendous faculty members such as Chad Turner and student leaders like Justin Hays, Saint Joseph's College could flourish. I was doing work I loved, with people I loved, and for a place I loved. In retrospect, these were among the happiest days of my life.

It was all about to come to an end.

Alfred Hitchcock once said the definition of suspense is showing the audience a time bomb beneath a table where a group of people sit unaware and playing cards. That January, the faculty and students of Saint Joe's happened to be those card players. Something ominous lurked just outside of our sphere. Like Hitchcock's hidden bomb, it would wait, ticking away until its appointed time. When the counter decremented to zero the bomb would detonate, searing the landscape until all became unrecognizable.

We knew about the problems of course. You would have to be a special kind of oblivious not to. Financial issues plagued Saint Joseph's for decades, all the way back to when I was a student. As of that cold January morning in 2017, the College carried an egregious amount of debt, rumored to be somewhere more than $20 million. The reasons were myriad. Some known. Some speculated. Some spoken. Some unspoken. The construction of new buildings in the mid-1990s and renovations to old ones in the 2000s burdened the institution with this growing debt. Compounding matters was an enrollment level that remained either stagnant or falling at just under 1,000 students. Almost all the students we did recruit received high tuition discounts.[8]

Quite a set of challenges, to be sure, but they did not seem out of step with the obstacles that plagued most small, private colleges. We received assurances from our administration that while serious, the matters were not insurmountable, and years remained to handle them. Faculty held no direct control over finances, so the issues became the equivalent of potholes on Highway 114, or the compacted ice that built up in wintertime on Rensselaer side streets and alleyways.

"Man, somebody should do something about that. Who do we talk to?"

"Call your representative."

Or in this case, a Board of Trustees member. I had my own "in" with a Board member. My father served as a Trustee for many years. At family dinners, I would sometimes bring up the matter of the College's debt. He would tell me something that sounded like a financial plan, and with it being such, I confess that I never understood it.

"And if we do that, we can make our way out of it," he would say, referring to the debt.

"Great. Then when is this board actually going to *do* something?" my mother would counter.

My mother's comment echoed the sentiments of a few faculty members. Despite the assurances from the top and the malaise of "When has there *not* been a financial struggle?", something percolated in the undercurrent of the zeitgeist. American academicians as a whole could not help but notice the death toll of small schools from the previous decade. Moody's Investor Service published a prediction in September of 2015 that the closure rate of small colleges would triple in the coming years and the rate of mergers with larger universities would double.[9] Much of higher ed certainly took note of the study.[10]

The college closures of the 2000s did share certain commonalities, namely declining enrollments coupled with debt and deficits aggravated by high tuition breaks. Even larger for-profit institutions were not immune to the shifts in higher education. In fact, as Saint Joseph's College began the 2016-2017 academic year, ITT Technical Institute closed all of their franchise campuses.[11] That occurrence, devastating as it was to students, faculty, and employees of ITT, was viewed by analysts as yet one more dot on the downward-sloped line. As a not-yet-tenured professor, the fragile situation haunted me without question.

However, I can't say that college closures occupied much of my mind that sunny January morning, not in a dominant sense, anyway. I stood in line for the copier with my syllabi in hand and cursing myself for procrastination. A colleague in front of me in the queue turned around with an expressionless face.

"We had almost a whole month to get this done, didn't we?" she said.

Both of us laughed. I told her the wait at least gave me time to decide my setlist for songs I would play before lectures.

She said she liked my practice of connecting rock music to my lecture's theme and said she might start doing the same. We conjectured that in time we could have enough songs for a "Core 2 mix tape." The banter and laughter continued, expanding even to involve fellow faculty members who stopped into the room just to check their mailboxes, perpetuating that "first day of the new semester" energy and vibe.

Not a word about closed colleges, though. The same could not be said for all in America. For as we talked that morning, Dowling College sat vacant on the shores of Long Island, New York.[12]

The previous July, Dowling's Board of Trustees voted to close the college after conferring its final degrees on August 28th, 2016. Just as most other colleges welcomed students both new and old onto their campuses, Dowling College shut and locked its doors for the final time, its entryways barricaded. A skeleton staff of maintenance workers continued to mow lawns, keeping the grounds attractive to salivating real estate developers eyeing the former college's waterfront location for new residential properties.

--

Far to the west sat another set of empty husks once filled with professors and students. Dana College in Blair, Nebraska came to end on June 30th, 2010.[13] It fell prey to a familiar fanged, multi-headed monster of declining enrollment, shrinking endowment, and increasing debt. In the summer of 2017, I would make the acquaintance of Milt Heinrich[14] who taught art at Dana College for his entire professional life. That January morning as I prepared for class and drank my coffee, Heinrich drove into Blair for his own coffee. To do so, he needed to pass what remained of the Dana campus, the empty remains of a community to which he devoted his life.

"You have to mentally callous yourself," he would tell me. "August comes and school's supposed to start. But it doesn't. And it doesn't. Year after year it still doesn't. This has been like a death…and everything that comes with it."

One need not go so far east or west to find other such college cautionary tales. Just over the border from Indiana, St. Catharine College once stood in Kentucky. Less than a year before I stacked and separated syllabi that January morning, St. Catharine had spent 10% of its annual operating budget on financial aid. Enrollment declined from 600 to 475 students. Struggles ensued involving litigation with the U.S. Department of Education and by June of 2016, a gruesome decision needed to be made.[15]

"It is with great sadness that I announce today, after exploring all possible options, the Board of Trustees has determined the challenges facing St. Catharine College are insurmountable and we will be closing the college at the end of July," Board of Trustees chairman John Turner said.[16]

I could not fathom hearing that from our Chairman of the Board. The end of Saint Joseph's College? The idea of me, untenured and still earning a terminal degree, set adrift in the modern higher ed job market? The end of our community? The end of all my father worked for? This couldn't happen to us.

Could it?

Yet it happened to others. Three colleges. One moment they were there, the next they weren't, leaving behind a cluster of buildings, often old and run down after struggling for years from what boards and business staff termed "deferred maintenance", a warm blanket of euphemism if there ever was one. The empty, dusty structures awaited buyers to turn them into new educational facilities, or even demolish them to turn the land into golf courses the way things go today. For many, these closures gave cause to shrug shoulders or wag fingers at the troubles and deficiencies of current higher education.

For others though, the colleges represented entire lives.

Not every college that closes stays closed, though.

"Well, Sweet Briar was able to come back," a colleague once said to me.

She said this in the cafeteria as we discussed Saint Joseph's finances.

"What do you mean? That line of young adult novels for girls?" I asked.

She took a beat to look at me blank-faced before speaking.

"No. Sweet Briar College. You're thinking of *Sweet Valley High*."

Indeed, I was.

Sweet Briar College is an all-female school in Virginia. Set amidst bucolic hills and trees, the college featured a curriculum centered on the liberal arts. At one point, it even allowed students to bring their horse, if they had one, with them to college, quartering the equines in campus stables. On March 3rd, 2015, the Sweet Briar Board of Trustees announced by unanimous vote that it would close the following August.[17] The faculty, the students, and the alums, would not go quietly into the night, however.

"I couldn't be shut up," John Ashbrook, a Sweet Briar Professor of History would later tell me. "I gave interviews, wrote an op-ed piece in the Pittsburgh *Post-Gazette* about one of our former presidents, and made appearances at functions to keep the college open."[18]

Local media launched investigations and called on the board to resign.[19] Amherst County filed suit against the board, claiming the board was negligent in their fiduciary responsibilities to the college and in doing so had broken a number of Virginia laws.[20] Students and their parents launched a class-action lawsuit of their own[21] while alums organized and pushed back against the decision. In the end the fight was won.

The “Save Sweet Briar” slogan changed to a celebratory, “We Saved Sweet Briar”.

Antioch College achieved a similar triumph. Situated in the pastoral environs of Yellow Springs, Ohio, Antioch became somewhat legendary as an innovative school for the humanities and the liberal arts. Since its founding in 1850, Antioch boasted alums ranging from luminaries of humanity such as Coretta Scott King to Stephen Jay Gould to a few of my own personal heroes, such as Leonard Nimoy and Rod Serling. Antioch was known for being a community of faculty and students with fierce devotion to both one another and their college, and a spirit of activism to go forth and change the world for the better. Students there went through what they called “co-operative education,” where they were expected to not only attend classes but to work jobs as well. All of it came crashing down in June of 2007 when the Board of Trustees announced they did not have sufficient funds to continue and would close indefinitely at the end of the 2007-2008 academic year.[22]

“There was a very angry reaction,” Dr. Hassan Rahmanain said.[23]

Rhamanain felt loyalty to Antioch College for deep personal reasons. As he completed his PhD at the University of Pittsburgh in the late 1970s, his home nation of Iran plunged into revolution and he knew there would be no going back.

"Antioch offered me a home, a sense of community. I knew it was a place to fight for. At Antioch, students are politically active, part of change. They learn about the problems of the world and are then expected to go out and do something about them. So, both students and alums filled campus upon hearing the news. They *organized.* This surprised the Board of Trustees."

Alumni, students, and faculty fought a fight that lasted for years after the announcement. Following an unrelenting campaign of fundraising, political sparring, and legal negotiations, Antioch College achieved independence from its former board and emerged to accept students once again.[24] On that same January morning that found me juggling syllabi, warming my chilled fingers on them as they spat straight out of the copier, Antioch began a winter semester of teaching young people to "Be ashamed to die before you have won some victory for humanity" as their founder Horace Mann instructed.

Would the Saint Joseph's College community stand and fight if need be? The Sweet Briar and Antioch stories stirred the blood and inspired the spirit, but I held no interest in experiencing such fights firsthand. For every successful campus revolt, there existed too many other grim tales of colleges that did not come back.

But we would be different…or so we were told by our administrators. A strategic plan was in effect. We would "grow our way" out of the financial troubles. Already underway were combined efforts of fundraising and recruitment. As faculty members, our charge was to make our programs "revenue positive." We were given to understand that such corporate-speak translated to taking all possible measures to never have a class of fewer than eight students. Of course, faculty met this initiative with a modicum of grumbling as getting a collective of professors to agree on anything is something akin to herding cats. For people trained to have minds open to the ideas of the world, it's amazing how firm our opinions can sometimes be.

– –

Understandable in this case. Faculty and staff at the college already endured sacrifices such as stagnant wages, significant drops in retirement contributions, and daunting insurance deductibles. We all hoped these sacrifices would be temporary and through campus-wide collaboration, we would find ourselves in better days. It could be done. There were case studies to follow, not the least among those being Antioch and Sweet Briar as to how a small college can work together as a community and overcome bad times.

None of it was to be for Saint Joseph's College.

What follows on these pages is fundamentally a story of loss. It contains every aspect of a classic human drama to the point where it verges on the Shakespearean. There is hubris, and there are even bits of mendacity and cruelty thrown in for good measure. At the same time, there is the very best of what humanity has to offer. There is valor, there is love, and there is the strength of community.

Now, before anything else, we must look to history, both the institutional and the personal, and examine how everything came to be.

The Core program taught me that.

NOTES

1. Davich
2. Gerlach 145
3. Ibid.
4. I interviewed Professor Chad Turner on 3/28/2017 and by email on 4/11/2020. Notes in author's possession
5. I interviewed Brian Capouch several times, most extensively on 4/4/2017. Notes with author.

6. "Electron"
7. I interviewed Justin Hays many times over the course of a year and half, primarily on 3/30/2017. Notes in author's possession.
8. Saint Joseph's College Fact Book, p 4.
9. Woodhouse
10. "Small U.S. Colleges Feeling the Squeeze"
11. Puzzanghera and White
12. Booth and Bolger
13. Abourezk
14. I interviewed Milt Heinrich by phone in July 2017. Notes in author's possession.
15. Douglas-Gabriel
16. Blackford
17. Bidwell
18. I interviewed Dr. John Ashbrook by email in July 2017. Notes in author's possession.
19. Editorial board
20. Commonwealth of Virginia v. Sweet Briar Institute, Paul G. Rice, and James F. Jones Jr.
21. Pounds
22. Mytelka
23. I interviewed Dr. Hassan Rahmanian by phone in July 2017. Notes in author's possession.

24. Donahue

CHAPTER TWO: History…Institutional and Personal

It must have been around Easter.

I'm three years old. I'm holding a stuffed bunny whose body is something of a green unitard that is thready to the touch. Holding me is my Grandma. I tilt my head and rest it against her coat, the fuzzy, bumpy fabric pressed to my soft cheek. Grandma is talking to me, but the words now sound muffled, lost to the dimness of memory. My mother is also somewhere in the scene, but I don't quite remember where. The early spring air is cool but the sunlight on my face is warm. The light is bright, almost a whitish yellow, so I'm guessing it must be sometime in the morning. We are standing by the reflecting pond of the College with the Chapel to our backs.

That is my first memory as a human being. The fact that it is at Saint Joseph's College is both telling and central to everything I write in this book. Saint Joe was far more than an alma mater. It was far more than a job or even a career. It was home. I know more about and am far more bonded to both the people and the physical campus of Saint Joe than I am to the vast majority of my blood relatives and to most other places I've lived. How could that be? It all begins with my parents.

Dr. John Paul Nichols and Connie Neese arrived at Saint Joseph's College in 1968. They found a comfortable apartment in Rensselaer. On March 6th, my mother's parents, Maxine and Donald Neese, came to town and met my father by the Saint Joe reflecting pond. They followed Dad to a Christian church in Rensselaer where my parents were then married in a simple service with only my grandparents and the clergyman in attendance. In my youth, I never asked my parents about their wedding as the subject never really interested me, but as I interviewed them about their early days at Saint Joe, I found myself wishing for a little more pageantry for them. Various dignitaries, champagne, fireworks, maybe Dad dancing while playing the accordion. I don't know.

The reception celebration was, in truth, far more modest. My grandparents came to my parents' apartment where my mother proceeded to make everyone beef stroganoff for a wedding dinner. That was the extent of the nuptial revelries as Dad needed to get back to his academic duties at the College.

Almost all at once, the new couple began making friends with several of the faculty.

"The very first thing that impressed us about Saint Joe was what a friendly place it was," Dad said. "I was made to feel welcome immediately. I didn't have to prove myself in any way to earn that welcome."

This spirit of inclusiveness was essential for my mother. I tend to share her psychosocial makeup, meaning we're both shy and not what one would call social climbers. So, I have often felt for her in regard to what the experience of coming to a tight-knit community like Saint Joe must have been like for the daughter of Ohio farmers from a rural town with a population of 200.

"It was a totally new experience, hard to grab a hold of," Mom said. "It had its own distinct, unique identity."

Identities can be strong when an institution has been around for a while. By the time my parents got there, Saint Joseph's College was set to celebrate 79 years of educating minds since its founding by the Society of the Precious Blood.

Who are the Society of the Precious Blood and how did they get such an eyebrow-raising moniker? I will admit that I heard the name tossed around so much in my youth that I never gave it much overt thought, yet my subconscious always wondered why anyone would want “Blood” in the title of their organization as the word seldom connotes anything good going on. I mean, unless you’re a production house for horror films, I suppose. Well, the story behind the name and thus the very foundation of Saint Joseph’s College begins with St. Gaspar del Bufalo.

Fr. Dominic Gerlach, longtime Professor of History at Saint Joseph’s College and the author of an official history of the institution, described St. Gaspar this way: “He was a Roman priest who headed a group of missionaries in Rome to preach religious renewal in Italy after the French Revolution and the subsequent Napoleonic Wars had severely damaged people’s faith, both that of the clergy and the laity.”[1] St. Gaspar himself endured four years of exile and imprisonment after refusing to swear obedience to Napoleon, but returned, believing the renewal of the church and the restoration of the people’s faith to be his true calling from God.[2] As is the case with saints, St. Gaspar was said to have performed miracles. Almost every entry on his supernatural CV involves the healing of the sick, with one instance of a prime tobacco crop harvested well outside of season thrown in for good measure.[3]

Here's where the "blood" comes in. St. Gaspar organized his priestly followers under the name "Congregatio Pretiosissimi Sanguinis," or "Congregation of the Most Precious Blood," because "people responded so well to the suffering of Jesus as a sign of the great love by which He had redeemed them through the shedding of his blood on the cross."[4] To this day, members of the order add the initials C.PP.S. behind their names, referring to the original Latin title, and wear a large crucifix and chain at formal occasions as physical representation of their membership.[5]

Missionaries of the Precious Blood arrived in Rensselaer, Indiana to build a school in the late-19th Century that would serve the educational needs of Rensselaer and the surrounding communities. The institution began as St. Joseph's Orphan Asylum as the Civil War rendered great need for such institutions. The 1870 U.S. Census shows that 69 orphans called the school home in that year. Since this was the first, and only, parochial school in Jasper County, Indiana at the time, Catholics in the area began sending their own children there for an education. By 1876, the orphans transferred out to another location. As the institution was already transitioning from orphan home to educational facility, the Society of the Precious Blood saw an opportunity.[6]

Bishop Joseph Dwenger was bishop of Ft. Wayne, Indiana. He was one of the first Precious Blood priests to be born in America and established a name for himself as a builder of schools. He directed that the Rensselaer location become a college.[7]

On March 20th, 1889, the College published its "Act of Incorporation":

"The name of said college and theological institute shall be SAINT JOSEPH'S COLLEGE. The purpose of said institution shall be the education of young men in all branches of science and instruction secular as well as religious."[8] It was stated in the clearest of terms that the college "shall be immediately under the supervision and control of the Society of the Precious Blood..."[9]

“College life” at that time bore little to no resemblance to its modern-day counterpart. My friends and I spent our undergrad days complaining about cafeteria food, all while going back up to the line for more pizza with a trip past the salad bar and then washing it all down with milk and cookies. Students at Saint Joseph’s College in 1889 would’ve seen us as living in the lap of luxury. The early College needed to be self-sustaining. That meant all students at the institution aiding in daily chores such as the growing and harvesting of food on farmland and in vast gardens. These efforts also included tending to College livestock, such as hogs, cows, and turkeys. If any daylight remained after completing those tasks, resting was not an immediate option. A list of tasks still required attention, including firewood cutting, thatching, and ditch digging. This labor was not done for a paycheck or a college work/study program. It was done for survival.

This was not unusual. The insipient era of Saint Joseph’s College saw several variations on a similar theme. Christian missionaries moved to rural environs of the Midwest, finding flatlands, stony fields, and sheltering hills where they could build schools.

It happened in Ohio, as The Christian Connection, a religious collective that espoused no one creed and instead relied entirely on the Bible, later came to land in Yellow Springs in 1850 and decided to build a college upon it. In 1852, Antioch College opened with the legendary political reformer and architect of the American public school system, Horace Mann as its founder.[10]

It happened in Nebraska, as Dana College was formed in 1884 by Danish immigrants who had left the Conference of the Norwegian-Danish Evangelical Lutheran Church of America who came to that picturesque land overlooking the Missouri River Valley.[11]

It happened in Springfield, Kentucky in 1839, as the Kentucky Sisters of St. Dominic obtained a charter to grant educational degrees and a campus was built along Bardstown Road, today's U.S. Route 150. They built towards the time when they would be St. Catharine College, conferring two-year degrees from their own Roman Catholic liberal arts curriculum.[12]

In these landscapes, missionaries with a passion for education saw a vision of what could be: self-sustaining educational institutions providing liberal arts curricula to students and service to their surrounding communities. It would mean toiling brick by brick, but the buildings would go up. It would mean long days in fields, but the clergy and students alike would be fed. It would mean, at times, digging deep into pockets and treasuries, but the costs would be met. The colleges grew because those who sacrificed to build them and to lead students and faculty alike to prosperity, would not allow the colleges to do otherwise. Those who worked and sacrificed were, in many regards, the same hands that built America.

Reading through these histories, I would sometimes take a moment and reflect on my tiny place in it all. Most of the buildings of Saint Joseph's College dripped with a sense of antiquity. It wasn't just their age or the musty odor that came with the years. It was all the "ghosts", the knowledge and the near visceral sensation of those came before me and invested themselves, sometimes all of themselves, into a place that develops the mind. By teaching and devoting myself to my discipline and the humanities, I helped carry these intentions on into the future. I might be a tiny cog, but the machine was mighty and more important than me. I could not let it down…not after all the struggles and sacrifices the people of small colleges endured.

One of Saint Joseph's own worst tribulations took place in an era Fr. Gerlach called, "Crisis and Rebirth."[13] Like all small colleges, Saint Joseph's College took a beating during the Great Depression of the 1930s. Student bills did not get paid and enrollment began to shrivel. In 1932, the Board of Trustees decided to allow lay students to enroll at the college once more. This change did little to affect enrollment numbers and many C.PP.S. priests expressed that it was simply time to close the College. Father Joseph Kenkel, then president of the College, would hear none of that. To counter such blithe cynicism, he proposed a bold new plan to the Precious Blood. This plan was to convert Saint Joe to a four-year senior college as there was an emerging market for such a Catholic institution of higher learning.[14]

Though the College began to grow, it was not an easy fix. After retirement, Father Kenkel was asked if he knew the student nickname for him. He replied that he did and that it was "The Great Stone Face." He went on to explain his demeanor on campus: "What other expressions would be appropriate if you didn't know where the money was to come from to feed the students for the next day?" Indeed, breakfast in those lean times was limited to "shavings and belly wash," meaning corn flakes and a beverage sort of like coffee, but not really. Contemporary college students might consider this meal before complaining their cafeteria food offends their taste buds. This austerity, and especially Father Kenkel's stewardship, paid off in the long run and Saint Joe emerged from this time of difficulty to transform into a four-year institution fully accredited in 1950 by the North Central Accreditation of Colleges and Schools.[15]

While not quite Elysium, better days had most certainly arrived. They came about because of decisive leadership.

Like other religious schools, Saint Joseph's College gave its students a thorough indoctrination of the institution's principles. Throughout the existence of Saint Joseph's, these very guiding principles would be evidenced on the College's great seal: "Religios, Moralitas, Scientia." Those words must be in that precise order, as explained by Fr. Gerlach: "...it was a clear statement that in the College's motto, 'religio' was to take precedence over 'moralitas' and 'scientia.' Or, why else have a college?"[16]

Religion before morality.

The three components of the Saint Joe motto are best considered together while setting them square within the context of the human story. That was the pedagogical theory of Dr. John Nichols and that was what made him a perfect fit for the College.

Born to a Catholic family in Cincinnati, Ohio, my father went off to college at age 16 at the University of Dayton. He arrived to major in mathematics, but while in undergrad he also discovered literature, particularly in courses dealing with French literature and a "mind-opening course" in World Literature. He ended up graduating with a BA in philosophy. That launched him on an eastward trajectory across the Atlantic, landing in Switzerland.

"I went on to study Theology at the Catholic University of Fribourg, a leading international university with an outstanding Faculty of Theology," Dad told me. "My life-changing discovery there was *synthesis*."

He emphasizes that last word, squinting through his glasses and shaking his open hands. To hear him tell me this was eye opening. Dad seldom spoke much about his younger years. Friends in my teen years would chide me about his European travel combined with his taciturn ways, telling me he probably worked as a spy. There was no such excitement I'm afraid.

He was pursuing academic synthesis. "You're not just a citizen of America," Dad would tell me as a kid. "You're a citizen of the world. Hell, you're a citizen of the universe. A constantly evolving universe." This was the "synthesis" he spoke of, every single thing being part of a greater whole and needing to be considered together, and it is what I would later encounter in Core, thus making those comments in boyhood make sense.

The journey towards synthesis did not end in Fribourg. Far from it. From Switzerland, Dad went on to Belgium.

"I went to the Catholic University of Louvain to do a doctorate in Philosophy," Dad said. "To stick to my metaphor, Louvain added many other voices to the chorus of synthesis. I was putting it all together: saints, sinners, agnostics, and atheists. The years I was at Fribourg and Louvain were the years when the Second Vatican Council was in session down in Rome."

The Second Vatican Council took place between 1962 and 1965 with the intent of renewing the Catholic Church for a contemporary world. The new church would hold its masses in vernacular languages rather than Latin, prayers were reworked and reworded, clergy began to eschew ornate regalia, and most critical for Catholic education at Saint Joseph's College, there was a change in thinking. Vatican II stated that the church accepts all that is true and holy in non-Christian religions and called upon all to work towards a spirit of "Christian Humanism." Many professors at Louvain at the time were active experts at that Council, so that made the Council's openness to other religions, to all humanity literally, part of Dad's worldview. The message that Louvain and Vatican II taught him in particular was to respect history.

"What Louvain added to my previous commitment to synthesis was an equally powerful dedication to interdisciplinary inquiry," he said.

It turned out that "synthesis" and "interdisciplinary" were exactly what Saint Joseph's College wanted when my father arrived to teach philosophy in 1968.

An excitement permeated the air on the campus as faculty challenged the old paradigm of what a general education program should look like at the college level. The "same old, same old" would not do anymore at Saint Joseph's College and the atmosphere of both campus and the nation set the stage for the beginnings of something daring, maybe even as "radical" as the 1960s themselves. Just as Dad moved into his new office, a committee of faculty had already been hard at work on a proposal for this new program. It would become an educational curriculum that would set this small, Indiana college apart from any other higher education institution in the United States.

So to fully understand Saint Joseph's College and what made it unique in higher education, one must understand its curriculum. This understanding will, in time, allow one to also see that despite the academic quality and the amount of grant money the curriculum brought in, it may also have created a number of complex difficulties for the institution. Deep breath in, everyone. We're going to take a rollercoaster ride through what faculty call "curriculum development" and as any professor will tell you, it's a little like watching sausage get made.

John Groppe[17] along with his wife, Rosemary, moved to Saint Joseph's College in 1962 to teach English. He was therefore strategically placed to be among the very first faculty to "ride this new wave" hitting education and become one of the full-fledged catalysts in reinventing the Saint Joe curriculum. He, along with the other members of the faculty, would be charged with channeling and responding to changes not only in society such as the Civil Rights movement, but from within the Catholic Church itself.

"Vatican II hit the College in a significant way," Groppe said.

As Saint Joseph's College was the only Catholic college in its diocese, lay and church faculty knew it would play a special role in the implementation of Vatican II decrees in the community.

"We were re-thinking what it meant to be a Catholic intellectual," Groppe said. "We wanted to reflect Vatican II, but we also wanted to be distinctive."

This distinction, it was thought, should be something that would answer the question of "Why go to Saint Joe and not Ball State or Indiana University at Kokomo?" As Groppe explained, there was an opportunity to break out of the old mode of Catholic education in the United States. You could take a class in 1920 and the same one in 1950 and get the same lectures. General education was viewed by college and university students as "that stuff you get out of the way."

What if these courses could be meaningful instead? What if instead of isolated classes serving as mere boxes to check off for graduation, the general curriculum could show a relationship between fields of study? What if the curriculum started where the students are, in the contemporary situation, before jumping back anywhere in time? What if the general education program lasted throughout all four years of college, integrated and united many disciplines, all while complementing the student's major?

When I describe this kind of academic program to peers in higher education, their mouths often drop and they give me a look like I'm wearing a fish around my neck, just before they say, "We could never do that where I'm from." However, Saint Joseph's College possessed a unique advantage in addition to its small, homey size that would help make a curriculum like this happen.

"All of our priest faculty were already multi-disciplinary," Groppe said to me in a voice that hinted at his New York City roots. "They knew philosophy plus something else. So, the idea of being 'interdisciplinary' didn't seem so foreign to them."

A small enrollment came to be something of an advantage in this regard. Discussion classes could be capped at 12-14 students each. This allowed for not only intimate, in-depth discussion of the concepts and texts, but for students to get to know one another as individual views are debated and reconsidered. "I learned just as much from the person sitting next to me in class as I did from the professors," a student once said of Core. That student comment is but one of many testaments to the success of the program, but in the late 1960s, the viability of Core was anything but clear.

Having just arrived at the ground floor of Core in 1968, Dad could attest to that fact.

"The spirited debate over this proposal and all the changes it would demand in the total undergraduate set-up gave me a rapid and in-depth introduction to the entire academic scene at Saint Joe," he said. "There was much arguing, but there was also much *esprit de corps* and even euphoria about the possibility of doing something momentous. Still, some feared it wouldn't work. Some wanted to give up on it after just two or three semesters; but there was a critical mass of faculty members who just would not let it fail."

"I never heard specific stories, but I always knew when he'd get home, there had been an argument with someone," my mother said of that time. "But what was really attractive to me though, was that everyone was at least committed to the same idea. There was no disparity between the clerical and the lay faculty. There was integration."

In November 1968, the Faculty Assembly passed 60 to 20, a margin of three to one, the new Core Curriculum. The director would be Father William Kramer.

Then the truly arduous work began. Each of the ten new Core courses would be interdisciplinary and team-taught; their faculties would be responsible for teaching writing, encouraging discussion, and working toward integration of content into the concept of "Christian Humanism" that came out of the Second Vatican Council. A radically new type of academic community would have to be created to make this "true Core" succeed. Indeed, every faculty member at the College would have to be involved in teaching the curriculum because every professor's discipline and perspective would be essential to the "marketplace of ideas." This would no longer be a campus where an academic could say, "I teach English and that's it." They would also have to be involved in Core.

This meant teaching subject matter ranging from examining contemporary issues and ideas to finding their roots in ancient and medieval history and periods of thought such as the Enlightenment. It also involved the incorporation of scientific research to foster an understanding of humanity's place in the universe. It was also critical that non-Western cultures receive close examination. All of this then culminates in the senior year where students and faculty alike ponder the question, "What does it mean to live as a Christian Humanist?" This all stood as a challenge to faculty for it always meant that at one point or another in the semester, the professor would be out of his or her academic depth. That meant modeling for the students what an engaged learner does in order to come to an understanding of the material.

Thus, the full faculty of Saint Joseph's College sat down together to teach Core. This meant academics of, at face value anyway, disparate fields of study working in concert to cover a common curriculum. Biologists and chemists worked with humanities professors on how to best present the themes of Dante's *Inferno*. English and philosophy faculty gave their perspective along with scientists on the theory and practice of environmental sustainability. All of these subjects and all of these professors came together under one roof to present the human story viewed as a single beam of sunlight spread through a multidisciplinary prism. Lest this description give the false impression of complete harmony, it should be duly noted how "multidisciplinary" can also produce views in conflict. In the beginning, however, such conflicts fell to the wayside.

"We were so busy, there really wasn't any more time for arguments. We had to get this thing started for God's sake!" Groppe said. "When we first taught Core 1 [the first semester freshman class in the sequence], we hadn't planned Core 2 yet." he said.

As one might imagine, this did not allow much time for getting the entire faculty clear on pedagogical intent. Groppe spoke of a text the Core faculty agreed to adopt and one faculty member volunteered to lecture on it.

"And I'm sitting there in the balcony of the auditorium while he lambasts the book. Just blows it off the stage," Groppe said. "Yes, we could have used a little more discussion."

A mild way to put it, I thought. I couldn't help but place myself in Groppe's shoes as a faculty member. I doubt I could have kept myself from bellowing out, “Look, I’m all for diverse views, but we all agreed on this book and we’re trying to *build* something here, Ricky!”

That, however, was just the point. As with any new idea, Core did not go without constant revision. Dad took over as Core Director in 1973. He insisted that what could be “unique and powerful” about the Core program is that students could graduate from Saint Joe with eight semesters of their major study and eight semesters of Core. The courses of study would constantly bump up against one another, even further demonstrating that no discipline exists in a vacuum and that everything is connected. This did not come without its share of disagreements, failures, and revisions.

Among the objections was the nature of the audience: college students. A subsection of the faculty thought that the age group, fraught with the usual college distractions of sports, parties, and the tendency towards laziness in youth, could not succeed such an integrated curriculum focused on critical thinking. Other professors protested, arguing “I was hired to teach (fill in the blank), not Core!” This was often countered with, "Judging by enrollment, not many students want to take (fill in the blank). So, how will you earn your salary?"

"It was very hard to design each Core the first time around," Dad said, stressing the syllables in "very hard." "So faculty not yet in Core collected all student criticisms…and stimulated more negativity against Core themselves…trying to prove that Core was not 'academically respectable.'"

Would Core survive? Not just the established curriculum but the very idea of it? Decisions needed to be made by leadership. These decisions would chart the future of Saint Joseph's College. In 1976, Father Charles Banet, President of Saint Joseph's College, realized Core as the means to take the College into the coming decades and beyond, and made the decision to throw his full support behind the curriculum. Banet succeeded in convincing the Lilly Endowment to award Saint Joe $500,000 and to invite Saint Joe to join their "Continuing Conference for the Liberal Arts." This began a years-long series of grants to support the enormous amount of faculty development that was necessary to turn Core into a long-term success, meaning the provision of training that would help faculty feel more comfortable in the inevitable "blind spots" that crop up when teaching in an interdisciplinary curriculum.

In 1979, the National Endowment for the Humanities bestowed a grant to support a week-long institute on campus titled "On Designing a Core Curriculum." The announcement of the institute attracted eighty faculty and administrators from forty different institutions. Success has a way of breeding more success and approximately $5,000,000 in grants came to Saint Joe specifically for Core over the following 25 years from the federal government, foundations, and private individuals. The NEH issued Challenge Grants that ultimately put $3,000,000 in the College's endowment to support Core. At the same time, faculty began to get involved with different higher education associations, giving talks about Core and publishing articles about this program, resulting in Core becoming well known in higher ed circles.

It was around this point in my interview with Dad where I needed a break. Get coffee, walk around, or something. All the numbers and the acronyms and the…yeah, all the flora and fauna of academia and even sectors both public and private…I

- -

struggled to absorb it all. He really did all that? For the place where he worked? Such dedication to a workplace was, in all honesty, unheard of my experience and for many in my generation. Yet Dad did it. He kept doing it, too.

Since NEH had awarded several grants to Saint Joe by 1984, William Bennett, the NEH Chair and future Secretary of Education under both the Reagan and George H.W. Bush administrations, turned to Saint Joe when he was writing *To Reclaim a Legacy*. In that work espousing the value and the need for greater attention to the humanities in higher education, Dr. Bennett called Saint Joseph's College in Indiana "one of three bright spots in the nation" for humanities education, the other two "spots" being Brooklyn College and Kirkwood Community College.[18]

Due to this attention, other colleges sought advice as to how they might adopt a similar curriculum. Both Dad and John Groppe served on a blue-ribbon panel of Saint Joseph's College professors consulting for other colleges on constructing an interdisciplinary program that stretched across the curriculum. The idea received the same initial resistance at a few of these other institutions as it did at Saint Joe. Groppe recalls one such instance of skepticism from a professor of German.

"I asked this professor if her curriculum covered German art and history in addition to language," Groppe said. "She of course said that it did. Then I told her, 'Well then you're already being interdisciplinary. You're just not getting the benefit of expertise from other faculty in those fields."

All this work with Core gave my father experience with not only teaching and curriculum development, but administration as well. In light of this experience, he was named as the College's Vice President for Academic Affairs in 1984, an office he held for the next eight years. During his time in office, Dad not only further grew the Core program, he expanded Saint Joseph's College. In 1986, Saint Joe partnered with St. Elizabeth's Hospital in Lafayette, Indiana to provide a degree program in nursing. This partnership proved to be both long and fruitful, as nursing became the major with the highest consistent enrollment at Saint Joe.

I came along about two years into the Core program's existence. There isn't much I remember from those early days apart from the aforementioned Easter moment at the pond. I have no recollection of the Core program's foundation, nor do I have any memories of another pivotal moment in Saint Joe history: the burning of the Administration Building.

The Administration Building or "the Ad Building" as it was known in campus parlance, was a massive, three-story structure, wider than it was tall and situated perpendicular to the Chapel. Completed in 1891, it was the tallest structure in all of Northwest Indiana at that time.[19] The building served a potpourri of academic needs, including classrooms, faculty offices, and records storage.

In the early hours of February 4th, 1973, a fire ignited in the south end of one of the upper floors of the Ad Building. Several area fire departments responded but by then the blaze was well out of hand and efforts had to be focused on protecting the nearby Chapel. All could be thankful that no one was hurt, but the building was a total loss. Classroom space was gone, and professors lost entire libraries and papers. College records would have gone up in the flames as well were it not for the valiant actions of a few intrepid students running into the building and retrieving the filing cabinets.[20]

"Got the news about it first thing in the morning," Dad recalled. "Went out to the College and saw recent alumni from Chicago and Indianapolis were already there, standing around the pond in the snow. Since it was Sunday we went to mass in the Chapel. I remember being angry with the priest because he didn't mention the fire or the College in the Prayers of the Faithful."

After the removal of the rubble, an empty space would forever stand in front of the Chapel and Merlini Hall. The loss of the Ad Building was so devastating that many speculated that Saint Joseph's College would not recover.

"Even before then there were obvious signs of just scraping by," Groppe said. "The windows rattled. Sashes went unpainted. Retirement contributions were cut."

The February 1973 fire plus the dire financial situation placed the College at a true crossroads once again. Decisions would need to be made if there was to be any future at all for the school. Indeed, expenses far outweighed income at the time and

Saint Joe declared financial exigency. This resulted in four tenured faculty members losing their jobs. This exigency prompted many Rensselaer residents to realize the need for Saint Joe in their community and thus the town launched the "Brick by Brick" fundraiser. The funds rolled in and the financial situation stabilized for the time being.[21] Also helpful was an insurance settlement for the Ad Building that was far in excess of the building's value.[22] Despite the hardships and the loss, decisive action and community cooperation ensured Saint Joseph's College would live on.

I only knew about the inferno from a painting.

Years after the blaze, my first-grade class visited Halleck Center to see a mural in progress. It wrapped all the way around the inner wall of the Halleck Student Center's central floor, telling the story of Saint Joseph's College from its humble beginnings to its late 1970s incarnation. I wasn't much of an art critic in first grade, but the mural made an impression on me. The bright colors, the storytelling…complete with obvious characters…in a sequence of visuals all spoke to me. No doubt because I was already a fan of comics. I remember staring for a time at the depiction of the Ad Building's demise. A field of dark red and bright orange flames cast light against an empty, black husk of a building. Figures silhouetted in the foreground, I could only guess they were firefighters from the helmeted shape of their heads, watched in hapless futility. Like many six-year-olds, I viewed firefighters with a combination of excitement and awe. Something deep in me was struck by the fact that even brave, capable people were unable to stop this destructive blaze once it started. It was without a doubt the most visceral and evocative sequence in the entire mural.

Any notion of Saint Joseph's College being "home" was just forming in me. I only knew I was connected to the place via my family. Interviewing my mother, however, has retrieved dusty records from the deep archives of memory. At the time of first grade, I was connected to Saint Joe not simply by my family, but rather I was one of many nodes on an intricate web of community.

"Most of the faculty had large Catholic families and many of them lived out in College Woods," Mom said, referring to a small, tree-crowded subdivision less than half a mile from campus to the south.

I went to elementary school with the children of these families, often riding in carpools driven by the parents. These kids became my boyhood friends, particularly John Groppe Jr. In fact, when I decided to join Boy Scouts, John Groppe the professor was the Scoutmaster. The wife of Saint Joseph's College's Vice President for Academic Affairs worked at St. Augustine's for many years. On Sundays, many of the families would attend mass together at St. Augustine's. I would often spend the services in the balcony as Dad sang and played the church's pipe organ.

Later as a Saint Joe student and then as a professor, people would ask me with sly smiles, "What was your Dad like at home when you were growing up?" They asked because they only knew him as a professor or an administrator, and they hoped for a glimpse of the real human being. I'd shrug and answer, that he was just…Dad. As such, he did a lot of "dad" things.

When I was a child, I just knew that "Dad worked at the College." It was that red brick place near the Hook's Drug Store.

In my pre-kindergarten days, I would ride on a seat on the back of Dad's bicycle out to campus and then home. On the way home, Dad might stop at Hook's to pick up prescriptions. That meant I might be able to cajole him into getting me candy or a comic book, or at a longshot, green plastic army men. At home, I would hear him utter phrases such as "I'm going to correct a few papers" or "I have a Core science lecture to prepare," and then off he would go to do those things in his den, a room walled with bookshelves. The shelves all held texts on subjects ranging from world history to theological treatises to the odd tomes in Latin, Greek, or French that discuss…well, I still really don't know what they say.

I'm sure I was also a mystery to him in a way. As new comics came in the mail, as I acquired more pulpy paperbacks like *The Shadow* and *Perry Rhodan*, and as he surveyed the groove formed in our floor before the TV, caused by my posterior sitting there every Saturday, watching b-movies and then later bingeing on British New Wave on MTV, Dad was no doubt flummoxed as to just how I developed such strange interests. Teetering on the edge of college age, I read and wrote more about bands like Duran Duran, U2, and The Cure than I did any subject that sat on my father's bookshelves.

Fortunately, there was hope for Dad.

My brother Michael was born in 1977. When I wasn't antagonizing him, and he wasn't playing pranks on me, the same burgeoning attachment to Saint Joseph's College began to take root in him. In fact, Michael reminded me that it happened at a much earlier time for him, for he attended a preschool at the College, run by a faculty wife on the upper levels of McHale, a building adjacent to the Chapel that came to house several administrative offices. When school would finish for the morning, Mom would sometimes take Michael over to my father's office in Dwenger Hall for a visit.

"I still remember the creak of those wooden floors," Michael said.

On a few other occasions, Dad would bring him to the science lab where Michael would study the replica skulls of gorillas and early human ancestors. Michael also got to know the faculty lounge. My high school marching band would go to tournaments on Saturdays in the fall and Mom would often accompany us as a chaperone. On select Saturdays, Dad, as Vice President for Academic Affairs, would need to attend Board of Trustees meetings. Not wanting to leave Michael home alone, Dad set him up in the lounge next door to the Board room. There Michael would have a TV, books, comfortable chairs, and a stocked refrigerator. It was in the Saint Joe faculty lounge, he tells me, that he learned he liked ginger ale, thus leading to the eventual Ginger Ale Taste Test of 2000.[23]

Given our difference in age, Michael was just starting middle school when I left for college. That is if you can call moving the span of what is essentially walking distance "going away to college." As I mentioned before, I decided upon Saint Joseph's for undergrad, astonishing most anyone who knew me. Why did I do it? The fact is, during my senior year of high school I attended a number of activities and events on campus, such as computer contests and even a student entrepreneur day, and I realized a feeling of deep connection to Saint Joe. This was beyond my familiarity with the place as my Dad's son. It was the stirring in my gut when I sat down on the railroad ties plopped as benches in front of Merlini Hall, the dorm where I would spend the next four years. That stirring said, "You're home."

It was right. I took to Saint Joe right away.

My first fall at Saint Joseph's College, I discovered an absolute love for the stage. I acted in my first play and got a special thrill seeing family and friends in the audience.

"Could you ever imagine seeing Jon Nichols do this?" a former high school teacher in the audience said to a family friend.

Something about Saint Joseph's College was changing me and for the better. All of the reading from my early years, be it novels or comics, gave me a love of narrative, but I never gave serious consideration to the creation of narrative as a profession. Ignited by the Core coursework of Saint Joe and my introduction to the literature of the world, I decided that I might actually make a go of this writing thing. I started writing for the Saint Joe newspaper, the literary magazine, and the student-produced TV sitcom. I held a shift on WPUM College radio each semester. Radio work likewise involved writing as I would script comedic bits and even full-blown radio plays for my shows, my favorite of which being "Jonny Nichols—Angry Youth." In the course of all this, I formed friendships with six guys who are my best friends to this day. No, they are more like brothers in their own right. I never worked so hard nor partied so hard. That latter activity did, I will admit, interfere with my academics on occasion. One said occasion involved my Dad.

I was crazy enough to take him for a Core class I needed my senior year. In all honesty, he really was the best choice out of all the professors. The final exam for the class came at 8:00AM on a Thursday in December. I went out partying the night before and woke up the morning of the final…at 8:20. I sprang from my bed, tossed a ballcap backwards on my head, and then ran from Merlini to the second floor of the Science Building, my head pulsing and pounding like Mario and Luigi were having a hammering contest inside my booze-addled brain. I reached the classroom, turned the knob and slowly crept in through the door. The entire class, along with Dad, looked up at me as I tiptoed to a desk. They then, likewise including Dad, fell into mocking laughter.

I got all As that semester…and one B.

My revelries should have been confined to weekends like Little 500. During my time at Saint Joe, I came to understand the reverence "Little 5", as it is known in Puma parlance, holds in Puma culture. It is usually held on the second to last Saturday in April. It began as a simple pushcart race in April of 1963. By 1971, the race evolved into racing go-carts with gas-fueled engines past hay bale chicanes as campus streets become an Indy-style racetrack. For one Saturday out of the year, Saint Joseph's College is alive with the buzzy roar of dozens of engines and the smell of gasoline and motor oil.[24] That festival was just one of so many factors that made Saint Joe so special to me.

Which explains why I broke down on May 9th, 1993. In the early hours of that day, I found myself sitting on a brick and cement bench outside of Halleck Center. I started crying, induced by a cocktail of sadness and terror. In just a few hours I would graduate from college. Many graduates feel trepidation over their futures and I was no different. I was at a crossroads in my life and needed to make a decision, but I was bereft of a clue as how to do so. There was something else at play, though. I was going to have to leave Saint Joseph's College. At the College, I lived among my friends in a close community. Soon, I would more or less be all on my own. It shook me to the depths of my being at that time.

That was when I realized just how much Saint Joseph's College was a part of me. The College had taken me from my earliest memories to the dawn of my adult years. It fed me, both in the physical sense of food bought with Dad's salary to the intellectual sense with the Core program, though it would still be a few years before I would be humble enough to say that to Dad. In regard to that intellectual growth, I was far from the only one who could say that about Core. I shared something with everyone who attended Saint Joe with me. It fostered a sense of community and a spirit of belonging. Through the place meaning so much to us, we all mean something to each other. How many people can say that about their college? Regardless, I was still required to leave on May the 9th.

No. More like pried from it like a nail from a finger.

Michael took his own place at Saint Joe four years later. He likewise wrote for the newspaper and even became its editor, but his tenure with the publication carried something special with it. When he started as a freshman, the Core Building was completed, and it became the central location for faculty offices. That pretty much emptied out Dwenger Hall for other uses, including the College newspaper.

"The editorial office was in what used to be Dad's office," Michael told me.

He followed Dad's footsteps in other ways as well. At Saint Joe, Michael realized he wanted to be a college professor and his discipline would be philosophy. Specifically, he wanted to study the various religions and myths of the world and how they interrelate. This included a keen interest in Eastern spirituality, especially Buddhism. Michael's dedication to his discipline is evidenced by his earning the title of Valedictorian of the Class of 2000.

Beyond the classroom, Michael was elected student body president. This role not only provided him the honor and experience of serving the College and its students, it also came with an additional distinction that would be with him well past graduation.

“I met an intelligent and beautiful woman named Jeannette,” Michael said.

They worked together as members of student government. They married in the College Chapel in 2002.

Soon after that, Michael landed a fully-funded position at Northwestern University where he would earn his PhD in what he described as “a herculean academic struggle.” In addition to the customary trials of teaching, researching, and writing that come with most doctoral programs, Michael needed to commute from Evanston to Southside of Chicago to reach the University of Chicago, the only institution in the area where he could learn Sanskrit.

“After the orientation on my first day at Northwestern, I sat down on a bench in the hallway and wondered if I could actually do all this,” Michael said. “The day I successfully defended my dissertation, I saw the same bench and said, ‘I am definitely sitting down on this thing again.’”

It all paid off. In 2011, a hiring committee at Saint Joseph’s College asked Michael to join the Puma faculty.

"I still remember hanging up the phone, walking into the living room of our Evanston apartment, telling Jeannette that I'd gotten the job, and feeling her jump into my arms and cry with joy," Michael said.

While Michael went through his own Saint Joe experience and subsequent triumphs in graduate school, I spent my time in the Western Suburbs of Chicago, going through my "lost years." I give the 1990s such a name because despite whatever I might have said at the time, I never possessed any clear idea of what I wanted to do. I worked hard at my jobs, but I believe I failed to live up to the work ethic my father modeled for me. Why? My efforts were not focused in a direction to really take me anywhere. Complicating…perhaps even creating…this process was confirmation of something I suspected for a long while, even during the overall happy years of Saint Joe: I suffer from anxiety and depression.

Although it's been said many times, many ways, depression and anxiety suck. They are these…things…living inside your head and alter how you see your experiences and most of all, how you see yourself. Throughout the years, my mind needn't even look to the outside world to create a distorted view of my "shortcomings." I could just look at my own family and what my father and brother accomplished. Dad, along with many other professors, endured long days and nights of mental exhaustion and built an academic program that attracted millions of dollars in grant funding for Saint Joseph's College.

I, by way of comparison, managed to survive eight hours outside in the rain, squatting on a concrete sidewalk while waiting to buy tickets to *Star Wars Episode I: The Phantom Menace*, and bedazzling my friends in the line with my *Star Wars* trivia prowess ("How the hell do you remember the name 'Commander Jerjerrod?'")

Dad mediated intellectual and pedagogical conflicts between fellow academics, who drew their arguments from deep wells of knowledge in realms such as literature, history, and philosophy.

I once jumped in to break up a bitter spat between my best friends about who was the greatest Green Lantern. "When you're ready to admit it was Alan Scott, I'll listen," my friend George growled.

My brother could read and write Sanskrit.

I could recognize Kryptonian when I saw it in a DC Comic, and I could sort of speak the lines in Klingon from *Star Trek III: The Search for Spock.*

Yep. Me and the other two Nichols men. Our lives ran almost parallel.

These thoughts are more than demoralizing. They are paralyzing. They kept me from trying many things and they convinced me to abandon entire endeavors after just one failure. That latter point is hampering indeed if one wants to be a published writer. On the positive side, this condition can be tackled and managed with the proper medical professionals. Millions of people are successful in facing these issues with vigorous courage every day.

After reflection in the early 2000s, I realized that it was this engagement of the mind, or lack thereof, that contributed to my depression and anxiety. I realized that the universe was telling me to go to graduate school. Finally, I listened and attended DePaul University to study Writing and Rhetoric as academic disciplines. I also found a true calling to help students who struggle with writing or who arrive at college underprepared to learn. Later I would enter Bay Path University to pursue a terminal degree in Nonfiction Writing. But never once did I think all that grad work would bring me right back to where it all began...back to Saint Joe College.

This was not without its downsides. Like Michael, I met my own "beautiful and intelligent woman" named Debbie and somehow convinced her to marry me. My accepting a position at Saint Joe, two hours away from where we lived in suburban Chicago, did of course place a strain on my marriage with Debbie. Physical distance, in our case, helped lead to miscommunication, slow resolution to problems, and yes, a few terse words. Debbie hung in there, though. Her giving nature allowed me to continue work that she came to realize I was rather good at. Though connected to Saint Joseph's College only by her marriage to me, Debbie even came to see what Saint Joe meant to me and to my family, and what it meant to be teaching on that hallowed campus.

It is difficult to describe that glorious experience of teaching at Saint Joe. There I was, working alongside professors that I had as a student. One colleague was, as I said, my own brother. We would see each other at lunch quite often or I'd be giving him rides home. Sometimes he would creep into my office and just wait until I'd turn around from whatever I was doing and then let out a startled yelp.

"Best of all, you have no real idea just how long I've been standing there," he'd tell me.

We would also work, of course. Sometimes it would be advising one another on a lecture or we would be doing actual curriculum development. An image would pop into my mind as we worked. This image is a precarious comparison and thus I will tread lightly. I once saw a black and white photo in *Life* magazine of John F. Kennedy and Robert F. Kennedy. Jack was leaning against a white pillar outside the Oval Office, his arms crossed and his face down as he listened. Bobby stood in front of him, mouth open and gesturing with his hand.

In those moments with Michael, I found the photo most relatable. I do not in any way mean to either state or imply that we had the Kennedys' talent, eloquence, stature, or anything else. The common ground I saw was two brothers in their adult, professional lives, working together as peers despite however many years might separate their births. Both of them invested in bettering an institution they cared about so much.

Saint Joe was indeed something of a "family business." For my brother and me, we were also custodians of our father's work, maintaining the Core program while revising it in order to keep it relevant and updated. We could also strengthen the program's commitment to a Catholic mission with the Extended Core curriculum, giving a chance at college to students who might be overlooked by other institutions. I sometimes shook my head in bemused wonderment at how life brought us back to the College, not knowing quite how to express what it meant. So it was Michael who placed it in the most eloquent terms, doing so through his own discipline.

"There are Native Americans who believe our lives have two points in a cycle," he once told me. "In terms of Saint Joe, you and I actually have three points in our cycle. We were here as children, as teens, and now as adults."

Yes, we had aged, but then so had the campus.

Dwenger Hall was closed off to entry. Given the amount of decay in the structure, it was deemed too expensive to renovate. Given the amount of asbestos in the walls, it was too expensive to tear down.

It was not unusual to see buckets in the Science Building, catching the steady *drip drip drip* of water from the ceiling whenever it rained. Several other buildings suffered from years of deferred maintenance.

A nice set of apartments had been built for senior class housing between Justin and Noll Halls, but Saint Joe long since lost the student facilities arms race. That was thought to be a contributing factor in stagnant or declining enrollment rates. Regardless, it was all part and parcel of a worsening financial situation. The faculty shared a desire to thrive, but the physical and financial infrastructure creaked like rotting timber. Still, we were assured there was hope and that closing the doors was not an event anywhere on the horizon.

Then the president abruptly resigned at the end of the 2014 academic year and the Vice President for Academic Affairs announced his own departure but a few months prior. The Vice President for Business Affairs likewise resigned later that fall.

Dr. Stephen Hulbert[25] was brought in from The Registry for College and University Presidents as an interim president as the Board searched for a permanent hire. Hulbert's tenure was brief, but I recall him as a level-headed man with a solid understanding of higher education. Meanwhile, presidential candidates came to campus for interviews. An offer was extended to a candidate.

That man was Dr. Robert Pastoor.[26] He came to Saint Joseph's in 2015 from Marietta College where he served as Vice President for Student Affairs. After a gala inauguration that October, President Pastoor set out his plan for getting the College back on solid financial footing. In his words, "we would grow our way out of the problem." This included plans for increasing enrollment, offering online degree programs, and opening opportunities for residents of Rensselaer and surrounding communities to enroll in certification classes.

While we were "growing our way out," the administration also grew. Pastoor hired a Vice President of

Enrollment Management to work with the Director of Admissions, a Dean of Students to work with the Vice President of Student Affairs, and finally a Vice President of Mission. It became a running trivia question for faculty and students alike: "Can you name all of our vice presidents?" I will admit that I could not. Many of these new administrative hires drew executive level salaries. Employees naturally wondered how this could be when austerity should seem to be the rule of the day, but once we received a 2% raise in our own salaries, we began to think the financial situation might be taking a turn for the brighter. Exteriors of buildings also received a spruce up. We hired new faculty to start in August of 2016. Why would any of this be happening if we were not already climbing our way to drier ground?

By November 2016 and there was a new sense of urgency. The Higher Learning Commission (HLC), the institution's accreditation authority, placed Saint Joseph's College on probationary status. In certified correspondence dated November 16th to President Pastoor,[27] HLC announced that the College was "out of compliance" with Component 5.A of the criteria for accreditation: “the institution’s resource base supports its current educational programs and its plans for maintaining and strengthening their quality in the future.” Key factors cited in this decision were:

-Continued loans from the endowment to meet liabilities and expenses;

-Institutional losses resulted in approximately $10 million in losses to net assets;

-Deferred maintenance backlog continued to increase; and

-While the College had established short and long-term goals to balance the budget and hired outside consultants to help with strategic planning and fundraising, few of these goals had been implemented.

By no later than January 8th, 2018, Saint Joseph’s College was to submit an Assurance Filing “providing evidence that the College has ameliorated the findings of non-compliance.” Among the evidence required was achievement of financial stability including reduced reliance on endowment withdrawals, successful implementation of an enrollment and retention plan, and successful monetization of the Waugh land.

"The Waugh land" is a wide stretch of farmland south of Rensselaer. Juanita Waugh, a local farmer and businesswoman, gifted the "*usufrucht*" or "fruits of the land" to Saint Joseph's College prior to her death. Stipulations of the gift said that the land, valued at over $40 million, could not be sold outright and must continue to be worked. Saint Joseph's College collected approximately $2 million each year from farmers and a wind energy company who installed a protracted line of massive windmills on the property. Should Saint Joseph's College no longer exist, *usufrucht* would fall to the Mayo Clinic. College administrators began negotiations with the Mayo Clinic as the other entity named in the trust. The idea would be to have Mayo take over as recipients of the annual $2 million in exchange for the value of the land.[28]

Pastoor assured faculty that Saint Joseph's College still held options and the Waugh land was a strong one. We could withstand the financial pressure and there was no immediate cause for alarm. As for the HLC report, we had been given years to fix the problem.

"I did *not* come here to close Saint Joseph's College," Pastoor assured us at a 2016 faculty meeting.

Meanwhile, faculty received their own marching orders. The Office of Business Affairs directed that each academic curriculum needed to be "revenue positive." That meant having enough rear ends in classroom seats paying enough tuition to justify the major or minor's existence. It also meant that no single class could have fewer than eight students enrolled. While a few of us wondered just how this would save money and others outright asserted that it wouldn't, the re-envisioning went ahead both for the major studies and for the Core program. Though frustrating and at times grueling, the process yielded positive results and many of us saw our programs in new ways, bringing the promise of exciting opportunities.

We also started new academic programs. Saint Joe partnered with Valparaiso University, just half an hour to the north of Rensselaer, to offer an engineering curriculum. I was in my second year of directing Extended Core and that program was yielding measurable results in terms of retention. Our most populated major, the nursing curriculum at St. Elizabeth's, already underwent an expansion with an "RN to BSN" program for nurses returning after serving in the field for a time.

Good news also came from the Office of Admissions. Brian Studebaker, Director of Admissions and a fellow Puma friend from my undergrad days, reported that the number of admitted students was up 19.8% from the previous academic year and incoming freshmen deposits up 57%. The Fall 2017 freshmen class looked to be on track to break records.[29]

One item did arise that fall that is relevant, but only in retrospect. On the Board of Trustees, there was always a faculty representative and a student representative, each with voting rights. The student rep was the President of the Student Association as elected by the student body. Faculty elects the faculty rep. A proposal came before the Board of Trustees to render the faculty and student representatives as non-voting members. Faculty met this proposal with natural skepticism, as did a few Board members. The matter was tabled.[30]

Overall though, as we left for Christmas Break that December, the general mood among faculty was both energetic and positive. We could make changes, we could adapt, and we could work to get the College back on the right track. Best of all, there was time to do it.

Little did we know what lay ahead of us.

NOTES

1. Gerlach 2
2. "Founder – Missionaries of the Precious Blood"
3. "Saint Gaspar del Bufalo"
4. Gerlach 2
5. ibid.
6. Gerlach 6-7
7. Gerlach 8
8. Gerlach 9
9. ibid.
10. "Mission and Vision" [Antioch College]
11. "Mission and Vision" [Dana College]
12. Blackford
13. Gerlach 119
14. Ibid.
15. Gerlach 118-119
16. Gerlach 35
17. I interviewed John Groppe on 3/10/2018. In addition to the interview, he provided me a written precis on the early years of the Core program. Notes in author's possession.
18. Bennett
19. Gerlach 26
20. Gerlach 20-22

21. Ibid.
22. From the interview with Groppe.
23. The winner was Canada Dry, notes in author's possession.
24. Gerlach 192
25. I interviewed Dr. Hulbert by phone on 24 Apr. 2019. Notes in author's possession.
26. Dr. Pastoor politely declined to be interviewed for this book.
27. HLC document in author's possession.
28. DiMento and from an interview with Brian Capouch.
29. I confirmed this with Brian Studebaker on 6/21/2020. Email in author's possession.
30. 11/2016 Board of Trustees minutes in author's possession.

CHAPTER THREE: Gethsemane

A new semester, an old faculty meeting.

That's what it felt like, anyway in the late afternoon of Wednesday, January 18th, 2017. I walked into the Courtney Auditorium with a Diet Coke and a McDonald's bag containing two cheeseburgers. I picked a meeting agenda up from the back row. Chad Turner came in behind me as I scanned the sheet of paper.

"This isn't good," I said to him.

Chad looked at me and scrunched his nose. I held up the paper.

"Short agenda," I said. "Those usually turn into the longest meetings because people think there's room to argue."

He smiled, snorted, and took his own copy of the agenda as well as the minutes from the previous meeting. I walked down the steps of the center aisle, headed for my usual seat. Funny that. The clear majority of us on faculty probably haven't had assigned seating since high school, and yet we would all migrate to "our spots" in the small auditorium like swallows back to

Capistrano. A psychologist might have made a fair study out of the phenomenon. I took my "spot" next to my brother. He looked over at my McDonald's bag.

"Did you bring something for me?" Michael asked.

"I haven't eaten today," I responded.

"So, what you're saying is you didn't bring anything for me," he said.

"I didn't know you wanted anything."

His trademark look of haughty derision, reserved most often just for me, came across his face as just he shook his head.

"Jonny…" he said in a quiet tone and through a smirk.

I bit into one of the cheesy, salty sandwiches laden with more artificial constructs than I could count. As I chewed the morsel, I glanced over at Michael's stack of papers. He was scheduled to present the revamped Core program that meeting. The directors hammered out the modifications before Christmas break, streamlining the curriculum and collapsing courses in keeping with the new "revenue positive" directive. Regardless, there would still likely be spirited debates over the new plan because as academicians, that's what we do. I would joke from time to time that like lawyers, if a faculty member fell asleep during a meeting and then snapped back awake, the first words from his or her mouth would be "I object."

We prayed. That's how these meetings always started. After the "amen," I scanned down my agenda. Things kicked off with a few *pro forma* obligations, and then the update from the President followed by yet another update, this time by the Vice President for Academic Affairs. Next bullet item read "Old Business," which assuredly there was none from the last meeting before break. New Business held Michael's presentation on Core.

In the middle of it all, I would no doubt start daydreaming about books I could write, or classroom discussion topics for the following week. By mid-semester I concentrated on grading my students' papers during these meetings, but given it was the beginning of the year those had yet to materialize. I supposed I might ponder on my own distinctive brand of Zen kaons, such as, "Could Matter-Eater Lad from the Legion of Super-Heroes eat Captain America's indestructible shield?" Those reveries would not really get into full swing until

“Concerns of the College” where rhetorical ground was most fertile for argument. By “Announcements” I would begin gathering my books and papers, ready to head to the faculty soiree that immediately followed each meeting. Before anything else, there was of course the President’s update. Dr. Pastoor, a barrel-chested man with a bushy moustache, walked to the front of the Courtney Auditorium and took the microphone. I thought he would probably give an update on the negotiations with the Mayo Clinic over the Waugh Land and other such financial matters with numbers and legalese that would result in my mind’s eye glazing over, turning my inner attention to matters of writing or maybe Galaga on my iPhone. Yes, haven’t played Galaga in a while and that might…

Our situation is dire.

Pastoor said that.

Or something like it.

I dropped my phone.

A series of cold pinpricks shot up my neck and into my jaw. My eyes locked on Pastoor. Everything else in my peripheral vision just seemed to disappear as I listened to his report. Mayo Clinic came back with an offer of $15 million after we asked for $35 million. Then they came back with $20 million and Saint Joe said "thanks, but no."

Money was running out. The College needed $20 million before June 1st to keep operating. Options grew fewer and fewer, or as Pastoor put it, "I now have a shorter runway to land this thing."[1]

I was critical of the rhetorical semantics of that analogy but felt no confusion as to his message that this was a time of crisis.

"I know you all worked on things like…no fewer than eight students in a class, revenue positive programs, and all that," Pastoor said to us. "Sorry but that's not going to help."[2]

Nothing like being told your work was pointless. How many days and hours did we spend on that planning? Pastoor then explained we faced a $50 million problem that doesn't include deferred maintenance. It becomes $80 million after that.

"Here's an analogy," he continued. "I look at Saint Joseph's College as a patient, treated with Band Aids and ointment. We opened up the patient and found a deadly disease."[3]

He paused for a moment and then drew in a breath.

"I need you to be really certain that you understand these dire straits," Pastoor said. "Are we closing? This is not my intent. But this institution is at a precipice. All the minutia we deal with from day-to-day doesn't matter. We are working diligently to try to resolve it. We will do what is in the best interest of the institution."[4]

I realized at that moment that I had not moved since he started talking. It was the same physical sense of immobilization one gets from reading a fascinating book or witnessing an engrossing scene in a movie. Only this time the captivation stemmed from burgeoning terror, like listening to a doctor unfold point by point what is wrong with you and sensing a build towards a grim prognosis.

"If this college is to continue in any way, then it will have to be something that looks drastically different from what it is now," he said.[5]

I'm not proud of my denial, but it was there that night. My immediate, inner response to that comment was, "So we'll change. That's fine. We can do that. Institutions should grow and adapt with the times anyway, right? Heck, I don't care if we become a school exclusively for circus acrobats. Just keep Saint Joe open. We can do this."

Pastoor continued to explain to the hushed faculty that he was still pursuing options. There was a donor he was in contact with who might provide the funds needed to help the College continue. Pastoor held out hopes that there was still a chance, but nothing was definite. In fact, he emphasized that nothing would be definite until the Board of Trustees meeting on February 2nd and 3rd when they would decide "how best to move forward." Until then, we were not to share any of this with students. A community meeting would be held soon enough, and it was important that everyone be given the same, consistent information. Then, Pastoor paused again and choked back tears. He asked that we continue to pray for the future of Saint Joseph's College and then concluded his segment of the agenda by walking up the center aisle of the Courtney Auditorium and exiting the room, leaving it in stunned silence.

Dr. Chad Pulver,[6] Vice President for Academic Affairs, took the microphone for his update. Dr. Pulver can best be described in one word: competitor. Standing at 6'4, his jawline chiseled, and his dark hair always kept military short, Pulver left quite a legacy on the basketball court during his undergrad days at Saint Joseph's College. His speech was often peppered with words such as "execute," "initiative," and "clutch." That night of January 17th, he wore a sharp, pinstripe suit with a Puma purple tie and matching purple socks. He swallowed hard before addressing the faculty.

"So, we have students," Dr. Pulver said. "We have to take care of those students. If there are things that need to be answered, reach out to me or reach out to Tom."[7]

Tom being Dr. Tom Ryan, Associate Vice President for Academic Affairs.

"We still have a semester to finish out. I want you to focus on that. That's all I have," Pulver said.

He sat back down. Again, the faculty remained in silence.

The meeting continued to unfold after that, but I would be hard pressed to tell you anything of it. It was as if I viewed the auditorium and everyone in it through a gauzy haze. The voices sounded as muted trumpets. The speakers looked like colleagues of mine, but they stood obscured in a gray fog generated by my own thoughts. Thoughts such as "Am I going to have to find a new job?" and "Who the hell would hire me?" and most chilling, "Does this mean a world without Saint Joseph's College? I love this place and everyone in it. We couldn't just…" That last, blighted notion broke my bleak reverie and brought me back to the meeting.

"Of course, after what we've just heard, you might wonder 'What's the point?'" Michael said during his presentation of the changes to Core.

A subtle wave of grim laughter rolled across the assembled faculty.

"But I have a job to do," Michael continued. "That job is strengthening Core."

We voted in favor of his proposed changes, then moved on to a few perfunctory matters and once again I drifted. I just wanted to get upstairs to the soiree. Not for any food or drink, but so that I could speak with my friends and attempt to process what the hell just happened. Well then again, a beer or nine might help that process. We motioned to adjourn and then stood to say the Our Father as we did at the end of each meeting. I prayed it with more fervor than I ever have in my life.

Michael stayed behind, speaking with the Chair of the Assembly about exact wording of the Core changes for the minutes, I presumed. I got up to leave, but made certain to grab my empty McDonald's bag. The whole building could have been going down in a blaze, and I still would have picked up that bag. Something my parents drilled into me from a very young age. You pack out your trash and you clean up your mess.

I left the auditorium and met Dr. April Toadvine,[8] a colleague of mine in the English Department, on the stairs. Her head of curly brown hair stood just beneath my shoulder as she gripped the railing and took the stairs with slow steps due to a back injury of long ago. As with any workplace, my level of comfort and familiarity varied with each coworker. I was most relieved to find one whom I knew and trusted.

“What the hell was that?” I asked her.

April shook her head as she looked down at the steps.

“Who knows?” she answered.

Indeed, we concurred that it sounded as though no one knew much of anything. That is, at least until the upcoming board meeting in February.

“It will be bad,” April said as we reached the second floor. “But it won’t be that bad.”

“You’re thinking layoffs?” I asked.

I opened the door to the second floor and held it for her.

“All I can think about is my Core 6 class and my Shakespeare class tomorrow,” April said. “It’s about all I have control of right now.”

We walked past the faculty offices and came to the lounge by the elevators. Our food services had already set up the typical tables of pizza, vegetable trays, and hors d'oeuvres. I skipped all that and took a beer straight from the tub of ice at the end of the serving table. I plotzed into one of the lounge chairs, took a gulp of frosty, hoppy malt, and just stared forward. What was happening to us? After sitting there for a minute or so, Jordan Leising[9] came into view.

Jordan was in his second year of teaching political science at St. Joe. A beard appeared and disappeared on his round face, or so I teased him. He kept a series of bobbleheads of political figures on his office shelves and a poster on his wall of the "Ron Swanson Pyramid of Greatness" from the television series, *Parks and Recreation*. He was young and new to teaching, but a man of great energy and keen intelligence. Like me, he was also a St. Joe grad and held deep appreciation for and devotion to the Core program. Over those two years, I came to rely on his insight while planning two different Cores together and cultivated sincere regard for him as a colleague as well as a friend.

"What the hell was that?" we both said in unison.

"What exactly happened over Christmas break?" Jordan asked. "I mean this is a dramatic shift in tone. One minute we're making plans, the next Mr. Hyde pops out and says 'run for the hills, we're all doomed?'"

We hashed and rehashed several versions of those same questions and got nowhere fast with them. I scanned the room for Pulver, but he must have already left. President Pastoor departed right after his statement, so who was still present who might have insight into the state of mind of the administration?

Over by the ice buckets of beer, Dr. Bill White[10] offered a counterbalance. He taught history at Saint Joseph's College for the past 30 years. He also managed to garner a reputation for himself in many regards. For one, he was a learned scholar and known far and wide among the student body as a merciless grader. If you really wanted to learn, however, then students also knew that Bill White could teach you as few others could. He was also known as a Cassandra figure of sorts, warning all who would listen of Saint Joe's impending financial doom.

How did he know? Bill served as a faculty representative to the Board of Trustees for many years. He also was a member of the faculty's Finance Advisory Committee. This allowed him a peek behind the curtain at the greasy, dirty machinery of the College's fiscal engine room. When asked of what he knew of our true financial picture, Bill would answer with his trademark dark humor. Motioning with his hand to mimic a plane crashing or look at me and say, “You’re a clever guy. You’ll be fine after this place closes.” Chad Turner told me about a dinner party Bill threw at his house for the History Department and their families.

“I told him that Jess gets nervous, and so to tone down on the doom and gloom,” Chad said. “He says okay, but then he gets a couple glasses of wine in him and what does he do? Launches right into it!”

In what must have been a moment of realization, Bill then changed the subject to the problem he was having with bats in his attic.

Those who knew Bill White, however, also knew that he harbored a heart of gold beneath that projected darkness and he cared a great deal about Saint Joe and the students that we served. That night in the lounge, a beer in one hand and his other hand placing his gold-rimmed glasses back on his face, he exuded an air of genuine confusion.

“What the hell was that?” I asked.

“The Finance Advisory Committee met about two weeks ago,” Bill said.

He went on to explain that Spencer Conroy[11], Saint Joe's Vice President for Business Affairs, did not give any kind of doom and gloom at the meeting. The report from Conroy, according to Bill, was that negotiations with Mayo were tough, but could work.

"It was positive," Bill said. "I left thinking we might have five years to get things right."

Even "the town cynic" expressed shock at the impending "precipice" President Pastoor spoke of.

"What the hell is happening?" I asked, not to Bill but just in general.

"I think the axe will really start swinging," Bill said.

One of our colleagues walked past who, like me, was untenured and a thesis away from completing a terminal degree.

"Dead man walking," Bill chided.

From anyone else besides Bill "Heart of Darkness" White, I might have taken it as an insult. Instead, I got another beer.

This cycle of drinking and questioning just what the hell was going on continued for about another hour. If someone told me that morning, "Guess what you'll be doing that day…"

After my second beer I went to my office, bundled myself for the frigid January night, and went to go see my parents.

"It's over," I said to Dad. "That's what Pulver and Pastoor told us tonight, anyway."

Dad sat in his chair in his study, a book across his lap, looking up at me with his brow furrowed. I didn't know how else to tell him.

"That's what they said?" he asked with no small amount of surprise.

I replied that those might not have been the exact words, but that was the "temperature of the room," so to speak. I relayed what was said best I could. Mom overheard and walked into the room.

"I knew it," she said.

A "pop" echoed out as she rapped a knuckle into the wall with a quick jab. Mom shared a few things with Bill White. She could likewise be cynical and often challenged him for the role of Cassandra, warning that poor financial decisions and, most of all, the people in charge over the years were going to run the place into the ground. Unlike Bill White with his experience on both the Board, the Finance Advisory Committee, and his firsthand viewing of financial reports, Mom's view came from her uncanny ability to see inside someone's character. Bereft of what seemed any concrete evidence, Mom could often tell if someone was a fraud, a do-nothing, or worse. This could be maddening for those around her who could not see the same without any evidence. It was likewise aggravating for her because, more often than not, she would be proven right. Plenty of nights she would be sitting at the dinner table and waving her arms while saying, "What's the point of having this board if they do nothing?"

Our family has had a few interesting meals together.

Dad stood up and went to his desk.

"There's a meeting of executive membership of the Board in Chicago tomorrow," he said. "I'll find out more then."

I did not sleep well that night.

- - -

The following morning, I arrived on campus and parked at the Core Building. I needed to give a lecture in one hour on Isaac Newton and the Scientific Revolution, but to say my head wasn't in the game would be an understatement. My stomach roiled with acid, my hands would not stop fidgeting in my gloves, and I fought with considerable resolve the urge to run back into bed and just watch TV all day, pretending nothing was happening.

Chad Turner, held the door open for me as we both went inside the Core Building to start our day. Dressed in his trademark blazer and bow tie combo, I have never known Chad to be anything but soft spoken, bright, and jovial. That freezing morning of January 19th, I noticed his eyes drooping lower than usual behind his glasses.

"Hi, how you doing?" he said.

It was his four-word, automatic greeting with a rhythmic cadence all its own. Only this time the delivery came across as forced.

“Got the same thing on my mind as everybody else after last night’s meeting, I imagine.”

“We just bought a house,” Chad reminded me.

After Chad accepted the faculty position at Saint Joe, he and Jess lived in Mishawaka, meaning Chad’s daily commute amounted to over three hours total. Not only did the drive involve precarious winter conditions at times, it also meant moving between Eastern and Central time zones. In the morning that wasn’t bad as he gained an hour.

“However, each afternoon I had to leave my office by 4:00 PM to make it home before 7:00 PM. Between it being the first semester at a new job and trying to carve out time to work on my dissertation,” he said. “It wasn’t so bad, though. The drive did not involve much traffic, and so it was easy to sit back, listen to the sports-talk radio shows.”

While that is all well and good, long commutes grow taxing in both physical and economic terms. Chad and Jess wanted to move to Rensselaer.

“One thing we quickly realized was that there is almost no rental market in Rensselaer,” Chad said. “We had a very hard time finding a place to rent, especially a place that was suitable for us and our dog, and so, as my job felt very stable, we began to look for a house to buy."

Saint Joe administrators even helped connect Chad and Jess with realtors. The administration likewise helped the Turners out of a jam as a gap occurred between dates of needing to leave their Mishawaka rental and closing on a brand-new house in Rensselaer.

"Jess and I just painted it, installed light fixtures. I mean, we both wanted to settle here. With the new hires and facility renovations, I thought Saint Joe was following the plan for growing," Chad said as we climbed the stairs. "Well we won't know anything until the Board meets. It could still be all right."

"That's right," I added.

What else could I say? The alternative was unthinkable.

I saw Dr. Tom Ryan.[12] Not only was he my colleague but in an added dimension, only possible in a small town such as Rensselaer and a small college such as Saint Joseph's, Tom was one of my high school English teachers. He was the first teacher to begin nurturing what ability I had for writing while

---

introducing me to writers who still stick with me, running the spectrum from Poe to the Transcendentalists. A mentor and patrician in educational circles, his gift for teaching and connecting with students is unique. During my time at Saint Joe, it was Tom's guidance and opinion on matters that always reassured me the most. He stood in his tweed blazer with the patches on the elbows, carrying a Styrofoam cup of coffee mixed heavy with creamer. I always thought he bore more than a passing resemblance to Art Garfunkel.

Many of us knew that he held a special connection with the C.PP.S. and deep friendships with several of their priests. Tom even kept an apartment in Carthagena, Ohio, where he would sometimes go for spiritual retreat. This position might have allowed him insights to the situation that the rest of us lacked. I asked him what he thought and set down his coffee cup.

"I think there are a lot of good things that could happen, but we just need to get past this crazy time and know where things are…" he spun his two index fingers in the air in a helicopter motion before bringing them to a sharp point towards the floor and finishing with, "Conceptually."

There's still a chance, I thought.

I gathered my notes from my office and headed back downstairs to the Shen Auditorium to give my lecture. I'll be damned if I can repeat anything I said because my brain just wasn't in the game. There I was, my mouth spouting words, my legs moving me in my customary shuttles back and forth across the stage, but my mind somewhere else altogether, ruminating on the greatest existential threat I've ever faced. Then somehow, per the order of the administration, I was to continue teaching classes that day and not say a word as to what was reaching critical mass behind the scenes.

Somehow, I managed. We all did. Really, helping a student adjust a thesis statement or talking with a student to help them resolve a problem gave my mind somewhere else to go, namely to work I enjoy. Later in the day, I overheard talk in the hallway between professors and support staff.

"Just last November we're told that there's a good chance we'll get money from the Mayo Clinic for the Waugh land. Now suddenly they say, 'It's not happening, folks,'" someone said.

In addition to the inconsistencies in messaging, decisions of expenditures came under scrutiny. You don't hire faculty and move them here when you're in financial distress. You don't give people a 2% raise, either. I'm no accountant, but I know that the line for 'net loss' in the budget of any functional organization should be *zero*.

More of the same questions and ruminations followed throughout the day. That's what people do though when something doesn't make sense and…even worse…we can't do anything about it. We just keep saying the same things to each other over and over only phrased and paraphrased in different ways, hoping we come across an incantation or unlock a rhetorical sequence that would bring everything into focus and clarity.

April came out of her office carrying a Norton Shakespeare reader and one of the Harry Potter volumes. My eyebrow arched at first, somewhat taken aback by the combo. Then I remembered she was teaching an electives course on the Potter books. I asked how she was holding up.

"The CW-verse serves a purpose," she said.

She explained that she spent the previous night catching up on episodes of *Arrow* and *The Flash* backlogged on her DVR. April wasn't alone. Another faculty member who passed by mentioned that he turned on *The Dick Van Dyke Show* in an effort to divert himself from reality. Upon changing the channel after the show's end, he learned that Mary Tyler Moore just died, and reality crashed in just the same.

But I envied my colleagues and their TV viewing. In times of crisis, the unmoderated nuclear reactor that is my anxiety is such that nothing, no matter how much I may otherwise love it, not even vintage 1970s sci-fi cheese like *Logan's Run*, can take my mind from the problem at hand. Nothing, save for a resolution. When would we have this resolution?

"Well, we won't know anything until the Board meets," April said.

Friday came. That meant the afternoon "community meeting" for all faculty and staff in the Shen Auditorium. President Pastoor held a similar informational meeting the night

---

before with the students. I watched the reactions come in on social media as students responded with a range of shock and dark humor. The quote that best matched my own thoughts was, “I just want everything to be okay again.” Students in class earlier that day asked me questions about what was happening. I wanted to take their pain away, but I lacked that super power.

“I know we all complain about how things are at The Joe sometimes,” I told my students. “But there are so many lives depending on this place. Lives with families. So what I ask of you is, if you are someone who prays, please pray for us all and the future of the College. Pray that there may be people working hard towards finding solutions.”

Would Pastoor give us any assurance of solutions at the afternoon meeting?

Pastoor’s spiel ended up being almost verbatim to what he told us at the faculty meeting. Dire financial situation. Drastic changes needed. Still working with donors, one big donor in fact. Won’t know anything until the Board meeting on February 2nd and 3rd. Someone asked him if we would still hold interviews for the Presidential Scholarship. Every year around January, high school students with exceptional and distinctive academic records received invitations to campus to be interviewed for the chance at a Presidential Scholarship, which was, for all intents and purposes, a full ride to college. Faculty and other staff served as panel members for the interviews.

President Pastoor said that we would indeed move ahead with the Presidential Scholarship interview day as planned. In fact, everything at the College would go forward as usual until we learned of anything different. Then at close to the same point as he did in the faculty meeting, Pastoor choked back tears.

"If we pull together, we'll get through this."

After the meeting ended, the building cleared out for the weekend.

I stayed behind. I spent an hour walking back and forth on the second floor. My footsteps were the only sounds, save for the hum of the fluorescent lights. As I passed each name on each office door, I realized that I could tell a story about almost every one of them. More than that, I realized that for over twenty years, I had worked with other professionals in other organizations and other fields of work. Never ever had I shared such a common spirit though, a mutual goal, and a genuine affection for my coworkers as I did with the faculty of Saint Joseph's College at that time. Where could I possibly find that again?

At my own office door, I touched my nameplate, running my fingertips over the indented letters of "J. NICHOLS". It meant something. It was a concrete manifestation of everything I had wanted and worked for since graduate school. My type of degree or where I got it from did not matter. I earned my place as an Assistant Professor by demonstrating time and again that I could teach. My students testified to such, as did my peers. I had built something. Working with my wonderful colleagues, I wanted to keep building. Everything I am was tied to Saint Joseph's College. I existed, my brother existed, and really my whole immediate family existed and was sustained by the work my father provided over fifty years to this College. It couldn't all be taken away now, could it? Something had to be done. This couldn't be the end.

I started out for home in the Chicago suburbs to be with my wife and dogs for the weekend. Driving through Rensselaer, my headlights cut through a thick fog. Rising temperatures and subsequent snow melt created a nocturnal haze, the kind that puts a halo around every streetlight. A "Raymond Chandler evening" as someone once called it. In a happier mood, I might also have quipped, "Watson, I believe we're on the moors." This time, as I drove down College Avenue and past the old bowling alley, I saw two figures outlined in the mist.

They were two students of mine, a dating couple who were holding hands as they walked back towards campus. The man held a plastic bag, inside which I could detect the outline of Chinese food containers. I could also see the silhouette of his bowler hat, a personal quirk of his. Both did quite well in their studies. Far more important, both were good, kind people. They seemed to be enjoying the night together, looking forward to a good meal and good company, not the sort of "party til you puke" stereotype one might figure for college students on a Friday night.

After I passed them, I pulled my car into a gas station and started to cry. Truth enveloped me, feeling like a blanket kept for two days in a freezer. I shivered and almost retched inside it as I saw how selfish I had been. Since Wednesday night, I dwelled

---

nonstop on the fear of losing both my job and the legacy of Saint Joseph's College. In doing so, I made an egregious error by overlooking one of the most critical populations of all.

If Saint Joe fell into the abyss, what would happen to those kids? Not just the ones I passed in the fog, but all of them? Where would they go? Would they be all right? I thought of the students in the Extended Core program. For a few of them, we were the only college who would take a chance on them. With our small size and the amount of attention and guidance we were giving them, we might be their only shot at an education. What would happen to them?

As it was with every other question that week, the answer was in unseen hands.

"Didn't they just tell you there was time to work your way out of this?"

That's what Debbie asked me when I got home and I told her about the community meeting. She was already in bed when I got there, wearing pajamas covered in cartoon otters. I crawled up onto the bed next to her and wrapped my arms around her midsection. Butterscotch, our girl dog, curled at Debbie's head while my boy Chewie came over and plopped across my legs.

"What about all that work they had you do over the holidays?" Debbie kept asking. "What about 'revenue positive?'"

"I guess things were actually going very badly," I said. "Far worse than anyone let on."

Chewie shifted and came up next to my face, panting. He started licking my cheek, wafting dog breath into my nostrils. I put my left arm around him and pressed his forehead to mine. Butterscotch stirred, looked up at me, and smiled.

"I can't let this happen to Dad," I said. "Hell, I can't let it happen to Mom. She made Dad's work possible by taking care of the family. She gave her life to the College in her own way."

"I know," Debbie said, her hand stroking both Chewie's head and mine. "It's like a family business. I just feel so sorry any of you are going through this."

Moving onto my side, I managed to position myself so all four of us could be piled on one another. I repeated what Pastoor said at the meeting earlier that day. There was a potential big donor in the works. I also knew that plenty of wealthy and accomplished Pumas would not let the College collapse. Something needed to happen. As I hugged each member of my family, I knew I was responsible for their well-being. They were my responsibility, every bit as much as Saint Joe was. More even. My father taught me that and how could I live up to his work ethic if I didn't have work? I propped myself on my left elbow and looked in Debbie's brown eyes. She smiled.

"We all love and support you," Debbie said.

"Even the otters?" I asked.

I made a playful point at her pajamas.

"Yes, all the otters love and support you too," Debbie said, but then her expression turned sullen. "Except this one."

Pajama fabric bunched in her right hand, she lifted up one of the smiling otter faces.

"He doesn't care. He's an asshole," she said.

We both laughed harder than we had in a while.

I knew her head was spinning.

Free-floating anxiety.

That is the best phrase to describe the two weeks that followed. A bizarre production of *Waiting for Godot* might be another. No one knew anything, and rumors circulated. One of them was that Saint Joe might “suspend academic activities” after the current semester to return sometime later with a rejuvenated schema by which to move forward. It sounded crazy to me. How could an institution of higher education simply call “Time out, everybody!” and then think that any students would return to it with any kind of confidence? And weren’t they, that very day, still taking students’ money?

Interviews took place for the Presidential Scholarship just as scheduled. Jordan Leising served on one of the panels. He confided in me about his misgivings in both asking the prospective students about what they could bring to the College and extolling what Saint Joe could do for them.

“I wondered if this was ethical,” he said. “Was I selling them a false bill of goods? Did I have any right to sell this place at this time to those kids?”

Those who staffed Admissions held similar misgivings but followed their given orders: continue with “business as usual." Adam Current[13], who worked as a counselor in Admissions, was a graduate in Philosophy from Wabash College and was both a fellow writer and devotee of the humanities. I had gotten to know him rather well and he would stop into my office from time to time, talking about the state of things in Admissions. They were on track for a record freshmen class, he told me just as his boss, Brian Studebaker reported. In that "interzone" before the coming Board meeting, they kept on processing applications, meeting with potential students, and mailing out both promotional packets and acceptance letters.

Thus, hope remained. Talk continued of those wealthy donors mentioned by the administrative leadership. A real energy circulated amongst the students as marketing majors and art majors talked about ways they could help by designing campaigns to reach out to alums, community stakeholders, and anyone else who might help us in this time of great need. There was also the flipside.

"I went to talk to someone in leadership," someone in Philosophy said. "I asked him if we should be looking for other jobs. He said 'yes.'"

Though chilled by that news, I wondered if I should go talk to someone as well. Dr. Pulver would be a logical choice. He and I had built a positive working relationship. I held something of an avenue to him as he and my brother Michael were already good friends from their undergrad days at Saint Joe. Pulver and I also shared a love of comic books and the fiction of pop culture, so we held our share of afterhours discussions and debates in our offices. It was Pulver's idea to design and launch Extended Core as a bridge program for students in academic need. I always knew him to be a straight shooter and if he had any clue as to what was going on, I believed he would tell me. If I could just get an edge of the curtain to pull it back and get the merest peek behind it…

Then I ran into Michael. As Dean of Core, he went to Pulver and asked about faculty assignments for Core in Fall of 2017, a typical question for any January. Pulver told him not to bother with it.

"I'm going to assign faculty anyway," Michael said. "It's my job."

These secondhand statements from Pulver stood in contrast to the "there's still a chance" message from the other administrative leadership. Two choices stood before me. I could cultivate suspicion and skepticism, or believe that everything would work out all right. Perhaps like an idiot, I chose to go with the positivity of the latter.

"Evening, Jonny," Brian Capouch said to me that Tuesday night as I sat down with my dinner tray.

I did my best to make it to Brian's "Tuesday nights in the cafeteria" because mutual students of ours such as Justin Hays were among his dinner guests and the conversation was always lively. In sharing a meal together, the students could see another side of me, one outside the classroom that is…gasp…human. The generation of this bond between us only benefitted the educational process.

That night of January 24th, however, the tenor of the table was grim. I sat down next to Justin. For the first time in person, I congratulated him on his admission to Maurer School of Law at IU. He thanked me, but turned the conversation right back to the

---

future of Saint Joe. He and all his friends at the table, all seniors, shared similar concerns.

Jose Arteaga[14] sat across from me next to Brian. Jose was my student during his first semester at Saint Joe. A big teddy bear of a guy from East Chicago, Indiana, he once met Katy Perry after a festival concert before she achieved megastar status. He complimented her on her show and Perry offered to sign a CD for him. His reply was a bashful "That's okay, thanks" before sneaking away. Jose studied political science and communications, and ran a successful campaign to become student body president. As such, he served as student representative to the Board of Trustees before his term expired at the end of the previous semester. He knew how the Board worked and kept peripheral relationships with at least a few of its members. I asked him what, if any, word he might have gotten from the Board members he knew.

"Well, it's not like we hang out much anymore," Jose said in typical soft-spoken but droll response.

As I ate my salty meatloaf and mashed potatoes, Jose's remark sent a random quip streaking through my head.

"It's not like we're here for the food."

Much earlier on, I mentioned how complaining about cafeteria food was a time-honored tradition at Saint Joseph's, even as I tempered those complaints in perspective of what 19th and early 20th century students endured. No matter the cuisine, we enjoyed our time with each other. Looking down the table, I saw others like me who participated in this communal bread-breaking ritual as their family had before. Guys like Alex McCormick.[15] He reminded me somewhat of the character of Otter from *Animal House*: affable and just a bit slick, but with a sharp intelligence behind it all. Several members of his family were Pumas, but Alex developed his own, genuine attachment to the place. "Saint Joe came to mean more to me with every year," he once told me. If the worst happened, he would feel the hit just like anyone, graduating or not.

I heard another plate hit the table. Nate Wade[16] sat down across from me on the other side of Brian. Nate hailed from Indianapolis, Indiana, studied political science, and ran track with Justin. Freckled and redheaded, he was smart and funny, but also held a quiet intensity about him. Stephen Nickell[17] came to the table with Nate. I was curious to hear their takes on our troubles, but I figured Stephen might be preoccupied thinking about the job he would start by the end of the summer. Stephen had secured a position in the management training program at the Sherwinn-Williams company. I was happy to hear it, but somewhat surprised that he was going to sell paint because he majored in…you guessed it…political science. He was also often the voice of Republican conservatism at the cafeteria table. As one of the many either political science or soon-to-be law students at the table, he would be included in Brian Capouch's calls of "Lawyer boys!" Brian issued those cries when he wanted to challenge the students' knowledge of the law against his own.

"And the legal term for closing an institution is…lawyer boys?" Brian asked.

He waited, mouth hanging open in a smile. Nate and Alex sort of looked at each other and shrugged, but no answer came from the table.

"Dissolution," he said at last.

"You really think that's what's going to happen?" Justin asked.

This prompted a "Capouch story". This one was a tale exemplary of "the worst-case scenario" that harkened back to Brian's father working at a small, corporate farm that went belly up.

"One car came from this direction," Brian said, his flat hands moving in the air to represent the automobiles. "Another from this direction and they blocked the driveways. Guys got out and said that the bank now owned the property."

As the story went, Brian's father attempted to go inside one of the barns to get a few personals. The representative of the bank told Brian's father to turn around or else he would be arrested for trespassing. Brian added, "It can happen that fast if the bank calls the loan."

I stuck my fork into my meatloaf, dragged a morsel through mashed potatoes and gravy, and kept eating. The students at the table, much as the faculty did after our meeting, kept hashing and rehashing the same questions. We needed to know what was happening, we needed to know soon, but even with my father on the Board, none of us had any real avenue to answers. Even Jose found himself in this boat. Despite his service on the Board, Jose still could not in full piece together how we arrived at this point.

"Why did we start an engineering program?" he asked. "You don't start a new program if you're having trouble funding the ones you already have. And what was with all the new vice presidents and consultants? Does Pastoor not know how to do his job?"

"I'm telling you, when a college starts hiring a bunch of vice presidents and consultants, that's a sure sign of things going down the tubes," Brian said. "This whole place could shut down by March if they really did fuck up that bad and the money's not there."

More of Brain's doom-saying. Or so I told myself. I asked him how that could happen if the Board is run by successful businesspeople. He said something to the effect that for many of these "captains of industry," being on the Saint Joe Board was a side gig. At best.

"What do you think?" Justin asked. "Are we finished?"

I realized that Justin was talking to me. I also realized that no one from administration gave us any coaching on how to handle these questions from students. No manual or training existed for faculty to follow, no maps for these territories. There was no "single overriding communication message" to repeat as organizations are often so wont to issue in these matters. The most we got was, "The Board will meet on February 2nd and if there are any questions, refer them to administration."

In no way could I toss out such hollow and vapid buck-passing to students who meant so much to me. Then again, what could I say? I could say that I was hoping against hope that those in power loved Saint Joseph's College as much as we did and were devoted to pulling out every stop to save the place. I could say that I refused to believe that our financial problems were greater than the sum total of skill and knowledge of the entire Puma community. And yet…and yet…the dour rumors, the grim predictions, and the overall sense of a ticking clock haunted my thinking like nightmare demons from "behind the wall of sleep." If I answered Justin's question with the truth, that I feared for my life and was liable to break into tears at any moment, well…that would go against my sense of obligation to be a role model for my students. Did he need to know what I thought or what would be encouraging?

I swallowed hard. All I could say was, “I’m very glad you got into a good school for the fall, Justin.”

Justin nodded and looked down at the table.

“Ah! That’s like what my contact on the Board said when I asked him the same thing,” Brian jumped in, gesticulating. “When I asked he said, ‘Be a nice day if it don’t rain.’”

“That’s what a lot of people don’t get,” Justin said, looking square at me as if to make his message as clear as possible.

I didn’t know what he meant at first.

“They say, ‘Why are you worried? You’re a senior.’ I can see why new freshmen might say that, but Saint Joe means something to me. I care about it.”

“Yeah, from the alumni to the freshmen, we are one big community,” Nate said.

“Plus, my brother, Miguel goes here,” Jose said. “And he’s just a freshman.”

That slipped my mind. I explained that I never doubted any of their commitment to the community. I was just glad that whatever befell us in the coming days, it should not affect their academic or professional futures.

Unlike Jose's little brother…and hundreds of others like him.

We lingered over our meals for another hour, getting up for coffee and dessert. We joked, and we distracted, but in the end, we kept coming back to the same subject matter.

"Well, we won't know anything until the Board meets," Brian said.

That phrase. "Won't know anything until the Board meets." It kept coming up and it became clear that my fate, and the fate of my students and my colleagues, rested in the hands of the Board of Trustees.

But just who were these people?

Save for one exception…my Dad…they were, in a sense, abstractions to me. Nebulous entities. Our relationship was very much like the one I keep with local, state, and federal officials. I might know a few of their names, but to my shame in this participatory democracy, I did not know all of them or the many decisions they make that affect my life. With the Trustees, I'd met a few, while others I knew only by name or as passing faces at functions such as commencement or President Pastoor's gala inauguration.

Experiencing Saint Joe from a faculty perspective, I would hear administrative leaders say, "That will be a Board decision." I would then hear from colleagues that "the Board has nothing to do with that." Additionally, others reported hearing the phrase, "We're an *advisory* board, not a *policy* board," from Board members. What that even meant no one seemed able to elucidate. A joke, perennial going back to when I was an undergrad, asked, "What does it take to be a Trustee? Well, how much are you willing to donate?" All joking aside, the most honest comment I could make that January night would have been, "I don't really know what they do."

So I did research. Why?

On one of the summertime forced marches my Dad took us on through a national park, a ranger told us that in times of crisis, wild animals fall back on what's natural. Black bears have curved claws, so when threatened they will run and find a tree to climb. Grizzly bears have blade-like claws, leaving them unable to climb trees and no choice but to confront the threat with their deadly size and strength. Me? My academic training gives me a natural inclination to write and research. Nuclear tensions are high? I'll research every weapons system, every strategy, every possible effect brought on by a full-tilt exchange, then write essays and fiction about it. Beyond that, I'm pretty much worthless in such a situation.

My research that night showed me I was not alone in this puzzlement over the nature of college boards. There seemed to be a degree of bewilderment in higher education in general as to what a board's function is supposed to be. Are they fundraisers? Are they walking billboards and glad-handers for the institution? Are they a governing body charged with the well-being of a college and guiding it into the future? All of the above? None of the above?

I found an article by Jon Marcus in *The Hechinger Report*. It captured much of the murkiness and foggy perception held of boards by both students and faculty alike. Many blasted these entities as do-nothings, as self-serving individuals in it for a plaque on their business office wall or a line item on their CV. Others claimed the opposite, charging that orders from boards amount to obstructive meddling and in a few cases, altering what a college should be.[18]

It also seemed that challenges for boards of private Catholic schools might be the most acute. Dr. Carol Ann MacGregor, Assistant Professor of Sociology at Loyola University New Orleans, wrote in 2013 that Catholic schools "are closing at an alarming rate." MacGregor identified several factors in these closures, among them being the exorbitant amount of tuition at a private, Catholic school, and a much smaller pool of clergy to draw from to staff these schools. As mentioned earlier, one financial blow dealt to Saint Joe was the retirement of many clergy members who drew meager salaries as their living expenses were met by their status as priests, brothers, or nuns. Other Catholic schools faced this obstacle as well as they became forced to hire secular faculty at salaries that at least attempted to be competitive with other schools. In addition,

MacGregor also cited the ugly and long-running sexual abuse crisis within the Catholic Church, further deterring potential students and their families from attending private Catholic schools, both in secondary and higher education.[19]

In such a climate, board leadership for a Catholic school would need to be, one would think, aware, active, and with firm hands on the navigational controls. For as Marcus reported, despite being "largely unseen," "board[s] of regents and trustees oversee a $407 billion higher-education industry."[20] Given that considerable amount of capital at risk and the ever-escalating pressures on higher ed, boards started to come under increasing fire for being too complacent when it comes to reining in costs and increasing enrollment. Marcus quotes Anne Neal, president of the American Council of Trustees and Alumni:

"Sitting back as passive tourists is no longer a recipe for success in higher education…If they're not in charge, who is?"[21]

By repeated accounts, the Board of Trustees were, at that point anyway, in charge of the entire future of Saint Joseph's College. In fact, it was up to their sole discretion. A tremendous amount of power sat square in the collective hands of only a few people.

I decided to learn more about our Board of Trustees.

The Board consisted of 34 people. Many were alums, most of them possessed business experience, and four were priests from the Society of the Precious Blood. Among the key players:

Benedict "Ben" Sponseller[22] was the Chairman of the Board and a 1974 graduate of Saint Joe. He made his mark on the professional world as a leader in human resources, notably as Director of Human Resources at Abbott Laboratories for 11 years and then as Vice President of HR at Hospira and Baxter pharmaceutical companies. In 2011, Sponseller founded his own outfit, Straight Line Consulting, from which he provided guidance on labor/employee relations, union negotiations, corporate culture, and "directed change management".[23] I met him once at the inauguration reception for President Pastoor and at first mistook him for former Senator Bob Dole.

Stephen Ruff[24] served as Vice Chairman of the Board since 2013 and a Board member since 2003. He graduated from

Saint Joe in 1968 and then went on to the College of Law at DePaul University, so we had two alma maters in common. In his years of practice, Ruff had built a reputation as a competent legal mind, specializing in litigation and estate management.[25] He also accumulated extensive experience with several orders of the Roman Catholic Church and Catholic-sponsored schools. Additionally, Ruff advised these various clients on the lease, sale, and purchase of real estate.[26]

Fr. Larry Hemmelgarn[27] worked as the Provincial Director of the Cincinnati Province of the Missionaries of the Precious Blood. In other words, he was the boss of this particular chunk of C.PP.S. territory. He was also a 1979 graduate of Saint Joe. Through the magic of Google, I came across a personal statement from Hemmelgarn in a 2009 edition of the newsletter, C.PP.S. Today:

"When I was a little boy, I knew I wanted to be a priest. I pictured myself as the pastor of our little country parish, celebrating Mass on Sunday, presiding at weddings and funerals, leading the Stations of the Cross. True to my dream I was ordained 25 years ago, but God had other assignments in mind for me. Although I have been an assistant and have helped out at parishes, I have not yet been a pastor."[28]

Instead, he went into the clerical version of management. Not such a terrible thing in this situation, I thought, having someone who understands issues such as finance and physical assets while tempered with a spiritual compass and a sense of a Catholic college's mission.

Sounded good so far. Three people with experience in organizational leadership, negotiating their way through complex, real life problems, and each with a strong connection, spiritually as well as historically, to Saint Joseph's College. So, they had "buy in." They were, or should be, invested in seeing the College survive. Plus, it seemed that Hemmelgarn and his three other members of the C.PP.S. serving on the Board would be able to provide perspective beyond dollars and cents, because sometimes a college does things that a business wouldn't because our missions are quite different. Yet something about the presence of those four on the Board gave me pause.

I knew that sometime in the past decade, the C.PP.S. underwent a process of "alienation" from Saint Joseph's College.

This meant that the C.PP.S. wanted to be disassociated from ownership of and fiscal responsibility for Saint Joe. If someone sued the College for any reason, they could not include the C.PP.S. in the suit. Despite that, the C.PP.S. still retained voting membership on the Board and one of these members would always be the Provincial. In this case, Hemmelgarn.[29]

That's about as much of a sweetheart deal as you could get. What would that mean for us at this critical juncture in Saint Joe history?

I continued down the list of the Board Members. Then things got even more interesting.

Representative Todd Rokita, Republican, Indiana 4th Congressional District.[30] Our Congressman. His stint on the board went back almost ten years. He served at least a few different Catholic charitable organizations, including the Knights of Columbus.[31] Again, here was someone who appeared to have "skin in the game." He would have to be looking out for the best interests of his district, the economic well-being of his constituents, while also having devotion to a Catholic mission.

And…on drums…Dr. John Nichols. I knew Dad joined the Board in the 1990s and his voice was well-respected in terms of academics and best practices in higher education. Something troubled me, however. When I told him about President Pastoor's bombshell address at the faculty meeting, Dad seemed to be every bit as shocked and caught unawares as the rest of us. Were all 34 board members getting the same information? If not, who was on the inside and was Dad on the outside? If so, why? That in turn begs the question, who is really in control?

I decided that was the stuff of spy movies and *X-Files* episodes. This was the board of a small college. Shadowy alliances and secret cabals pitted against one another did not make any sense in this case. What purpose could it serve? Why would any of them want to say that they moved to close a college, especially if it was their alma mater, without even attempting to salvage it?

That's what I talked myself into anyway, as I turned out the lights and drew up the covers that night. The thinking was something of a departure for me as anxiety and depression often have my mind leaping to doomsday scenarios right from step one. Someone needs to see me in their office? I must have done something wrong. No, not just something wrong. Something awful. Could someone have planted cocaine in my desk? To frame me? Have they been looking at my browser history? Oh God, that's probably it. Look, I'm a writer. It's not unheard of to google "poison," "terrorism," and "water supply" in one search.

That time, I started to feel reassured. The Puma Community was wide. It wasn't just me, rather there were a lot of us in this thing together. Saint Joseph's College was too big and too important to too many people, including an entire order of the Catholic Church, for it to be allowed to fail.

Then "the letter" came.

Or to be more accurate, the email.

On Wednesday, January 25th, at 5:22pm, Saint Joe in-boxes all received a message with the subject header, "Presidential Discourse."[32] It was indeed a message from President Pastoor, addressed to the "Saint Joseph's College Community." After a tap dance opener of the "challenges and blessings" of being President, Pastoor went on to declare:

"After extensive review and analysis of our situation, I have come to the understanding that our financial challenges are dire.

"The truth I have come to understand is that in order for Saint Joseph's College to remain true to our mission to serve our students and to be successful in today's higher education marketplace, we would need to benefit from a cash influx of approximately $100 million with commitments totaling $20 million coming before June 1st, 2017. It is only through financial remedies of this magnitude that I could state confidently that we can provide the kind of educational experience that our students deserve."

The missive closed with what was becoming an all-too common mantra: "The Saint Joseph's College Board of Trustees meeting next Thursday and Friday, February 2nd & 3rd, will discuss a variety of paths forward for the future of the institution."

"What the hell?" I exclaimed at my office desk. "What the hell is that?"

A stretch of sidewalk away from me, Jordan ate dinner with the students in the cafeteria. He later told me about the reactions as students heard the tone of an incoming email and looked down at their phones.

"They were all flabbergasted," Jordan said. "I was too. Where did the $100 million figure come from? We were told $20 million."

"We were in shock. Everyone was looking at their phone in anger and confusion," Justin said.

Most troubling of all was just who President Pastoor included in the "Saint Joseph's College Community" that received the "Presidential Discourse." Current faculty, staff, and students got the message, as did the extended alumni network.

So did all the incoming freshmen enrolled for the fall. And their parents.

It does not require a bold leap of imagination to envision these new students jumping ship upon hearing the college of their choice needs "$100 million" in order to "provide the kind of educational experience that our students deserve."

The "Presidential Discourse", in effect, killed any chance at a freshmen class for Fall 2017.

Chatter spread from office door to office door, down the hallways of the dorms, and all down the line to Main Street, Rensselaer. A friend of mine who taught English at Rensselaer Central High School texted me.

"Hey buddy. Hear times are bad at St. Joe's. You're closing?"

I gnashed my teeth at the insinuation. How dare he say that? Stabbing my fingers into my iPhone's flat screen, I sent my reply: "Where did you hear that? That isn't true. We haven't been told anything yet." I slapped my phone onto my desk.

Fear and anger moved as dance partners in my chest.

So we made the front page of *Inside Indiana Business* the following morning.[33] The lead article more or less recapitulated Pastoor's assertion that "a $20 million cash influx is required by June 1st." The journal then published a copy of Pastoor's letter in its entirety. Though it's been said that "no press is bad press," I could not help but think how grant funders such as Lily viewed

Saint Joseph's College at that moment. Oscar Wilde once said, "There is only one thing in life worse than being talked about, and that is not being talked about."

Loved *The Picture of Dorian Gray*, but really disagreed with his philosophy of PR that day.

A follow-up message from Pastoor came to all Saint Joe employees the next afternoon. In it, Pastoor addressed "a number of erroneous statements" regarding his letter. He countered Brian Capouch's assertion that Saint Joseph's College would close in March, assuring us that the academic year would continue as planned and that "All of us are committed to providing the best possible education and services to our students." Also, Saint Joe needed $20 million by June 1st. "The $100 million dollar figure has been used by the College since June 2015 as a way to address its total debt and deferred maintenance needs. These two areas total approximately $60 million. Please understand that this figure is NOT what is needed immediately but, rather, should be raised over a period of time (5-10 years). The remaining $40 million will facilitate the complete transformation necessary for the College to continue to carry out our mission and remain competitive in the higher education market."[34]

That last sentence brought me a bit of hope, leading me to believe that the College was still planning to move forward and that we would still be here somehow. Perhaps the "mystery donor" would come through and in concert with us taking an offer from the Mayo Clinic for the Waugh property, we might buy ourselves a few years. Then again, the "Overlords" might be succumbing to the increasing "corporatizing" of higher education, where academic degree programs are marketed, bought, and sold the same as one would with Heinz ketchup, Crest toothpaste, or a Hooters.

Pastoor closed by saying he hoped this follow-up missive would clarify any confusion and that we should share these points when talking with students, alums, and the community at-large. I could not help but wonder however, if this clarification also went to those very people rather than just to Saint Joe employees. If not, then the new message seemed a mere awkward attempt to cram demons back into a Pandora's box opened the day before.

February 2nd came. It started as any other bright but cold winter morning at Saint Joe.

Except for the TV news vans parked across the street.

Security carried out their orders to bar the vans from campus, so the reporters and their crews set up on the other side of Highway 231. A newspaper, I never found out which one, published a cartoon of a hypothetical Saint Joe student sitting with woeful gaze at a large church collection plate containing a request for $27 million. Calls by media to the President's office went unanswered or got the response of "too busy right now."

The alumni jumped into action in just one week's time. Flabbergasted by the "Presidential Discourse," alums started to come together through social media, forming a "Save Saint Joe" group on Facebook that fast accumulated members. At the behest of Saint Joe's "overlords", the name of the group was changed to "Involved for Life," matching the College's tagline. No matter the title, the Facebook group served as a tool to organize alums and grassroots fundraising campaigns. Several alums arranged to be on campus for the duration of the board's meeting, attending the prayer of the rosary, mass, and the vigil scheduled for that Thursday night in the Chapel.

I stopped by the cafeteria that night for a quick meal before heading to those services. I met Brian and Justin at our usual table. Over dinner, Justin told us about how Fr. Vince Wirtner, campus chaplain and Vice President of Mission, went around campus boosting morale. He would grin, point to the sky, and proclaim, "God's got this!"[35] During the day, he appeared on campus radio, reiterating the "God's got this!" mantra, attempting to calm fears and return the attentions of both students and professors to academics. After the inspirational address, the station played "Amazing Grace."

"Ha! That's the song they always play at the end of funerals," Brian chimed in. "You know, when all the old ladies are sobbing and singing along out of key."

Even less assured than I was when I walked in, I finished my chicken stir fry and told the fellas I needed to get to the Chapel for the vigil. Brian reminded me he was "allergic" to churches and thus wouldn't be going, but to call him later if I got wind of any news from the Board session. Justin reported that he and Nate Wade would leave for an indoor track meet at Hillside College in the morning, so we probably wouldn't be seeing each other until after the weekend. I shook his hand and we wished each other good luck. I left the caf to make my way across the dark campus to the Chapel…

Where I dropped to my knees as soon as I slid into a pew. Along with the other attendees, I prayed the rosary. I prayed through mass. I prayed harder than at any other point in my life. Not just to God above, but to all the professors and alums I knew who had died. I prayed that they might be in the Board chambers that night in spirit, influencing the Board's decision. I prayed to my Grandma, deceased just three months previous. In my childhood, she never failed to get me what I wanted. I asked that she might come through just one more time somehow. All this I begged of the heavens and all its angels, saints, and other denizens. Not just for me, but for my family, for my students, for the friends I worked alongside of, for anyone who swept the floors, cooked meals, or helped keep the place running. So many with entire lives invested in Saint Joseph's College. Lives with families. People like Jordan Leising in a pew across the aisle from me. People like Tom Ryan, two pews ahead of me and a rosary wrapped tight around his own hands.

I looked around at the church. The statues, the simple wood carvings of the Stations of the Cross. I had seen them all a thousand times before, but that night they took on different meanings. The images of Christ's suffering recalled to my mind depictions of Him in the Garden of Gethsemane, on His knees, hands clasped before Him, and face turned skyward with a forlorn expression. That passage of the Bible haunted me since childhood. There Jesus was, caught in a free-floating "interzone" between the life He once knew and the horrors He knew to come. In terror and sadness, He begged, He pleaded that it might all be taken away from Him, so much so that His sweat turned to blood, or so the gospel says. I could muster no blood from my brow. I hoped stomach pains and an overactive bladder and colon might suffice.

The stained-glass windows of the Chapel sparked another memory. In 1953, George Pal produced a film adaptation of H.G. Wells', *War of the Worlds*. As the film draws to a close, Martian machines are blasting into Los Angeles, burning and killing everything in their path. Most of the city evacuates, but those who could not or did not wish to leave gather together in a church. As they pray and sing hymns, sounds of explosions and destruction outside grow ever nearer. Families hold each other for a final time. In an impressive piece of cinematography, light from the Martian heat rays flickers in spastic bursts through the stained-glass windows of the church.

Then it all stops. The outside is quiet. The ships drop to the streets and their crews collapse, felled dead by viruses and bacteria to which they had no immunity. The little things, "which God in His wisdom placed on this Earth." The invasion ended, saving all of humanity just when all looked lost. I took a bit of solace from that scene.

That I could take more comfort in that moment from a 1950s sci-fi b-movie than the Bible, well…I'm not sure what that says about me.

Services ended. Fr. Wirtner pointed to the ceiling and reminded us that "God's got this!" He also announced that the Chapel would remain open throughout the night for those who wished to pray. I stood up from my pew and greeted alums from back in my day. As I walked with them back out into the icy night, they over and over again expressed their bewilderment. Why wasn't anything said sooner? If things were "dire", why was there no sense of urgency in the typical communication to alumni the previous fall? This led to a back and forth of, "I know a guy at…" followed by a company name such as AT&T or a Catholic university such as Notre Dame…all holding the potential for philanthropic contributions to Saint Joseph's College. Yet never once were these alumni engaged to ask their network for help.

By this point we reached the edge of the Chapel, just in front of the frozen reflecting pond. We said our goodnights and they assured me they would be there the following afternoon for the announcement from the Board. I noticed an over six-foot tall figure walking through the cloister connected to the Chapel, a sporty fedora on his head. Only one person on campus stood at that height: Dr. Chad Pulver.

He came up the walk and I introduced the Vice President for Academic Affairs to our fellow alums just before they headed back to their hotel for the night. I then walked with Dr. Pulver back to the Core Building…and had one of the most surreal conversations of my life.

“Oh, the irony of this isn’t lost on me,” Pulver sighed.

I struggled a bit to keep up with his long stride. Ice on the sidewalk didn’t help matters. I followed his gaze as he looked at Siefert Hall and then made a sweep towards Merlini Hall and the Science Building.

“The campus looks better than it ever has. The faculty are more energized than they’ve ever been,” Pulver said, shaking his head.

“Uh, yeah,” was the only witty reply I could muster.

What was he telling me? What did it mean?

Glancing up at the stars glittering in the clear, cold sky, we chatted about a telescope his sons acquired over the holidays. By that point we reached the warmth of the Core Building. He told me to go home and get rest. I told him I hadn’t been able to sleep in days. He wished me better luck with it.

Pulver went to his corner office. I remained standing in silence in the lobby.

What did all that mean? Did he already know the Board's decision? Was it code? Why didn't he just tell me? Was Pulver trying to tell me we were closing but not really tell me because it can't be announced until the next day? Why the hell didn't I just ask him? What kind of idiot was I for not asking? Was it because I really didn't want to know? Too late now. Those little pinpricks started up again in my stomach. A cold tingle went through my shoulders. I did the first thing that came to mind.

I ran back to the Chapel, its gothic presence looming in the dark, only its front lit only by the floodlights at its base. I ran under those same icy blue stars that Pulver and I remarked about earlier. This time I didn't look up at them with sci-fi dreaminess and scientific curiosity as I did so many times in the past. At that moment, I saw them looking down at me, cold, uncaring, and burning just fine for the next few billion years despite whatever the Board would say the next day. Research on Board members bubbled up in my thoughts as I ran.

What did it say on Sponseller's LinkedIn page? He specialized in "change management." I'd been around corporate doublespeak long enough to know that often means downsizing and layoffs. And Steve Ruff…all those real estate deals he was involved in with Catholic schools…

This really wasn't looking good. Not in the way my mind was connecting the dots, anyway. I thought of something Lenny Bruce once said: "All businessmen are sons of bitches."[36]

My hand shook as I grabbed the smooth wooden handle of the Chapel door. Still heaving from running, my lungs welcomed the warm air inside after the dry bitterness of the outdoors. I looked around. Only one person remained in the church.

It was a lone faculty member.[37] He knelt in the first pew, still holding vigil. I stood in the back so as not to disturb him. His hands clasped, and his head bowed before the altar, he struck me in that moment as a concrete symbol. I said the phrase "This place means everything to me" many times in the days after that January faculty meeting. There kneeling before me was a physical representation of just how much it meant to so many others, no doubt begging in prayer for the same deliverance we all were.

Gethsemane.

I left the Chapel and went downstairs to see who I could see.

I found quite a few people.

The Board Room is adjacent to an older, smaller cafeteria that still fed the clergy. Outside of that is an open chamber with old, clunky folding tables and chairs where students would sometimes congregate to play games and drink coffee. This time the area held several alumni, huddled with pizza and beer. The head of campus security sat perched at guard duty in a chair next to the Board Room door.

"How you doing?" I asked him.

"Oh, hanging by the same thread as everybody else," he replied.

The whole somber scene reminded me of a hospital waiting room, a family gathered outside the surgical ward as someone they love goes under the knife just behind the walls. Everyone sat waiting for word on the patient's condition. Would it be upgraded from "dire"? Even the air felt heavy. The walls themselves seemed to breathe. Something bad was going to happen. You could feel it. The only real question was, "of what magnitude?"

I saw someone and felt a brief moment of recognition. Then I realized it was Jackie Bradway, one of the leaders of the Alumni Board.[38] I knew her by her maiden name, Jackie Leonard when she was two years behind me in undergrad. She was also a fellow writer, working in journalism and then public relations for Kohl's and also for the firm of Fleishman-Hillard. Her first husband, Mike Tackett, was also a Puma and friend of mine as well. He died suddenly in 2012. Though Mike was not from Rensselaer, Jackie buried him in town so that he would be close to where they met, a place they both called "home," a place where she and their two children would always visit.

By bitter coincidence, President Pastoor's "Presidential Discourse" reached her on the fifth anniversary of Mike's death.

"I just had to laugh and throw up my arms when I read it," Jackie said. "Like, 'Of course today is going to get worse.'"

We gave each other a "you doing okay?" hug, befitting the hospital waiting room motif. This led to us catching up a bit. Jackie had remarried and relocated to Milwaukee where she taught at the University of Wisconsin-Milwaukee. She told me she arrived the night prior was full-on committed to doing whatever it would take to save Saint Joe. On her drive down from Milwaukee the previous night, she said she reminisced about her very first visit to the College.

"I actually didn't want to go," Jackie said. "My dad made me and we just kept driving past all of these cornfields. I thought 'We're going the wrong way. We have to be going the wrong way.' But when we got to campus and we turned in through the front gate, and I immediately felt this sense of peace. I knew I had come home."

"This is where I'm going to college," she told her father.

"Could we get out of the car first?" he replied.

Jackie was just one other in a sprawling list of people who had an amazing, transformative experience at Saint Joseph's College.

"How can something like this come from cornfields?" she asked, expecting no real answer.

Jordan walked up to me, a single slice of pizza on a Styrofoam plate in his hand. We did the whole "you doing okay?" hospital waiting room greeting as well.

"I keep hearing this phrase, 'planned incompetence'," he whispered.

In turn, I told him about my bizarre exchange with Dr. Pulver. This resulted in two academics, for all our knowledge and means of articulation, giving one another a series of dumb looks, shrugs, and no answers.

"That night I kept thinking about all my experiences at Saint Joe," Jordan would later tell me. "I wondered if fear was making me misty-eyed and seeing things with rose-colored glasses. Then I remembered a lecture your Dad once gave on creation myths. He said those myths of our origins aren't about what actually happened but they're about you and me and who we are. Obviously, the board would want to continue this. Look at what it's done for me and for so many other people."

Speaking of Dad, I realized he was nowhere to be seen. I moved to make my exit.

"There's Father Hemmelgarn," someone said.

I stopped in my tracks, turned, and saw the priest emerge from the board room. I recognized him right away from the profile photo I saw nights before online, but in person he just looked so…golden. Golden hair, gold-rimmed glasses, a golden hue to his skin, and a smile that wouldn't quit. It was a smile I'd seen on many faces. Hotel managers. College presidents on Parents Weekend. Restaurant maître ds. Someone telling me I "can get it now at half price."

I wondered if he would try to sell me salvation or a used car. One of the alums offered him a beer.

"Well I just might do that," Hemmelgarn said, still smiling.

He sat in one of the "waiting room" chairs. It was then that I noticed he held a small, brown dog in his arms. Hemmelgarn placed the dog on the floor and let it sniff and poke about on the carpet. He watched the dog, looking down from the chair. Other Pumas gathered around to coo at the cute little canine. I stepped back and heard something crunch beneath my feet. Crumbles of plaster fallen from a crack in the dry wall...

Someone asked Hemmelgarn how things were going in the Board Room.

Hemmelgarn sighed.

"Oh, it's a lot of work," he replied. "But it's going all right."

The little dog kept sniffing and scurrying at his feet. When it began to walk its own path away from the chair, Hemmelgarn reached down and made a wall with his left hand, stopping the dog in its tracks and pushing it back beneath his seated legs.

I stole away to call Brian and give him his update. I told him things kept getting weirder. One half of the Saint Joe administration/Board of Trustees conglomerate broadcasted "There are still things we can do" while the other said "We're screwed." It all depended who you talked to. Two definite camps started to emerge.

"There's a phrase going around in rumors. 'Planned incompetence,'" I said.

"If that's true, then those motherfuckers are cooked," Brian replied.

Even through the phone I could sense the anger lacing his typical vigor as he hit the "ed" at the end of "cooked".

"It won't be long before the carpet is pulled back and everyone will see just what went on," Brian said.

But that was my point. Just what was the "it" going on and of more immediate concern, what would tomorrow bring? Brian said he would be there for the Board announcement, slated to take place sometime in the late afternoon when the meeting wrapped up. We said we would meet up then and continue to confer on what would be, I hoped, a positive outcome.

So, I went to bed that night, a night unlike any other. My phone read 12:06AM and I realized I had reached a day that would determine the rest of my life.

NOTES

1. From minutes of the Faculty Assembly of January 17th, 2017.
2. From author's own memory.

3. From minutes of the Faculty Assembly of January 17th, 2017.

4. Ibid.

5. From author's own memory.

6. Dr. Chad Pulver did not respond to multiple requests for an interview.

7. From minutes of the Faculty Assembly of January 17th, 2017.

8. I interviewed Dr. April Toadvine on 3/29/2017. Notes in author's possession.

9. I interviewed Professor Jordan Leising on 3/28/2017. Notes in author's possession.

10. I interviewed Dr. Bill White on 3/28/2017 and several other occasions thereafter. Notes in author's possession.

11. Spencer Conroy politely declined a request for an interview.

12. Dr. Tom Ryan responded to an initial request for an interview, stating he was unavailable. He did not respond to a subsequent request.

13. Adam Current provided me with his written thoughts on the subject of this experience. Documents in author's possession.

14. I interviewed Jose Arteaga several times, primarily on 3/20/2017. Notes in author's possession.

15. I interviewed Alex McCormick several times, primarily on 3/20/2017. Notes in author's possession.

16. I interviewed Nate Wade several times, primarily on 3/20/2017. Notes in author's possession.

17. I interviewed Stephen Nickell several times, primarily on 3/20/2017. Notes in author's possession.

18. Marcus

19. MacGregor

20. Marcus

21. Ibid.

22. I interviewed Ben Sponseller by email on 7/22/2018. Notes in author's possession.

23. Sponseller, Benedict, LinkedIn user profile

24. Steve Ruff declined to be interviewed, but sent a written statement. Statement in author's possession.

25. Ruff, Stephen, LinkedIn user profile

26. Stephen L. Ruff Jr. | Ruff, Freud, Breems & Nelson Ltd

27. Fr. Hemmelgarn initially accepted a request to be interviewed, but did not respond to subsequent questions.

28. Hemmelgarn

29. The official minutes from that Board meeting were unavailable to me. However, my father was Secretary of the Board and wrote the minutes for that day. He provided a signed memo attesting to the truth of the proceedings regarding the C.PP.S. alienation.

30. Indiana Election Results, 08 Nov. 2016

31."Todd Rokita"

32. Pastoor, Robert. "Presidential Discourse." E-mail in author's possession.

33. McGowan

34. E-mail in author's possession.

35. Holden

36. "Lenny Bruce—The Meaning of Obscenity"

37. This individual requested not to be identified.

38. I interviewed Jackie Bradway several times over the past two years, primarily on 5/18/2018.

CHAPTER FOUR: Damocles

Temperatures remained in the teens the following Friday morning.

I dressed in a purple shirt and a purple tie with flecks of scarlet. The College community had pledged to fly Puma colors and show the board our spirit and commitment. I then went out to campus and taught my class on Language, Grammar, and Society. We muddled through Germanic influence on English and then ended half an hour early. Campus ministry had scheduled another mass to take place just after class and I wanted to be at it. As an alum and as a professor, I could think of nowhere more important for me to be than in that mass that very day. Plus, the class couldn't focus that morning. How could they? Before going to the Chapel, I needed to swing by Halleck to drop off a form.

While there, I saw construction underway. Workers moved buckets of paint into a conference room undergoing refurbishment…all as the Board met to decide whether to keep the place open. It struck me how incompatible it all was. You don't spend money on cosmetics if you're under financial duress. Shaking my head, I jogged down the steps of the student center and headed for the Chapel.

Yet again I met Jordan Leising in the pews.

"I canceled class too," said Jordan Leising who arrived behind me in the church. "We're all buzzing around about so many different things. We've no bearing or compass."

Mass began. Fr. Wirtner led us through the ceremony and I prayed with the same urgency and despondency as the night before. In the Prayers of the Faithful, Fr. Wirtner asked that we pray especially for, "our Board of Trustees, who are meeting right now to decide the best possible future for Saint Joseph's College." I took comfort in that petition for it presumed a future. Mass ended, and I left in anxiety to continue begging and beseeching the Lord.

The day wore on. With no further classes, I didn't have an anchor or focus. Someone in the hall mentioned that the following day, February 4th, was the 45th anniversary of the fire that destroyed the Ad Building. Few expected Saint Joseph's College to survive that tragedy.

But it did.

Perked a bit, my desultory self met a few colleagues for lunch in the cafeteria. I don't remember who sat with me, but I had a breaded fish sandwich, fries, coleslaw, and a bowl of cream of broccoli soup. What the mind chooses to recall in times such as that Friday still puzzles me.

Alumni continued to arrive on campus to show their support. Eric Mills[1], a friend from my undergrad era, surprised me in my office. He drove up from Kokomo, Indiana upon hearing of the Board meeting and asked if I would show him around the College as a few years elapsed since his last visit. I welcomed the diversion. As we walked down the hall and I bundled myself against the cold, I heard a cry of "damn it!" from Bill White's office. I told Eric to hold off while I checked on Bill.

"Marian University," Bill said to me. "They're absorbing us. Our students, anyway."

He showed me to his computer. Marian's website displayed a posting, addressed to Saint Joseph's students in no ambiguous terms, telling students about the opportunities and transfer deals available with Marian.[2]

I wandered back to my friend in the hall, thinking the Marian announcement indicative of a brokered merger or a sort of partnership. Merging with a larger Catholic institution was an idea long bandied about with names like Notre Dame and DePaul. Such partnerships grew more and more common in the past decade, particularly for smaller, liberal arts colleges.[3] For many institutions, it is a way to retain as much of an identity as can be before there's talk of closing the doors. It would make sense that the Board made such a deal.

Right?

Eric and I went to walk the campus. He wanted to go across the highway and see Drexel Hall. Given the bitter cold and the duress of the day, I admit I did not want to, but then I realized he must not have seen the building since its restoration. When we were students, it was a dilapidated structure and off limits for safety reasons. It became the object of late-night, post-boozing expeditions as a "haunted house" experience. Indeed, in the dark of night and surrounded by dead trees, Drexel held a most Lovecraftian sensibility.

Things changed. Funds came about to renovate Drexel, a historic landmark as designated by the State of Indiana. It became an office building that housed the departments of admissions, marketing, and development. I relented to the excursion over to Drexel. Part of me saw it as fitting. On this day of all days, I would pay visit to where it all started, the first building on the campus.

Once inside the building, Tony Maidenberg[4] caught me in the hallway. He was Director of Major Gifts for the College and we'd met when I did an interview for a fundraising video. Even in the wake of the "Presidential Discourse," I knew Tony and his office kept working on wooing donors. I introduced him to Eric. Tony called over someone else from the marketing department, telling them to take Eric on a tour of the building. Tony said he wanted to talk to me.

"I heard from a friend a little bit ago," Tony began. "The board just voted to close the College."

The concrete block wall behind me tapped the back of my head…or rather the other way around. I must have lost my balance. I could feel my eyes get wider.

"I have no reason to doubt this person," Tony continued. "And they're sitting outside the board room right now."

I didn't want to be there. That is the most succinct way to put my thoughts at that moment. I wanted to be out of Drexel. I wanted to make apologies to Eric and run back to the Core Building.

And that's exactly what I did in that order. Frigid air burned my lungs as I ran across the campus once more. Steam pumped from my mouth. I slipped in my loafers as they didn't make for optimal running shoes, especially with icy sidewalks thrown in the mix. No matter. I needed to get back to my colleagues…my friends. I didn't know what would happen, but I knew that I wanted to be standing next to them in solidarity when it did.

There still has been no official announcement yet. It's all a lot of loose talk 'til then, I told myself as I entered the Core Building and scaled the stairs to the faculty floor. As I did, my phone vibrated to signal an email. I looked down at the screen and saw the announcement for the "Community Meeting" scheduled for 5pm that afternoon. Counseling services would be available afterwards, it said. Having slogged through more than my share of meetings in my professional life, I never once experienced one that might require "counseling afterward." A faculty member soon replied with an all-campus email that asked, "Why do we need counseling if we have not heard any facts?" A just question. I grew irritated with the dribbles of hints coming out and just wanted something solid. A small group of faculty huddled around Tom Ryan's office and I thought I might find solace among them.

Tom sat at his desk. A lamp at his right elbow glowed the only light in the room, giving his statuettes of Catholic saints shadowy tones. He looked up at the rest of us and piped into the conversation from time to time while checking text messages on his phone. The rest of us, including Jordan Leising, made sullen remarks about the same drips and drabs of information filtering out of the board room of the Chapel basement and our impending meeting followed by optional counseling. Most of us began to concede doom.

"I predict," Tom Ryan said, a broad smile on his face and two index fingers up in the air, "We are not going to close."

I didn't know if it was just another case of Tom's terminal optimism, but in that bleak moment I took it. Besides, if I had to guess, the text messages he kept glancing down at came from Dr. Chad Pulver inside the board room. Tom's view stood in stark contrast to what Tony Maidenberg and the recent emails indicated, but the fact remained that we still didn't know anything. We would, however. Time came to head down to the Shen for the campus-wide meeting.

Michael's office sat across from Tom's. I saw that he had just arrived and was hanging up his winter coat. I stood for a moment and waited for him so that he could walk with the rest of us. We acquired Chad Turner along the way as well.

"Feels like we're walking to the gallows," Chad said as we descended the stairs.

I made the sign of the cross over myself.

Hundreds of students, faculty, and staff already sat in the Shen Auditorium by the time we arrived. In fact, the only place left for anyone was to stand all the way in the back. From my position against the back wall, I could take in the entire auditorium. That allowed me to notice something.

Someone had placed fresh boxes of Kleenex at the end of each aisle.

People kept filing into the Shen. I learned from a passerby that through the wonders of mobile technology and social media, the announcement was being streamed live to alumni and other concerned members of the community across the United States.[5] Dr. Anne Gull,[6] Professor of Chemistry, walked in and stood next to me. We exchanged less-than-enthusiastic greetings given the circumstances. While I came to know her only in the past year, I knew Anne committed the majority of her professional life to Saint Joseph's College. She earned the rank of Full Professor as well as a reputation as an outstanding educator, inspiring many young women to pursue careers in the sciences. In that brief moment when we said hello,

I saw a legacy. Just one of many, so many, in the room. Then the buzzing of ambient conversation stopped.

President Pastoor, himself wearing a purple tie, went to the podium. The assembled paid polite attention.

"Father, please come up and say a prayer," he said.

Father Vince Wirtner came to the microphone. "Oh Lord, we need you here with us tonight," he began. He asked God to "help us open our ears, our hearts, and our minds." He prayed for "the continuing mission of the Society of the Precious Blood." He then returned the podium to Pastoor.

"We never anticipated to be here for this particular meeting, but here we are," Pastoor said.

He went on to explain that no questions would be taken today, but there would be Q&A sessions on Monday for students and for faculty. Then he yielded the floor to Chairman Ben Sponseller, who unfolded a piece of paper in slow, thick movements.

"The Board of Trustees is a huge, huge responsibility," he said. "A scary responsibility at times. We have in our hands the futures of so many and we have the responsibility to carry on what the missionaries of the Precious Blood established for me and my classmates and for you and your classmates."

Ferchrissakes, get on with it, man, I growled beneath my breath.

"We accept that responsibility," Sponseller continued.

Fear. It has a distinct smell to it. Like the charged ozone in the air just before a summer storm. It hung there in an ominous cloud over all of us. A floating sensation came over me, a sort of numbness where I was watching everything in a detached manner, like a child told to go in another room while the adults discussed something traumatic, but the child remains out of sight to listen around the corner.

"The last day and a half have been very difficult days," Sponseller said, his voice soft and somber. "We've come to the conclusion that we just can't align things from a financial perspective to keep the doors open under the current way that we operate."

My arms crossed. I dug my fingers into my shoulders.

"So, we voted today to temporarily shut down. There won't be any students at Saint Joseph's College in the fall of 2017."

I heard the wind go out of several stomachs. A single, sharp wail came from somewhere on my far left. A chorus of sobbing ensued. I couldn't speak. I could only breathe. Intentional, pained breathing, the kind where you have to force it. I stumbled, and Anne Gull took me in her arms, tears appearing on her cheek. My own wall cracked and I let loose with a cry.

This couldn't be happening.

I fell onto my brother's shoulder. We just stood there, saying nothing. We didn't have to.

"Our students, as always, are our number one priority. For you, we have…we will have… multiple choices of places you can go to continue your education," Sponseller said, his voice turning upbeat at the end. "And the reason we're taking such time for Q&A is that we want to have the right answers for you. So, I'm going to step out and be back later. May the Lord be with you."

He stepped away from the podium and began to make a quick ascent up the far aisle, escorted by campus security. Vice Chairman Steve Ruff followed behind Sponseller.

"Two days?" I heard someone shout.

With all the energy of a dying animal, I made a slow turn to my left to see the shouter. It was Jose Arteaga.

"We have to wait two days? That's pathetic! You're fucking pathetic!" Jose continued to yell at Sponseller and Ruff.

Sponseller and Ruff left the building together.

Everything seemed in slow freefall. The Sword of Damocles is swift, I learned. In fact, you're not even sure what the sharp, sudden trauma is until you realize your head has just been sliced off. I still held on to Michael, unable to get much of a bearing. As I did, ramifications started to dawn on me.

I had just lost everything.

My family just lost everything.

Sobs and wails came from every direction. Everyone struggled, looking about as if they just crawled out of a plane crash and didn't quite know where to go next.

Tom Ryan came up the aisle.

"I wish you had been right, Tom," I said.

"Oh, I was right," he said.

He smiled wide and brought his right finger up with a quick thrust.

"We didn't close. We're just taking a break," Ryan said.

He patted me on the shoulder and continued walking, leaving me where I stood.

I started shuffling and bumbling my way through the crowd, stopping at intervals to ask students and faculty if they were all right, as if we'd just emerged from a tornado or something. My phone buzzed in my pocket. It was a text from Debbie. She said that she saw it all on the Facebook livestream, announcement of "suspension of operations." I texted back, "Please find out the procedure for filing for unemployment in Illinois when you work in Indiana." She responded she would not worry about such things just yet. Instead, we would get through this crisis together. Everything she said came with the deepest, most heartful love. In that moment though, I found it feeble solace. Nothing, no one could have helped me.

Then I saw him. He wore his blue windbreaker and customary newsboy cap. His face betrayed no immediate symptoms of distress. Michael moved past me on my right and headed to him. We both took hold of our Dad's arms at once.

"I tried," was all Dad could say.

"That's when I lost it," Jordan Leising later told me. "Seeing the three of you standing there, seeing all that was lost…"

I, on the other hand, did not see Jordan. I could not keep track of anyone in the sullen, dispersing crowd. I did not see April Toadvine, either, who began a slow walk back up to her office. A student followed her.

"She came to see if I was all right," April said, amazed. "She was checking on me, when her own college trajectory had been upended…after the whole world ended in stunned silenced and punctuated sobbing. An end I didn't actually think would happen."

Jackie Bradway stood somewhere at the back of the Shen, steeped in a sense of disbelief. Not only in disbelief at the loss of Saint Joseph's College, but in the handling of the whole ordeal.

"I've seen crisis PR. I've done crisis PR," Jackie said. "I worked on the Firestone tire crisis. What I saw in the Shen is not how it's done. Such hollow words, such lack of emotion, and then they ducked out the door."

Brian Capouch attended the meeting, but I missed him in the melee of grief. After the announcement, an announcement he anticipated for months, he made a quiet exit to mosey over to Halleck and have dinner in the caf. He arrived to find a cafeteria barren of any inhabitants, save for student workers going about their tasks on blank-faced autopilot. A student worker, as always, sat at the front cash register. She looked up to take Brian's money with the same blank face…then exploded into tears. Brian hugged her and tried to tell her everything would be all right, before sitting down to a meal as the sole customer of the cafeteria that night.

Where were all the students?

A police presence arrived on campus as the administration anticipated a possible riot. A campus security SUV blocked the sidewalk leading to the Core Building. While

---

an expected part of planning and preparation in a moment like this, it was all for naught.

"No one wanted to do anything," Stephen Nickell said. "You could hear a pin drop in the dorms as people just stayed in their rooms. I just sat and stared at my desk."

On the other hand, the resident assistants of Saint Joe received marching orders. Jessica Robinson[7] was one of those RAs.

"The housing director at the time called all of the RAs into an emergency meeting," Robinson said. According to her, the RAs were told "not to show our feelings about the closing and that we had to pretend everything was ok for the residents."

This would prove to be a tall order.

Chad Turner went home to his wife, Jess. They poured themselves drinks and called their respective sets of parents. Chad tried to remain optimistic, but kept drinking just the same. Jess just started her own homemade party goods business. After a year of work, sales had started to take off and she had connected with people at craft fairs and flea markets in Indianapolis. Saint

Joe closing held ill portent for her crafts. She might have to go back to work and if that happened, she would have to give up her business altogether. And if they both needed to go elsewhere for a job…

Chad looked around their house, the house they moved into just the previous year.

"People won't want a house with blue walls," he said.

Bill White did not even attend the announcement.

"As soon as I saw the post on Marian's website, I knew," he said. "Everything else was just throwing dirt on us."

Nevertheless, he checked his computer for the emailed version of the announcement. After reading it, he left his study and said to his wife, "I won't be teaching in the fall."

I lost Michael in the dissipating crowd. I later learned he went home to be with his family. His wife jumped into his arms, just as when Michael learned he got the job at Saint Joe. Once again, they both cried. This time for a different reason.

Me? I couldn't go home. I needed to be with others, others who just had the same catastrophe befall them as I did. Where do academics go when the world comes crashing down and the chest cavity that once housed your heart is naught but a vacuum?

The bar, of course.

Through social media, I tracked down my soon-to-be-former colleagues at the Wagon Wheel Bar and Grill, just beyond campus and on the other side of the defunct bowling alley. Wagon Wheel was a time-honored watering hole not only for students, but for alumni during homecoming and Little 5 weekends. One of the bar's main attractions is the Wagonmaster, a burger unlike any other in the 48 contiguous states, if not the world. I did not feel like eating, however. I needed a beer.

Or 42.

I met Jordan Leising along with Dr. Michael Steinhour[8], Assistant Professor of Sociology. They were already two rounds in but were gracious enough to help me catch up. In less than an hour, we accumulated even more of our broken comrades and soon the small bar belonged to Saint Joe faculty and students.

You're not supposed to accept beers and shots from students. It's something I learned in teacher school. That night, however, I didn't see the harm in respecting their care and hospitality. In fact, the night saw the genesis of what would henceforth become a repeated refrain among many of my fellow faculty…

"What are they going to do? Fire me?"

We kept drinking, trying to prop one another up with booze and music from the jukebox. With his quirky sense of "right song, right time," Michael Steinhour played Billy Joel's "We Didn't Start the Fire" and it just seemed to…fit. I started scrolling through alumni and community responses to the video announcement streamed to Facebook. Most of them were variations on the following themes:

"How does this happen without us knowing sooner?"

"This is sickening."

"St. Joe was my daughter's first choice for school next year. She is heartbroken."

And from an actual member of the Board: "May God have mercy on the soul of the Chairman of the Board of Trustees."

More than a few comments called for indictments of President Pastoor and the full Board of Trustees, not that such action would be legally feasible.

"Jon?" a voice said.

I turned around and saw a woman. She had gray hair and wore a button-down shirt, her expression honest in its grimness. She held out her hand.

"Carol Wood," she introduced herself.[9]

I recognized the name. She was a board member. I stood up and shook her hand. I focused hard, trying to hear over the loud music of the bar so that I didn't keep retorting with a frustrating and impolite, "Sorry, what?"

"Your father and I didn't always see eye-to-eye," she said. "But we stood together today. We did all that we could."

This was but the first indication of a deep division in the board room that day. Word of it began to circulate, both in the bar and on social media. We, meaning the students and faculty there that night, learned that the vote to close, or "suspend activities" as the party line had it, came to 18-12.

All four priests of the Society of the Precious Blood voted to close.

When I heard it, I first thought the din of music and loud voices played interference with the words and I misunderstood. No, I caught it right the first time. Soon, several social media posts appeared, repeating the news.

"Yes, multiple sources have confirmed this for me," Jackie Bradway later told me.

Jackie used to be a journalist. She knew her craft. The conclusion seemed inescapable.

How???

The Society of the Precious Blood, the missionaries who founded Saint Joseph's College over 100 years ago, decided that it needed to be ended. I kept drinking, but the very idea, the betrayal of it all…it still made no sense to me. It made no more sense the later it got and the more alcohol that went through my bladder.

That night might have been a good Puma party, if not for the whole "world coming to an end" vibe hanging over it. But parties don't last forever and the Wagon Wheel closed, forcing us back out into the freezing February night. No symbolism lost on me.

As I stepped out of the bar and looked to my right, I could see the lighted Chapel just down the street, seeming to hover there in the icy dark. I gazed at the twin towers and spoke aloud the first words that came to mind.

"Without you what's left to believe in?"

Fierce, bright morning sun shot through my window a few hours later. It drew shadows and shapes on the scuffed walls. I thought I should feel something. Anything. All I did though was stare at the middle of the room where sunlight through the window panes made a cross-like shade on the floor. I got up and went to the bathroom and washed my face. The towel seemed to scratch my skin more than the day before.

I met Dad for breakfast.

I attempted to reconstruct myself from the night before with coffee and oatmeal. I asked Dad about the vote and if the Precious Blood all voted as a block to close. He nodded.

"Hemmelgarn was there in full regalia, big crucifix on his hip," Dad said. "I guess so that we all wouldn't forget he was the Provincial. He said that 'all things have a natural life cycle, and that includes colleges.' That's fucking ridiculous. Colleges last as long as people care about them and maintain them."

I thought of the priest praying over us so many times in the previous days and weeks. Did he know? Even as he said those prayers? Were we in that church praying for something that was already a done deal? I questioned if I could ever sit in a Catholic church again.

Dad and I went silent for a bit, just staring into our coffees. It may be a risky comparison, but it felt like the morning after 9/11. The morning held a somberness of certainty, a certainty of knowing that a sense of security was now gone, and nothing would ever be the same. Was it the apocalypse? Of course not, but it would for certain suffice for ours and other families until the Big One did show up. Our lucida, the gravitational center that held our universe together just vanished in the blink of an eye, and both of us, along with our entire community, found ourselves in freefall. Somehow, we would all have to find a new universe.

At the same time, I could not believe how ordinary everything was. Outside the window by the breakfast table, barren tree branches swayed by slight degrees in an icy breeze. Crystal clear icicles hung from the edge of the roof. It was all just…there. As if nothing had happened the previous day. The sun still came up like clockwork, painting that same rosy, fluorescent pink in the sky as it does every cloudless winter morning. "Tuesday, September 11, 2001, dawned temperate and nearly cloudless in the eastern United States."[10] That's how the report of the 9/11 Commission opens. Indeed I remember the pristine blue sky of that morning and the utter ordinariness of my commute that day. Life went along in Chicago at that moment and even later that night in a sense. Life was going along in Rensselaer the morning of February 4th, 2017. Because that's what the universe does. It goes on…no matter what just happened to you.

My mind tussled with two wild tigers at the same time: trauma from loss and grief and the panic of needing a new job in just three months. What would I do? I still needed to complete my terminal degree. In addition to that, I didn't exactly have an impressive record of publication because I spent most of my time teaching and serving Saint Joe. No articles or short stories in *The New Yorker* or *The Paris Review* or even some lesser known literary journal. I had been something of a lackluster custodian of my talents, if I may even call them such. Despite my accomplishments with students at Saint Joseph's College, I didn't think I was going to be a hot commodity in the higher education marketplace. Partly due to my own cognitive distortion, and partly my discipline being English. In 2017, English was not what you might call a growth sector in colleges and universities. For too long I had known that adjunct instructors were more common than not, all of them teaching classes with no insurance benefits and peanuts for pay.

I might have to try the private sector. Oh, who was I kidding? A quick spin through news headlines and job listings demonstrated to anyone that those with intellectual pursuits aren't exactly valued. I bore neither aptitude for nor interest in "branding" someone's box of cereal or line of trainer shoes.

Writing is indeed a needed skill, but the hapless job-seeking writer really ought to also know something about business or IT in order to be at all attractive. I didn't. Even if I learned those subjects, I'm not a good fit for a corporate office. That much I knew from experience. I am an outsider in such spaces, for I just see the world so differently. Sometimes I cannot even explain what I see. "The office" to me is something of pantomimic caricature. Did I choose this outlook or did my subconscious? Might the answer be "yes?"

Once, I recalled, there was a market for a sort of wandering scholar. These learned people would go from town to town and tell others about the books they'd read in exchange for a meal, a roof, and security.

Of course, that was in medieval times, but I wondered if I might bring it back. Why couldn't I? Nobody reads anymore. It would all be new to them, like a kid coming across old Bugs Bunny cartoons.

Was I going to have to teach high school? Oh God, I was going to have to teach high school, wasn't I? A high school teacher is someone possessed of Olympian mettle and superhuman fortitude. I'm not like that.

Wait, another possibility existed. I dropped my oatmeal spoon and grabbed my phone to check into this sudden, bright beacon of hope. After a Google search, my hopes became dashed upon the rocks.

I was too old for the Coast Guard.

All joking aside, just what *was* I going to do? What were my poor students going to do? Fear caused me to dig a fingernail into one of my knuckles. I watched the pink flesh peel upward in white flakes as a tiny drop of blood bloomed upon the surface.

Anxiety and depression would be here to stay for a while.

"We need to rewrite that opening paragraph in the Saint Joe literature about the history of the College," Dad said.

His voice broke the silence. I put my hands under the table.

"It should read, 'Saint Joseph's College…Founded by the C.PP.S.—and *killed* by the C.PP.S."

When something heavy hits me and I feel trapped under it, there's a question I sometimes ask: Has anyone else ever been through this? Not only does seeking an answer to the question sometimes provide pro tips on crawling my way out, but it also helps me feel less alone. Once again, I found myself turning to research.

In truth, I knew we were not alone. I already knew of the spate of closed colleges. What could I learn from others who went through this same variety of nightmare? How did they compare with the Saint Joe experience? What lessons might they offer for going forward and getting through our own tragedy? I found that the saga of our college community ran parallel in many ways to other collapsed colleges, yet we also possessed key differences. Just as important, I found students, academics, and whole communities whose experiences deserved telling every bit as much as Saint Joe's.

These are their stories.

NOTES

1. Eric Mills gave permission for me to use his name on 5/12/2020. Facebook message in author's possession.
2. Screenshot of this website in author's possession.
3. van der Werf.
4. I interviewed Tony Maidenberg on 6/18/2020. Notes in author's possession.
5. This video is available on the Facebook page, Involved for Life. It was livestreamed by Blake Sailors, a Saint Joseph's College student at the time.
6. I interviewed Dr. Anne Gull in April of 2017. Notes in author's possession.
7. I interviewed Jessica Robinson by Facebook messenger on February 4th, 2021. Notes in author's possession.
8. I interviewed Dr. Michael Steinhour several times between 2017 and 2019. Notes in author's possession.
9. I interviewed Carol Wood on June 24th, 2020. Notes in author's possession.
10. Kean, et al. 18

CHAPTER FIVE: Brothers and Sisters in Arms

Justin Carlson found it.[1]

Dowling College in Oakton, New York, sat on the water's edge of the Connetquot River, flowing in from Nicoll Bay and the Atlantic Ocean. Woodsy and small, the college held everything Carlson looked for.

"I originally chose to go to Dowling because it offered small classroom sizes," Carlson said.

The private liberal arts college was also only a short ride from his home in Port Jefferson Station, New York, more or less due north from Dowling on the other side of Long Island, keeping him close to friends and family. Athletic with close-cropped dark hair, Carlson participated in Army ROTC, affording him a three-and-a-half-year full scholarship to Dowling College. He majored in history while earning a double minor in political science and international studies. An apt choice perhaps as Dowling College is loaded with history.

The institution sits on the site of the waterfront mansion of William K. Vanderbilt, horse breeder and manager of the Vanderbilt network of railroad investments. After Vanderbilt's passing, the Royal Fraternity of Master Metaphysicians took up residence in the house. This organization sought to create "an immortal baby" in the 1930s by isolating the baby from any concept of death or illness.[2]

None of that likely factored into a Dowling student's decision to enroll. The school benefitted many Long Island students like Carlson, who wanted a college with many degree options while remaining close to home. Despite these attractive features, something started going wrong at Dowling. It did not escape Justin Carlson's notice. By his junior year, he knew things were different.

"Over my three years there, the classes kept getting smaller," he said.

He wasn't wrong. Enrollment at Dowling turned into a downward spiral. The student body at Dowling stood at 6,379 students in 2005. By fall of 2014, that population had shrunk to 2,453.[3] The incoming freshmen class dropped 50% between 2011 and 2015.[4] Also debilitating was the presence of an all-too familiar small college killer: debt. Dowling College carried $54 million in long-term debt.[5] Related to these figures was a high tuition rate. The cost of one residential academic year at Dowling for a standard 30-credit package was between $40,000 and $44,000.[6]

"The place looked like a mess," said Carlson. "Then they started laying off professors. I thought something was going on, but I couldn't transfer because of my scholarship."

Then a warning came in June 2014. The Middle States Commission on Higher Education, Dowling's accreditor, declared that Dowling failed to comply with three major financial standards…shades of the Saint Joe evaluation. In response, Dowling needed to submit to Middle States budget projections through 2019, plans for fundraising, a plan for paying off the $54 million debt, and…most ominous of all…a "teach out" plan for Dowling students should Middle States revoke accreditation.[7] In July of 2016, the Board of Trustees announced that the college would close after conferring its final degrees on August 28th, 2016. Middle States Commission on Higher Education would revoke accreditation at midnight thereafter.

"I was at dinner with some friends when I opened up my email," Carlson said. "I was totally shocked. I knew the college was in bad shape, but I didn't think that it would close before I graduated."

"I spent the whole day crying when I found out the news," Jessica Glaz, a Dowling freshman, said to the *Long Island Press*. """My mom wants me to go to NYIT, but I just can't get over it."[8]

While receiving the news by email would be traumatic enough, other students learned of their college's closure through the media. Jordan Beavers, a Dowling senior who studied physical education, also related his experience to *Long Island Press*:

"I feel like this was really shady…I didn't even receive an e-mail," said Jordan Beavers. He shook his head furiously. "I feel like the school lied to everybody."[9]

I stepped back from my laptop. So much about the Dowling experience overlapped with Saint Joe. The gradual deterioration of physical plant. The shock. The accusations of deception and being "shady." Scant hours after Saint Joe's announcement, we already started encountering all these claims and numerous "rabbit holes." Further reading into Dowling's story offered me insight into things to come for Saint Joe. Several Long Island-area colleges lined up to offer transfer packages to the displaced students. Molloy College of Rockville Centre offered to accept all Dowling credits, similar in a way to what Marian University tendered to Saint Joe. Drew Bogner, President of Molloy, even offered a few words on college closure in general:

"How can you let an institution run completely out of money? How in the future can we make sure that colleges have enough money to ensure a proper closure? I think we should start thinking about whether there should be something in place to make sure this doesn't happen again."[10]

Yeah. Would've been nice if somebody could've pulled that off in 2016. My reading of the Dowling case revealed another dimension Saint Joe would be sure to face: the matter of the what remained of the endowment. Funds collected for a college endowment often come from donations and gifts from wills that are given with the intent of ongoing higher education. Endowments are not considered college property in the case of a college's demise. At that point, the funds fall under the administration of the state's Attorney General's office. What all would that mean for Saint Joe?[11]

And would the fate of our physical campus be as that of Dowling College? Blocked off, and maintained just well enough to entice real estate developers and so-called entrepreneurs?

"One thing for sure," Carlson told me. "Was all of the faculty and staff laid off were left scrambling for new jobs," he said, adding that several of these professors had to move out of state entirely.

And where did Carlson end up?

He finished out his college career at…of all places…Saint Joseph's College, Patchogue, New York.

Milt Heinrich never saw himself in Nebraska.

He grew up in a working-class suburb of Cleveland, Ohio. His father was a craftsman, as was his father before him, who also lived with the family.

"Working with your hands was honest work," Heinrich said.

Art is, of course, a form of working with one's hands. Heinrich devoted himself to the study and teaching of art, leading him to a small college in Blair, Nebraska in 1976.

“My interview was at the dean’s house. We had coffee and cherry pie,” Heinrich said.

This would be indicative of what life would be like for him at Dana College.

“I felt at home,” he said. “Everybody smiled at each other at Dana. Everybody said hello to each other at Dana.”

With its small class sizes and overall close-knit student body, this allowed for professors and students to form a relationship of true mentorship which benefitted all.

"Particularly for students who needed a nurturing atmosphere rather than a competitive atmosphere," Heinrich once told the media.[12]

The Dana College community also provided a safe and friendly place to raise a family. The Heinrichs had two children together and raised them in Blair, a town whose population never rose above 7,000 in those years. This allowed the Heinrichs to know the people of their community and take full advantage of the small college atmosphere by attending concerts, plays, and sporting events together. I could identify. Just toss in a Catholic grade school and a College Woods subdivision and it would be the Saint Joe community experience.

Things began to change at the dawn of the 21st century. Enrollment at Dana began to flag. Budget deficits grew larger, to the magnitude of multiple millions of dollars. Donor campaigns did little to ease the burgeoning disaster.[13]

"It was multiple storms hitting all at once," Heinrich said.

Dana College sought a buyer. They found one in a private investing group. This group formed an entity called the Dana Education Corporation. It planned to retain the Dana campus as a for-profit institution while also offering online coursework.

"I really liked the people who were buying us," Heinrich said. "The president already sold his house and had been on campus for weeks."

One hurdle remained, however: approval of the purchase and continued accreditation by the Higher Learning Commission of the North Central Association of Colleges and Schools. This would prove problematic, for at the same time, for-profit colleges came under intense political scrutiny. In June of 2010, Senate Democrats with Dick Durbin of Illinois and Tom Harkin of Iowa leading the charge, vowed to crack down on "bad actors" in the for-profit sector of education in order to safeguard federal student aid funds from fraud and abuse.[14]

On June 30th, 2010, Durbin called for a ban on allowing companies to acquire accreditation through the purchase of nonprofit colleges. That same day, officials at Dana College announced that the college would close as HLC denied the request to transfer accreditation to its new owner. There would be no time for legal action, or any other countermove.[15]

"One of my friends put it this way," Heinrich said. "It was like a wedding. Then at the rehearsal dinner, somebody pulled the plug."

For Heinrich, the news reached him as he drove back to Blair from an appointment in Sioux Falls, Iowa.

"My son called and said, 'Dad, it's over. You have until Tuesday to clean out your office,'" he said.

In a matter of hours, over 500 students learned they would need to find new colleges, and hundreds of employees lost their jobs. Again, it all seemed so frightfully similar to me. A small, religious college in a small, rural Midwestern town, turned into a community shattered by familiar hobgoblins of declining enrollment, budget deficits, and in this case a bit of national politics tossed in on the side. Like Dowling, the physical campus of Dana College remained empty in February of 2017. A man named Allan Baer, leader of an organization called the Renewable Nations Institute (RNI), came in and pitched plans for the property of Dana. Baer sought the campus for educational programs in developing sustainable energy solutions. Talks ensued but little to nothing came of them. Dana College remained empty.[16]

Heinrich continued to work in his private studio in Blair, painting and sculpting on commission as well as producing his own work at his website, Heinrich Design. He planned to retire at the end of what ended up being Dana's last academic year, but that has been of no comfort to him. His community had been lost. He came to grieve that loss in the same manner as one would a family member or dearest friend. He came to practice a self-conditioned routine of just not looking at the empty campus he once loved.

Would I be able to do all of that? Sitting on my bed with my laptop that Saturday after the Saint Joe announcement, I feared I wouldn't.

St. Catharine College, as mentioned earlier, is located in Kentucky, south of Louisville. Look it up on Google Maps and you will find a chilling word in red beneath its marker: CLOSED.

The dawn of the 21st century saw a time of expansion for the college. In 2003 it received approval from the U.S. Department of Education to begin awarding four-year degrees.[17] Unfortunately, that was when the troubles started. The U.S. Department of Education issued notice to St. Catharine College in January 2015 that the college would be placed on "heightened cash monitoring" for "severe findings" resulting from an audit of the college's financial aid program.

Again, I couldn't help but feel I'd seen such a movie before.

However, St. Catharine administrators expressed uncertainty over just what those findings were, but stressed that St. Catharine College was in fine financial shape. Jeremy Pittman, then Vice President for Financial Aid and Enrollment Management at St. Catharine, made the following statement to *Inside Higher Ed*:

"We are fine…We don't have concerns over cash flow issues."[18]

I honestly got chills when I read that. It sent me back to the murky and nebulous days of November and December 2016 when Saint Joe faculty, students, and employees received an "all is well" signal from our own administration. Or at the very least a form of, "We took a hit to the hull, but the ship's not sinking yet. Can you pitch in a hand?" Was this sort of deflection of financial scrutiny part and parcel of small colleges in trouble?

For St. Catharine, the Department of Education contended that the college did not gain federal approval to offer financial aid for its new undergraduate programs initiated in 2011. College officials countered that they did not believe such approval was necessary as the new degree programs did not represent a notable change in the curriculum. One condition of the resulting heightened cash monitoring bore direct effects on how St. Catharine offered its students financial aid. Under the monitoring, the college would give students the aid and then later apply to the federal government to have the funds reimbursed.[19]

These implications were staggering. If the college faced sufficient lag time in recouping the financial aid funds, there would be serious budgetary consequences. If the college did not offer financial aid to the students, then few, if any, students would attend. In addition, an important aspect of St. Catharine's mission was to serve the underprivileged of its surrounding communities, thus making financial aid even more critical. Over half of the college's 600 students came from low-income Kentucky families who qualified for assistance and were reliant on various levels of financial aid to continue their education.[20]

Enrollment declined from 600 to 475 students. The college then filed suit against the federal government for $645,000 in unreimbursed financial aid funds.[21] The suit warned that without the sought monies, the college sat "at the brink of extinction."[22] The matter tumbled through the court system with a judge remanding the case to mediation, but as the federal funds never materialized, it became clear that a mass infusion of cash would be necessary in order for St. Catharine's College to continue into a new academic year. A grim decision was made.

On Wednesday, June 1st, 2016, the Board of Trustees of St. Catharine College voted to close.[23] Hundreds of St. Catharine students now needed to transfer, and 118 employees found themselves out of a job. While such losses are devastating enough, Roger Marcum, a former superintendent of Marion County, Kentucky schools who retired from St. Catharine as an administrator in 2013, described to *The Lexington Herald Reader* what the absence of St. Catharine College would mean to the local community:

"It's a very sad day. The college has made a difference in the lives of a lot of kids who were first-generation college graduates…It met a real need in Central Kentucky, and there's going to be a void. But without federal aid, St. Catharine can't survive because it has so many low-income students."[24]

Also in the same *Lexington Herald Reader* article, a community member spoke to just how important a small, accessible institution of higher education was to this rural area. Michael Lewis headed a local project that gave farming education to veterans. He studied at St. Catharine, learning about farming and community development.

"It's the economic anchor of this community," he said. "I think it speaks to the ways our communities and cultures are controlled from afar. It's really going to affect a lot of people, and it's something that didn't have to happen."[25]

Like the other two closings I examined in my bedroom that chilly February morning, the case of St. Catharine bore obvious parallels. However, two distinct aspects to that particular closing that bore a special kinship to Saint Joseph's College. For one, St. Catharine carried out a mission of educating low-income students, particularly those of its region. Saint Joe shared a similar mission and as I would learn in the months to follow February 2017, there would be those who would treat the humanitarian act with scorn and derision. "There's your business problem. You're teaching people who can't pay."

More serious than such capricious fiscal criticisms is the vast vacuum a closed college tends to believe behind in a small town. What would happen to Rensselaer, Indiana when Saint Joe became an ostensible hole in the ground? What happens to local businesses? What happens to a kid from a cash-strapped rural family and who has only known small classroom education? They try to stick it out because there is no other local option. Not without a small college like Saint Joe.

As I kept reading though, I found not every college closure ended in Armageddon for either the college or its base town.

In the foothills of Virginia's Blue Ridge Mountains, a testament to one of humanity's ugliest institutions gave birth to a place of higher education dedicated to justice and equality.

Sweet Briar College sits just 12 miles north of Lynchburg on what used to be the Sweetbrier tobacco plantation owned by Indiana Fletcher-Williams.[26] She willed that the property of Sweetbrier plantation be turned into an educational institution for women during a time when women did not even have the right to vote.[27] At Sweet Briar, the faculty taught three classes per semester and focused not on churning out publications and research, but instead concentrated their efforts on providing the best possible classroom experience for students. It is therefore no wonder that the college attracted top-notch faculty like Dr. John Ashbrook, a professor of history. In fact, it was this quote from him in *The Atlantic* that would prompt me to one day seek him out for an interview:

"Coming here was the best thing that ever happened to me."[28]

Definite Saint Joe familiarity in that statement, I thought. Same for Dr. Camilla Smith Barnes[29] who was likewise quoted in the same article and who I likewise would speak to.

"It's a very special place," Dr. Barnes said of Sweet Briar.[30]

A very special place with a very serious set of financial challenges, though. Sweet Briar carried a steep price tag for students. That factor, combined with a low demand for single sex colleges, particularly in rural areas, led to a decrease in enrollment. A student body that once sat at 700 full time students dwindled to just over 500.[31] As a consequence, Sweet Briar began offering deep cuts in tuition. Around 74% of the student body received financial aid,[32] with the average need-based scholarship at the time totaling $22,654.[33]

Those chills? I felt them again and not just from the Indiana weather. Sweet Briar's enrollment came close to our on-campus student population at Saint Joe. Not only that, but it sounded like Sweet Briar also offered a similar high discount rate for tuition in order to maintain enrollment. The similarities wouldn't stop there, though, as I would find, for their faculty received similar marching orders to what we did.

Faculty began to help strategize ways to dig Sweet Briar out of its troubles. One obvious suggestion was to make the college coed. Numerous legal hurdles blocked this approach, however, due to the will of Indiana Fletcher-James. As evidence, one need only look to the struggles in desegregating the college. Faculty then shared the burden of sacrifice, accepting freezes in salaries and cuts to their retirement benefits.[34] This was all in addition to Sweet Briar faculty salaries being well beneath the national average.[35] The college hoped these shared sacrifices would act as a stop-gap while Sweet Briar College climbed its way to more solid footing.

That eerie sense of déjà vu? Yes, I kept feeling it.

On the morning of March 3rd, 2015, the faculty and staff of the college received an email summons from President James Jones to a noon community meeting in the campus chapel. "Please make every effort to attend," Jones wrote.

"Those near me and I speculated that there would be an announcement of huge layoffs," said Barnes. "Of course, we expected that, if this were the case, tenured faculty would be spared unless their entire department was cut. As math faculty, we figured that our department was pretty safe, but that they might let go of me: I was the single tenure-track math faculty member and had expected to apply for tenure in the fall."

As members of the Sweet Briar community approached the chapel, they began to see signs that the news might carry more gravity than Dr. Barnes thought.

“What are all those TV trucks doing parked on campus?” one of the librarians asked.

Just before the meeting began, someone drew the alcove curtains, hiding the cross in the chapel.

“One can hear the noon bells tolling in the audio recording [of the meeting],” Barnes said.

The college’s president announced Sweet Briar would close. The next few seconds saw a wave of weepy and angry whispers wash across the assembled.

“It was a quick blow that shocked me to the core,” Barnes said in her *Atlantic* interview. “I was so traumatized that I did practically nothing except cry, hug people.”[36]

I wasn’t there in 2015, of course. Yet from my experience in The Shen Auditorium of Saint Joe, I might as well have been. Adding to the similarities, President Jones, like Saint Joe’s own Ben Sponseller, continued his address undaunted by the display of emotion in order to outline the reasons for closure. These factors included debt, deferred maintenance, lack of interest in rural colleges, and low donation rates from alumni.

"I don't think that [Jones] mentioned the real reasons for what put the school in this position," said Ashbrook. "A disengaged, unimaginative board; a succession of mediocre to poor presidents… an out of control discount rate to attract the students…the abandonment of the traditional liberal arts curriculum that was one of the few strengths of the college; and the inability of the college to hire the right PR to get SBC's message out to prospective students and their families."

Camilla Smith Barnes didn't think of all the ins and outs that led to the cataclysm. She spent most of the day sitting and staring in shock.

"But I rallied a bit in the evening and started my job search by posting on social media that I was suddenly back on the market," she said.

Laura McKenna, writer of *The Atlantic*'s "The Unfortunate Fate of Sweet Briar's Professors," interviewed several faculty members of Sweet Briar College, Ashbrook and Barnes among them. In the following paragraph, McKenna encapsulates just what it means to be a professor at a closing college:

"And in my discussions with faculty, I learned that while some are considering work outside of academia, few have knowledge of how to pursue such opportunities. Even those in the math and sciences—industries generally highlighted as ones poised for immense job growth these days—aren't sure that their skills will translate to another sector. The school, they say, hasn't offered them career counseling or transition services. (The administration for its part says that information regarding severance pay and outplacement services will be available in April.) And there is little hope for a severance package, some faculty told me. With most of the endowment tied up in legal restrictions or designated for creditors, little spare money exists to provide a soft cushion for employees."[37]

That read like the Saint Joe situation in a nutshell. The endowment. And all of its legal entanglements. What would that mean for Saint Joe? Back to the matter of employment, Ashbrook offered me a blunt take his situation at the time.

"For me, this was a devastating blow," he said. "I had given SBC ten years of my professional career and served as visiting professor for six years before that in various institutions. I was mid-career, tenured, openly conservative, and in my mid-40s. In other words, unemployable in academia."

Just like those of us at Saint Joe, Sweet Briar faculty faced the additional hurdle of being let go at a terrible point in the academic hiring cycle. A few professors considered taking adjunct positions, jobs that "won't pay the bills, but at least we won't have a gap on our CVs", as Ashbrook told *The Atlantic*.[38]

Sweet Briar students learned of the closure in a meeting just after the president told the faculty and staff. *The Richmond Times-Dispatch* described the student response:[39]

"Will someone please tell me if this is a joke?" one cried.

“I had all my hopes here,” said Madelin Santos, a freshman originally from the Dominican Republic. “It’s like crushing us. It’s crushing our dreams.”

Shock. It seared the campus. Students, faculty, and staff all found themselves in freefall with nothing solid to grab hold of. As one faculty member pointed out though, the shock came not from naivete in regard to the institution’s financial shape, rather it came from the lack of open discussion as to just how near the precipice was.

"It is impossible to say that any of us lacked information to understand how dire the situation was," said John Casteen, an Associate Professor of Poetry. "At the same time, not a single person thought there was any possibility that the college was going to close at the end of this year. It was very abrupt, a huge surprise."[40]

Someone else, I realized once more, lived my experience. I wouldn’t have wished it on anyone, but there it was. In the case of Sweet Briar though, the alumnae organized and went into action. *The Roanoke Times* conducted their own review of Sweet Briar's publicly filed financial statements. The newspaper published their findings in a March 14th, 2015 editorial under the particularly unambiguous title of "Our view: Sweet Briar board should resign."[41]

"Something just doesn't add up here," the editorial began.

Sweet Briar faculty began to mount their own concerted effort of resistance. On March 16th, 2015, professors broke one of the rules in their own handbook and called together a special meeting. The product of this meeting was an adopted resolution that condemned the board's decision to close and demanded a meeting with the Board of Directors to discuss ways and means of continuing the college.[42] Fifteen days later, the faculty would again meet, this time to issue a vote of no confidence in Sweet Briar's Board of Directors and President James Jones, arguing that said parties shirked their fiduciary responsibilities and refused to engage in dialogue with staff over the matter of the closure. The vote also called for the resignations of Jones and all board members.[43]

Coming on the heels of both votes, an attorney for Amherst County filed a suit against Sweet Briar, arguing that President Jones and the members of the board failed in their duties to keep the college open, failed to consider other options to continue the college, and in the course of doing so breached a number of Virginia state laws. The complaint pointed out that the will of Indiana Fletcher-Williams stipulates that the land Sweet Briar sits upon must always remain a college and may not be sold for other purposes. The suit entered the will as Exhibit A. It is Exhibit C of the suit, however, that offered a glimpse at what might have been happening at the board level. The attachment is a 2014 letter of resignation from a former Sweet Briar board member. After being asked to resign, this board member cited numerous areas of disagreement with the board, including "secretive governance, where few people make decisions."[44]

On the faculty side of things, Dan Gottleib, Associate Professor of Psychology, rose up to become one of the luminaries of the Sweet Briar drama.

"Dan was our intellectual guru," Ashbrook said. "Debunking all the 'Killing Sweet Briar' arguments. He illustrated, with statistics and studies, that we were not in the death spiral that the board and administration said we were [in] and showed that we were viable with changes. His participation was invaluable in the 'Saving Sweet Briar' crusade."

In a May 29th 2015 op-ed to *The Washington Post*, Gottleib wrote:

"Sweet Briar's own problems were self-caused and reversible, leadership made no changes to address the problems, and there are still many options moving forward. Sweet Briar faced a short-term financial problem because leadership made bad decisions and refused to admit them or change course."[45]

Resistance to the Sweet Briar board continued to rise on all fronts. On April 15th, 2015, an Amherst County judge issued a 60-day injunction against Sweet Briar, halting the administration from spending solicited funds, such as donations from alumnae, towards shutting down operations. This did not stop the closure but did slow it down.[46] On April 20th, 2015, over 50 faculty members sued the college, seeking $42 million in compensatory damages for tenured faculty plus $2 million for non-tenured faculty. In addition to these funds, faculty sought "temporary and permanent orders to stop the closure of the college, reinstatement of their jobs, and a declaration of their right to continued employment."[47]

Yet another lawsuit hit the president and the board five days later, this time filed by the students of Sweet Briar and their parents. This suit argued a breach of contract and "tortious acts" by President Jones.[48] The legal back and forth kept going, all the way to the Supreme Court. Then on June 19th, 2015, Virginia's attorney general announced mediation led to an agreement keeping Sweet Briar open for the fall of 2015 with a new president and an all-new Board of Directors. Plans came out for increasing enrollment, trimming the number of majors, and recalling as many of the faculty and staff as possible.[49]

Sweet Briar was saved.

“Was this the way?” I wondered.

As I stepped away from my computer once more and took up a bottle of water, I considered whether all I just read provided a blueprint for saving Saint Joe as well. If lawsuits, alumni, and faculty all worked together in concert, might we have a way of turning all of this off? Closure of Saint Joe need not be fait accompli. Sweet Briar showed that.

Or did it? Might this victorious revolt against the imposed will of a college board be a unique case? Reading further, I found it wasn’t. Another happened a few years before Sweet Briar.

In the middle of otherwise conservative and agrarian southwestern Ohio is a “hippie enclave” called Yellow Springs. The town was founded by social reformers who wanted a utopian community similar to that of New Harmony, Indiana. That latter experiment went bust, but Yellow Springs’ Antioch College survived.

Jeanne Kay[50] came to Antioch as a student in the fall of 2006 to major in Postcolonial Studies.

"Antioch was my miracle," Kay said. "I knew immediately that my life was changed forever and that I was home. There was a place for me in the world and I had found it."

I could completely relate.

It happened to be a troubled home, however. An article in *The Chronicle of Education* dated one year after Kay's arrival, described Antioch campus in the following manner:

"Once a prominent countercultural institution, Antioch is a wreck today. The campus looks almost abandoned. Bricks on buildings are spalling, steel-cased windows are decades old and rusting, and weeds push through cracks on buckling asphalt walkways…Over the years, the college could not keep up with maintenance of its buildings. The residence halls, with group showers and inconsistent Internet access, are a generation behind buildings at other colleges. Many point to the cafeteria as the nadir of the Antioch experience — resembling a school lunchroom, it is open at limited hours with terrible food, current and former students say."[51]

So far, so similar. As Kay emphasized however, that Antiochians, much like Saint Joe Pumas, did not attend the college for food or facilities. They came for community atmosphere and the actual quality of the education. Not only that, students at Antioch learned valuable practical skills as each one of them was expected to work either on campus or in the community while studying. This proved to be such an attractive model that it was "franchised" to other locations in the nation in a system called "Antioch University." Such growth did not come without an economic cost that faculty found burdensome and uneven.

"This system drained administrative resources and the energy of the faculty, making the college financially weak," said Dr. Hassan Rahmanian, calling attention to a unique administrative facet of this arrangement: "We had a chancellor of the university system and a college president."

The reverse seemed to be true as well. The Antioch University system began to view Antioch College as more of a burden than an asset. Antioch archivist Scott Sanders told Bill Donahue of *The New York Times Magazine*:

"To the university, we were the aging family member who needed to be put in an old folks' home. They didn't want to take care of us. Pipes burst on campus. Roofs didn't get repaired. Downspouts went forever without being cleaned out, and we saw constant budget cuts."[52]

Enrollment declined as well in the 21st century. That situation, combined with physical plant challenges and cash troubles, snowballed into a sudden and shocking announcement in June of 2007. Citing insufficient funds to continue operation, the Board declared that Antioch College would indefinitely close in June of 2008. After this "suspension of operations" as the Board called it, thought would be given as to how the college might retool itself for the future.

“I never imagined the decision would come to that point,” Rahmanian said. “It was a big surprise to everyone.”

“Learning about the college's imminent closure…was as traumatic for me as learning of the death of a loved one,” Jeanne Kay said. “It wasn't just that I would not get to graduate- it was that the whole community would be disbanded and destroyed.”

Yes, I thought as I read her account and scribbled notes on Saint Joe stationary. At least someone else out there gets it. Someone else knows what it’s like.

After the shock, however, came an organized revolt…which surprised the Antioch Board of Trustees. Jeanne Kay described this shock board members felt at the pushback from students, faculty, and alums, but emphasized that the reaction stemmed not only from the grievous loss of the beloved college, but a betrayal of one of Antioch’s fundamental principles: community. As explained earlier, faculty, staff, students, and administration all share governance at Antioch.

"This top-down, unexpected decision- even our president at the time, Steve Lawry, did not suspect the board would vote to close the college at that board meeting- went against all of our values, and felt like an attack on our livelihoods, our community, our homes, our principles," Kay said.

I wanted to jump up from my bed and pump fist in the air while yelling, "Preach!" Better, I thought though, to still myself and take careful note of how the revolt at Antioch played out.

Alumni got the Antioch College Revival Fund off the ground with an enthusiastic response.

"They had over one million dollars by the Saturday morning following the announcement [of closure]," Rahmanian said.

Resistance to the board decision continued to mount, crossing most sectors of the Antioch community.

"Faculty were, I think, the most deeply affected," said Jeanne Kay. "Because many had been tenured faculty members for years and years, had given their whole lives to the institution, and were at an age where they had very little employment prospects at other schools- and also not the slightest desire to pick up and move their whole lives."

Tell me about it.

"'Antioch is my home' was our slogan, all year- it's what we wrote in chalk on our red brick walls, on our banners and signs," Jeanne Kay said. "When we came back, there was an atmosphere of joyful resistance: we were going to spend the year fighting to save Antioch."

It would be a "beautiful struggle" as Jeanne called it, borrowing a phrase from Ta-Nehisi Coates. The organized resistance took their arguments straight to the University Board of Trustees.

"I have never seen community meetings so well attended," said Rahmanian, reflecting on the process. "There was no anger. It was all constructive."

As the rebellion made its move, so did administration. Antioch Chancellor Toni Murdock announced that Antioch College President Steve Lawry would be stepping down. Faculty responded with a vote of "no confidence" in Murdock.[53]

Distrust in Murdock and the University system as a whole continued to build. Speculations as to motives in the move to suspend operations emerged in a series of editorials written by Jeanne Kay in *The Record*, Antioch's college newspaper. Kay references a summer 2006 commencement speech by Murdock to a new class of PhDs. In this address, Murdock is quoted as saying that "Antioch College has more nostalgia than dreams." She went on to say "Can the College be reinvented and sustainable without the University? Can the College survive on its own? My question is - why would it want to?"[54]

Kay ended the editorial with hopes that the University might separate itself from the College in a manner "closer to the decolonization of India than that of Algeria. Otherwise we just might have to start building the Barricades."[55]

Though that assertion may have been stirring to say the least, Hassan Rahmanian explained that the copious amount of writing and research done by student journalists at *The Record* were invaluable to the anti-closure movement, both in terms of uncovering fact and in ongoing connection and communication with the Antioch alumni diaspora.

"Every issue they had investigative reports," said Hassan Rahmanian. "Students did a wonderful job. They retained objectivity."

Yet despite these student efforts, the legal actions, the fundraising, and the seesaw, back and forth challenges of the university trustees, and an attempt to buy Antioch College away from the university system, the unthinkable occurred anyway. Negotiations failed, and Antioch College closed at the end of June 2008.[56]

"We all acted like survivors of trauma," said Jeanne Kay. "But I was even more heartbroken by the knowledge that my comrades in arms, even those with whom I'd disagreed or fought most vehemently throughout the year, would be without a job, without a home, in just a few weeks. That we were simply going to disperse, go our own wounded way after this terrible collective defeat while the new Antioch would be started from scratch, as if we'd never been there to fight."

Kay transferred to another college. She described her experience at the new campus as "unimpressive" and "sanitized." It also lacked any of the sense of identity and community once found at Antioch. Something else, something greater, also tore at her spirit.

"How could I have left my community and chosen to save myself?" she asked. "I wrote about my homesickness -- for Antioch was my home, undeniably – to a classmate."

This friend read Kay's message in the Antioch library, just as a former faculty mentor of Kay's happened to walk past.

"Bring her home," the professor said.

"I got the message," Kay said. "Ten minutes later, I was hauling my suitcase out of my dorm, towards the admissions office to sign my "discharge" paperwork. That night I spent at an airport motel in New York. The next day I was back in Yellow Springs."

But back for what? Did not Antioch College close?

It did. What happened after the closing, however, may be one of most unique and inspiring stories in all of higher education. It is the story of Nonstop Antioch.

After the closing, a few of Antioch's students and faculty operated in a sort of exile. The alumni fund allocated $1 million to pay the salaries of these professors as they continued to teach classes. Tuition for a Nonstop student was a meager $1,500 per year.[57] The classes took place in locations all over Yellow Springs as the community opened their doors wide to the exiles. Hassan Rahmanian was one of the Nonstop faculty members.

"I taught economic development classes that were connected to local efforts," he said. "There was a full integration with the community. The classes took place in old industrial buildings, in churches, in coffeeshops…where you'd walk in and see a sign saying 'Class in session' in a corner. I taught a class in someone's living room. Out the window you could see the dead campus. Just eerie…"

Without any of the trappings of a traditional college experience, students remained and professors kept teaching, providing concrete testament to the allure of Antioch and the loyalty of its community members.

"They have the body, but we have the soul," Hassan Rahmanian told fellow Antiochians.

In 2009, Nonstop Antioch even held a commencement exercise. Jeanne Kay described the experience, referring to a journal entry she made in 2007.

"I wrote that there is nothing in the world that can stop me from graduating from Antioch College," Kay said. "A month and a half later, I learned there was indeed something that could stop me from graduating from Antioch College and it was called Antioch University."

Even as the commencement exercise transpired, activism continued in meetings between supporters of Antioch College and trustees of the University system with the Great Lakes Colleges Association acting as mediator. On June 30th, 2009, there was at last a breakthrough in these talks. As stated in a Great Lakes Colleges Association press release from that day, both entities, "agreed to move expeditiously to create a new, fully independent, Antioch College to reopen at an early date."[58]

The name "Antioch College" once more sat in the hands of alums, free and independent of the university system with its own board of trustees and jurisdiction over funds. A new college president was unanimously selected, Mark Roosevelt, the former superintendent of Pittsburgh Public Schools.[59] They could even begin recruiting new faculty and students, eventually gathering a starter set of six professors and 35 students, and all of these students would attend tuition-free.[60] By 2012, Antioch received an overwhelming 3,000 applications for its 75 slots, making it one of the more selective colleges in the United States.[61] Hassan Rahmanian even reported that all of the first four cohorts graduated tuition free, while also receiving discounts on housing and meals. Speaking of Rahmanian, he became Vice President of Academic Affairs.

"There have been financial pressures since day one," he said. "But I am optimistic about what we are doing and our future. We have a large population of First-Generation college students, and diverse students."

Why do all of this for a college? Particularly when it seemed lost? Simple.

Because it was home.

Just as Saint Joe was for me, and for so many others. Sweet Briar and Antioch did it. They resisted the edicts of their respective boards and fought back to keep their homes. Somewhere in the story of their struggles, was there a formula for Saint Joe?

I aimed to find out.

NOTES

1. I interviewed Justin Carlson by email on July 6th, 2017. Notes in author's possession.
2. Jahn.
3. Booth and Bolger.
4. Smith, Kate.
5. Ferrette and Schwartz.
6. Roy and Ferrttee.
7. Ibid.
8. Booth and Bolger.
9. Ibid.
10. Ferrette and Schwartz.
11. Smith, Kate.
12. Gibbs.
13. Abourezk.
14. Field.
15. Huckabee.
16. Rohman.
17. Blackford.
18. Stratford.
19. "Kentucky's St. Catharine's College…"
20. Ibid.
21. Douglas-Gabriel.
22. "Kentucky's St. Catharine's College…"
23. Blackford.
24. Ibid.
25. Ibid.
26. Gore.
27. "History."
28. McKenna.
29. I interviewed Dr. Smith Barnes by email. Notes in author's possession.

30. McKenna.
31. Ibid.
32. "Here's How Much You'll Pay to Attend Sweet Briar College."
33. McKenna.
34. Ibid.
35. "Sweet Briar College Faculty Salaries."
36. McKenna.
37. Ibid.
38. Ibid.
39. Kapsidelis
40. McKenna.
41. "Our view: Sweet Briar board should resign."
42. Friedenberger.
43. Pounds and Petska.
44. Commonwealth of Virginia v. Sweet Briar Institute, Paul G. Rice, and James F. Jones Jr.
45. Gottlieb.
46. Pounds, "Judge issues 60-day injunction against using solicited funds to close Sweet Briar."
47. Pounds, "Sweet Briar faculty file complaint seeking more than $40 million in damages."
48. Pounds, "Students, parents join with alumnae on Sweet Briar College legal action."
49. Pounds, "Transfer of power complete at Sweet Briar College."
50. I interviewed Jeanne Kay by email on 28 Sept. 2017 and 13 Mar. 2018. Notes with author.
51. Carlson, Scott ""A House Divided."
52. Donahue.
53. Chiddister, "Faculty vote determines no confidence…"
54. Kay, "Editorial."
55. Ibid.
56. Holden, "The fall and rise of a college."
57. Donahue.
58. "Antioch College Alumni Association Creates Framework…"
59. Fuoco.
60. Donahue.
61. Chiddister, "Mix of big dreams, hard reality."

CHAPTER SIX: Wolverines

On Saturday, February 4th, 2017, Justin Hays and Nate Wade rode a team bus back to Saint Joe from their track meet. Using their smartphones and laptops, they accessed financial data for Saint Joseph's College and reviewed all official correspondence from the Board and administration over the previous months. Again and again they pored over documents.

Justin texted Alex McCormick, Stephen Nickell, and Jose Arteaga back on campus, telling them they would meet upon the track team's return and begin to mobilize. Nate bit into a granola bar as he leaned back in his seat.

"Giving us three days to plan a counter-attack was the dumbest thing they could have done," he said.

The following Sunday I got an email. The entire faculty did. It came from Dr. Pulver, inviting us to a Monday evening informal meeting at Dr. Tom Ryan's house.

"It is possible that we may not be part of the new campus," he wrote. "But we can provide insights and guidance to those who will be in that position."[1]

"Unwashed arrogance," I said in gut reaction.

Reactions from others came quick.

"Colleagues, is it just me or did we just get an invitation to provide input on a future we will unlikely be a part of? This goes from bad to worse," one longtime professor wrote.

"Who am I giving guidance to? You are getting rid of all of us but I should want to help whoever they recreate this place with?" asked another.

So it went. Back and forth between professors. I read these emails on my phone, sitting on my couch and watching the New England Patriots overcome an enormous point deficit to beat the Atlanta Falcons and win the Super Bowl in overtime. There is always a way to come back, I thought. They kept us in the dark about the impending closure. Might it also be so that there is a plan for resurrection and it's under wraps too?

I returned to campus Monday morning. Someone hung a Saint Joe flag upside down in a window of the Core Building, accompanied by a sign which read, "UNDER SIEGE." I scaled the stairs to the second floor. Somber chatter filled hallways. I heard that the "suspension" announcement took the human resources staff of Saint Joe every bit by surprise as the rest of us. That meant they started their Monday morning scrambling to begin the process of following a joyless procedure: typing layoff notices for 200 employees.

Other talk said that the nursing program would continue at St. Elizabeth's Hospital in Lafayette. That way Saint Joseph's could still hold on to accreditation as it transformed into…whatever the Overlords had in mind. All of it sounded like the spread of loose rumor at that point. Such things tend to happen in the wake of disaster and the breakdown of communication.

Shuffling around the corner, I entered the faculty lounge where I poured a mug of coffee, just as I did every morning. I then made my way back into the hallway where I saw April

Toadvine, unlocking the door to her office while holding three empty cardboard boxes.

"Starting already?" I asked her.

"I don't trust how much longer we'll have access to our offices," April replied.

Dazed by the notion, I went into my own office and sat down in the chair by my window. Winter sunlight fell on my face. I took a drink from my mug, felt the welcome jolt of java on my tongue, and then picked up *Candide* by Voltaire, the text we would be discussing in Core 2 that day. Flipping the book open, I started to read. If you could call it that. My eyes darted from a word at the top of the left page, then to one in the middle paragraph of the right. I attempted to correct my gaze, but it snapped to the bottom of the page. I tossed the book back on my desk and looked out my window at the campus.

Just down the hallway and unbeknownst to me at the time, Michael spent time in his own office behind a closed door, preparing to give a lecture that morning in the Shen. How to prepare? Five minutes of uncontrolled weeping seemed to be the only sensible choice at that moment.

– • –

Both our mornings, though separate, indicated what was to come. Somehow, we would be expected to keep teaching. All of the faculty were going to have to keep teaching as everything came apart around us. As students shifted their focus…and who could blame them… to where they would go next, as pressure mounted for professors to find new employment, as everything we loved crashed down piece by piece, we needed to keep teaching. How will any of us concentrate? What would be the point?

The point, I decided, was that it was my job and regardless of the circumstances, I needed to leave my students with at least a modicum of academic value. It was my obligation.

I went to my class. Nothing seemed different. All my students showed up, or most of them did, anyway. They looked the same as the week before. They wore that "Saint Joe uniform" I described so much earlier: Puma athletic sweats and hoodies, black socks in thick Nike flipflops. Everything looked the same, but of course none of it was.

"So…how was your weekend?" I asked, hyperbolic fake smile and all.

My response came in the form of grumbled laughter. One of them told me that chicken bacon ranch sandwiches would never be the same to her. I furrowed my brow and she reminded me that she worked part-time at Subway.

"That was the sandwich I was making exactly when the email came through last Friday," she said.

After placing the sandwich in the toaster, she heard her phone ding on the counter. She glanced down and saw the email on the screen.

"I broke down," she said. "I just kept saying, 'What am I going to do?' The customer had to ask if I was all right."

Others responded with grim nods. I could not help but think of Justin Carlson and how he learned of Dowling College's closing. I guess people really do learn of disaster through email.

I said they would be fine. As already admitted students, most of them would be known quantities to college admissions departments. That's a golden commodity in higher education. When the other colleges showed up, and they would, the students would have numerous offers to choose from. More than that, they were Pumas. Our education prepared them to face many challenges, no matter how egregious.

"What will happen to you?" one of them asked.

They all looked at me. I went quiet, somewhat taken off guard by the question.

"I have no idea," I said with all honesty.

I would get a little more of an idea that afternoon…I and every other employee of the college that is. In a meeting hosted by Ben Sponseller, we would learn about severance, final days, and when our health insurance would end.

We entered the Shen Auditorium for the first time since the awful pronouncement three days earlier. Counting, I saw just about every faculty member there, seated among those who cleaned our buildings, staffed our administrative offices, kept the heat and the power running, cooked our meals, and maintained our beautiful landscaping. I took a seat. I can still remember the smell of the bottle of hand sanitizer in front of me...right next to the fresh box of Kleenex.

Ben Sponseller took the stage. Accepting the microphone from one of our AV techs, he began to speak.[2]

"I'm an alumni too," he began. "I have a lot of skin in the game, but not more than you do and I'll never lose sight of that. It's a driving force. Where does the buck stop? Right here with me and the board. I accept the weight, even though I don't want to, but I will. It's important there's someone here who makes sure we do this with class and the right way and with dignity."

He paced for a bit, taking a pause.

"What led up to this? We're running out of money," Sponseller continued. "It's a reality. HLC has a gun to our head because we haven't satisfied their demands financially. We could find ourselves without accreditation in the middle of a semester."

I squinted my eyes and scribbled on my notebook: "HLC withdrawing accreditation in the middle of a semester???????" Yes, I used that many question marks. Even underlined them.

"Our tuition discount rate is about 65%," said Sponseller. "So they're [students] only paying for 35% of the operating cost, and we can't afford to run the institution this way."

He continued to rattle off more reasons. In fact, they sounded like they could have been plagiarized straight from President Jones of Sweet Briar years previous. Deferred maintenance. Lack of alumni giving. We did have the income from the Waugh farms, he said, but there were multiple restrictions on converting it to the cash Saint Joe needed.

"Since we can't use it today, we'll use it later for Catholic education," he said.

Later?? My suspicions of an unspoken plan grew emboldened. Sponseller paced a bit and looked up towards the back of the house. His eyes open wide, his gestures gentle but definite, his vocal tone upbeat…almost like a pitchman.

"Over the next several months, we will be downsizing all departments. We expect severance to be paid from the rest of our endowment. We are working with the Indiana Attorney General tomorrow and should know within three months," Sponseller said.

Yes, just as I found in the case of Dowling College, any dispersing of endowment funds required approval of the Indiana Attorney General. Thus, getting any kind of severance pay by the end of our contracts in the summer was entirely incumbent on the AG's decision. A lot could go wrong. A lot.

Sponseller opened the floor to questions. Employees wishing to speak approached a microphone on a stand in the stage-right aisle.

QUESTION: "What if the Attorney General doesn't let us use the endowment? Do we not get a severance?"

Sponseller: "Fair question, I don't know the answer. I said I wouldn't speculate and I'm not going to."

QUESTION: "When will the first round of downsizing take place?"

Sponseller: "I can't give an exact day and time. But knowing what we know there are positions that will disappear overnight. I'm not trying to be a wise guy, but we don't know."

I started to notice an unsettling trend. However, I thought it might just be my own perceptions askew from bewilderment and duress.

QUESTION: "A variety of us are under different contracts. What does that mean for severance?"

Sponseller: "I don't know, I haven't read our contracts. We'll have to get back to you."

No, it was a trend.

QUESTION: "You stated all means had been exhausted, but I haven't heard of anyone going out into the community to ask them for donations and help? To the industries around us?"

Sponseller: "I don't know the answer to that either."

Still trending.

My mind couldn't keep from going back to the fact that we met for the express purpose of getting answers to the terms of "ending our professional relationship," as it's put in corporatespeak, with Saint Joe. Not to put too fine a point on it, but the whole reason why the executive membership of the Board said they wanted three days of additional time.

Bill White approached the microphone.

Bill: "How much longer will employees be covered by health insurance?"

Sponseller: "I don't know. We'll have to get back to you on that."

Bill: "That's all right. Our lawyers will find out."

Applause and cheers roared up from the assembled. A new petitioner took his place, a woman wearing a gray hoodie. I knew her. She cleaned the second floor of the Core Building. Sometimes she would stop in my office and look at my action figures and we would talk about the superheroes her little boy loved. As she breathed in to speak, she wiped tears from her eyes.

QUESTION: “We know we will be let go. Will this happen before students leave, or right after they leave? How long do I have before I have to tell my son, sorry I can’t feed you and sorry we’re homeless?”

Sponseller: “It’s extremely unlikely it will be before graduation. And I’m sorry.”

He added an impotent shrug at the end of his statement. I did not personally discern this as a gesture of discarding, or capricious dismissal. I got the genuine impression Sponseller wanted to do something for her, but possessed no powers to do so at that time. Once activated, a closure is difficult to stop.

QUESTION: "I don't trust anything people have said here today, because you haven't answered the questions. Was the board given only one option for the continuation of the college?"

Sponseller: "No. We looked at many."

The meeting ended not long after that. Somehow, I left knowing measurably less than I knew walking in.

Across the street in Drexel Hall, employees in Admissions experienced no less surreal of a day.

"That morning, we denied an entire recruiting class," Adam Current said. "We returned deposits, cancelled visits."

They also fielded a substantial amount of calls from angry parents. A similar scene unfolded at the office of the Registrar, who like every other division of the campus, learned of the closure just two days prior. Students packed the place to request transcripts, "like a bank run during the Depression," as Adam called it. A weekend gave no time to change policy and with no contrary direction from top administration, a customary fee still came with each request for transcripts. The Registrar's office held no unilateral power to change this fact. Again, outraged parents hit the phones delivered scathing epithets. Eventually, administration rescinded the fees.

"Parents had every right to be outraged," Current said. "All of us felt equally shocked and betrayed. But as their kids packed their dorm rooms, we packed our offices."

I ended up going to Ryan's house for the evening meeting.

A smattering of colleagues chose to do the same, including Bill White. I put together a plate of snacks from the spread the Ryans graciously prepared, and then sat down in one of the living rooms where Dr. Pulver was holding court in front of the Ryans' fireplace. After the chitchat of opening pleasantries, he fielded a natural first question. "What the hell happened?" Pulver responded that Spencer Conroy, Vice President for Business Affairs called him on December 23rd 2016. He said We're out in May. Pulver said, what do you mean we're out? We're out of money, Conroy told him.

The matter dropped as conversation turned to ideas for a "re-engineered Saint Joseph's College" and what such a College might look like.

Tom Ryan suggested that the College could become a place for underperforming high school students. I built off that, saying that we experienced considerable success with the Extended Core bridge program, so we already held a track record in such matters. Dr. Pulver pointed out that many of the families of said students could not afford full tuition, so that would not go far towards correcting the financial problem. Whatever would emerge from the campus needed to be financially sustainable, but both Ryan and Pulver agreed that Core must be an integral part of it.

"In that case, I'll go ahead and say I'd be perfect for it," Bill White said. "I've taught every Core except 5 and 6, and I have been a director of Cores 1 and 2."

At that point, Pulver's face went ashen. Ryan looked down at his living room floor. I'm not certain what their exact response was, but it was something along the lines of "we'll think about it." Little more was said, concrete or otherwise, of any specific plans to jumpstart Saint Joe back to life. Instead, the gathering disbanded, amounting to not much more than more talk about the loss of the College and an hors d'oeuvre buffet in Tom Ryan's living room.

Driving the snow-compacted roadway out of the subdivision, two thoughts started to gnaw at me and yes those came in addition to the sadness of the loss of Saint Joe and the fear of a jobless future. One was the growing sense of still more plans and machinations underway behind the curtain. Someone…more likely a group of someones…already formed definite ideas of what Saint Joe would become. The other realization being only a mere fraction of us would be part of it. Despite mostly petty disputes, Saint Joe faculty shared a powerful sense of comradery. We believed in the mission of the College and we worked in collaboration to provide a curriculum while at every turn being asked to do more with less.

But the human drive to survive is strong and that drive becomes something of a "mono-thought" when terrified. Would we fracture? As our *Titanic* continued to sink for the coming three months and when the icy water reached waist-high, would

100 colleagues knock one another aside to get in one of only two or three lifeboats?

Would I?

Even though it was going on 9:00pm, I returned to campus. The students would meet with Sponseller in the Shen, the late hour due to the large population of student athletes not getting out of practice until that time. Once more I found myself in that damned auditorium. Once more it filled to standing room only. Would there be any more answers provided at this meeting than the previous? Given the number stood at zero from earlier that afternoon, I realized the bar was so low it was in the Earth's mantle.

I saw Justin Hays first. He wore a dress shirt colored Puma purple and a silver-gray tie. Stephen Nickell, Jose Arteaga, Nate Wade, and Alexander McCormick were with him and each wore button down shirts with ties and in Nate's and Jose's cases, jackets.

"We wanted to be seen as professionals and taken seriously as professionals," Justin later told me. "We were mobilized. We had junior and senior meetings beforehand, so we were ready with questions."

A sophomore named Blake Sailors,[3] the same student who live-streamed the announcement of the closure the previous Friday, set up to video the meeting and livestream it to the Involved for Life page on Facebook. Towards the beginning of the video, you can hear a man's voice asking Blake questions.

"Are you the one who did the video from last Friday?"

Blake confirmed it.

"This meeting is probably going to go longer than that one did. Is this going live to Facebook?"

Once more, Blake confirmed it.

"Well thanks for making me famous."

An uneasy laugh came from Blake.

A beat went by. Blake can be heard asking the person sitting next to him off camera just who that man was.

"That was the Chairman of the Board of Trustees," came the reply.[4]

The session began, much as the previous one did with Sponseller reiterating the rationale of those who voted to "suspend operations."

"We may very well lose our accreditation next year mid-semester. Do you know how irresponsible it would be for this board to be in the middle of a semester and we lose our accreditation?" Sponseller asked.

He turned the floor over to the students for questions. It was a setup similar to the faculty and staff meeting, two microphones, one at each of the center aisles. Stephen Nickel came to the microphone first.

"You say we could lose accreditation in the middle of next semester," Stephen asked. "How is that possible when the Higher Learning Commission said the earliest we could lose our accreditation is December of 2018?"

Sponseller responded that Saint Joseph's College needed to show a balanced budget by "this time next year" and one year would not be enough to correct the budget. Justin Hays came to the microphone for the first of many rounds he would fight that night.

- - -

JUSTIN: "Since the buck stops with you and since $27 million of debt is not an overnight catastrophe, how do you plan on being accountable for a problem of this magnitude?"

The Pumas erupted in cheers and clapping. Both Justin and Nate waved their arms and made "shhh" motions to the students. Sponseller answered that Saint Joe took out loans and decided to pay them off later, that they invested in students, but just never got the enrollment numbers needed to pay off the debt.

"Why did we do it? We did it for you, my friend," Sponseller said with a point to Justin.

At that point, Jose Arteaga came to the microphone.

"Hi Jose!" Sponseller beamed.

Jose took a beat before responding, "Whatever." He returned his attention to the notes in his hand.

JOSE: "Who authorized the letter from January 25th?"

SPONSELLER: "I'm Chairman of the Board, the buck stops with me, I authorized it."

Well, at least one of my questions was answered. Nate Wade then came to the mic.

NATE: “You mentioned a going concern by auditors. When did you learn of the going concern?”

SPONSELLER: “In the last…six to eight weeks?”

For confirmation, he looked to President Pastoor, seated in the front right row.

Sponseller began to roam the stage, saying how Saint Joe experienced the financial bind for years because the Board wanted to “keep this place open.” To remain open would be “rolling the dice that we won’t lose accreditation. We’re looking out for you.” He then squared his body towards the assembled students.

“I tell you what,” Sponseller began. “You’re going to be facing disappointments a lot greater than this in life.”

A low grumble rolled through the student body. One student’s jaw dropped, aghast in disbelief. Another looked away in disgust. Yet another placed her cheekbones in her fingers and seemed to squeeze back tears. Again, Jose spoke.

JOSE: “You said you won’t resign, but I think you should really look into that.”

The Puma brothers and sisters cheered, and once more Nate and Stephen urged them to quiet.

JOSE: "My next question is for President Pastoor."

He asked why Pastoor hired a Vice President of Institutional Advancement who had no fundraising experience. Pastoor countered that the VP of Institutional Advancement accrued numerous years of fundraising and donor outreach experience at several institutions. Jose pointed to the laptop in his hands.

JOSE: "Then he needs to update his LinkedIn page."

Laughter ensued and Pastoor admonished Jose to "Have a little respect." Justin and Stephen motioned for their fellow students to quiet down. Good, I thought. Just as Hassan Rahmanian said of student assemblies at Antioch, our engagements with the Board would need to be constructive and free of anger.

There came more questions. One student asked why the College's alumni did not receive notice of the dire financial situation far in advance of Pastoor's letter. Also, is all the secrecy ethical in this case?

SPONSELLER: “I believe if you go back and look at our correspondence, you see an increased sense of urgency. There’s even one that says, ‘This is a call to action.’ As for ethical, I have no problems sleeping at night over our decision.”

The wave of grumbling returned to the auditorium. That whole “all constructive, no anger” tack started looking more untenable with each answer.

Gabi Pepple, a junior philosophy major, came to the mic.

GABI: “I want to say this is not just a disappointment for the students, but for the faculty and staff who make their lives here. Is it responsible or irresponsible to give us a few months to figure out our lives while you’ve had decades to work on this problem?”

Sponseller, again, reminded her that “accreditation loss could happen as soon as the middle of next semester.”

GABI: “Higher Learning Commission says we have until at least 2018.”

SPONSELLER: “That’s just one piece of the story. The other is that we don’t have enough money to continue and you then wouldn’t be eligible for loans.”

Someone else asked just where the financial deficit came from.

SPONSELLER: “That’s not a difficult question to answer. It’s the tuition discount rate. We give you too much financial aid.”

More grumbles ensued from the audience. Sponseller rushed to respond.

SPONSELLER: “Given gladly by the way, because we like seeing you here.”

“Is he blaming us?” I heard a student whisper.

Shaking my head, I began to shuffle in my perch in the back. It was all surreal. Sponseller’s smiling and joking, no doubt meant as conciliatory gestures, did nothing to blunt the angst of the room. My wandering led me over to where Tom Ryan stood, wearing his customary tweed jacket with the patches on the elbows. I watched as Shannon Mauger, a senior and one of my students for more than a few of her Core classes, went to the mic to ask her question. She began by explaining the reason she and her fellow Pumas endured mold in the windows, mice in the dorms, and frogs in their bedrooms is because of how the professors treated students.

SHANNON: "We are not another number to them. They really care about us. You're making arrangements for students, but what are you doing for faculty? They've had their jobs ripped out from under them with no notice. Are you helping them find new jobs?"

Tom Ryan scoffed as he turned his back and walked towards the rear wall of the Shen.

"Are we going to buy them a car? Are we going to get them a blanket?" he said in the softest of voices while looking at his shoes.

I gave a nervous laugh, then coughed and stared at a blank spot on the stage.

Clock hands ticked and the night, a night that never should have happened, drew to an end. Justin Hays, selected by peers as the final student speaker of the night, came to the mic.

"I have been asked to make a closing statement for the evening," he said.

It seemed to me that day that Ben Sponseller often didn't know what to say. The exact opposite of that mindset came to the microphone in that moment. Anton Chekhov said, "Cut a good story anywhere, and it will bleed." Therefore, and because Justin's words likely synopsize the thoughts of anyone who has endured a college closing, I present his oratory here in its entirety:

"We were told earlier that we would have greater disappointments than this in life. Frankly, I think that was a slap in the face to our mission of Involved for Life. If there is one positive that has come from this tragedy, it is the community. We have seen countless alumni come together to try to save this school. We have seen our professors crying and we have cried along with them. We have seen people worried about not having a house for their kids and we have seen people worrying because they are single parents.

"We as Pumas feel like we were let down. Honestly, we feel we were a little bit betrayed and a little bit sold out. I think it is so terrible that we have to go through these next three months knowing essentially this is the end of Saint Joseph's College. We have professors who have essentially given their whole careers to this school. We have freshmen who signed on believing that in four years they would graduate from Saint Joseph's College. They may go on to get a degree from somewhere, but they won't get the full Saint Joe experience of Homecoming and Little 5. I don't think it has been fully grasped how big of a letdown this has been for students, for faculty, for alumni, and for those Board members who fought tirelessly to keep this place open.

"People have cried so many tears over this closing, and we have been told this is essentially not a major disappointment. This is such a tragedy for those who have given everything to Saint Joseph's College. I played three and a half years for this College as many other people in here have..."

He made an animated wave of his arms, gesturing around the Shen.

"If we didn't care, we wouldn't have sat here [tonight]. This was a huge disappointment for us and probably will be for the rest of our lives. Professors who have given 30 years to this place? I cannot even comprehend that as a person who isn't even 30 years old.

– · –

"So I think going forward, what you need to know is that this was not the best for the students and the faculty. You took the easy way out. We have alumni fighting tooth and nail on Facebook, trying to pull together funds and they were let down. And my heart is let down for my heroes such as Jon Nichols, Mike Nichols, John Nichols Senior, Brian Capouch, who have given everything to this college. Now it's nothing. It's never going to be the same again."

This brought the loudest cheers, claps, and table poundings of the night. I did not expect my name to be dropped and certainly not in such a context. Calling myself humbled in the moment would be an understatement. More than that, I marveled at the execution of it all. Justin delivered a true closing argument…and I got the distinct impression I just witnessed the birth of a political career.

Later, I sat alone in the dark. Just me in my bed with a flask-sized bottle of Crown Royale and those same damn stars outside my window pane, just watching everything turn to dust. I reflected on my takeaways from the evening. In the months to come, I would see several points of commonality between what I heard and saw in the previous four days and what other colleges experienced.

Like Sweet Briar and Antioch, the students and faculty knew full well Saint Joe experienced financial difficulty, but we had no idea that closure loomed anywhere on the radar. Like Sweet Briar and Antioch, the professors of Saint Joseph's College were teachers. A few did research and published, but the preponderant population of the faculty invested their efforts into developing curricula, teaching it, and mentoring and caring for students. This form of "teaching-centered" professorship would not translate well to the current job market in higher education, where competition is fierce and publications the highest of currencies. Also, as with Antioch and as Justin Hays pointed out at the meeting, a considerable amount of faculty devoted their entire professional lives to something that in one scant flash, no longer existed.

In the current incarnation, anyway. I grabbed my notebook where I wrote down the *sotto voce* comment made by Tom Ryan, our Associate Vice President for Academic Affairs.

Again, and again I reviewed the words. All these years of studying rhetoric and I still could find no truly benign interpretation of a comment most kindly assessed as tone deaf. I coupled Ryan's words that night with his "we're just taking a break" response to me after the "suspension of operations" announcement. Once more I suspected people on the inside of something. Something percolated, but remained known to few. Worse, people I once knew and respected, it seemed in the fog, took the reins of the thing and no longer held any regard for the faculty. In a sensation that took me all the way back to 7th grade, I realized someone was planning a party and I wouldn't get an invitation…and neither would most of my colleagues. As the ship sank, those who worked behind the curtain would row away in a self-serving lifeboat. The rest of us would tread the ice water, hoping Rose might scoot over just enough and let one of us hang on to her wooden plank.

I rolled over in bed and checked my phone, curious about alumni responses on Facebook to the live video feed of the night's meeting. Reaction to Sponseller's presentation seemed nigh universal. Comments included:

"Don't get defensive in your tone with these students. You just destroyed their lives."

"If he [Sponseller] is sleeping well at night, then he's probably one of the only ones in the room who is."

"This guy is an embarrassment to SJC, open or closed."

"I'm in serious shock that's the Board right there."

Not all the comments served as vituperative spitballs and philippics. Countless comments blunted the vinegar and reminded me of the truest value of that evening. Rightfully so, many alums and concerned supporters commented on the students. They praised their professionalism, their poise, and their preparation of fact-based arguments.

"This is what a Puma education means! This is Saint Joe's!"

"All their professors did their job to perfection."

For yet another time in four days, I shed tears. This time they welled up from pride and affection. That night in the Shen, I could see right before me in real life and real time, our students putting into practice what we taught in Core: have a clear thesis, support what you say, be prepared to look at things from multiple views, and do it all with professional, academic language. We pointed the way, but in the end the students did it on their own.

My thoughts drifted back to Sweet Briar and Antioch. Fighting the Board and their decision as those colleges did might be a Quixotic notion at best, but it bore consideration. Saint Joseph's College produced intelligent and articulate students, past and present. Our extended community included alumni with years of professional accomplishments and social, technical, and financial resources to draw upon. Two populations motivated, connected through a central hub on social media, and feeling very, very pissed off.

Also, the Saint Joe community members no longer seemed to have the market cornered on surprise. Indeed, the Board at this point behaved every bit as taken aback by the alumni backlash as the Antioch trustees did in my reading. Our Board also did not appear savvy as to the power of social media and how it can be used to organize people.

Yes. We could fight this thing.

“We’re going by the Bible and they’re using *The Art of War.*”

Brian Capouch said this as I closed the door to the empty classroom. I volunteered to stand rearguard, glancing out the door’s window at intervals.

It was Tuesday, February 7th, 2017, the very next night after the student meeting with Sponseller. As usual, Capouch and I met the students for dinner in the cafeteria. While a jolly affair under most conditions, I attended with a most gloomy demeanor. The guys still cracked jokes. I wanted to join in, to revel in their company for I knew our time from that point forward grew short. But I couldn’t.

We mulled over the events of the previous night’s meeting and went over how the news of the closing hit the local and regional media. *The Daily Herald*, a publication in the area of my suburban Chicago home, ran a story with the headline, “Saint Joseph’s College Says Financial Woes Led to Suspension.” The article featured an interview with Sponseller, who again pointed to HLC as the primary motivator.

"We've got HLC pretty much with a gun to our head," he told the *Herald.* "Not because they're not good people, but because we haven't satisfied their demands - not academically, but financially. They want a house in order that I could not see, and that my advisers on the board could not see, we could do in time to avoid our accreditation being pulled."[5]

This statement to the press brought puzzlement and consternation at our table. No matter how many times students, with hardcopy of the HLC notice right in their hands, pointed out that HLC would give us both time and guidance to get our “house in order,” the Board narrative ignored the counterargument marched on to the next prepared talking point. I sucked down a Coke float and tore into a stack of cookies.

“Did you just get double desserts?” a student wearing a poofy cap cocked to the side asked. “I thought you’d get more veggies.”

“Look kid, I just lost everything. At this point it’s either a sugar binge, or hookers and cocaine,” I said, joking.

With that I tossed back the rest of my sweet cola-chocolate concoction while the guys laughed.

"There's got to be something we can do," Justin said.

Brian Capouch pushed away his plate and swiveled his head, looking around the cafeteria.

"A rebellion is forming. But we can't talk about this here," he said. "Too many eyes and ears."

Nate Wade suggested we go across the street to the Core Building and find an empty classroom. We needed to be cautious, however. We didn't know everyone's allegiances, and if the wrong person should overhear any of our cussings and discussings, the results would be assured. We headed out of the caf. Jose said he needed to drop off an assignment but if we texted him the room number, he would meet us.

The rest of us walked through the hallway. As I did, I kept looking over my shoulder and around corners. In addition to depression and fear, I could now add paranoia to my self-destructive cocktail. Or is it really paranoia if there are those who do in fact mean you harm, even if not in the physical sense? I could also feel the beginnings of an intense bond with these fellow Pumas. Seven men, with Alex in absentia due to a night class, moving together in service of common mission. As we saw it, and as did most of the Saint Joe community it seemed, a gaggle of powermongers decided long ago the outcome of our College and we in turn decided that "the fuckers have gone too far this time," to quote Brian, our erstwhile leader.

Justin spotted an empty classroom and we all filed into it, taking seats in the long tables arranged in a u-formation. That's when Brian started in on the *Art of War*.

"A key point in the *Art of War* is surprise," Brian said. "The announcement hit fast and everybody's shocked. There's no time to organize a coherent response. They state as little as possible publicly to avoid their asses getting sued. I'm telling you, things did not go their way at all in that meeting with you last night. They said things to deliberately get you riled up, hoping the students would get out of hand and they could call an end to the meeting and get escorted out by security without saying one word more, but you guys fucked them."

Brian slapped his hand hard on the plastic-wood surface of the table at the end of that statement, sending the sound of the impact reverberating throughout the classroom.

"You all were so professional, so polished, so prepared, that you never gave them the opportunity," Brian continued. "They still have the plan in motion, though. They want to hold the baby's head under the water and drown it fast as possible before any more questions get asked."

Motion. Something at the door. My stomach churned my half-eaten dinner. I went to check, and found it was Jose.

"Excalibur," he whispered when I opened the door.

"Huh?" I responded.

I allowed him into the classroom and shut the door behind him.

"I don't know, I just figured we should have a password," Jose said.

Head shakes and good-natured laughs came from all around, but from that point forward, "Excalibur" would indeed become our "code word," indicating whatever information followed would be regarding underground action to save Saint Joe's.

Jose sat. Brian continued his point.

"So, they drown the baby fast, we're all too shocked and in disarray to do anything about it, then they switch things over to the new plan, making it look like they saved the place. I'm telling you, it's Munchausen Syndrome by Proxy. Y'all know what that is?"

I said it was, as near as I could recollect, a mental condition where a parent or other caregiver exaggerates the symptoms of child or other dependent's illness or deliberately keeps that dependent sick in order to feel needed and get attention.

"Well, sort of," Brian said, his eyes squinted and shoulder shrugged. "It's really where someone creates a problem or makes a problem even worse, just so they can swoop in and solve it and look like the heroes. That's what's happening here. Keep making the financial situation worse, drive it into the ground, let it all fall apart, and then scatter everyone away, so they can create the NEW SAINT JOE!"

He shouted those last three words and made a mock thrust of his fist into the air. I fidgeted and looked out the window to the hallway. For a man aiding in the insipient stages of a clandestine revolution, Brian seemed to still need to understand "noise discipline."

Talk returned once more to what we could do about it. The guys had already compiled a whole slate of media outlets to speak to, both local and national. Jose got in touch with *The Indianapolis Star* and *The USA Today* and both papers agreed to interviews. I told them they would need a clear timeline of events to present in order to get a straight story out to the press. Together on one of the desk tables, we sketched out just that on a yellow legal pad.

Then there would be the following night. The Student Association called an emergency session and a motion of "no confidence" would be brought to the floor. As student representatives, Justin, Jose, Stephen, and Alex would all be voting on the motion. Those subject to the vote would be Ben Sponseller, Steve Ruff, Bob Pastoor, Chad Pulver, and Spencer Conroy, the Vice President of Business Affairs. They would also add the Vice President for Institutional Marketing and Advancement. I cautioned the guys. Just as they did the night before in such an admirable fashion, they must have a clear thesis and evidence provided to support why such a statement on these men was necessary. Throughout it all, they must present their case with cool and level heads, and any documentation on the matter must also be written as such.

"Well gentlemen," I said. "Welcome to the Resistance."

"And... Lawyer Boys..." Brian said, standing up. "What do you always do?"

Silence.

"Be situationally aware," Brian said. "Tomorrow the AG could move. HLC could move, because it's sounding more and more like they [Board and administration] have not followed the proper procedures for shutting down a college. Someone could file a lawsuit, because a few of the Board members who voted to stay open are looking into legal avenues. Only time will tell."

"What do you think our chances are?" Justin asked Brian.

Brian grabbed his winter coat from the back of his chair and tossed it around himself.

"I think the most likely outcome is this remains set in motion, it all shuts down, but maybe later the carpet can be pulled back and we see exactly what they did us," he said. "But

Jon is still out of job. It reminds me of a documentary I once saw about a young man diagnosed with terminal brain cancer. It changed my life. He had this concept of 'happy death.' He did not choose his circumstances, but he could be happy by…"

Brian went on with one of his "memory dumps" about the documentary and I concede my mind tuned out. I did not want to hear it. It sounded too much like other alumni on social media, far removed from the war on the ground, planning an "epic" Little 5 to drink and laugh and then skip into oblivion. I wanted to fight. I began to envision myself…and all of us in the room…printing "underground" literature and distributing it on campus.

I would once more wear my old black duster coat from the goth days, keeping the printed leaflets stuffed inside its enveloping length, hidden from the scanning eyes of the regime. A student would walk by and I would make a furtive handoff. They would take the sheet and read the bold heading: "RESIST"…followed by instructions. Like France in 1943 all over again. Better this than plunging myself headlong into the abyss of the academic job market. If given but a moment's consideration, the thought of a job search enshrouded my mind like some giant, loathsome bat and frightened me into paralysis.

"And that is what, Jon?" Brian asked.

I made a loose shake of my head.

"I'm sorry. I was thinking about something else," I said.

Yeah. Mainly the real threat of my whole world coming apart.

"GODDAMMIT, YOU HAVE TO FOCUS!" Brian shouted.

That brought me all the way back to undergrad. He was right, though. In more ways than one.

Brian zipped up his coat and made a fast exit for he had yet other projects at home that would take him well into the night as usual. After walking out the door, he popped his head back in once more.

"And for Christ's sake, find somebody for this group who doesn't have a penis," he said and left.

People sans penises already went to work elsewhere, forming a smart and organized network essential to the resistance. Jackie Bradway and Elysse Ruggles continued their work on the Involved for Life page. Board member Kris Sakelaris,[6] who voted to keep Saint Joe open, suggested that the page be used as a platform for fundraising the money necessary for retaking the College. This came after Sponseller and Pastoor pledged at the student meeting to step down if $20 million was raised by June 1st.

"I think Dr. Pastoor and I would go and have a beer," Sponseller joked at the student meeting in response to the offer.

But for Kris Sakelaris, Jackie Bradway, and the members of the Alumni Board, the proposal came as a match to a fuse.

"What if we started a fund?" Kris asked. "If they need money, then let's go get it."

"Let's show them what we can do," Jackie said.

Jackie began writing letters and social media posts to alumni. As a member of the Alumni Board, she tapped into a database of over 8,000 email addresses and positioned all fundraising pleas with the face of the Alumni Board square upon it.

“We knew we were one of the few SJC-affiliated groups that had any trust left,” Jackie said.

With Jackie’s experience in PR and journalism providing the guidance, the alumni organization launched a press release to hit February 9th.[7] Headlined, “A Statement from St. Joseph's College (Rensselaer, IN) Alumni: We Demand Transparency after Board Votes to Close Campus,” the release detailed the objections the alumni community raised to the Board’s decision. It quoted statements from several alums, but perhaps the most succinct of objections came from Mark Andrew Zwartynski, Saint Joe class of 1974.

"I have been able to view and read the transcripts of both (Faculty and Student) Q&A sessions and I am embarrassed at what I saw. Because I saw nothing. I saw a decision made long before the faculty, staff, students and SJC Community had any opportunity for input, the sharing of experience or intellect," Zwartynski said. "There has been a lack of transparency from the Board of Trustees at SJC and their spokesperson. I know several alumni have reached out to try to help and have not received anything but ridiculous condescending remarks.”

The story went to the press. The rallying cry to alumni echoed out as well. Raising multiple millions in four months' time might indeed sound like chasing windmills or an even worse kind of impossible, but I decided that the definition of "possible" was, therefore, inadequate for my tastes. Because "against all reason" sure as hell beat the alternative.

The following night, just as planned, the Student Association voted "no confidence" in each target they painted. All but one, that is. The vote on Dr. Pulver did not pass. The Student Association argued that those who sustained a vote of no confidence:

-"Failed to directly communicate issues to students as pertaining to our right to know the financial state of the College."

-"Did not exhaust all options to keep the campus open for the Fall 2017 semester," citing specific failure in engaging state government, the Rensselaer community, and the greater alumni community.

-"Allowed athletes to pass Signing Day and signed with the College."

-“Failed to address the questions of the students in the February 6th, 2017 Q&A session in a tone and manner that was required for as somber of an issue as it was.”

-“Allowed the cash flow of the College to reach a point so low that we are declaring a state of financial exigency in the middle of the Spring 2017 semester and hoping for a favorable decision from the Attorney General in order to free up endowment money to pay out severance packages.”[8]

In addition to the statement, a student petition asked that President Pastoor not attend the last-ever Saint Joe commencement ceremony in May. The President of the Student Association distributed the statement by email to all in the Saint Joseph’s College community.

It did not go unnoticed. President Pastoor called a meeting of his cabinet the following morning.

Justin Hays received a summons to Dr. Pulver’s office on that Thursday, February 9th. Justin arrived in the corner office of second floor Core around midday.

"He acted grim," Justin said of Pulver. "His upper lip quivered, and he looked like he'd been crying. He told me he was working furiously to help faculty find new jobs."

As Justin tells it, Pulver expressed concern that Justin's anger would become consuming. He went on to encourage Justin to shift all of this energy towards helping plan the new Saint Joe.

"Will our suggestions actually amount to something?" Justin asked.

That would be up to the C.PP.S., Pulver responded, according to Justin.

Downstairs, Alex McCormick packed up his books after class. Then Tom Ryan's face hovered into his view.

"Hello!" Ryan said. He requested that the two of them talk. They went upstairs to Dr. Ryan's office.

"He said that he knew there were a lot of conspiracy theories going around about him," Alex said.

Alex said Ryan expressed bewilderment as to how anyone could think he could do something to harm Saint Joseph's College and that every time he drove onto campus, Ryan saw a tree he helped plant during his time as an undergrad.

His own grandson just started at Saint Joe as a freshman on the baseball team. Why would he do anything to upend his grandson's college career? Tone everything down and look towards something positive, Ryan urged. Yes, positive things. Nobody *wanted* this to happen. Don't vilify Pastoor, either. He just got here, so get rid of that petition. According to Alex, the meeting ended with one last, clear message for Alex and his fellow seniors.

You need to be very careful about what you're doing.

Perhaps the harshest and likewise most befuddling administrative rebuke of the students' "no confidence" vote came from a campus priest. This cleric sent Jose Arteaga a text message that morning. In it, the priest professed to being "ashamed" of Jose and that Jose was "not after truth, but justice." According to holy man's text, the last time he saw something like that was when "they crucified Jesus."

A clear "pushback against the pushback" was underway. That point received a chilling underscoring later in the day. Kris Sakelaris messaged me on Facebook, asking that I warn Dad to not use Saint Joe email when contacting any of the Board

--- -

members working with attorneys on a "stay of execution" for the College. She believed the Overlords hired an organization to monitor emails. I shut off my phone's WiFi and sent a private message to Brian Capouch, asking him about it. As a former Professor of Computer Science and the architect of the College's computer network, he would know better than anyone.

From his response, I could almost hear him laughing at me.

"Long since done," he said. "My side is clean, but exposed on yours. Make sure everyone knows. They've got the old stuff, but nothing new. Is your Dad clued in?"

He would be.

It's not unreasonable. Any time you use your employer's computer network, all you send or receive over it is subject to the employer's purview and review. What did I previously say about the Board and the administration on email? Dear God. I used the word "incompetent." I used the word "duplicitous."

I used the word "shitheads."

Oh no.

Sakelaris's warning served as kerosene to the hellish fire of my anxiety-prone brain. I envisioned the administrators, along with their masters in the Board and the C.PP.S., meeting in an ominous, skull-shaped headquarters that could rise and submerge from the swamps of Lake Banet, just like the secret base for the Legion of Doom on *Challenge of the Superfriends*. In a chamber of the base lit only by large monitor screens, the Overlords studied photographs of student and faculty "troublemakers." One of the photos would be a snapshot of me and not one of my most flattering looks, either.

"The kid's getting close," one of the shadowy figures would say.

"Deal with the problem," another would respond.

I decided to decline every single call that came to my cellphone, regardless if I recognized the number. Otherwise, I might very well answer and hear a husky voice say, "You need to be very careful about what you're doing" before hanging up. Damn, I realized. Since I found myself searching for a job, then I probably *should* answer.

Go for a middle ground, I decided. I'll disguise my voice. I toggled between options sounding like either Christian Bale or Paul Lynde. Figured either way the caller would be put off.

Which utterly defeats the purpose of a professional job search. Damn again.

I decided I should also change up the routes I took home at the end of the day. Keep them guessing. But never drive past Lake Banet at night. I could just see a black SUV coming roaring out of nowhere, ramming me off the road and into the depths of the lake. That or men in black suits would quickly flip a rubber bag over my head and drag me off to somewhere that I "couldn't cause any problems." My God. How far would they be willing to take this if they felt threatened?

The most realistic scenario, however, promised to be far more nightmarish than any of my other paranoid reveries. The Overlords could easily dismiss a non-tenured "troublemaker" with immediacy. No severance. Instant loss of health insurance for my wife.

In modern America, that might be one of the most damning sentences for anyone.

Turns out the administration broke its silence with the media earlier that day.

The Rensselaer Republican printed a front-page interview with President Pastoor. The paper excerpted one pertinent quote from Pastoor and placed it as an inset in large type amid the article. The quote read:

"I don't know why it was a surprise to anybody" and attributed to "Robert Pastoor, President of SJC."[9]

It is impossible to overstate how much this quote vexed the Saint Joe community. Several students posted the results of the "no confidence" vote to their social media channels, accompanied with the phrase "I don't know why it was a surprise, Bob."

Dave Bangert at the *Lafayette Journal & Courier* picked up Pastoor's quote and the paper paired it with a Saint Joe file photo of a smiling Pastoor.[10] Bangert included the Pastoor quote from the *Republican*, but reported Pastoor also said "Context might have been lacking." Meaning, Pastoor admitted to the quote, but maintained that he never shied away from open admission of the precarious financial situation of the College when dealing with the public. Others, as one might expect by this point, saw things in a different light.

One of them was Bill White. He told the *Journal & Courier* that as a member of the Finance Committee, he learned that Saint Joseph's College "probably had about five years to live" unless the institution underwent drastic changes. Then, the faculty received pay raises and new hires came on board, many of them VP-level positions drawing high salaries.

"So people looked and thought, well, we're continuing to hire, we got a pay raise in the fall, we were not asked to take cuts and our budget went up $3.5 million, well, of course it's a surprise," White said. "It looked like we were in good shape. Why did you give pay raises last September if we weren't in good shape?"

I knew my students planned to contact the *Journal & Courier* and sure enough, I found a photo of Jose next to the column, posing with a far-away look of subdued contempt on his face, all with the Chapel in the background. In the article, Justin pointed to President Pastoor's November 30th, 2016 meeting with students in the aftermath of HLC's announcement of probation.

"He basically told us the class of 2018 would be able to graduate from St. Joseph's College and we would not have to worry about things," Justin said. "Then he went out and told the papers that no one should have been surprised."

"There was no talk on Nov. 30 about closing down," Jose told the paper. "Look at the vote of no confidence. Why did they do the things they did? Why did they recruit a new class to Saint Joseph's? Knowing the financial situation, why did they allow athletes to pass the Feb. 1 signing day? There's a whole list. If they knew about this – if it shouldn't have been a surprise, like he says – why would they do these things?"

I soon learned though that not everyone felt sympathy and support for our situation. *Inside Higher Ed* ran a story on our "suspension of activities."[11] This article covered much of the same territory and talked to the same characters in the drama, such as Bob Pastoor and Bill White. It mentioned our parallels with Sweet Briar, including the alumni response to save the school. Such comparisons came with warnings from experts that every situation was different. It was the comments on the article, however, that took me by surprise. They included:

"Maybe they could go do something in the private sector. Start companies, be a good employee, etc. The market is saying we don't need as many college professors."

"The faster they learn that the cushy world they've know [sic] for the last several generations is imploding, the better off they will adjust."

"Only in liberal la-la land would a college last this long with a business model whose customers can't pay." Never mind that poster's obvious misunderstanding of the mission of "Christian Humanism."

And…my favorite…

"PhD trained Obama voting extreme Leftists lose their jobs? Oh no!!!! Actually, time for celebration and Schadenfreuede [sic]."

I knew of the attitude, but, perhaps due to my upbringing and perhaps from the type of friends I tend to keep, I never before encountered it with such vehemence. The ethos of this attitude states that if you don't turn a wrench or sell a widget, then you must be somehow involved in a dodge or a hustle at society's expense. Don't like what's happening? Well, read up on Libertarianism. Employment troubles? Then that's purely due to your poor life choices. The situation is the will of the almighty Market and we bow to its omniscience…and you'd better too. If the act of doing so reduces you to a screaming mass of jelly, it can be no one's fault but yours.

Not much love from the Catholic Church in this regard, either. Brian Capouch reported that he learned we weren't getting empathy from the more, shall we say, conservative wing of the faith.

"They see this closing as God's divine justice," he said. "We're a Catholic college that has an LGBT student alliance and taught in Core that it's okay to follow other religions. We just weren't 'Catholic enough.'"

But another news story, this time from WNDU in South Bend, Indiana, featured voices from a sector of our community not yet heard from: parents of our students.[12] And as any educator will tell you, few forces are so strong as a parent scorned. This article described the parents as "completely blindsided" by the announcement, keeping with the common theme among Pumas.

"As parents we have not even received any communication from the school, our communication has been coming through our children," Kim James, parent of a Saint Joseph's College freshman, was quoted in the article. She continued on, describing her daughter's experience: "Starting this process all over for her is just truly devastating. She found Saint Joe to be the perfect fit for her."

Another parent, Diane Faus, described her son Blake's struggles. A Puma football player, his scholarship was "basically gone. Blake is having to start all over."

"Our daughters are lost, they don't know where they're going from here," said James.

"Obviously something is not right and they need to be investigated," said Kendra Brouwer, whose daughter was a freshman.

The news piece ended with a link to the petition for the Indiana Attorney General's office to investigate the Board's decision.

- - -

Brian's words echoed in my head. Yes, a rebellion was underway.

As enthusiastic as I might have been over that prospect, I must confess my continued cowardice. I woke that Friday morning, reached into my closet and took a shirt from a hanger. I wondered if I might find "BACK OFF" scrawled across it in red, showing how they could get to me at any time without my even knowing. When I arrived on campus, I made tentative steps towards my office door. Would I find "MOVE ON" slapped across it in crimson paint? Not only that, but with the human urge to survive being so ingrained, who could I trust? Who, besides Brian and the guys, supported the resistance and who remained loyal to the establishment? Who might be watching me? Who might report me?

I went to the lounge and took enough coffee to last me through the morning. That way I would not have to emerge from my office until lunch. What would I do for a midday meal? I didn't want to go to the caf and travelling off campus made me too visible for too long. Why couldn't full meals be available out of the vending machine?

The door to the lounge opened. I whirled around and squared my shoulders to meet the intruder. My fingers clinched around the handle of cup full of hot liquid, keeping ready to fling it in their face, just in case.

It was Michael. I exhaled and let my shoulders drop.

"You all right?" he asked.

"Apart from the obvious? Yeah. I guess," I answered.

We started talking over the aftermath of the week. Michael had been busy. Academic Affairs worked overtime that week, finding ways to get as many juniors as possible into accelerated courses so that they may graduate early. For his part, Michael would have to manufacture a Core course that would combine two semesters of material and be delivered over 11 weeks. Calling it a Herculean task would be an understatement. Beyond that, we mulled over the various statements of finality and the issuing of plans for "wind down" coming from administrative offices.

"It's all coming apart," Michael said, a sad smile of disbelief on his face.

"It's not an accident, either," I said.

I started listing off the numerous factors creating suspicion. Among them, the suddenness of it all, the complete and utter lack of transparency, and the flippant responses at both of the Q&A sessions.

"Oh, there was no conspiracy," Michael said. "It was all just accidents and incompetence."

After a beat, I told him I could not reconcile just how so many people degreed as MBAs and CPAs did not realize we would be out of money until just last December.

"Well, if you don't know what you're doing, one might not recognize the flashing warning lights," he said.

"So, you think it was…what? Well-intentioned bumbling?" I asked.

Michael agreed that was essentially the case. I nodded my head. His contention caused me to re-evaluate all I'd heard until that point. It was something of a more comforting notion. Our destruction came not from nefarious collusion, but by mistakes and fatal, but honest, decisions. My mind needed to consider it.

The growing rage in my chest, however, remained unconvinced. I left the lounge and walked down the faculty hallway. I saw a quote affixed to Tom Ryan's office door. Printed in blue type on an ivory white stationary with a floral imprint border, it read:

"'The true voyage of a sailing ship is to reposition and correct and begin again.' Emerson-'Self-Reliance'"[13]

At lunch, I drove across the street and parked in the lot of Wal-Mart. From there I called Jackie Bradway in Milwaukee. I told her I would, as much as possible, call her each day and feed her as much information as I could from the ground. The Wal-Mart parking lot seemed the best place to do this as it was far away from prying eyes and ears of the Core Building. I kept the engine running so as to…you know…drown out any possible listening devices.

I started to feel like I was in a John Grisham thriller. Or a piece of film noir. I wondered if I could switch these phone appointments to nighttime. Under the lights of the Wal-Mart parking lot. I could wear a trench coat, light a cigarette, and maybe crack open a flask. Better have that shoulder holster handy, too. And a pocket full of fake passports.

Back to reality. Sitting in my car, I told Jackie about the student vote of "no confidence" and the subsequent talking to's and leanings on conducted by administration on the principal organizers of the vote. A second or two of dead silence passed on the phone.

"They need to leave those kids the hell alone," Jackie said at last. "Enough harm has been done to them."

I told her about a find from my email earlier in the day. A faculty meeting was scheduled for next week. For that meeting, a professor already submitted a motion for a vote of "no confidence" on the same suspects as those brought before the Student Assembly. Jackie reported that at that moment, Alumni Board members already proposed their own vote and again on the same figures. The massive fundraising effort also continued.

Kris Sakelaris volunteered her house for an all-day, all-night session of stuffing envelopes with Alumni Board members.

- - -

The envelopes contained a letter appealing to the thousands of alumni and other members of the Saint Joe community, asking for an opening of hearts and wallets to save the home we love.

"Last night, my husband said 'You're putting a lot of time into this. This will be over soon, right?'" Jackie said with a slight laugh. "I had to tell him, 'No. This is going to be a thing for a while."

She then explained her situation to me. She just married her second husband, Jack, in October 2016. Not only was it a new marriage, but her and Jack were in a "Brady Bunch" situation as Jackie called it, blending a family with her kids and his. Jack, not being a Puma, also admitted to being somewhat mystified as to the hold Saint Joe kept over its community members.

"Now I'm in this full force, balls to the wall effort to save the place I love," Jackie said. "But he knows. He knew from day one how much I love Saint Joe."

So much for Jack to absorb in this new marriage, adding even more strain to something already new and forming, to say nothing of the ordinary efforts of keeping a family functional.

Jackie's tale indicated even more, though. This thunderclap which hit the ground Friday, February 3rd…it reverberated, sending ripples and tremors into far corners of lives many miles removed from Rensselaer. As awful and fearful as I felt, I wondered what might be going on at kitchen tables and at coffeeshop meetings in other locales of the United States. Even if on a minimal level, the announcement of closure changed the lives of thousands. People I had not even met were at that moment shaking their heads and saying, "I can't believe it's gone."

Jackie then admitted a hurdle ahead in the fundraising efforts. It sounded familiar as Antioch faced a similar situation in their resistance fight.

Alumni Board members already reached out to Pumas in their immediate circle, checking the financial pulse and the willingness to give whatever they could afford. Many reported the same concerns: Why would I give my money to an organization where the leadership that allowed the financial situation to deteriorate still remained in place? I could not argue against that business sense and roles reversed, I can't say I'd be reaching for my checkbook, either. The message from alums grew clearer: nothing would happen until the entire Board, or at the very least Sponseller and Pastoor, resigned.

Word of this obstacle circulated throughout the alumni community, meaning it eventually made its way back to campus. Students took it upon themselves, in whatever small way, to try to move those roadblocks to the side. That night, white cloth sheets dangled from the terraces of the campus apartments, scrawled with bold black ink:

"SPONSELLER MUST GO."

"RESIGN, PASTOOR."

I sat in bed watching an awful movie called *Red Dawn.*

At its heart, the 1984 film is quite a valentine to the far right in its "red scare" paranoia and unabashed uber-patriotism. The story takes place in a small town in Colorado as the then Soviet Union invades the United States. A group of high school students effect escape during the initial attack and go into hiding in the mountains. Upon learning of the execution of their

- - -

families, the youths soon form a guerilla outfit and fight back against the invaders. There are even two brothers who fight to avenge their father. Together, they called their guerilla band, the "Wolverines" after their high school mascot.

The movie fails on most every objective level. Writing, acting, conception, it's all indefensible, save for arguing that all axiological arguments are essentially subjective. I know I often fall back to that position in justifying my love of b-movies as an intellectual pursuit. In truth, however, my heart has a serious weak spot for *Red Dawn*, despite all its egregious flaws. It stirs the blood, showing a group of young people who cry out to their oppressor, "You will not take our home from us. Or if you do, it will only be after you pay a grievous, grievous price. We guarantee your victory will be a pyrrhic one."

We lived here…not the majority of the Board members who could go back to their jobs and one of their multiple homes, at least one or more states away in several cases. The sentiment of "We live here" echoed in the cries of "Antioch is my home" on that campus in Yellow Springs, Ohio during their struggle. How often in the preceding month did I hear or say, "Saint Joe is my home"? Then I would later read in Jeanne Kay's writings that she wondered if it was time to "man the barricades" and I would know just what she meant. The exigency of the previous month transmuted to an atomic pile of rage in my gut. How could I let Saint Joseph's College be taken from me while I flaccidly sat there and did nothing? While political and financial leadership did nothing but argue? Could we, the ones who stood to lose the most, take up arms and retake the campus by force? I would be a rider on a pale horse for the C.PPS. …and Hell would come with me.

"I'd rather die on my feet than live on my knees," my inner self seethed, imagining a military solution to our problem with the C.PP.S. Board members. "Everything has a natural life cycle…and you're at the end of yours, motherfucker."

No. Too crude. I then instead imagined a scene in a distant and improbable future where I sit in an armchair before a fireplace, dressed in black and a glass of Pinot Noir in my left hand. Beethoven's Symphony No. 7, Allegretto plays on speakers. A man in a butler's uniform walks up to my left side.

"It is done," he says, and then leaves.

He of course refers to "Project Red Water." I smile, bringing the glass to my lips to stain them blood red. The flames of the fire flicker.

These stand as far from my proudest thoughts, but they were the truth of the moment at 2am. They were demented…and so was I. As a great philosopher once wrote, "If a man is considered guilty for what goes on in his mind, give me the electric chair for all my future crimes." Matters of sanity, ethics, and the law guaranteed I would do nothing I imagined.

I did make one decision, however. The next day, I would tell Justin and the other guys our name would be the "Wolverines."

It didn't stick.

Maybe it was the boys' good sense. Maybe they thought we were already Pumas, so no need to bring other mammals into the mix. Justin also preferred another phrase for us: "Freedom Fighters." It didn't roll off the tongue quite like "Wolverines," but it became our moniker nonetheless. Although they did grant me a Photoshop tribute in the form of a still frame from *Red*

Dawn with my face pasted over C. Thomas Howell's. Jose got Patrick Swayze and Justin ended up with Charlie Sheen. I embraced that casting, as Howell's character makes a noble and memorable last stand against a Russian attack helicopter. And "last stand" is how things felt to me by the end of the day.

The directors of H.R. came roaming down the hall of second-floor Core. Each one held a stack of white business envelopes, making "fnip fnip" sounds as they sifted them, looking at names. One of the H.R. reps raised his sad eyes from an envelope and looked at me as I stood in my office doorway.

"Jon?" he asked.

Hesitant, he handed me the envelope.

"It's a non-renewal notice," he said,

I already knew. Sympathy swelled in my gut as I could just how bad this guy felt, carrying out the dirty duty of dispersing termination notices to his fellow Pumas. I nodded with a grim smile, hoping to convey that I understood, and took the envelope.

Many years previous, a guy, I'll call him "Glen," told me about his divorce. He could not stand the thought of losing his wife and was legally contesting her filing. A courier appeared at Glen's workplace to serve him with the divorce papers.

Glen ran. Glen made a full sprint down the aisle of office cubicles, bolted out the emergency exit (yes, setting off the alarm), and bounded down the stairway. If the papers did not touch him, so Glen's thinking went, then the divorce would not be real. As I sat across from Glen in the bar, I could not decide whether to hug him or kick him. I felt crushed on his behalf by his pathetic account, and I mean pathetic by the strictest, Aristotelian definition of the word. But why, I asked myself, would anyone struggle so hard and go to such embarrassing lengths to be with someone who so clearly did not want them?

In my office doorway at that moment, I was Glen.

I wanted to run from H.R., straight down the hallway, through the door, and down the staircase, doing my best rendition of how I envisioned Glen's run. Of course, I didn't. I opened the envelope with my full, legal name on it, all ominous and official-looking.

"Given the Board's decision of February 3rd," blah blah blah…

"Regret to inform you that" blah blah blah…

"We encourage you to look for work as soon as possible" blah blah blah…

I folded the letter and tossed it onto my desk. Turning, I leaned my right forearm against the wall and looked out the window. Once again, the setting winter sun painted the sky blood red over Bennet Hall. My fingertips gripped the white, grimy drywall, clawing at it.

This can't be how it ends. This just can't be how it all ends, I kept thinking. There must be a way to fight. I just could not shrug, pack my office, and start applying away for new jobs. This was an eviction. My colleagues, my students, all of us, thrown out of our second home, and I would not go quietly.

I saw myself in a noble last stand. As external forces conspired to collapse our world down upon us, I would rise against it. Regardless of odds or probable outcomes, I embraced the struggle itself as worthy and the only course of action my conscience could reconcile. I would reject quasi-Buddhist philosophies of just rolling over and "letting go of what I can't control" and "surrendering to what is." I would eschew with great disdain Capouch's recommendations of "happy death."

I decided to fight until burnt.

Students and alums already fired their initial retaliatory salvos in the war. On the afternoon of Wednesday, February 15th, the faculty would have the chance to empty a few missile tubes from our submarine with the vote of no confidence at the regular faculty meeting. Word soon arrived that Father Larry Hemmelgarn, Provincial of the C.PP.S, would be in attendance at that meeting. In fact, he would be on campus attending a series of meetings, with one rumored to be focused on the so-called "reinvention" of Saint Joseph's College.

"I was told they want to turn us into a Catholic prep high school," Brian Capouch told me. "With Tom Ryan as headmaster."

I asked Brian where he heard that. Did he have any documentation to support such a claim? "I can't say, I can't say," he told me. I had just been klonked in the head by what I started to call "rumor debris," kicked up and swirled about in the wake of last Friday's tornado. Given no foundation for the claim, I could only file it as gossip…even if it tracked with certain behaviors, and even if made sense in its own unsubstantiated right.

The day bore another tidbit. The *Lafayette Journal & Courier* ran a story in response to Board Chairman Sponseller's numerous claims of the threat of accreditation loss, possibly as soon as "the middle of next semester."[14] The *Journal & Courier* interviewed Steve Kauffmann, media spokesman for the Higher Learning Commission.

"We would never do that," Kauffman said, referring to pulling an institution's accreditation mid-semester.[15]

What was more, Kauffman told the *Journal & Courier* that none of the Saint Joseph's College leadership had engaged with HLC about the "temporary suspension" prior to the public announcement. Kauffman also stated that HLC, at that point, had yet to receive any teach-out plans from the College. These plans constituted all protocols and agreements with other institutions our students may transfer to in order to continue their college careers. Review and approval for such protocols might take months, Kaufmann added.

We marked day 12 of life after the announcement and May approached in two and a half short months.

The *Journal & Courier* contacted Sponseller for an interview. He did not respond.

I tossed on a blazer and went to the Courtney Auditorium for the first time since the infamous January meeting. Michael sat with Tom Ryan two rows ahead of me, both of them laughing about something. I sat with Chad Turner and Jordan Leising.

"Right now, I'm trying to look for a job, teach classes, and finish my dissertation," Chad said. "I'm finding each day that I can only do any given two of those three effectively."

"This is the lowest point of my life," Jordan said. "Right alongside the deaths of two of my family members."

I gritted my teeth and made repeated, nervous clicks of my pen. With that pen, I planned to cast my no confidence vote. What would that do? I hoped it might serve as evidence for alumni and dissenting Board members building a case and pursuing legal avenues to overthrow the current leadership, if such a coup could be possible. If not, my vote would serve as a gouge in their sides, or a bloody nose, that kind of nice little scar that follows you into new professional endeavors. My bull-sized taste for revenge wanted more, but what else was there, really?

The meeting came to order and President Pastoor came to the stage in the front of the auditorium, just as he did the month before.[16] This time, his tired eyes drooped a bit more. His movements appeared slower. He reported that payroll would be good until the end of August. Any severance would be contingent on work undertaken by legal counsel with the Indiana Attorney General. Pastoor then opened the floor to questions.

At last, someone asked it. As quoted in that day's edition of the *Journal & Courier* and as pointed out by our own students at their Monday night meeting, a faculty member asked about the discrepancies between Sponseller's claims about our proximity to accreditation revocation and the actual and ironclad rules of HLC.

The president of the Board misspoke was all Pastoor said. As to how we arrived at and eventually fell over the "precipice," to use Pastoor's own terminology, Pastoor offered a rundown of the years of borrowing and deficit spending.

"The alumni giving has been fairly stagnant. The financial situation didn't just happen in the last two years," he said in what could be interpreted as self-defense. "The last 20 years this institution has been living foot to mouth. No savings over this period. We built a building in 1998 without fundraising, another in 2000."

"I couldn't trust anyone before. How can I trust people now?" a professor asked.

"I can't give you any personal promises," Pastoor replied.

Behind me, Bill White stood up to speak.

"For 32 years I have taught here," he said, brushing the lapels of his suitcoat back away from his chest and placing his hands in his pockets. "Like many of my colleagues, this has not simply been teaching but a calling. That has been taken from us. You have your lawyers—we have ours. If we're not paid out according to the handbook, we will file suit and our lawyers tell us we will be entitled to triple damages under Indiana law. And then there will be *no* future for Saint Joseph's College."

Roars and claps came from the rows behind me. I flinched. I wanted to stand up and cheer. While it did not represent the end I wanted, Bill showed the war footing I believed we needed. Yet something held me back. Who was watching and what could they do to me? Being non-tenured, I could be dismissed. That's what. I was spoiling for a fight. On the spot though, fear tempered my flames as I wondered if I actually possessed the guts to accept the ramifications of said fight. For as James Baldwin wrote, "To act is to be committed and to be committed is to be in danger."

To my shame, I just sat.

Pastoor stood stone-faced through the cheers. When the acclamations for Bill subsided, Pastoor gave the summation of his presentation. His mouth went into a tight line and he made a sharp point of a finger at his two Vice Presidents in the room.

"[They] have busted their butts for you the past several months," Pastoor said. "They deserve a lot of thanks whether you believe it or not."

With that, Pastoor exited the auditorium…not up the aisle through us and to the exits but through the stage left door, closing it behind him with a hearty slam. The sound echoed out as a thunderous, low-fidelity burst.

As chief academic officer, Dr. Pulver still needed to present. He gave a brief report, but one longer than his January address. It included updates on the teach-out plan, the one that still needed HLC approval according to the day's news. He then left the meeting.

Then Father Hemmelgarn stood to address the assembled faculty. Despite the occasion, he still smiled.

"Thank you for asking me to come," Hemmelgarn said.

He then explained that several C.PP.S members are Saint Joe grads and that this whole affair broke their hearts. However, "everything has a natural life cycle" and "ministries are constantly changing." The change, he alluded, would be to an educational institutional that serves underserved populations. Michael Nichols raised his hand and asked what the future would be for the Core program.

"Ah yes! Something near and dear to your heart," Hemmelgarn said. "Core, I think, is one of the gifts we've given the community. Hopefully we can continue to wave that banner. Wish it would catch on."

He laughed and shrugged.[17]

I patted the pockets of my jacket and realized I didn't bring enough rum to the meeting. Another faculty member piped up with a question.

"Go back 60-90 days. Why haven't we done outreach to the mayor, the community, and so forth?"

"At the end of December, it was obvious," Hemmelgarn said. "That's why we moved the Board meeting up. I actually think very highly of Ben Sponseller. He's a pragmatist. He forced the Board to look at this seriously. We were looking at a lot of ways to do this and were putting together contingency plans. Marian University leaked information and caused an infuriating situation. This was from Chad [Pulver] working on plans in case it went this way. Marian jumped the gun."

Someone asked why they didn't cut spending earlier.

"Does anyone remember when Saint Joe wasn't in financial trouble?" Hemmelgarn responded. "I was a sucker too.

I dug deep and gave money, too. I say this just to tell you we all believed in what we were doing."

I thought for a moment, parsing the rhetoric of "I was a sucker, too." Who are the other implied "suckers"? Board? Faculty? Or the students and their parents who sent their children and their money to the College in the fall only to have both plunged into a sinkhole? I rhetorically analyzed it again and again, yet came up with nothing complimentary from the term "sucker."

And what did the Pelican Group, the consulting firm hired to help plan a resurgence, do that was positive?

"They involved the community," was Hemmelgarn's only answer.

"I've been let go before," one of my brother faculty members said. "I've never been disrespected like this, though. We aren't all in this together like they say."

Still beaming the omnipresent smile, Hemmelgarn said, "I am sorry for the impact this is having."

A few faculty members who lauded him for honesty, compassion, and being the first person serving in any

Title	REQUIEM FOR A COLLEGE
Condition	Good
Location	Walden Aisle Q Bay 03 Item 13522
Description	May have some shelf-wear due to normal use. Your purchase funds free job training and education in the greater Seattle area. Thank you for supporting Goodwill's nonprofit mission!
Source	Prescanned
SKU	0KVOFY00JXHM
ASIN	B0B14MBLHQ
Code	9798825403311
Employee	1mmendoza
Date Added	1/23/2025 12:24:53 PM

administrative capacity to apologize for the situation…something irrefutably true. I later asked Bill White how he felt about the moment.

"I hate that he is always smiling. One may smile and smile and be a villain," Bill said, quoting *Hamlet*.

That was nicer than my appraisal.

Father Hemmelgarn exited along with any other non-voting members of the faculty assembly. The doors to the Courtney were sealed. Time came for faculty to, in essence, put six men on trial. Their charges? Poor judgment, dereliction of duty, and overall just screwing up. In other words, leadership that the faculty assembly, like the students, could no longer follow with any trust or assurance. We motioned and approved to consider and vote upon each man separately. These votes would come by anonymous paper ballot, a simple "yes" or "no" scribbled upon them in pencil, pen, or the odd felt marker.

Deliberations over Sponseller, Ruff, Pastoor, and the Vice President for Institutional Advancement and Marketing went fast. Each vote passed. Michael Nichols took the mic and spoke in defense of Chad Pulver, asserting that as Vice President for Academic Affairs, Pulver bore no responsibility for the financial disaster. Tom Ryan followed that up, "piggybacking off it" as is so often the phrase in higher ed discussions, by saying that he knew of many nights in recent months where Pulver remained in his office after dark with the lights off. "Be positive," Ryan implored us.

Whether the two men's pleas made the difference or not is uncertain, but the vote on Pulver failed in spectacular fashion: 7-49.

The criticisms of Spencer Conroy were mild at best and the vote on him failed, 6 to 28 with two abstentions.

Word of the "no confidence" votes spread to the students and to the alumni off campus. We gathered in the forums of cyberspace and meatspace, discussing what to do next. The moderates continued to call for fundraising and pressuring the Attorney General to investigate. The militants called for an uprising.

And the Board and the administration said…nothing at all.

The following days got warm. Warm to the point of befuddlement. In mid-February, the temperature reached 70 degrees. Students wore shorts. My winter coat stayed in the back seat of my car as muggy, uncomfortable air adhered to my skin. A foggy mist fell over the campus at night, making me consider my imagined scene in front of Wal-Mart once again, film noir mixed with rural Americana.

Nothing, not even the weather, made sense anymore.

I sent Brian Capouch an email. An innocuous one, asking for his arrival time at the cafeteria that night. He replied with the time but added, "My nerves are shot. The intensity and duration of this combined with everything on edge. I can only imagine how it is for you guys."

About the same. I spent my days in a sort of blind haze. A hammering in my cranium paired with an acidic burn in my gut.

"Everybody I've talked to understands that nobody is more screwed than the faculty," Capouch also wrote.

Tell me about it. The College sent word about a placement agency coming in to help support staff. It's always miserable to lose a job, but at least they would have a resource for a search. Dozens of colleges in addition to Marian announced their willingness to take Saint Joe students. A student's options would be many. Faculty? We found ourselves in a downhill drift in all departments, straight into an oversaturated job market and at the wrong time of the hiring cycle at that.

I didn't accept it. Not one bit. I still believed in the fight. Board members who voted to keep Saint Joe open, "the loyalists," continued to work behind the scenes, pursuing legal and financial avenues for a "stay of execution." I never saw Dad work so hard. He sat at his desk in the study, single lamp shining and a yellow legal pad covered front page to back in financial numbers and sources of donations and revenue.

Seldom in my years did I meet someone as good with numbers as my father. He could perform long division in his head while I struggled to add single digits. There was a requirement in my teen years that I bring my homework for checking each night in an effort to raise my woeful math grades. He would move the numbers around on the page in what looked to me like a sort of medieval alchemy. I had no idea how he did it and he could not understand why I didn't. I remember one particular night of teeth gnashing and desk slapping as he saw my answer for a "solve for x" problem.

I don't know why. I thought it was a fine sketch of the Batmobile.

If the numbers on Dad's legal pad could be demonstrated as concrete financial proofs, then they could form the basis of new proposals to bring to the Chair of the Board…which did not fill me with much confidence. For trustees like Dad, that's how you do it, though. He spent his formative years deep in the rigor of not only academia, but the Catholic Church. There is an order in things. You put forth your intentions through a hierarchy and work up through the system. Surely if your motion is logical and supported well-enough, then the Overlords should agree and concede your request.

I didn't spend my formative years in that milieu. I grew up in front of MTV. I still at times wear combat boots and my black leather jacket. I distrust hierarchies and often the intentions of their decisions. That punk/metal ethos, still lodged somewhere in a section of my brain that remains in permanent adolescence, said that I have as much right as anyone to scream out what I wanted to say, to stand at the top of Halleck Center and howl at the heavens anything that came into my head. "CRY HAVOC! Let slip the dogs of war!"

I didn't want to wait around for lawyers and fundraisers and other guys in suits, hoping to "work with" the Overlords. I wanted to act, to kick down doors and kick in faces if the need arose. The Overlords might accuse me of "a negative attitude" or "losing grip on reality." Given their rendering of our "reality," I couldn't see any other rational response to the absurdity. And it was most unambiguously absurd…of Camus-like proportions. Only unlike Camus, I felt no desire to accept and laugh at the absurd, and to give a mere shrug and say, "happiness is fleeting." Instead, I want to kick, bite, claw, punch, and spit.

Of course, that doesn't work well for a career or much of anything else anywhere in polite society. At one point or another you have to yield to hierarchy if want to get anywhere, or you wander about in delusion. You also have to watch what you say, lest you trail the unsightly and unbecoming behind you like a bridal train of stained toilet paper stuck to the bottom of your shoe for the rest of your professional life. Oh, but by God, wouldn't I like to…

A media blitz. Yes. A freshman suggested throwing a big mixer for the press. College student logic ran that people would show up to anything as long as there's free booze. I needed to explain to him how much that costs.

Professor Emeritus Groppe found no difficulty getting press. Press in the Saint Joe newspaper, anyway. He wrote a wordy, full-page screed called "SJC: A History of Subsidies" for *The Observer*. It ran down a list of financial hardships similar to those provided by the Chairman of the Board.[18]

"Throughout our history, St. Joe's finances have always been precarious…" Groppe wrote.

Tuition discounts, declining enrollment, loss of professors who were also clergy and thus requiring higher-salaried replacements from the lay world, it was all in the article, almost with a hand ringing of "whaddaya gonna do?" Still, he offered a few crumbs of praise for Saint Joe and its strengths. The strength he saw as "singled out more frequently than others" was the sense of community and family generated by close interactions between students and between students and faculty. He closed with, however, “that this closeness to faculty and staff and the personal attention to it bears witness to, including small classes, is in part, a factor of our enrollment problems.”

So, even our strengths, in Groppe’s nihilistic shrug, were weaknesses.

I tossed the newspaper with an indiscriminate throw. One of the pointed, crisp edges of the fold hit the wall of my office with a “TACK!” I dropped into my wheeled chair. Force of impact sent me in a slow roll backward until I tapped against the wall. The familiar, dusty smell of the Core Building flowed into my nostrils. One of the last times it would.

Come on fundraisers.

Come on lawyers.

Come on Attorney General.

Why was I not fighting harder?

The hits just kept coming.

In a message dated February 27, 2017, Sponseller sent out “A Message from Saint Joseph’s College Chairman of the

Board."[19] It came written in a Q&A format. In my rhetorical analysis, whoever wrote the Q end of things came at the text from Sponseller's point of view. No doubt the writer worked for an Indianapolis PR firm hired by the Board.[20] The genre format allowed for Sponseller to control the narrative and once more lay out the rationale for "suspension of operations."

"These have been some very hard truths you've shared," the writer said at the close. "Do you see any positives in this situation?"

"My dad always told me to look at the donut, not the hole," was Sponseller's response. "At SJC, the donut is 127 years of educating people who are out in the world, contributing to society in ways that go wider and further than anything we can imagine."

True as that might be, I could express from faculty and student experience the great difficulty of seeing the cakey sides of the donut as we all dropped straight down into the gaping hole.

I went back to the Wal-Mart parking lot and called Jackie to chew over the prose that got dolloped into the collective Saint

Joe inbox. She pointed out that the 18 Board members who voted to close and walk away should do just that. The other 11 could remain with the Saint Joe community and work together to solve the problem.

"We want it [the College]. They don't. Why is this so hard?" Jackie asked.

I bore other news for Jackie as well.

Dr. Pulver sent an email at 9:07AM that morning.[21] It included a rough plan for how Saint Joseph's College might continue in the fall and for the 2017-2018 academic year, which up until that point seemed like so much vapor. The first draft plan, formulated by six faculty members in addition to Pulver, allowed us to keep HLC accreditation, cater to students not reliant on federal loans for tuition, and above all be financially sustainable. The attached document called for a college with three majors, business, education, and biology, four minors, the same subjects plus communication, Core courses, and eight full time faculty.

Eight.

I told Jackie about this brave new world of "The New Saint Joe" as Brian Capouch shouted in previous weeks, a "leaner, meaner" college model that would fit the bill of "fiscally responsible" as the Overlords called it. None of which made much pedagogical sense without supportive data. Something like propping a corpse up and still making it move and appear work. "They're trying to *Weekend at Bernie's* this place," a colleague called it. But what the hell? Why worry about the details? Whatever got us back up and running and me and my friends kept in the game of teaching. As I explained to Jackie, I earlier ran my finger down the smooth, cool computer screen, looking for a place for me.

Nothing.

I found nothing. I started to think about just how few lifeboats the *Titanic* carried back in 1912.

I told Jackie the majority of faculty knew nothing about this until opening their in-box. Indeed, Bill White made this known through an email he sent just before I left for my secret parking lot phone call.

“Big thanks to all who planned the future so quickly and inclusively. It is great to see that the Christian humanism of Core will still brightly shine,” he wrote.[22]

Bill’s years in and tenure stature afforded himself the ability to say that. The most I could do was nitpick the original message for grammar. I asked Jackie to keep this proposed “New Saint Joe” on the QT until when and if it may become public knowledge. Being a former journalist…hell, once a journalist, always a journalist…in addition to being a trusted Puma in this war, she agreed. We hung up and I drove out of the parking lot, headed across the street and once more into the breach.

After sundown, I sat in my office and sized things up. The alumni fundraisers would have to be the heroes of the day. Up until that point, all I had done was feed them information of what was happening on the ground. While it felt good as it gave me something to do and a small sense of accomplishment, it didn’t take a college professor to see that more would be required. Much more. In fact, it would mean throwing a Hail

Mary and engaging in an activity so contrary to my personality it made my skin crawl.

I needed to shuck, shill, and fundraise.

My mind cycled through classmates from all those years gone by, trying to think of anyone who could help. Once names bubbled up, I picked up my phone to track them down on social media. I would make a list and compose a personal appeal for each one of them. I had to try.

Someone knocked on my half-open office door. A colleague of mine came into my office, high heels of her black boots clacking on the tile floor. She sat down across from my desk, saying she hadn't had a chance to talk with me since this "shift in the universe" as she called it. I told her I was emailing and phoning alumni.

"Commiserating?" she asked, smiling.

"No," I answered. "Fighting. Working with them to find financial and legal actions we can take."

"Ahhg!" she grunted, tossing her hands up into the air. "Our severance!"

I just looked at her for a moment. I knew she meant nothing personal by the remark. Legal action, such as a suit or an A.G. investigation that found a case that could stick, could tie up the release of endowment funds for months on end. As mentioned in the case of Dowling College, a college endowment is tricky in the legal sense as a hefty portion of the funds more often than not come from donations. When such funds are used for purposes other than the intent of the donor, such as the paying out of someone's contract, that requires approval from the state attorney general. A thorough investigation, such as the one I and alumni petitioners called for, could extend that process into the foreseeable future. In retrospect, the comment from my office visitor also ran along lines similar to what happened in the battle for Sweet Briar. While many faculty voiced their opinions in that fight, I was told a subsection of them remained silent for fear of losing their severance. My colleague in my office was thinking in practical terms and who could blame her?

I could.

In that moment, I could. I felt an incandescent rage for anyone who wouldn't stand and fight for our homeland. Yes, it may be a "last stand," but anyone who could dismiss the loss of all we had built and worked for over so many years with a blasé feint of "It's just a shift in the universe," stood as incomprehensible to me and therefore we could have no common ground. To me they became as pandas who wouldn't even fuck to save their own species. I turned in my chair, shifting my shoulder towards her, and fixing my eyes on my phone and notebook. I asked her to please excuse me, for I was a busy man.

After all, I had a goddam war to fight.

Only it turned out to not be much of a war. No more than you could call a mass of people hurling vocal and digital cries toward an obscured and unresponsive cabal a "war."

The Alumni Board and Involved for Life, God bless their indefatigable spirit, continued to fundraise and fundraise all hours of the day. The tally hit the one million mark and continued to rise. Alums posted photographs on social media of their envelopes containing checks, all addressed and sealed for mailing. Many people stood ready to fight, and that faint chance grew.

Thus, I inhabited a weird interzone of wanting with all vehemence for something to work while beginning to doubt it all at the same time. I tried to write the sensation off to anxiety and depression, inwardly chastising myself for not having faith in those ardent alums working so hard. As I learned in my years however, hard work and noble character do not always beat machinery in motion. So much could still go wrong, even more wrong than it already had.

On March 3rd, something did go wrong…even though it was understandable and foreseeable. The St. Elizabeth School of Nursing, our partner and the provider of our largest number of majors, broke away from Saint Joseph's College and announced it would seek a new college with which to partner.[23] In previous days, the Overlords expressed intent to retain the nursing program as a means of holding on to accreditation, perhaps without the burden of maintaining a Rensselaer campus. Leadership of the nursing school at St. Elizabeth's Hospital naturally turned their thoughts to protecting themselves and their students in the wake of the "suspension of operations" announcement and a self-pronouncement from their partner institution that the financial situation was "dire." This severing meant that even if the rebel factions gained the funds, the injunction, or what have you, to save the College, a substantial portion of the student body and their tuition dollars would already have broken away and were unlikely to rejoin with an institution still on fragile ground.

Even if we won, we might still lose.

Days ground on, turning into weeks as March evaporated with nothing much happening. Bill White did send a message to the entire Board of Trustees regarding the termination letter they served to tenured faculty. He called the letter "cruel," "possibly illegal," and "on the border of being immoral." "I realize that the Board is focused on the future of the college," he wrote. "But please take some time to look in the rear view mirror at the debris you left behind."[24] I nodded with admiration as I read the email. Bill skewered the bastards as only Bill could. I relished the words, but it all grew hollow and fleeting for me. I couldn't join in the game for lacking tenure, so that left me cheering like a dingbat on the sidelines. It just added to my sense of impotence that March.

Because there never came any fierce legal fight to save Saint Joe, as happened at Sweet Briar. No protests or demonstrations, as happened at Antioch. Just…tumbling. Yes, tumbling, like a sock in a dryer. It was a sense of freefall where somehow you never fully touched bottom, but were cycled back up to the top to fall once again. What's more, rumors about possible programs happening on campus in the fall kept getting tossed in with you like Snuggle sheets, only nowhere near as soft or fragrant.

"I have little confidence of there being anything here in the fall," one of my colleagues, a philosopher, said to me. "But if there is, I know I won't be asked to be any part of it."

If the Overlords pulling the levers behind the curtain made the decisions, precious few of us would be. I suspected that those who remained would likely not be solely selected on need, but on "loyalty." Of course, any secret scheme would require sustained accreditation, and that grew more tenuous by the day. Both Pulver and Ryan drove up to Chicago at least once to meet with HLC. The results of the parlay, it was rumored, did not go well. In fact, one of the Overlords was said to have described HLC as "unworkable."

Dr. Pulver echoed this sentiment during a March faculty meeting.

"HLC wants us to fail," he told us, reasoning that a failure would spare HLC the expense of ever sending a site visit team.

Didn't matter. March came to an end and the Board of Trustees made the decision for us. On Monday, April 3rd, the Board of Trustees voted to surrender HLC accreditation, effective June 30th. In a press release, the Overlords said they made the move in order to "preserve resources, protect all current grades and degrees, and prepare a path for a future partnership."[25]

This also effectively ended the fundraising efforts of the Alumni Board and Involved for Life. Although the campaign efforts managed to raise $2.5 million in a little over a month's time, no amount of money would make a difference without accreditation. True to their word, Involved for Life announced they would be returning the money to all 852 donors.[26] While the outcome was not at all what we hoped, the effort itself remained a testament to nobility.

"We did all that without any support from the actual college," Elysse Ruggles, one of the alumni fundraisers, said to the Lafayette *Journal and Courier*.[27]

I sat dumbfounded in quiet when faced with the news. This is not how it's supposed to go. I have read fiction and nonfiction all of my life and this was not a proper, sensible narrative arc. No reader would ever accept this as a satisfactory ending to a story. In fact, it was about as anti-climactic as it could get. No final conflagration. No Ragnarok, where my side would fight to the last, even in fiery, bloody defeat. I came at that time to an intimate understanding of T.S. Eliot: "This is the way the world ends/Not with a bang but a whimper." But there wasn't even a whimper.

It just…ended. We lost. Finished. I felt idiotic for having ever felt it could have been otherwise.

What follows next is how a college dies.

NOTES

1. Email in author's possession.
2. Much of the dialogue is from minutes taken by Josh Lemieux, who at that time was Area Director for Housing and Residence Life. Lemieux distributed these minutes to all campus employees after the meeting via campus email. Minutes in author's possession.
3. This video is available on the Involved for Life Facebook page.
4. I confirmed with Sailors in email on 3 Feb. 2018 that it was Sailors' voice and that indeed he was speaking to Ben Sponseller.
5. "Saint Joseph's College say financial woes…"
6. I interviewed Kris Sakelaris on 18 May 2018. Notes with author.
7. "A Statement from St. Joseph's College (Rensselaer, IN) Alumni…"
8. Document in author's possession.
9. Photograph of this quote in author's possession.
10. Bangert, "Bangert: Saint Joseph's closing no surprise?"
11. Seltzer.
12. Chronis.
13. Photograph of this quote on Dr. Ryan's office door in author's possession.
14. Holden, "Can Saint Joseph's College keep its accreditation?"
15. I contacted Steve Kauffman at HLC to ask if there was ever a case where HLC revoked the accreditation of a college or university in the middle of a semester. His response was a simple "no." Email in author's possession.
16. What follows this sentence is taken from that day's faculty meeting minutes in the author's possession.
17. From personal memory.
18. Groppe, "SJC: A History of Subsidies."
19. Email in author's possession.
20. According to Board members interviewed, the hiring of a firm was presented by the Executive Membership to the full Board as fait accompli.

21. Email in author's possession.

22. Ibid.

23. Press release from President Pastoor to Saint Joseph's community. Photos in author's possession.

24. Email in author's possession.

25. Holden, "Campaign to save St. Joe's raises $2.5M."

26. Ibid.

27. Ibid.

CHAPTER SEVEN: Funeral for a friend

A deluge of rain came with the opening week of April. Angels weeping for Saint Joseph's College.

Yes, even then I recognized that as a forced and trite metaphor. Didn't stop me from thinking it. The rains caused the waters of the Iroquois River to swell. When the rain clouds at last moved on, the water levels in time subsided, exposing banks of mud. This brought long-winged buzzards circling slow and patient in the sky. Waiting…

"They feed on smaller organisms left in the mud," a colleague in biology told me.

You could find other interpretations as well. As the wormy, smell of wet earth permeated the air, water became something of a theme.

"I'm rereading *Moby-Dick*," Adam Current told me.

He said it while sitting at the desk for the administrative secretary for faculty. She needed to be somewhere else that day, perhaps a job interview, and they assigned Adam to cover phones. It grew most difficult to find work for admissions counselors to do. I leaned against the wall, listening to Adam talk about his interpretations of the book, and new insights he gleaned from this second or third go around on it. The phone rang, interrupting our literary criticism. Adam answered.

"You need to talk to the Registrar about transcripts," he told the caller.

I needed to be at lecture by nine. I left the room and made a listless shuffle towards the stairs to the Shen Auditorium.

I am one of those odd ducks who, most of the time, enjoys college lectures.

But I'll be damned if I could tell you what any of them covered post February 3rd, 2017. I sat during them, staring straight ahead at nothing in particular. My mind would flip between notions. In my trance that day, I realized why Adam chose to reread *Moby-Dick*. There we all were, serving aboard a collegiate *Pequod*. Like Ishmael, none of us signed on for a kamikaze hunt for a white whale, but the Overlords locked the wheel on course for disaster and long since abandoned ship with a shrug of "Welp, whaddayagonnado?" Behind them, our

Pequod would splinter and sink after ramming the great white whale, sending us all into a dark and salty abyss beyond our ken. I would wage my futile fight against the sea, my nose going up and under the waterline at intervals as the churning waves toss me and I reach out for Queequeg's coffin.

My mind then drifted back to the lecture. From my seat, I could see the laptops of many of the students, what few students who still showed up for class, that is. In any regular year, lectures would often be time for them to do other coursework, check their fantasy football teams, or even watch full movies. On that day, almost all of them looked at web sites of other colleges. They checked their applications, or they worked to fill out applications as the professor at the podium made a half-hearted attempt at delivering a talk. No doubt the speaker's mind struggled to think of where they could find a new job, all while trying to dispense their immediate duties.

"There was a cloud of heaviness over the campus, so melancholic," Gabi Pepple later put it for me. "Personally, I kept dreading the future. I didn't want May 2017 to come and go and

SJC to just become more distant in the past. Sometimes I got anxiety thinking about it."[1]

I looked at the student seated next to me. She pored over the website for a university in West Virginia. I leaned in to whisper to her. She recoiled, raising her right hand to somewhat block my view of her screen and I suspected she braced to be chastised for not paying attention in lecture. I pointed at her laptop.

"Could you let me know if they have a job?" I asked her.

When classes finished for the day, I saw April Toadvine in the hallway. She described her life as "a combination of fury and chaos" as she fielded repeated inquiries from people about her future.

"People think they're helping, but they're not helping," she said. "None of us chat anymore. We just ask how the job hunt is going or as someone asked me 'What's next for you?'"

What April said…it forced me to realize an ugly conclusion. I found myself in a position, an annoying and infuriating position in life that I never thought I would be in again.

It starts in high school. Graduation day approaches and everyone asks, “Where are you going to college?” I came of age before social media, so there could be no single cover-all announcement. That meant answering that same redundant question in what seemed like endless variations. Something similar happens as you near college graduation. “What’s next? Where are you working?” The question is especially uncomfortable if indeed you have not yet found employment. You then are blessed with a job and are doubly blessed if you start dating someone nice. After perhaps as short as three months, artillery shells of interrogatives rain down upon you once again. “Are you getting married? When are you getting married?” Then say you did hit the jackpot like I did and decide to spend the rest of your life with an amazing person and you get married. You might think the storm of question marks has subsided, but give it a week you’ll be playing *Meet the Press* once again over all manner of things.

“So when are you two having kids?”

– – –

But I thought I at last sailed through the question storm of life. Except maybe for "picked out your headstone yet?" But suddenly I found it wasn't over. Not for any faculty, student, or employee at Saint Joseph's College. Again and again we would be asked, "Where are you going next? Where are you landing? What are you going to do?"

In my inimitable snark, I would sometimes respond, "I'm getting loaded."

"What I tell them depends how optimistic I feel that day," April said. "I usually just tell them, 'I've applied.'"

She shook her head, looking at the floor, and then looked back up at me and drew in a deep breath, gesturing to the building around us.

"This is my side job," April said. "My main job is finding a job, and this place is a sloppy damn second. I need to figure out what's next."

I told her I still could not bring myself to undertake any kind of robust job search. Yes, I knew it should not be a demanding activity to just type "English" into a higher ed jobs site. But it was. When depression hits hard, someone can encounter what's called "the impossible task." This could be something as routine as a phone call, making a bed, or even taking a shower. It's just too much at that time. While one of the most "life critical" actions I could have been undertaking at that moment, a job search became my "impossible task" and I told my colleague as much. I also worried I wasn't doing enough to help our students transfer.

April offered an analogy of sorts for me. Imagine us in crashing plane, the airliner corkscrewing downwards. The oxygen masks drop from the ceiling. Procedure in such a scenario is you get your oxygen mask on first and then help others with theirs.

What do you do though if you have no idea how to even start getting that mask around your own face?

I went to my office and curled into a tear-soaked ball on my office floor. That's an unflattering admission, but I could take no other action at the time. Many would no doubt grouse, ridicule, or chastise me for doing so. Some perky, "life's all in your hands" son of a bitch might have screamed at me to instead execute a Nietzschean "Will to Power" and to rise up and face,

---

even embrace, the cocktail of sadness and fear which poured down on me. Life can be dominated and will in fact yield easily to intelligence and hard work.

Easy for Nietzsche to say. Then again, there's an aphorism of his that goes, "Terrible experiences give one cause to speculate whether the one who experiences them may not be something terrible." That, without question, played on my mind.

As I faced my new forever, I didn't feel like any rising or embracing. I wanted to cry. I wanted to scream. I either wanted to go into fetal position or punch walls, depending on which minute you asked me. I wanted to go back to that Chapel, kick down the door, and march straight towards the altar, telling God the whole time just what He could go do with Himself. For good measure, I would pull up a pew and read aloud *God is Not Great* by Christopher Hitchens in its entirety.

Unproductive? Well, that's how it goes. Depression can cover you like a tar that is colored black and endless like the infinity of space. It's not a hot tar. In fact, it grows cold quite suddenly, hardening like that old "Magic Shell" ice cream topping, leaving you frozen, immobilized. I could not move. I could not act underneath this cold, black, heavy thing, left without a clue of what to do next and able only to see all that was lost. Every time I tried to assess my faculties and capabilities, I came up with nothing. No hope.

Thoughts went through my mind that my only means of supporting my family might be my life insurance. I would need to research the most physically painless way to get it to them.

That night, after a half hour or so of solitary pillow-hugging, I gathered my wits. I'm a husband and a dad to two dogs. The three of them depended on me for income, so I had to do something. I emailed friends and asked about jobs. I updated my CV and even applied to two colleges. A bit more searching and I identified one more I would apply to the following day.

If you've never applied for a faculty or administrative position at a college or university, it's an experience. It's not a mere matter of submitting a resume and cover letter, then filling out a page-long application. Faculty applications are bureaucratic and byzantine affairs, stretching on for pages at a time. Franz Kafka himself could not have hoped to conjure up anything like them. The applications not only require a CV and letter, but often a "Statement of Teaching Philosophy," a "Diversity Statement," and three letters of reference from colleagues as well, along with perhaps even samples of your own writing. Wouldn't surprise me if a few universities even asked for recent blood and urine tests and your tax returns from the past six years.

Many of these teaching positions I found were short term. "Visiting lecturers" they're called, lasting only one or two years at most. Despite their impermanence, the qualifications quite often remained the same. "Must have PhD, good record of worldwide publication, willingness to teach welding as well as English, and relocate to what's left of a derelict oil rig in the Gulf." I found if I worked with true diligence, I could get through two applications in a night, but it meant skimping on class prep and grading.

Which made me feel even worse.

I called Debbie. I assured her I would do whatever I could to find a new teaching position, but I could not guarantee where in the nation that would be. She told me she knew I would work hard at it, but repeated that she needed to stay in the burbs to help her own family.

"I don't know what to do," I said. Before I even realized it, I mumbled out, "So tired."

"You always do this," Debbie said, soft concern in her voice coming through the phone. "You follow a pattern: obsess, obsess, collapse."

Point taken. It's my superpower.

"What are you going to do to take care of yourself while all this is going on?" she asked.

Staring out the window at the dark again, thinking for a moment, I found only one answer.

"The only thing I really can do," I said. "Going to get my kids out of here."

Think of Saint Joseph's College as a mid-sized sea creature of one sort or another. Maybe a manatee. If you're into manatees, that is. It is mortally wounded and trailing a crimson necklace of blood behind it. The ruby red droplets disperse and defuse in the water. One after another, sharks swim in fast and loose, circling towards the easy prey. The nearly 1,000 Saint Joe students became a sanguinary flow, irresistible to the sharks of admissions departments of other colleges.

Our own admissions department arranged for three transfer fairs for our students. Over 100 colleges and universities responded to the call and a few colleges had to be turned away due to space issues. Admissions counselors crammed themselves into the ballroom of the Halleck Student Center, each college taking a table. These included Ohio Wesleyan University, Olivet Nazarene, Goshen College, Manchester University, and of course…Marian University.

For one junior studying Mass Communication, her Media Ethics professor canceled class one day and walked all the students over to the college fair. She half-cried while discussing her options with admissions counselors, but also expressed gratitude for having a Saint Joe professor willing to help during such an abrupt and life-transforming predicament. Another student described going through the fair with "just a sense of panic. I thought I had it all figured out and made the perfect decision of where I wanted to get my degree and [the] thought of having to start my college search over breaks my heart."

The admissions fairs weren't always a smooth process in the Halleck Ballroom. During registration for the fair, a college admissions agent from Marian University is said to have stopped and stared at one of our student lounges.

"That furniture…" he asked, eyes narrowed. "What's happening to it after you close?"

An admissions counselor from another college was far too outraged to eye any furniture.

"He found out his director sent him without being registered," Adam Current said.

This visiting counselor, "now frog-eyed with rage" according to Adam, slapping his hands against his marketing fliers while stomping his feet on the floor, demanded a table for he "had a job to do."

"That must be nice," Adam later said to me in response. "Me? I'm staffing my own funeral."

I felt the same. While indeed most grateful that so many colleges and universities came to the aid of our students, giving them multiple and competitive choices of destination and sometimes…if the kids were lucky…a waiver of application fee, I still could not subdue my sense of possession. These were our students, on our campus. How dare they be taken from us? Jealousy. The whole surreal scene made me think of the visiting colleges as rescue helicopters spiriting our students away to safety. Good. However, I knew there would be no helicopters coming for the faculty. Pastoor warned us that night in January: nobody was coming to save us. Employees would be left to fend and fund for ourselves.

Back on second floor Core, I saw someone had taped a sheet to their office door. A memo from the College Business Office bore the title "Notice Concerning College Assets." It warned that "it is important for all employees to understand the importance of stewardship of the various College assets. It is the expectation of all employees that they do everything in their power to ensure that College owned assets are appropriately secured and maintained."[2]

Beneath that, someone wrote in deep blue marker, “Why is there so much concern about assets now? What about cash? (Stewardship of)”

Couldn’t argue.

Others selected milder sentiments to express with “door art.” I visited my brother Michael’s office one day, just to see how he was doing. He uttered brief responses and remained flat-faced in expression. An awkward pause passed between us and I at last, despite my better judgement, asked about the elephant in the room: did he find anywhere to apply? Michael shrugged and nodded. He then pointed at his office door. He had clipped off the front of a box of a Celestial Seasonings Sleepytime herbal tea and taped it to the door’s dark wood surface.

“That bear,” he said.

Michael pointed to the famous illustration of an anthropomorphic bear in a sleepshirt and night cap, dozing before a fireplace while seated in an overstuffed, green armchair. Also in the tableau, which appeared to take place inside the kind of cozy domicile a hobbit might inhabit, was a blue, old-timey radio set and a cat curled behind the chair.

- - -

“That bear has everything,” Michael continued. “He’s got a cat. He’s listening to NPR. Sometimes I just imagine myself as that bear.”

I certainly couldn’t fault him. Indeed, I found the image most appealing. It prompted dreams of a bucolic, Narnia-like setting where furry animals lived lives of peace and goodwill, and me sitting before a warm fire with the only sounds in the air being the voices of Terry Gross and her guest that day on Fresh Air. Like that bear, I could fall asleep with the security of my basic needs met.

Instead, I woke up with a sudden, violent jolt the next morning in my own bed with a job application half completed on my laptop. I turned to the bright, dawning sun with a mumble of “Christ, here we go again.”

Easter came and went.

Not since age seven had I hoped with such glittery wistfulness that the Easter Bunny would visit. He might bring me a rescued and revitalized Saint Joseph’s College.

Or failing that a bottle of scotch and a couple cartons of smokes.

Things buzzed for a little while on campus. An entity called the Renewable Nations Institute (RNI) expressed interest in acquiring Saint Joseph's College.[3] It would reopen the College and use it as a home base for teaching students from around the world about sustainable energy. They might even keep a few Saint Joe faculty on board as RNI wanted their students to have an interdisciplinary education. My Mom called the prospect, "Mana from Heaven."

Of course, I recognized RNI as the same organization once interested in Dana College, but nothing much came from that affair. Rumors circulated of several closed door and backroom talks, but just as in the case of Dana College, the idea of any partnership between RNI and Saint Joseph's College just kind of came and went. Hopes rose and fell like changing tides. Things like these took their toll.

"There were several 'bringing back to life' ideas which really were not great for my mental health, since I felt the death again each time these fell through," Dr. Anne Gull said of that time.

We did find one bright spot in the downward spiral. Both faculty and students of the College community clutched to one another in an increased sense of comradery. If we were a tightknit community before, we became doubly so after Easter...even if that sense would not be extended to the administration and to the Board of Trustees. I spent my lunchtimes with colleagues like Chad Turner, sharing the struggles of non-tenured, non-terminal-degree-having faculty in search of new full-time teaching positions. Who was going to hire us?

"Facebook memories keep popping up in my feed," Chad told me. "I see all the happiness and false hope I felt when I took this position two years ago. Sometimes I feel like this is a clown college and that's why they hired me."

While comradery and support ran high, we often felt unsure just what to say to each other.

"A coach said hi to me in the caf the other day and asked how I was doing," Jordan Leising said. "I said, 'Oh…you know…' He said to me, 'I know. It's like asking people how they're doing at a funeral.' And of course, he's right. This is our second home and we've been evicted."

He let his words linger for a moment before continuing.

"My bed is positioned in a corner of my bedroom facing a blank wall. I try to close my eyes at night, but I just end up staring at that blank wall. Yesterday I asked one of my classes how many of them sit up at night asking, 'What the hell am I going to do?' A lot of hands went up…including mine."

Jordan also brought to light another aspect of this process. As in the wake of a friend or family member's death, there would be constant reminders.

"I was doing laundry last night and saw at least three Puma shirts," he said. "Seeing them puts you in that 'Oh God' mood. Meaning, we're looking at things that aren't going to be around much longer. Things that aren't going to happen anymore, like Core lectures, or Little 5, or graduation. We're heading into a lot of 'lasts.'"

Lasts. Yes, it escaped my mind to consider it, but Jordan's keen insight and precision identified what all waited ahead of us. A long list of "lasts." For just how many of us, I wondered aloud, would it be our last time teaching college?

"I don't know," Jordan said, exhaling and shrugging. "I might have to leave academics and do something like work for a community coalition for agriculture back in my home town."

Indeed, that would be a decent option for a former farm boy. For others?

"How do you reinvent yourself in your late 50s?" Jordan asked.

He referred to our more seasoned faculty, in particular the ones who invested 20 or 30 years into both Saint Joseph's College and the town of Rensselaer. Just as with those of us on the non-tenured end of the spectrum, the veterans asked "Who is going to hire us?" I decided to ask Bill White where he was at in this whole debacle.

"I am laser-focused on us getting paid," he told me.

Bill unfolded a letter printed on plain white business paper with the Saint Joseph's College aegis in Puma purple at the top. I recognized it. Yes, the "pink slip" the rest of us got, but in his case worded for tenured faculty. As I glanced over the letter,

I saw quite a sticking point. Severance for a tenured faculty amounted to, according to the handbook, a year's salary paid out in twice monthly installments as if they were still teaching courses. This letter said that if the faculty member acquired new employment, they needed to notify Saint Joe HR and the severance payment would be the difference between the Saint Joe salary and the professor's new salary…if any difference existed.

"You got to be kidding me," I said.

The phrase was something of a mantra for us at that point. Every day seemed to bring a new insult from the administration. Just one more slap in the face for good measure. I tossed the letter onto Bill's desk. It landed soft and listless against a framed photo of his daughter and his grandson. I looked over at Bill. He sat in his chair, emptying a file folder of papers into a recycling bin already bulging and straining to hold its contents.

"Handout sheets from lectures stretching back over the past few years," Bill said. "All those moments will be lost in time, like tears in rain. Time to die."

A quote from *Blade Runner*, a favorite film of ours that we would discuss at length from time to time. I knew what he meant. Much of the paper getting tossed represented curriculum planning for classes taught, never taught, and only Bill knew what else. The sheets represented decades of work and personal investment. Behind him sat banker's boxes up against now empty bookshelves. He started telling me about Blackburn College in Illinois, where he taught history before coming to Saint Joe in 1985. The administration and the history department of Blackburn didn't like it when he decided to jump ship.

"But the bosses, the President, and the Dean treated me with respect to my last day—not the contempt so many of us are experiencing now."

Bill White, and others of us at either of the polar ends of the academic tenure spectrum at Saint Joseph's College, may have to adjunct. How long could we last on that? I asked Bill what he most wanted to see happen now. He paused his clearing and packing, rolled his chair back, and put his feet up on his desk.

"A Hellmouth," Bill said. "I want Saint Joseph's College swallowed by a Hellmouth."

On the television series *Buffy the Vampire Slayer*, a "Hellmouth" is a portal to Hell personified as the gaping maw of a hideous monster with the kind of visage common on covers for so many Eighties heavy metal albums. His comment stung for a moment. I loved Saint Joe and wanted it to live on and survive. Then again, oh to have sweet justice. To consign the perpetrators of this nightmare to Dante's underworld, to leave them no campus to "redesign," to leave them no carcass to pick at, to leave them lonely and ultimately with nothing…ohhh so nice.

Neither Bill, nor I, nor anyone we knew had a clue as to how one might conjure or otherwise produce a Hellmouth. So, Bill and a few others of the tenureds could only do the next best thing in America.

Sue.

Six of the tenured faculty, led by Bill White, filed a lawsuit against Saint Joseph's College in Jasper County Superior Court 1.[4] The plaintiffs argued that the College was not following the terms of the handbook by stating that the College would cease or decrease severance payments if the tenured faculty members found another job before March 14th, 2018. There was also great question as to the continuation of health and retirement benefits as stipulated in the contract. As the complaint read, the plaintiffs are "entitled to receive payment of their current salary and benefits through March 14, 2018 regardless of alternative employment."[5] Thus, the suit argued, the College would be in breach of contract to do other than what the handbook specified.[6] The complaint also argued that the administration failed to follow the procedure for financial exigency as defined in the faculty handbook as they did not "seek the concurrence of the Faculty Assembly."

Such litigation, like others of its kind as seen with the Sweet Briar faculty, would likely take months to play out and with no guaranteed outcome. But the lawsuit would make life tougher for the Board as they devoted more time and resources from themselves and the endowment to fight it. The whole thing looked and felt like being in a bloody barroom brawl. Your opponent has you in chokehold and the brain damage is already done, but dammit, you might still get a knife in their gut and they'll never get to a hospital before they bleed out.

In the meantime, professors, tenured or not, kept teaching. Faculty realized that juniors fell into a distinct and nebulous category. How difficult would it be for them to transfer out and do just one more year of undergraduate at another college? Faculty noticed, however, that about half the junior class could graduate with the 2017 seniors if they took accelerated classes between February and May. We could get them out in time. Professors then worked together with Academic Affairs to create and offer courses that could be taken and completed in such a short amount of time.

"I taught seven courses during those months," Michael Steinhour said. "I was exhausted mentally, physically, emotionally. I was doing what I love, helping students…but all while everything came unraveled around me."

As mentioned before, Michael Nichols took on the task of combining two semesters of senior year Core into a single nine-week class. This compressed class held in the evening ended in the same way Core ends for any senior, a lengthy capstone paper presented in class to fellow seniors. While this meant students would be engaged in the backbreaking act of reading and writing for this accelerated course along with the work for all of their other studies and perhaps even athletic practices to boot, it also meant that Michael undertook the equivalent efforts in teaching. I still don't know how he did it.

I found him in the cafeteria one night in the waning weeks of April. By happenstance I walked in just before his evening class. He sat by himself at a round table in the corner, the dying light of the spring sun falling on him through the window. Slouching his right shoulder into the back of the chair, nursing a cup of coffee, he stared straight ahead at his tray. His eyes looked half closed, his face somewhere between flat and a frown.

My heart broke in three places.

I felt as horrible as I would seeing any person sitting by themselves, trying conceal exhaustion, sadness, bewilderment, and disbelief. This hurt grew compounded by knowing he was a fellow faculty member, going through the same unimaginable experience as the rest of us while straining with a course load beyond reason…all so that we could get as many of our kids out as possible before the whole place got swallowed up by the ground. All this anguish grew amplified by the obvious.

He's my own brother. No matter our professional stations, regardless of our being middle-aged men, my formative years and the difference in our ages meant that a small corner of my brain would forever cry out, "It's your job to help take care of him." Even when we fought terrible fights as kids, even when my teenage-self belittled him so that I wouldn't be embarrassed in front the "cool kids," nothing ever overrode my sense of guardianship, no matter how much I concealed it. This relationship is written into our very names.

I've gone through life by my middle name, Jonathan. Michael's middle name is David. In the Old Testament, David became king. His friend Jonathan, however, looked out for him and even saved David's life a time or two.

What could I do for Michael David that day in the cafeteria? What could I do to save him from drowning? I just wanted to hug him, but it was neither the place for such a thing, nor was it really "our way."

I took a seat next to him.

"Hey," I said.

"Hey," he replied. "Just so you know, I won't be staying much longer. I'll have to get to class."

"That's no problem," I said.

An awkward silence followed. It happened with us even under the best of conditions. Despite our family ties and the numerous things we hold in common, we are also quiet and introspective by nature, with Michael being especially so at times. I broke the silence by releasing just a trickle of bitter bile, describing what I'd like to do to the people who caused the whole nightmare.

"Hmp," he responded and then went silent again.

That stoic, non-verbal utterance is something my father does too, even when confronted with disturbing information. It leaves the interlocutor mystified as to whether their statement is being considered or dismissed.

Michael started telling me about his wife, Jeanette, and her current work. She made friends with a local farm family getting into raising organic foods. While being just a start-up venture, they liked Jeanette, appreciated her knowledge of environmental science, and wanted her on board. As with all nascent businesses however, it would be a lot of work and the initial pay would be low. Maybe $20 per hour.

"I hope it takes off," Michael said. "Then maybe my drinking can become more than just a hobby."

There. The hint. The glimpse at the true goings on with him. His silence in the previous months and his coziness with administrators caused me to wonder just what he thought about this whole ordeal. Did he somehow get insulated from it? Had he found, perhaps written in Sanskrit in one of his arcane Buddhist texts, a means by which he could disassociate himself? No. In truth, he sat in the caf that night every bit as broken and battered as the rest of us.

And there was nothing I could do to help him. And there was nothing he could do to help me. How do you save someone from drowning when you're drowning too?

~ ~ ~

Michael got up to bus his tray and go to class. I went to the line and got a burger.

I ate half of it.

I still needed to teach. That might have been what saved me.

The combination of classroom responsibilities and my obligations to my students forced me outside of myself. I prepared, taught, and graded lessons just I would any other year. But I didn't always bring my "A" game.

It must have been apparent one day for as I shambled into the hallway after class, one of my students grabbed me in a tight hug.

"You're going to have a great future, Professor Jon, because you deserve a great future," he told me.

I thanked him. I'd taught this freshman student for only one semester, but his kindness and his compassion were unparalleled in my experience with students. I knew he believed every word he said.

Now if only I could've gotten myself to believe it.

The whole hallway of second floor Core looked a pigsty.

Recycling bins overflowed with papers and trash cans fought to contain food waste as streaks of various sauces dripped down the sides of the cans. Dust bunnies mingled with spider webs as they all congregated in the corners. Sometimes you could see food crumbs in with the mix. Air grew mustier and mustier in odor. The faculty washrooms approached a level of filth that rivaled that of a male dormitory, but thankfully never went quite that far. I thought of Justin Carlson's descriptions of Dowling College and its decay into disrepair, just before the New York institution closed its doors for good.

Our own situation that day came from laying off half the custodial staff in a flash.

Administrators decided on waves of "rolling layoffs." For example, if assistant coaches and trainers worked for teams not in season that spring, they found themselves gone by mid-April. Same went for the entire staff of Admissions. What work could they do at that point anyway? As for physical plant and the cleaning crew, only an "essential staff" would be kept on for the remainder of the semester and commencement. All the buildings would get a minimal, pass-through cleaning, and it would take longer for it to happen.

Then big blue monstrosities came into the hallways. Industrial-sized recycling bins. Provided for us by the Overlords so that we might better clear out our offices. Professors tossed entire binders and folders of curricula that represented whole careers into those gaping bins. Outside office doors you would often find stacks of books with handwritten signs reading, “FREE”. Workers rushed past me pushing dollies stacked with banker boxes or entire metal filing cabinets. Word came that a deadline loomed to get all valuable documents over to a temperature-controlled room in Schweiterman Hall at the far end of campus.

The random scraps strewn on floors…the offices in gradual states of emptying…the framed art either taken down or hanging askew…administrators moving at brisk pace while carrying envelopes and file folders…the rapid evacuation of sensitive documents inside heavy metal cases…it all looked like the fall of Berlin, only without all the pesky artillery shells.

Professors would pass me, tugging carts laden with boxes of personal effects.

"Sad times, Jon," one of them said to me as he carted his life away.

Later, I would think of this moment after talking with Milt Heinrich from Dana College about the closure ordeal of his own community. Recall that the announcement of Dana's closure was sudden and swift, like the drop of a guillotine blade. The news came to Heinrich on a Friday. By Saturday morning, he was moving out of his office. One of his recollections from the day brought the experience into human terms.

"The most heartbreaking thing I remember was hearing one of my faculty colleagues crying out in the hallway," Heinrich recalled. "She was carrying boxes of her things and told me that she was crying because she just lost insurance for her and her child."

No such outbursts in our hallways. Not that I heard, anyway. The same or similar thoughts occupied many of our minds though, I'm sure. I know they did mine. Unlike the poor folks at Dana College, we found ourselves with a few months to let the loss wash over us. By April of 2017, most of our cries went inward. I know I quashed one when I saw the dumpster.

Steel, stained, and bus-sized, it sat in a far corner of the faculty parking lot. Someone from the Business Office ordered it placed there, I guessed. “For our convenience,” you know, as we cleared everything of ours out of the Core Building. I walked up next to the dumpster. It stood a good two heads taller than me and so heavy, long, and wide it could only be moved by a semi-truck that hauls trash.

This time it would carry people’s lives.

Students held their annual art exhibition in the Core Building foyer outside the auditoriums. One last time.

I wanted to be there as I always was, trying to support the students in their creative efforts, but grading kept me from the reception. I went anyway in the late afternoon of that day after as the dying spring sunlight turned to a rough orange. I ambled through the exhibit. No one else was on the floor. All the faculty went home, even the ones known to stay late and get work done…really, why would they now? Many of the students had athletic practice or work. So I walked alone, taking in the paintings, the sculptures, and the sound of my own footsteps.

The temporary, folding blinds held solid work from our art department as usual, featuring the wide range of subjects you might expect. Portraits, still life, a couple punky skulls and "shock pieces", and explosive examples of abstract expressionism alive with vigorous color spread out before me. I lingered on a landscape painting, no doubt one drawn from a local subject. A single, lonely shed built of wood planks sat in a rustic locale of tall grass turned tan. Patches of snow splotched the roof in white. The sky hung over it all in shade of a deep, hazy blue-gray.

A well-rendered in its own right, I couldn't help but think of artist, Cornelia Parker. Decades ago she created an installation called Cold Matter (an Exploded View). Using explosives, Parker really did blow a small shed apart and then hung the fragments and pieces in a form that was a rough approximation of shed's previous form. Those among us who might not describe themselves as art lovers may be prone to ask, "What the hell for?" It has to do with what the shed represents.

"Where you store things you cannot quite throw away," Parker described it. "Like the attic, it's a place where toys, tools, outgrown clothes and records tend to congregate."[7]

Exploding the shed removes a place of shelter and erases the safety of "the normal". And even if you recover every single fragment and piece of the shed, there is no way you can put it back together just as it was before the blast tore it apart. No way at all. Just the ashes of everything…

I didn't know the student who painted the particular shed featured in the exhibit. I therefore couldn't ask her if she was familiar with Cornelia Parker. The likelihood, I conceded, was small that the student artist meant the shed to convey any reflection on Saint Joe's closing. Rather, it was a more likely meant to be a pretty, even if a bit lonely and melancholy, rendition of a rustic barn on a winter's day. Anything else indicated projection on my part.

And just another case of me seeing "lasts" wherever I went.

Students would later tell me that when they played pool or went to the rec center for a game of pick-up basketball, they asked themselves: was that it? Was that the last time they would ever do those things on campus? Would they ever see each other again after they went their separate ways? "The last" so often comes without warning…like a speeding shot from a sniper so well-concealed you'd fail to see them with a neon sign.

Glimmers of good came amidst it all. We did talk more. We talked to people we might not have otherwise.

"Met a lady who worked for SJC for 27 years," one of my students told me. "And she was so heartbroken to be searching for other jobs. 27 years and throughout my three years I've only seen and met you ONCE? A very humbling experience to say the least."

Our dinner conversations in the caf seemed to last longer. I found myself wishing the caf workers would start stocking the soda fountains with quarts of rum, but you can't always get what you want. I knew that in the acutest of ways. The meals also left something extra to be desired. Sodexo, the food service that ran the cafeteria, no longer saw us as a worthwhile investment for obvious reasons. Stock and fare received in the kitchen amounted to the minimum needed to keep a campus of kids fed. Every day, fewer options were available and more dishes repeated in the lineup. Many students found it intolerable.

"Don't blame Sodexo," Brian Capouch told the table one night.

Brian relayed that the corporation got screwed over as much as anyone else in the whole nightmare, given they spent over a million dollars renovating parts of the student center in exchange for a long-term contract reaching into 2029. Of course, there would be no Saint Joe in 2029.[9]

"They'll probably sue," Brian said of Sodexo.

Justified or not, it didn't change the culinary monotony. Brian, in an act equal parts magnanimous and merciful, took us all out to his favorite Mexican restaurant in Monon, Indiana. Burritos, laughs, photos, a guzzle or two of that rare nectar known as "Mr. Pibb" made for a good time had by all, but all of it acting as a sort of paperweight so the old, thin typing sheets wouldn't fly away in the chilly spring breeze. That's what I thought, anyway. The wind being the coming end. The sheets being all of us. The dinner being part of just another "last".

We returned to campus after dinner and I ran into Michael Steinhour. He told that me he just finished teaching night class, and he liked to walk the campus in the dark as his way of trying to say goodbye. Sometimes he would see students and he made sure to stop to talk with each one of them. Steinhour then put into words what I couldn't, and as a writer that kicked me in the teeth. We all knew the College to be dead on its feet, but none of us wanted to believe it. We wanted hope and there simply wasn't any left. I believed it a kind of drawn out torture to see part of the campus still alive, but headed towards a terminal point. Steinhour named this period of our lives:

"It's a three-month funeral," he said.

Little 500 weekend came. One last time. As I said before, it tended to be a real rager most years. The campus streets turn to a raceway lined with hay bale chicanes and the students and faculty all mill about in friendship.

And beer. There is no shortage of beer at Little 5. When I was a Saint Joe student, each race weekend involved dozens of Pumas acting as drivers, pit crew, or just staff workers to help make the event come off with few hitches. Everybody else, and that was a lot of us, was drunk. There might be a race going on, but we wouldn't know. Memories were made…or erased…that weekend. Though raucous, it was overall harmless fun, free from serious injury or property damage.

All right, one time we lit a couch on fire, but the Men of Merlini Hall extinguished the flames with extreme prejudice. And with our own precious bodily fluids, no less. It was Earth Day, after all. Besides, Saint Joseph's College was no stranger to the destructive force of fire and someone needed to take action for the error in judgment.

Dionysian overtones aside, Little 5 weekend was something of a symbol. It was a physical manifestation of the Puma spirit. People of the entire community would gather and revel in the kind of friendship and comradery that is seldom found elsewhere.

"If I'd known it was like this, I would have gone to college here," a Purdue visitor said to me one Little 5 weekend.

"It's like nowhere else," I told her.

In April of 2017, a couple thousand alumni descended on the campus for one last go around. The wide-open grass in front of the football field turned into a "village" of RVs, tents, and campers. At first I didn't want to go. The online chatter amongst alums kept boasting of how the beerfest with a slight side of racing would be the party-to-end-all-parties. I didn't feel like a party. Whole thing felt more like a graveyard dance to me, but there would be no telling the alums that. They would have their beer and brats, they would get their Wagonmasters at the Wagon Wheel, in between there would be more drinking and backslapping while talking of "good ol' days", and then they would go home to their lives…and their jobs.

Current faculty, staff, and students? We'd be left behind. Standing in the flotsam of the festivities and waiting for the bad things to come. I'm not one for dancing at funerals. Particularly if the body's still warm.

But if you're doing it right, you learn just as much from your students as they do from you. Justin and the other Freedom Fighters said they would miss me. They said that this was, indeed, one of our "lasts" and while that carried a melancholic tone, I might be sadder still for passing up the moment. Would I later regret staying away and opting instead to languish even more in sadness while staring in vacant desolation? Their appeal came across as both well-reasoned and a tug at the heartstrings. They must have had a decent rhetorician teach them argument. It still felt odd to party at Little 5 while the metaphorical tide kept rising, but what the hell? I figured I'd just ride the weird log flume of a weekend to the end and see where it took me.

My memories of the day are hazy. Navigational beacons are few, but one of them is starting out at the beer tent around 11am. Alcohol just started to fill my veins and bladder when a separate and distinct high kicked in from endorphins. I met a few Pumas from my undergrad days, people I hadn't seen in decades. Then more Pumas. Then even more. Thousands upon thousands crowded the campus under a bright spring sun with but few clouds in the sky. We hugged. We caught up. We bought each other more beers. That started to be both currency and custom for the day. Meet an old friend, even just in passing? Get them a beer if they don't have one. If you don't have one, they'll provide. And if need be, provide a "heavier" beverage.

"I've never faced being without work before. It's heavy."

That's what I said in the back of giant U-Haul truck a set of intrepid alums tricked out into a mobile bar.

"Speaking of heavy, let's do a few shots of Jager," the wheely-bar owner said.

He dropped two 1.5-ounce glasses with heavy bottoms onto the wooden bar and a thick, opaque, purple fluid drizzled into them like cough syrup. What the hell? Down the hatch. Even more alcohol mingled with the warm sensations of Puma friendship and nostalgia. A sweet burn and then more of the numb. I thought back to all those prevention filmstrips in junior high health class that described the chemical effects of alcohol. Why all the theater and the over-complicated explanations I'll never know. The process is fairly straightforward. It makes all pain disappear and everything ugly turn beautiful.

I continued to wander around campus and Alumni Village like Leopold Bloom through Dublin, only even more chock full of booze. I went from RV to RV, camper to camper, my typical shy self-emboldened by liquid courage. It didn't matter if I knew the alums or not, they welcomed me as I welcomed them. I started to notice that all I needed only introduce myself and a pattern would emerge.

"Nichols??" they would ask, their expression one of surprise then growing to wide smile. "The professor's son? I had your Dad for Core class!"

Then they'd give me more hooch. After twenty minutes or so of bon vivant banter, I moved on to the next RV and the whole thing started over again.

I saw the Chapel's twin towers jutting up above the budding but still bare trees. The sun had gone down by this point, though when that happened exactly I bore no recollection. I just stared at the cross-topped towers illuminated by the floodlights at the Chapel's base.

"Jump back and soak it in," my head told me. "It's the last time all Pumas will be together."

- - -

Monday the cards came.

The kids took the time to write notes to professors of their choice to let us know how much they valued and appreciated us. Even as their own lives turned upside down, even as they searched for new beginnings all while wondering when would be the last time they would see their friends, they gave thanks for our work and stood with us in solidarity. I am blessed to say I received a few of these cards. I opened them all in front of my mailbox and read them. As I did, I heard the sound of someone crying.

Not an altogether uncommon sound at Saint Joe those days.

Jordan Leising's office occupied the slot just outside the mail and copy room. I saw him at his desk, quite a pile of student cards in front of him. He wiped tears from his red cheeks when he saw me in his doorway.

"It wasn't us," he said and then waved about at the cards. "We weren't the problem. We did our jobs."

We stood in sullen silence for a bit. Then Jordan punched his desk.

"We did our jobs!" he seethed. "The bean counters and the Board didn't."

I nodded and looked down at the floor, kicking at the dust balls amassed outside the doorjamb. Would exoneration of faculty make us feel better or worse? Or both? Jordan lifted a student research paper and returned to grading.

"We have enough to do right now. So, all this probably won't really hit us until June," he said.

On the following Friday we buried the Core program.

While planning the 2016-2017 academic calendar, we slated the year's final lecture for that morning. We Core Directors didn't know just how final it would be. A wrap-up for Core 6: Humanity in the Universe turned into a eulogy for the entire curriculum. Many classes cancelled that morning so that students and faculty alike could fill the Shen Auditorium and say a communal goodbye to the curriculum that enriched so many lives and helped make Saint Joseph's College the rare jewel it was. One last time. Once again, a student would serve the gracious and vital role of impromptu videographer and livestream the event to the Involved for Life page on Facebook via her iPhone. That meant Debbie could watch from home. Five of the previous Deans of Core would speak that day, including Michael and Dad.

I found Jeanette and my two little nephews sitting in the front row. I smiled, waved, and took a seat across the aisle from them. Both the boys smiled back, each one fair-skinned with rosy cheeks, the youngest, with his blond hair askew like a bird's nest, revealed a missing a tooth or two with his grin. The lecture began, but I found myself unable to pay attention…Educator! Heal thyself!...and instead kept my eyes on my nephews. They tilted their heads forwards and up, swinging their legs while watching their daddy move about the stage, his voice projected from the lavalier mic on his lapel and cascading throughout the auditorium.

Did those little boys know? Could they know? I wondered. I know their mother must have impressed upon them the importance of that day as she helped tie their shoes and zip their hoodies in the morning. I knew they must have sensed their father's and grandfather's sadness in the months previous. Through the years they accompanied their parents to plays, ball games, homecomings and so forth on campus, so I knew the boys must already be well underway in forming their own attachments to Saint Joe, just as their parents and I did over our lives. My nephews promised to be "future Pumas."

No. It would never happen for them. There would be no future at Saint Joe for them or any other kid. Likely they didn't realize it, sitting in their blue and green hoodies, swinging legs ending in dirty Spider-Man and Hot Wheels sneakers. Judging by the fresh, black mud on those shoes and the cuffs of their little sweatpants, they played in the woods outside their house that morning. Their mother helped the boys turn the house into something of a biological field station, bringing leaves, caterpillars, and frogs back from the woods to the kitchen table for study and then release. They grew vegetables in the backyard garden. Each of them loved that house and those woods.

And they would probably have to leave it all.

How much time wasted? That's what I really needed to ask. Depression and anxiety derailed my train of thought once more and I lost out on listening to at least fifteen minutes of the last ever Core lecture. I even missed part of my father's talk. I forced my eyes, ears, and brain back to the present. In Dad's ten-minute segment of the lecture, he would be offering the summation of his life's work. How does one do that?

He did it, though. Best as anyone would be able to under the circumstances. The circumstances? They came to be summed up to perfection by one of my students as we all milled about after the lecture, warmly shaking hands and giving supportive hugs.

"This is like a funeral," he said.

My nephews came up and both hugged me at the same time, their arms around my waist.

I was wrong earlier. They knew.

Wonder of wonders I got a job interview.

A military academy in north central Indiana wanted to talk to me about teaching Humanities. I needed a job, so of

- - -

course I jumped on it. Preparing and preparing, poring over their curriculum and student demographic data, I worked until I built a sufficient amount of confidence…or what passes for confidence in my case. On the assigned day, I set out driving to the school in the late afternoon, for the interview would be a two-day process. As I drove, I saw the sun setting in my rearview mirror and the Twin Towers of Saint Joseph's College growing smaller and smaller in the distance.

A sense of guilt percolated up from my stomach to my heart and then my mind. I saw myself like a husband with a wife hooked to life support, and he decided to leave the hospital to go out on a date. I didn't want to make the drive. I didn't want to do the interview. I just wanted to turn around and go back home to my people.

"I'm thinking about how all those students would need to find new schools, but I guess every faculty member needs a new job now, huh?" one of the interviewers, an administrator at the school, remarked to me. "A whole college coming to an end. It must be tough."

"It's been a three-month funeral," I said.

- - -

I didn't get the job.

No real surprise. The place just wasn't my style. That and despite my diligent preparation and fiscal motivation, I didn't sink my heart into the interview. I couldn't really start something new until I made peace with the coming end. Who knew how long that would take? For as each one of the day-long gauntlet of job interviewers asked me questions, an inescapable truth haunted me. The last ever commencement ceremony at Saint Joseph's College barreled towards us all like a freight train bereft of brakes.

"I felt a funeral in my brain,

"And mourners to and fro…"

That's Dickinson, of course.

Those verses came to my mind the morning of commencement as students and faculty fought their way into their regalia. Just like every other year, we lined up in Halleck Student Center to make the processional over to the Richard F. Scharf Alumni Fieldhouse. Everything about it was…normal.

Just so damned normal. No words, no outward actions gave any indications that this graduation bore difference in any way from all the others. In that regard, I suppose it was very much like most funerals I've attended. You execute the order of the proceedings, you do everything which must be done, and you do it without any real commentary for to do so would only bring unnecessary attention to the sorrowful task at hand. Don't bring anyone down. Keep this as upbeat and celebratory as can be for the graduating students and their families.

"[We're] here not because it's an emotionally easy thing to do, but because we want our students to have the best graduation — the graduation that they deserve for putting in as much effort as they have, especially over these past few months," Dr. Jordan DeLong, professor of psychology, said.[9]

Right on point.

The wind became the most concrete disparity of the day. A spring gale howled across the campus, smacking all of us again and again in the face like a thin sheet of cold steel wool. Caps and tassels went flying. Students and faculty darted out to grab them and then dashed back into the moving line. Flag bearers gripped flagpoles until their knuckles turned white, fighting to keep hold of standards and flags turned into sails in the force of the wind. Holding his cap to his head, a colleague leaned over to me.

"This sucks," he shouted over the gusts of air.

It kept going on like that. There came only hints and glimpses of the added dimension of the day, this last of the lasts. A few tears down a cheek here. A sad smile there.

Alex McCormick, as the class president of the final senior class in the history of Saint Joseph's College, gave the customary speech afforded the office at every commencement. He stood tall at the podium, reminding us that "We're Pumas and Pumas always persevere." More than half my age, he possessed twice my strength. I stifled the too familiar feeling of panic as it welled up again, that kind of hopeless bitterness when someone you love is slipping away from your life and there is not one damn thing you can do about it.

When do we light the candles? When do we place the flowers over the grave?

I thought of what Jeanne Kay once wrote of the initial fall of Antioch, how their community members “were simply going to disperse, go our own wounded way after this terrible collective defeat while the new Antioch would be started from scratch, as if we’d never been there to fight.”

All the speeches made. All the degrees conferred. Then the time came at last. The end of ceremonies. Dr. Pulver returned to the podium after the benediction and drew in a heavy breath.

"Faculty, staff and those who have served our institution, please stand," he said.

The faculty stood. Applause sounded as rain driving on the roof. Pulver made a hard swallow, surveying the fieldhouse. I kept trying to interpret his words in a somehow less final way, denying all to the very end. Then the echoes of applause and cheers died out, replaced at once by the requisite “Fanfare and Recessional” played by the College band as we marched out of the fieldhouse. It all, at last, was put to rest.

Outside, amid the clusters of tearful students, I encountered a Board of Trustees member, one who I knew from the February meeting minutes voted to close Saint Joe.

- - -

According to his CV, his experience with higher education matters was confined to being vice-president of an Ohio engineering firm. He never attended Saint Joe. His face said "Sure is a shame" as he shook his head and the tone of his voice took on the same "whaddyagonnado?" so commonplace among the Overlords as he said, "Yeah, well the end was probably when we lost accreditation."

I possessed no strength that day to fight this man, a member of the Board of Trustees and as such ostensibly "in the know" on the point that we never lost accreditation. This fact should have been clear to him as the Board themselves voted to surrender accreditation one month previous. He asked me if I had anything "lined up after this." I said I didn't. He said he hoped I would find something soon.

"I hope you die," I thought. "Hell, I hope we both die."

Breaking away from the Trustee, I found my graduated Freedom Fighters and hugged each one of them. We took pictures and I tried to focus on the other meaning of the day. These young people, and all of their fellow students both graduated and not, lived up to and exceeded the meaning of

"Puma." While all about them came crumbling down, they persevered and did what needed to be done. And yet even though those seniors had every reason to start moving on after February 3rd, they stayed and fought. They handled everything with a grace and a determination I so often felt I lacked. Because of that, I could at least see the day as one for celebrating who they are and what they accomplished. No other factor could or should occlude their triumphs.

To my utter surprise they gave me gifts. A framed photograph of all of us with Brian Capouch on our last night at the caf. A class of 2017 t-shirt, complete with the adopted Billy Joel slogan, "We Didn't Start the Fire" on the back.

"We consider you a member of our class," Nate told me.

Then they handed me an old book with slight creases and bends in the corners of the cover. *The Art of War* by Sun Tzu, referencing of course Brian Capouch's quip, "we're going by the Bible, and they're going by *The Art of War*."

"Open the cover," someone said.

I did it. I found signatures and notes blanketing the inside cover and the front page. Messages to me that left me humbled, flattered, honored, and warmed on a day so otherwise bitter with chill. I could not find the words to express my humble gratitude.

"Guess where we got the book," Jose said, smiling. "We took it from the library!"

We all laughed. Yes, I recalled, I indeed instructed the Freedom Fighters to "liberate" as many books as they could if we ever suspected the precious treasures might be headed for nowhere but a dumpster. I teared up. I tried gathering as many of those students into my arms in one single hug, but that was a physical impossibility.

Like so much else that day.

One other typical aspect of a graduation day came like clockwork, but this time with added gravitas.

By around 5pm after any commencement, the campus would go deathly quiet. All the graduated seniors, along with any other students remaining on campus that weekend to assist with the proceedings, clear out with their families in a matter of an hour. An utter stillness falls. One moment the College is full. In the next it is not. It's like the silence that follows a torrential rain.

Commencement represents the closing of a chapter at any college, but for us? Everyone "graduated" that day. The children did not just grow up and leave home. No, the family moved and left the keys behind, the electric shut off, and the house foreclosed.

I walked the campus in the utter silence. Something reminded me of a line by Raymond Carver, "There is a silence that comes to a house where no one can sleep." Even the wind died down as if to add the effect. Scraps of trash lay in the grass in small pockets outside the dorms. Plastic bags, old student papers, even discarded shoes, all left as detritus in the wake of fast-departing students. I thought of pictures of Pripyat, the empty Ukranian city that is home to Chernobyl. After the nuclear disaster, Soviet authorities gathered up the citizenry, told them to leave whatever they were doing and go. Bring nothing because they would come back later.

Of course, they never did.

Pripyat became an "exclusion zone," off limits to all due to the insidious magnitude of the radiation. Today, if one takes the risk, they can visit the abandoned buildings to see toys left behind in school classrooms, dusty clocks with the hands stopped at the moment the electricity was cut, bottles and plates left on tables, and all manner of domestic wares dropped in place but never picked up.

No loss of life or limb at Saint Joe as with Chernobyl, but I wondered…would Saint Joe become another "Pripyat"? The garbage left behind on the grass might be cleaned by custodians, presuming any remained employed. The "winddown," however, called for the sealing of buildings. One physical plant staffer told me they would begin boarding windows on certain structures, which ones he didn't know. Finally, an actual "exclusion zone" would be declared around the campus.

Yes, according to the "non-renewal" notice I received, May 12th marked a red line. After that date, no faculty or student could set foot on campus.

The morning of May 12th I walked the campus again. The concrete of the sidewalks crumbled beneath my feet in a few places. Blades of grass and the bright yellow petals of dandelions poked their way through the crevasses, reaching for sunlight. A rusted bedframe, chipped and peeling in places, sat in the lawn outside Gallagher Hall. “Discarded like the rest of us,” I thought, but that voice came followed fast by Debbie’s, “You obsess, obsess, collapse.” She’s probably right.

She’s definitely right.

In the grotto I took a small knife from my pocket. I cut my hand. I squeezed the fleshy bulb on the outside of my left hand and my blood fell into the soil, causing tiny bursts of deep red firework splatter patterns in the dirt as each drop hit. I fused with the College in the physical sense. My DNA mixed with the actual terra firma. My land. My home. My people.

I went back to the Core Building. The heavy, truck-sized dumpster neared overflowing with discarded office and educational items. A veritable “sandbag bunker” made of full, black garbage bags formed a piled line at the edge of the lawn along the parking lot entryway to the building. A poster-sized plastic picture frame rested atop one of the bags, its transparent cover cracked in a forked pattern like a lightning strike. The poster inside it? One of those vapid motivational ones reading: “TEAMWORK”.

- - -

Once inside, I maneuvered through the trash cans outside offices and the boxed belongings stacked in the hallway. Dust covered everything. Part of the dust came from pulverized dry wall as physical plant workers ripped decorative paintings down from hallway walls, leaving behind a series of raggedy, crumbly holes.

"I will show you fear in a handful of dust…"

I came to an empty faculty office acting as a temporary H.R. station. There I handed the H.R. director my faculty ID, my parking pass, and my office key, then capped off the merry occasion with signing my name on a line. I looked at the three items I just placed on the desk. It struck me how ordinary they were. How many times a day did I use that key with no thought? How long did the parking pass dangle from my windshield mirror? Now a voice inside me screamed, "Give me those back. They're mine."

"I want to thank you," the H.R. director said, swallowing a lump in her throat.

I could not imagine what I needed thanking for.

"My niece was a student here," she continued. "She said that you helped her, that you and your brother always put students first."

"None of this could have been easy on you," I said. "And so I thank you for being the most human of Human Resources officers I have ever known."

It helped. It helped to be reminded that at least I did a little good. I needed that boost so that I might carry out my last remaining task. I looked at my now-empty office a final time, slid my nameplate from its holder on the door before placing it in my pocket, and began the slow walk away. That's all. It's a matter-of-fact process, so just keep it at that. One foot in front of the other and leave. It's just another day and you're just leaving work. As I made that walk, I passed April Toadvine's former office. A sheet of newsprint paper hung from the door with a black marker message written on it in Latin that said:

"Nolite te bastardes carborundorum!"

Or, "Don't let the bastards grind you down."

"Well it's getting harder to give a shit these days," I said to no one in the hallway.

- - -

I got in my car. I saw an empty space beneath the windshield mirror where the parking pass once hung for years. Turn the key and put the car in gear. Do everything like it's just another day. Just take a left out of the parking and a left onto the highway and leave campus.

Even if it's for the last time ever.

"The pattern of things to come faded away."

NOTES

1. Gabi Pepple's statement was a comment made on a Facebook update I made, asking for student recollections of that time.
2. Photos of these printed emails in author's possession.
3. Dimitrova and Sievers.
4. Wilkins.
5. Vizza
6. White et al. v Saint Joseph's College
7. "The Story of Cold Dark Matter."
8. "Food services company sues closed St. Joseph's College."
9. Holden, "St. Joseph's holds a tearful final graduation."

CHAPTER EIGHT: Haunted

There are good reasons we bury or burn our dead.

The sanitary benefits for society are obvious, but really, who wants to watch as nature take its course on anyone you love? Or with anyone else for that matter? We also need to "put them away," to finish the psychological cycle and begin to say, "This is relationship is done and gone."

Unless they come back to haunt you. I saw many ghosts in the summer of 2017.

I returned to Debbie and the dogs in the Chicago suburbs. Debbie or her mother would asked "How are you doing?" once a day. "Perfect" I'd say. Of course, I wasn't. Nothing was perfect. Hell, I would have settled for everything being perfect for just five minutes. Because though I appreciated being back with my family full time, I never felt like I really came back. I just felt so damn lonely. So much love flowed around me, so why did I only feel pain? Something to do with the utter disintegration of my community and being 100 miles from the campus of the former (had to get used to saying that) Saint Joseph's College, I reckoned. That and I kept seeing Pumas everywhere. Rather, I thought I did.

I would be in a grocery store and see someone in the produce section. My mind would swear it saw a former colleague and I would rush over to them, eager and relieved to find a fellow survivor of the disaster. Ended up startling a poor stranger trying bag their green peppers.

"Sorry. Thought you were someone else," I would mumble through an uneasy laugh before shuffling off.

While driving, I would sometimes see cars that looked identical to ones driven by former colleagues. So it must be them, my mind would reason. That blue Ford Fusion is Jordan

Leising. It has to be. Thank God. A friend. They're not really gone after all.

Of course it wasn't him. How could it be? I wasn't there anymore. He wasn't there anymore. None of us were. It was all gone.

The ghostly phenomenon just kept happening. I would answer my cellphone no matter what the caller ID said. I had to. It might be someone responding to one of my job applications. More often than not, I answered a robocall or a telemarketer, the kinds that let a good 10 seconds of dead air static crackle by before saying a damn thing. In that empty space, I could hear the faint sound of someone I knew from Saint Joe. Who exactly, I could not discern, but they were struggling to tell me something and I just could not hear them. This wraithlike phenomena did not confine itself to people, either. I found that out while walking the dogs.

Debbie insisted that I wake each morning by at least 7:30am.

"The babies have to be kept on their schedule," she said. "They need their walks and morning feeding at regular times each day."

Smart. While true enough that dogs need routine for good health, the directive also served to get me out of bed. Otherwise I might have stayed beneath the covers all day. Then maybe migrate to the couch and watch a few Godzilla movies. Instead, I got out the door each morning with leash in hand and a dog at the other end of said leash. One morning I walked Chewie in the park by my house. I saw something purple in the grass.

Not just purple. Puma purple. I could see a circular, raised, and wavy seal printed on the fabric. Could it be? Here? How? I ran up on it fast, almost breathless, with Chewie keeping pace beside me. My hand reached out and took hold of the slick hide of a drawstring bag. I turned the label up toward my face.

"Converse."

Ghosts are real. They're as real as the shirt on my back right now. They're as real as the air you're breathing as you read. They're the gestalt of despair and loss. They're everything you would have said to someone if you just had more time. They're the places and people left in our wake as life throws us somewhere else.

And they haunt us.

"You really didn't say much of anything at the time," Debbie said when I asked her to look back and describe me that summer. "You were just sort of catatonic."

No truer words. My baked brain soared off to that vibrant Saint Joe campus that still existed somewhere beyond the sunset. I was and still am astonished at the visceral, physical effects those first eight months of 2017 visited upon me. It scorched my stomach lining, it blocked my airways, made me shiver with a chill as cold as December while in the heat of July, and jumbled my brain to the point that I could only suspect that a fresh new hellish disaster lurked behind every corner of life. I grew bitter with the merest of things, like advertisements for "big savings" and perky cashiers asking "how are you doing?" (yeah, wouldn't you like to fucking know.) My short-term memory amounted to nothing. I found myself stuttering and flubbing words. Sort of a hindrance in my line of work. Wavering or not, broken and pathetic even, I still spoke of a ghostly, glowing mirage I saw just beyond that line of the horizon. Vision over visibility!

Debbie confessed how it unsettled her to hear me talk about all the ways the campus might still resurrect for…Spring 2018 even? It's all right, I told her. We would bring it back. There would be something soon.

"There was nothing I could really say or do," she said. "It took everything I had to keep from just shaking you and saying, 'it won't happen.'"

"Didn't you see the raven?" I asked her.

As Poe wrote:

"And the Raven, never flitting, still is sitting, still is sitting

On the pallid bust of Pallas just above my chamber door…"

The poem no longer served to cement an image of me as "the creepy goth kid from English class." It became real to me in a way I never would have expected. There is, of course, no raven in the poem. It's all in the poor guy's head. "Can't you see it?" that hapless man seems to scream to the reader at the end. "Can't you see that thing sitting there? Haunting me?" And so for me with all the memories of Saint Joseph's College.

Silence. So often in life I need it. It brings me calm, allows me to collect my thoughts, and helps me find myself. Not so that abysmal summer of 2017, a summer of dreadful speculations. Quiet then amounted to an open door for the ghosts. Their spectral forms manifested as memories of voices, both friend and otherwise. One moment I heard Chad Turner saying, "Hi, how you doing?" Then came Larry Hemmelgarn's smiley and smarmy, "Everything has a natural life cycle," and his invoking of his holy book while the rest of us suffocated. While slumped on the furniture in my living room, I heard a colleague say my name. I just knew I did. Next day, same place, same position, I heard Jordan Leising singing showtunes just as he would in the hallway of second floor Core. Then I found I could still hear the bells of the Chapel. I could still smell my office in the Core Building. Somehow, I could feel the presence of Saint Joseph's College in those weeks in ways and means I never could before, even when I actually stood upon the campus soil.

You might think writing would be my go-to drug for amelioration. I tried. I went back to blogging. I did a post on Mothman, the supposed otherworldly cryptid being that menaced the small town of Point Peasant, West Virginia as chronicled in John Keel's seminal *The Mothman Prophecies*. I even got my brother in on the blog post as we both enjoyed that book. Great fun! But collaborating on the post reminded me of how we once worked as a team at Saint Joe. The attempt at distraction only accentuated the pain all the more. When the shades find a home in a depressed head, they don't take long to root deep.

I scrolled the TV channels. Then when the selection of programming became irredeemable in nature, I found myself lamenting the absence of tuner knobs on modern televisions. I could remember being a kid and jamming the dial just so between two stations, creating a black and white field of super static and white noise. I wished I could hear it again. Apps for generating such a sound are disingenuous and if there is something an existentialist can't stand, it's goddam inauthenticity.

If TV proved insufferable, then the radio made an acceptable alternative. Yes, the radio and not a streaming service…though that would do in a pinch. Radio connected me to the outside world. I could know something and someone else was out there beyond the firmament, and I was not really adrift alone on an ocean. So, I learned to practice each of these methods as availability dictated.

And always always always sleep with the lights on.

Because in the darkness it seems to get worse. The questions. Did any of my…now former…colleagues feel this way? Or was it just me? Probably just me because no one else looked or sounded this weak.

It was the summer, I decided—the infernal, damnable season of summer magnifying these sensations of grief and loss. Jordan nailed it. The deepest sense of loss would not to set in until the damnable summer, when there would be no more work to do and the community dispersed in all the practical, concrete senses of "disperse." In that sensation of utter absence, I learned the difference between grief and mourning. Grief is something you feel, like a low-grade, omnipresent frostbite just beneath the skin. Mourning is something you do.

And I did it all the time that summer.

Chris, one of my best friends from my undergrad Puma days, flew me down to his place in Tampa-St. Pete. A magnanimous gesture to try to get my mind off of things, but magnanimity is part and parcel of close Puma friendships. Chris and I are the kind of guys to eschew the beach and sun, choosing instead to go on a tour of every book and comics store in the bay area. One store said the ghost of Jack Kerouac still made the rounds among its shelves. Given the writer drank himself to death in a house just down the street, I could see how he might come back from time to time, check for any enticing new reads, all while giving the staff the sensation of presence, presence imbued with literary gravitas, but icy, invisible, and just ever so slightly out of reach. All like being alone in a dark room but sensing something else is always there.

I knew the feeling well. I stood in Florida, but my mind could not shake the presence of a place 1,000 miles away in Indiana.

Another bookstore covered its front windows with flowy, greasepaint renditions of book covers. The usuals showed up, like Joyce, Tolkien, and Baum. Then I saw the book with the blue cover and the title written in gold down the spine: *Malleus Maleficarum*. I thought back to the previous Christmas break and how much honest fun I had sifting through research for my lecture, cobbling together all the features and facets of literature, history, and philosophy that came together at nexus points to produce the awful-but-still-fascinating story of the *Malleus*. I remembered the hours in my office, reference books stacked around me like bricks in a medieval castle wall, designing each PowerPoint slide and writing their content, losing myself in the work that really didn't feel like work at all. I recalled the compliments I received on the lecture from colleagues and students as I passed them on the sidewalk on my way to the caf in the abrasive January air.

Then I remembered it all disintegrated and would ever happen again. I stood in the hot Florida sun, chilled and cheerless as Norwegian gloom.

Just summer messing with me. There is a certain rhythm to the academic life and certain agents in a professor's DNA activate the deeper we press into summer. When the humidity rises, when the air currents are thick and slow, when the cicadas hum, when the fireflies dot the dark, when the smell of magnolia is heaviest, when the sunsets are a honeyed haze, it all acts as a signal. I should start writing my syllabi. I should meet with my Core 1 faculty about the semester ahead. I should check my planned writing assignments. For in but a few weeks, vans and SUVs would clog the main drive to campus as students moved back for the year.

But they wouldn't. Part of me left forever and I no longer held any real grip on who I was. What happens when you lose the place you come from? What happens when you must find somewhere else and all the while knowing no one will share your language, the "Puma language?"

I rolled in a sense of upheaval. I remembered a time as a kid when I went swimming in the ocean and I lost control in a wave. Left uncertain as to direction, I tumbled. Exacerbating the sensation, I have a complete inability to open my eyes under water, adding blindness to it all. Yes. That was summer 2017. My reading of *Moby-Dick* brought me in contact with this description of the sensation:

"There is no life in thee, now, except that rocking life imparted by a gently rolling ship; by her borrowed from the sea; by the sea, from the inscrutable tides of God. But while this sleep, this dream is on ye, move your foot or hand an inch, slip your hold at all; and your identity comes back in horror. Over Descartian vortices you hover."[1]

"Vortices." Something Milt Heinrich from Dana College said came back to me, underscoring the damnable summer: "August comes and school's supposed to start. But it doesn't. And it doesn't. Year after year it still doesn't," he said. "This has been like a death…and everything that comes with it."

For everyone who worked, taught, or studied at Saint Joe, we confronted our inaugural "it doesn't" that August.

Saint Joe exerted a gravitational pull on me like a dead star. Its light snuffed out, the star's husk remained, sufficient in mass to draw all of my thoughts back to it. Over time and incubation, those thoughts grew deranged.

More than before?? Oh sure. I thought I needed to be back there in Rensselaer, because what if they find a way to reopen Saint Joe? What if I wasn't there when that happened? I would need to be right there on the spot, first in line for the new faculty jobs. Otherwise they might forget all about me.

Delusion. Go back to what? Students went on to many other colleges, with Marian University taking maybe as much as 40% of them. As for my colleagues, our once close-knit community came apart like the bird house I built in 6th grade shop class. Splinters. I'd get news of someone getting a new faculty appointment somewhere else and feel glad for them that they had a job. Then the feeling would sour as the news underscored my own failures and I fell into envy. I'd hear that someone else still searched for work and feel heartbroken they remained in need. Then an odd and ugly sort of comfort would come over me as I thought "At least someone else has it as bad as I do."

Many of those professors fortunate enough to find new jobs uprooted themselves from Rensselaer and moved to other Midwest states such as Iowa, Michigan, and Wisconsin, or in other cases went to states as far away as Washington and Texas. Others achieved positions a bit closer to campus. Dr. Anne Gull stayed in Rensselaer, her family somewhat cemented in place as her husband taught business at the local high school, the same high school her youngest son attended as a freshman.

"What kid wants to move right in the middle of high school?" Anne asked.

Besides, her parents moved to Rensselaer in 2003 to help take care of her kids. If Anne and her family moved, her parents wouldn't want to stay either.

"Then we would have two houses to sell," she said. "Who wants to do that in this housing market?"

Staying would not be without its share of expenses, however. Anne said she would need a new car because it took her an hour each way to her new teaching job. During the interview for the position, an interviewer asked Anne how, after spending so many years investing in Saint Joseph's College and co-constructing a whole new science department, would she be able to start all over somewhere new. Anne came close to crying at the question.

The loss of community also weighed on her mind as it did with all of us. She wondered how many people she would end up still knowing in town.

"I was reflecting on it at church," Anne said. "I look at people and think, 'that person might be gone soon.' I think about it at school sports events, too. Kids might be wondering how much longer they'll have a teammate."

So, who else was still left in Rensselaer? My parents of course. There also appeared to be one other member of my family staying put in the town.

A message came through official channels from Saint Joseph's College. The former Board of Trustees completely dissolved…with the exception of its four C.PP.S. members. In fact, Fr. Larry Hemmelgarn would become the Chairman of a new Board of Trustees working with the intent of envisioning a new Saint Joe with a new business model. There would be a new president…or "Rector" as he would be termed…also a priest from the C.PP.S. Most of all, there would be a team of three former faculty and administrators charged with reinventing the College and breathing life into it once more. They would be called "The Phoenix Team," as if to symbolize a rise from the ashes. The team would consist of Dr. Chad Pulver, Dr. Tom Ryan, Spencer Conroy...

And Dr. Michael Nichols. He would be Director of Core in whatever new incarnation the College would take.

"How do I see this? How am I supposed to see this?" I asked aloud to an empty room.

Well, Chewie and Butterscotch were in the room, but the most I got out of them was a tilted head from Chewie before he returned to licking himself.

Michael got a job because he deserved it, but so much of the rest of the news placed him smackdab in the middle of a dubious context. The strong suspicions could all be put away in a drawer, right beneath my Puma sweatshirts folded with the neatness of hands on the chest of an embalmed corpse. After all, suspicions just turned into facts, or so it seemed. As the ship sank, a pre-planned lifeboat indeed stood by for a select few. Not too many seats on that thing, though.

In my heart, I know Michael took that seat in the interest of doing something good. He isn't someone to leave others behind and the whole situation probably gave him a fair amount of "survivor guilt." Without question he took the position because he must have seen an exciting possibility to bring Core back. He likely wanted to save, even if on a small scale, everything our father built. Michael acted out his part in this Euripedes play or far-too realistic production of *Hamlet* just as I did.

I wouldn't know any of this for sure, of course. We talked less and less as happens sometimes with siblings. Geography hindered us. Focus did too. I could not stop thinking about what happened and who did it, and Michael spared no time for that. He could only devote energy to move past the catastrophe and try to create a new Saint Joe.

What of the rest of the abandoned campus? Day by day, I learned of just how much hope crumbled in the most literal of senses.

A skeleton crew of maintenance workers and groundskeepers remained employed on campus. Their task? Keep the place from falling apart. As best they could anyway with their few numbers and limited resources against such an expansive property. They might have waved to Sisyphus as they worked. Their tireless efforts served as a stark reminder of how hard physical plant employees strained each day just to bubblegum the buildings together while the professors taught. Years of "deferred maintenance" manifested unchecked in the now empty buildings.

In the Science Building, an entire wall crumbled to bare, skeletal remains. Sections of the ceiling gave way in the theater. Ill-fitted windows in Halleck Center let in rainwater, thus leading to mold. A leaking pipe didn't help that matter, either. A group of cats made their home in the basement. Yes, I always heard a population of feral cats lived on campus as they kept the rodent population in check. But with little human presence left, they could at last execute their foolproof plan to take over. By reports, the smell of their excrement rendered Halleck toxic, an enormous litterbox in a nifty pentagonal shape done up in the artsiest vogue of the early 1950s. The cat dominion might not last long however, as the raccoons started challenging them for turf.

I made a quick visit to Rensselaer to see the campus, or rather get as near as I could to it. Grass grew tall on the IM field and really anywhere else not visible from the highway. Must keep that front property well-manicured. Rather like presenting a body at a viewing. Not a hair out of place. Just enough makeup on the cheeks and lips to keep it lifelike, prompting all the friends and relatives to lie to the bereaved. "Ohhh she looks so good." But the body itself is at least still full, even if it be with preservatives. The red brick bodies before me that day stood empty. Not one resident in a dorm. Not one professor in an office. Not one student in a classroom. All of those chambers accumulated dust in incremental layers like snow floating to the ground on a dim February morning.

What is it about an empty house that makes all of us so sad? I've seen plenty of them from streets and highways, their roofs sagging, their paint peeling, and the grass overgrown so as to look like a field of green wheat. Each time I would think someone somewhere labored over the house, even if just in the beginning and even if just to sell it for profit. Somebody cared. More than that, it was home for somebody. It might even have meant the world to them and maybe even represented so many dreams. Then, for whatever reason, they had to leave it all behind and let it go empty to rot.

Same might be said for Saint Joe.

Concrete barricades sprung up at all points of entry to campus. Upon thick gray blocks hung signs reading “PRIVATE PROPERTY—NO TRESPASSING.” Necessary for Rensselaer, of course. Empty and derelict buildings invite trouble. Isn’t that what they did to Dowling College after they closed off that campus for good? And Dana College? See? Reasonable.

Didn’t matter. Didn’t stop me from standing and staring at the barricades, half-out-of-my-mind-crazy with resentment at a sign calling me a trespasser in my own home. “This is what will happen if the commies win the war,” adults warned me as a kid. Well, it happened anyway.

“You have to mentally callous yourself.”

That’s what Milt Heinrich told me of having to drive past his beloved Dana College as it sat empty and derelict, year after year after year.

“It was surreal.”

That's how Hassan Rahmanian described the sensation of teaching a Nonstop Antioch class from someone's living room, in full view of the dead Antioch Campus.

I came to understand those professors in a whole new way. I also felt the presence of Saint Joe in a way could not have anticipated knowing. It was right there. Right in front of me. But I could not go to it. I could only look at the land where my father and others helped so many to learn and then go on and do great things. I could only stand and look at a campus that once made me so proud, stand and look at the finger-like green blades of grass and weeds coming up from the cracks in street and sidewalk pavement. Nature points up the folly of humans if given only half a chance, and will overrun and break down whatever artifice we create. Everything Pumas loved would soon just be memories.

That's why we bury the dead.

We also bury, burn, or entomb to keep the scavengers away. For the scavengers of the natural world, the vultures, the bugs, the bacteria, and the many others, come fast and furious when they sniff out a meal. So do business opportunists it would seem.

The Phoenix Team decided to sell off a number of the campus assets.

I should have seen it coming. It's part of the ritual, right? Someone dies and then you clean out their closets. You take their clothes and any other items you or other family members don't have an immediate use for, and you give them away or you hold an estate sale. What would be sold at the Saint Joe closet-clean-out sale? "Things we know we won't need anymore," the Phoenixes said. This left Puma Nation flummoxed as no clear plan for what lay ahead had been presented. Just the same, the liquidation sale would take place for 12-weeks, starting in mid-August.

The same time classes would have started.

New signs joined the "NO TRESPASSING" warnings by the barricades. These bumblebee yellow and death black placards read:

"STORE FIXTURES FOR SALE!"[2]

Two businesses came in to handle an almost total liquidation. Air conditioners, dorm furniture, science lab contents, radio station gear, kitchen equipment, light fixtures, and so on and so on. Just about everything that wasn't of historical value or wasn't nailed down.[3]

Oh why let "nailed down" stop anyone?

Under the direction of the "new" Board, the sale expanded to Saint Joseph's College memorabilia, including plaques and golden nameplates of athletes in the Puma sports hall of fame. Yes, even names were for sale.

This did not sit well with alumni.

"May I have the plate with my name on it?" one former women's basketball player asked online. "I can't imagine anyone else wanting it."

Others pleaded that their grandfathers or other departed family members had their names on the honor wall. Could they please have the plates? A response came from Drexel Hall. They could indeed get the memorabilia back…by having first dibs in the auction and paying but a small fee, maybe around 20 bucks.

They even hung a sign in the sports hall of fame of the fieldhouse to make it official:

"Plaques $20. Family members only."

To sweeten the deal, they threw in a hammer so you could pry the plaque loose yourself. Because if there's a fundamental axiom that overrides all else, it's the right to make a buck. Everything must go, go, go! Out of the way, Jesus! You're blocking the comeback!

An outcry, united, damning, and near immediate sounded out. Alumni came up with several adjectives and metaphors for the whole scene. The Phoenix Team got called many things. "Vultures." "Ghoulish" was tossed around a few times. "The fuck???" ended up being one of the more succinct responses.

"But don't blame the auction businesses," someone said. "They're just doing their jobs."

I could only think of John Mellencamp's words in response: "Saying it's your job ol' hoss sure don't make it right. But if you want me to I'll say a prayer for your soul tonight."

The new Overlords saw the error of their ways and all the resultant bad PR. "We blew it," they said in their honest mea culpa.[4] They then refunded money to anyone who purchased a personal nameplate, hall of fame plaque, or the like. The rest of the sale kept on rolling.

For the supposed resurrection of Saint Joseph's College required both cash and space, or so they said. I could see the cash needs of course, but space? Space for what? Well, if the new Board of Trustees intended to follow a "new business model" of higher ed, then maybe the library could be redone as facilities for income generators. Like a new football team. Or manufacturing space to pump out widgets or "product." Or space rented out for a strip club. Yet more revenue streams! Besides, you can toss out a library because you only really need to teach a small handful of books, right? *Atlas Shrugged* and anything by Tony Robbins or Zig Ziglar will do, and they can all be e-books at that. All the science labs could be turned into training facilities for "shovel-ready jobs" in growth sectors such as coal mining, and warehousing and manufacturing. Automation, schmautomation. We've never been forward thinking before, so why the hell start now? It's the job trends right now that count!

Speaking of jobs, I really needed to get one. Badly. Unemployment grew to be the strangest sensation. Since I started working full time at age 22, not once did a day go by where I didn't earn income. That summer of 2017 I found myself in unknown country, but economic realities are paused for no one. Feelings over banishment from Saint Joe often got shoved down in order to afford the mental bandwidth for an employment search. I went on at least a dozen phone or Skype interviews. I submitted at least five times that many applications to places. Not all colleges, either. I included private high schools, businesses (yes, I realized I had to try), nonprofits, and even locations like Target and Wendy's just to get income. Rejection emails came back fast, sometimes even in under 24 hours in the cases of the last two venues. What would I do if I didn't qualify to work even retail or food service? Someone put me in touch with a career counselor and I went to plead my case.

"It's because of your education," the counselor told me. "Employers in service jobs may see it and think, 'He's out of here the second he finds something better.'"

Well…true. I would've been. However, that did not mean I would not work as hard as I could for them in the meantime.

"Have you thought about doing corporate training? Or sales presentations on branding? There's nothing to say you couldn't learn it," the counselor offered.

No, she really didn't know me. I told her that I didn't want to become imprecise and make career decisions out of desperation. I already doubted myself for decades, but that summer I started doubting just about everything else as well. My former job held meaning for me, I explained to her. All the meaning in the world. But both that job and that meaning evaporated, leaving me lost and swimming against the tide.

"Wow. This really did a number on you, huh?" was her response.

She didn't know the half of it. She didn't know the panic. How it never went away. Every minute of the day it was in the back of my mind somewhere. Terrifying realities became parts of daily life and contemplation. My house wouldn't be called luxurious by any means, and probably isn't expensive as the market goes. Absent any real income though, its mortgage, especially added in with all the other bills, became real expensive, real goddam fast.

Could the Board of Trustees ever understand that, I wondered? Could the C.PP.S.? Have any of them ever known need? Have any of them feared hunger? Could they even conjugate the verb "suffer"? Oh one or two of them may step up to the challenge, crying "Me! Me! Me!" but that would only serve to make their votes all the more mystifying and thoughtless. So just what help did the Saint Joe Board of Trustees…many of whom viewing themselves as living embodiments of the most American of equation… "wealth=virtue"…provide? Besides a severance equivalent to 47 days of pay for the untenured and ongoing litigation for the tenured?

I was aware of it. I want you to know I was. I want to assure you a thesis crossed my mind that went something like "On the Annoying Circumlocution of Self-Pity and the Pointlessness of Paralysis."

This self-examination and castigation served only to drive me further into myself. Because that's really what went on that summer. I kept feeling these urges, these callings to go back to someplace that really wasn't there anymore. Yet it still pained me as if it remained, but could not be seen, like a phantom limb. As so much of my life fell away, I felt I could only fall into myself. That is the type of self-pity Joan Didion describes in the wake of a profound loss in *The Year of Magical Thinking*:

"We are repeatedly left, in other words, with no other focus than ourselves, a source from which self-pity naturally flows."[5]

All this I dwelled on while listening to the cicadas in failing sunlight. I cursed the fact we kept no booze in the house. Debbie and I both agreed it would be a bad idea. Not just for the expense, but for what I might do with it. But damn it if I couldn't have downed a bottle of scotch at that time, lying on the couch and giving my TV a good 1,000 yard stare. I thought about what my therapist told me the day before about how to get through such a deep, muddy trench. "Just keep going," she said to me. "You just keep putting one foot after the other." A shibboleth, I thought. She also said that I was right where I was supposed to be. For whatever messed up, crazy reason, this was right where I needed to be. And the way out was to go through it. Wonderful. Love to. But how?

Then my dog Chewie jumped up on the couch. He licked me once on the face before plopping himself onto my lap, his floppy-eared head turned and resting on my jaw. After heaving a deep sigh, he fell asleep, drifting into heavy "puppy snores." In a slow glide, I ran my hand down the soft fur of his back as his body raised and lowered with each snore. His heat radiated onto my midsection. I melted into the couch as his 80-pound weight held me to the cushions. I could go nowhere. Not that I wanted to. I at last found my perfect five minutes.

"Not everything is bad," I said.

Chewie got up about twenty minutes later to stretch out on the floor. I got up and went to the bathroom. After splashing cold water on my face, I looked in the mirror. I did not like what I saw. I was tired. Just so tired of feeling bad. All reserves depleted, no more could I broker any energy to pain, fear, sorrow, or rage.

I lied earlier. I could see how you "keep putting one foot in front of the other." You accept your situation. You surrender to what is. For whatever reason, things were what things were. My therapist was right. For whatever reason, this was where I was supposed to be and what I was supposed walk through by taking care of whatever was right in front of me. Only by shifting to such thinking could I begin to really put myself back together. And I could only make that shift when I was ready. That night, standing in my downstairs bathroom with cool water running down my cheeks, I was ready.

Just turn on the news and you can see it, I thought. How many people in the world aren't able to claim a "downstairs bathroom?" How many people went without food in their stomachs that day? How many starved at that very moment in Sub-Saharan Africa? How many people squatted in warzones in Afghanistan or Syria that very night? How many people did not have a loving family supporting them and instead sat alone in the dark?

It was time to stop complaining and climb back up. When making such a tedious and crumbly climb, however, a good model or scaffold can help. To find such a model, I did what I often do: I turned to literature.

Many academicians and literary critics would no doubt be repulsed by my choice of heroic model. I don't care. For regardless of any seasoned or cultured opinion, the Raven was at last chased to flight by a bat.

There before me stood the image of Batman.

Give consideration to the character's story. One moment he is but a small boy, a naïve innocent, walking with his parents through an alley…one of the basest and most ordinary facets of a city.

Bang.

Bang.

A pair of sudden muzzle flashes from a robber's gun. His mother and father fall dead to dirty, ordinary asphalt. His whole world disappears for good in those flashes. Everything he once recognized is erased in an instant. One moment his life is secure, knowable, and…again this word…ordinary. In the next, all that is gone. He can only kneel next to the corpses in an homage to the *Pieta* as the alabaster orbs from his mother's broken string of pearls roll across the gritty pavement.

This is Batman's origin story. No rocketship ride from a dying planet. No bite from a radioactive spider. Just a frail, human boy experiencing one night of unthinkable and indifferent cruelty, and then a lifetime of forging himself into a weapon for revenge. With every pushup, with every punch to his face from a martial arts master, with every long night studying in a library, Batman welded his broken self back together, but this time with mind and body honed to near perfection. And that's the key. Any one of us with enough drive, enough resourcefulness, and enough hate, could be Batman. Through Batman's story, though it's as fictional as any story could be, I began to believe I could be a survivor. I would climb out of the pit. For as James Baldwin wrote, "Deep water and drowning are not the same thing."

So I got up. I went to my doctor and she adjusted my depression medications. In addition to searching for full time jobs, I assigned myself day-to-day "missions" to hold myself accountable. These included cleaning bathrooms, shopping at the grocery store, staying laser-focused the whole time on that budget. I also took a position as an adjunct instructor of English at a local community college and another as a tutor in the writing center of a nearby university. Neither paycheck really amounted to enough to pay the bills, but I knew if I could stick with it for a while, this work would keep me in the classroom, it would add experience to my CV, and it would show hiring colleges that I remained dedicated to my discipline.

"Thanks, that really helped make sense of things," a student said one night in the writing center after I helped revise a paper. "Do you teach any classes here? I'd really like to take one with you."

That comment wasn't just me getting my car waxed. It was evidence. Saint Joe collapsed, but I could *still* be a good teacher somewhere else. This invigorated me. Maybe that student from the hallway back at Saint Joe was right. Maybe I did deserve a good future and the student I just helped served as evidence for it. Plus, the two jobs kept me busy most of the day and into the night when I worked the writing center, giving me more contact time on two campuses and that might bring opportunity. I also found the more active my mind and body became, the less energy I devoted to feeling bad.

One way to be active? Fall back on my training. Tucked away in a corner of my local public library, a thermos of Irish creamer-laced coffee to my left and a window looking out at green trees and gray rocks wet with river water to my right, I returned to a path I started down in the throes of those grim nights of late January. I went back to reading and research. Yes, I surrendered to my circumstances, however in order to accept said circumstances I also needed to understand. I needed answers, as best as I could gather them, as to the exact means how and reasons why Saint Joseph's College came apart. Despite the palliative statements from Board members and administration, I still did not know. Despite all the dead-sure accusations I made and despite the numerous conspiracy theories batted back and forth by students and alumni…or perhaps because of them…I still did not know the full truth.

I had no clear answers.

I had no solid reasons.

I did not really know how this all came to happen.

I resolved to find out. I would no longer be Ishmael adrift. I would be Ahab. The truth, the capital "T" Truth, would be my white whale and it tasked me…oh it tasked me and I would have it. I would chase it round Good Hope, and round the Horn, and round the Antares Maelstrom, and through perdition's flames before I gave it up. The truth demands a champion, and I would pursue that truth with icy determination and if need be, become a literary man-at-arms to confront the darkest perpetrators of injustice in the Saint Joe saga. For as Joan Didion once said, "Writing is a hostile act." Why me, though? As Batman once said:

"Because no one else will."

An important caveat existed in this quest, however. So important that I knew it must temper all else: intellectual honesty. As the poet Ingeborg Bachmann said, "Once one has survived something then survival itself interferes with understanding." To at last harpoon that Truth whale, to get the real answers my mind and soul held such frantic thirst for, I needed to seek out facts and not inventions. For as I read and researched and pecked away at my laptop, I began to wonder if I had not, in fact, created many inventions.

These inventions spoke to or corroborated my rage with such precision, like the black and white blobs of the yin-yang, nestled in and fitting each other. Nothing is ever black and white and cut and dry. Anyone in a fact-based profession would tell me that. That and information vacuums often create falsehoods. As case in point, a rumor once flew on campus that in return for shunting so many students to Marian University, Bob Pastoor would receive a cabinet-level administrative position at Marian.

A falsehood. No such thing happened. In fact, the alumni chatter I heard that August placed Pastoor as an interim administrator at a university somewhere around Fort Wayne, Indiana.

Through the fires of emotion, my objectivity, without question, became compromised. The sad, ludicrous truth is that for close to a year, I had not been thinking. I had been reacting. My fists overrode my brain.

I needed to separate integral facts from all the spurious and the adventitious. I would have to spend many a day and night in "the Batcave," applying every scrap of skill, analysis, and knowledge I gleaned from both studying and teaching in Core. Even then, I wondered if I would be up to the task.

Oh and where to start?

The answer, it turned out, came to me months previous on the somber and foreboding day we buried the Core program in the Shen Auditorium.

After the lecture's end, I met a man with wavy white hair and an easygoing demeanor. He carried a briefcase at his side and told me that back in 2014, he worked with three of his fellow Class of 1971 Saint Joe graduates on the outline of a plan that -if implemented- would have been the first step toward putting the College back in good financial health. They called it "Fight for Saint Joe." When they pitched this plan to the Board of Trustees, however, nothing much came of it.

"I have several boxes of documentation to back it up," he said and handed me a business card.

And that's how I came to meet Bob Neville.[6]

NOTES

1. Melville 157.

2. Bangert, "Bangert: After St. Joe's: Where are they now?"
3. Holden, "Memorabilia, cars for sale at St. Joe's asset sale."
4. Bangert, "Bangert: Shuttered St. Joseph's College apologizes selling hall of fame plaques.
5. Didion 195.
6. I interviewed Bob Neville on many occasions starting in 2017 and carrying into 2021. Notes with author.

CHAPTER NINE: Gang of Four

I went to the Red Pecker Invitational.

You read that correctly.

On April 21st, 2018, they held it at Lou Malnati's Pizzeria in Schaumburg, Illinois, about ten miles from the city limits of Chicago. The operative "they" being a group of close friends from the Saint Joe graduating Class of 1971, along with their spouses and a few friends from the other classes of the era. For a few of them, this meet-up marked their first time together in several years.

"Red Pecker" was in fact Bob Neville. Though white these days, his hair was a shock of bright red when he first arrived on campus back in 1967, earning him the nickname of "Red Pecker" by way of comparison to the redheaded cartoon character, Woody Woodpecker. In March of that freshman year, Bob and about a dozen other intrepid young men scaled the bleachers at the football field late at night and snuck into the press box. They brought a case of Pabst Blue Ribbon quarts, priced cheap at the local grocery and purchased by upperclassmen. A $5 box of potato chips they bought from the student food concessionaire served as victuals. They sat and drank, and talked in the dark. It was a smashing time.

"Or we thought it was, anyway," Bob said, laughing. "The bar was set pretty low that freshman year at SJC."

It became an annual affair, continuing on even after graduation, but at somewhat more erratic intervals and in more upscale venues. As Bob initiated and then perpetuated the event, it became known as the "Red Pecker Invitational." Bob invited me to the 2018 edition, the momentous 50th anniversary of the RPI, so that I might "get a little background flavor" for my writing and research. He was right. To work together on getting the answers I needed, and to understand why he and his friends made the effort they did to attempt to save Saint Joe, then I should know something about these people and what our College meant to all of them.

Bob, clad in a plaid, purple, button-down Saint Joe shirt, stood up and looked over the two dozen or so Pumas crammed into a side wing of the pizza place. He clinked a glass with a fork and the chaos of conversation dimmed to a low mumble.

"Welcome to the 50th RPI," Bob shouted. "Only a few basic rules. One, take care of our waiter. Two, no talking politics."

Someone a table over from me whispered.

"And three, don't talk over me!" Bob said to the commenter.

The assembled laughed.

"You never change," said the target of his admonishment.

"You know what…hey could we get Metamucil for everybody here?" Bob shouted across the room to the bar, cuing more laughs. "Maybe Pepto?"

He then took a moment to introduce me as the guy standing behind him and off to the right a bit. I made an awkward wave to a sea of unknown faces. Bob told them about the book. I saw perhaps two or three sets of eyes widen. The Pumas then returned to kibitzing and ordered their pizzas as well as drinks from the bar. They compared pictures of grandkids, engaged in a fair amount of "remember when" from undergrad days, and even toasted a few deceased classmates.

I realized I was wrong earlier. I did know these people. Regardless of whatever difference in our ages, I knew them. Our levels of life experience differed, but we remained kindred. I recognized the repartee and the deep comradery. In their own sense, alums of small colleges such as Antioch and Sweet Briar might have recognized the RPI-goers as well. For while years may have elapsed since the last RPI, these Saint Joe alums could sit down that night and reminisce, chide, and one-up as if no time passed at all.

I shared the same deep and unbreakable bonds with my own friends from Saint Joe. Were it us in the pizza place that night, I could hear my best friend George heckling me as I made announcements. I could see Chris, bursting at the seams to tell the tale of how I once thought the muffler that came off the rear end of his '76 Maverick would cripple the car and leave us stranded on the shoulder of I-65.

Yes, I really thought that.

I kept that less-than-flattering tale to myself as I sat across from Mark Nestor,[1] one of Bob Neville's best friends. Mark is a man of broad shoulders, flat hair, a white goatee, and that evening, a slight tan. Bob and Mark roomed together at Saint Joe on the third floor of Gallagher Hall. They lived next door to the only dorm room with a refrigerator as the neighbor student needed it for his insulin. The appliance also did well for chilling beer. A few of the dormmates on their floor once mixed up two gallons of screwdrivers and hid the concoction in two dozen smaller bottles in the drawers of the rooms. They kept finding them for weeks.

Like Bob Neville, Mark also acquired a nickname during his Saint Joe days: "Catman."

"I'd be at a party. Then I'd disappear for a while. People would wonder where I went. Then out of nowhere, they'd notice I was back in the party. 'Geez, you're like a cat,' they'd say," he explained.

Mark is welcoming enough, but he sizes things up fast and speaks in a straightforward style with short, declarative sentences. Things are this or things are that. He impressed upon me just how tight this collection of Pumas became over the years. If one of the group told Mark they needed $10,000, his answer would be one word: "Okay."

"We have strong bonds. We care about each other. We care about the school," Mark said. "I talk to Bob at least once a week, which is more than I talk to my own brother. Many of us have been best men at each other's weddings. We've done eulogies for each other's fathers. Paul's become a deacon, so he's got to be the last of us to go so he can bury us."

The "Paul" he referred to was Paul Muller.[2] A big man with the warmest of auras and a straight smile, it is easy to see him as a church deacon. There is a strength of spirit about him and that night at the RPI, he underscored that the same spirit extended through the rest of those gathered.

"Of our graduating group, almost every single one of us is still on their first marriage," Paul said.

A few of them even married women from the very first co-ed class at Saint Joe. I asked one of the ladies about being among the first female students at a previously all-male Catholic college.

"It was strange because although we heard so many of the guys opposed going coed, they all wanted to get to know us as soon as we got there," she said.

She opened one of the Saint Joe yearbooks stacked against the wall just past the remains of a Chicago deep dish sausage and mushroom. Flipping the pages, she pointed out all the black and white pictures of yesteryear, of women moving onto campus, and students in class with their professors or having fun in the odd, silly manners that tend to arise on college campuses. Speaking of silly, I spotted a picture of a billboard from that time meant to announce the College's new coed status: "Now We Have Brains and Beauty."

Shudder.

As I kept flipping the pages of yearbooks, two familiar faces caught my eye. The photo was of the inside of a living room. A man with dark, thinning hair sat in profile on an ottoman, holding up a baby that could not have been more than a year old. He held the child towards a woman with long, raven-black hair and wearing a pair of striped pants so in fashion for the early 70s. I deduced the identity of the baby from the other two people in the photo.

"Bob," I called out. "I'm in your yearbook."

I showed him the picture, right in the section of the yearbook labeled "the other side of faculty life." It depicted my parents in what must have been that first apartment Dad told me about, the one just outside Rensselaer.

"Well thanks, Jon," Bob said. "Now I feel really old."

Despite the blow to Bob, we later found the photo to be a sign of synchronicity. By chance I ended up in the Class of '71 yearbook. Somehow, I was supposed to be with this very Puma class that night. Destiny paired us on this intellectual and spiritual path towards discovering and uncovering.

As if to add further evidence to this connection, a gregarious man with a ruddy complexion and high forehead caught me. He wore a faded gray Saint Joe sweatshirt. He introduced himself as Doug Monforton.[3] He said he knew of me by way of Dad, having taken him for a class in what must have been Dad's very first years at Saint Joe. Over the years, Doug often received invitations to come back and guest lecture in business classes, making him well known to several faculty. I told Doug I knew him from his comments on Facebook, his criticisms of the Board of Trustees and administration being among the most direct, scathing, and honest anyone offered. As Johnny Cash once termed it, I admired the "gravel in his gut and the spit in his eye."

"He's our own General Patton," Bob said of Doug. "The 'alpha dog.'"

"How the fuck do they sleep at night?" Doug asked when the subject of the Board of Trustees came up. "I just remember sitting at home in Maui last year, watching the announcement online, hearing Sponseller say those words. I'm just like, 'I can't believe this.' Sponseller…him and the puppetmaster, Hemmelgarn…"

He closed his hands into fists and shook.

"If Saint Joe had been a publicly owned company, people would be in jail right now," he said.

Discussion turned to the final commencement on that chilly, windy day in May the previous year. Doug was there, along with Bob and Mark and their respective spouses.

"I remember the day I walked," Doug said. "The day my daughters walked and the LAST walk."

"The last graduation came exactly 50 years since we were introduced to Saint Joe as freshmen in 1967," Bob said. "It was like watching the house you grew up in burn to the ground."

Perfect description.

"There's gotta be a special place in hell for those rubes," Doug said of the Board.

It got quiet for a moment, and I excused myself to go to the bar for another Coke.

I've often wondered if something about me allows me to go unnoticed. Either that or perhaps most humans are so absorbed with themselves that they speak with abandon, unaware of others sitting or standing around them. This has served me well as a writer. I have taken descriptions and vignettes overheard conversations in coffeehouses, on train rides, and other locales, later to incorporate them into my texts. One might call it “literary espionage.” Waiting for my soda, I kept my face forward but tilted my left ear toward the RPI palaver.

“Think anybody’s going to read that kid’s book?” an old voice croaked.

“Why the hell the faculty couldn’t see it coming I don’t know,” someone else said.

Another voiced chimed in, agreeing. The men talked about the closing, about “diversifying revenue streams,” and “opening new markets.” “Hope is not a plan,” the initial speaker said. “They just weren’t smart.”

I paid for my Coke and went into a corner booth by the window to sit off by myself for a while. The roar of conversation washed over me as I incubated with my thoughts. The words hurt. Sometimes that doesn’t take much though. My anxiety, as well established before, magnifies things. The overheard conversation did force me to confront my own rhetorical stance. In a way, the eavesdropping acted as a psychological and philosophical plunger, unclogging the black and gunky and forcing me to look at it all with grim intellectual honesty.

Survivors do it, I once read. People can start looking for signs and symbols they missed leading up to the traumatic blow. Did I get a warning, seeing that poor woodchuck carcass in the middle of the street on my way to campus in December 2016? Earlier in 2016, we lost Bowie, Prince, my Grandma, my Grandma's family farm, and my Mom's cat. Shouldn't I have seen there must be more dominoes to fall? In September of 2016, my State Farm rep called me to ask if I'd be interested in additional life insurance. All those symbols like tea leaves and tarot cards that I just did not read…or at least I did not parse the correct meaning. Maybe.

Was it right there in front of us the whole time, within every moldy dorm room, every projector failure during lecture, and every gloss-over about the debt? Did our deep devotion to Saint Joseph's College blind us to the fiscal realities of our situation? Deep down, did I meet the grumblings and warnings of someone like Bill White with dismissal, thinking, "the community won't let it get that bad"? In the wake of the 2008 recession, banks, auto makers, and a few other businesses were deemed "too big to fail."

Did we see Saint Joe as "too beloved to fail"? I started questioning everything in that moment. Like I heard, would anybody even care about this story? And if I wrote it, would I just come off as stupid for being blindsided, or worse, would I cast my fellow faculty in an ill light? I questioned if I should even write anything at all.

The party broke up for the night and I said farewell to those I'd met. One man, whom I met only in passing earlier, looked me straight in the eyes as I shook his hand.

"Get the book done, please," he pleaded in a soft, hopeful voice. "Do it for all of us."

I told the sweet man I would finish the book. Then I wanted to go find the critic in the crowd, grab him by his coat lapels, and seethe Frank Miller's words straight into his face.

"What are you, dense? Who the hell do you think I am? I'm the goddamn Batman."

Fade out then fade in to a hotel parking lot. Bob Neville and I walked towards the hotel door. Thick plastic wheels rumbled against the asphalt as Bob dragged a briefcase tote behind him. I eyed the tote, hoping it held at least one magical document that could help everything make sense at once.

"Don't worry. We'll get you out of here soon, so you can head out to the Mothman Festival in West Virginia," he joked.

I felt my eyebrow arching. Bob knew Mothman? Then I remembered the post I wrote as I fought from sliding into the vortex.

"Yes, I read your blog sometimes," Bob continued. "I imagine that festival to be a more subdued version of Burning Man."

We went into the hotel and greeted Mark Nestor sitting in the continental breakfast nook. He came down from Michigan the night before. Like his friend, Mark also kept a heavy document case next to him. Bob rattled the handle on his own wheeled tote.

"Mine's bigger," Bob chided.

"You know how much other shit I have in my trunk?" Mark snarked back.

After we all got our coffees and fortified ourselves with hot, liquid caffeine, I set about right away to know something. These two men loved Saint Joe as much as I did. However, Bob gave me a sense at the end of the last Core lecture in April 2017 that he, Mark, Doug, and also Paul Muller brought specific sets of skills to the table that made them well qualified to, of their own volition, construct a plan that might have saved the College. What exactly were these qualifications?

"I started my own business working in commercial insurance," Mark said.

He continued, telling me about performing infrastructure and risk management analysis for insurance companies who specialize in the public sector. A third of his business is auditing claims. The day before we met, Mark even completed a performance review for the Rensselaer Public School Corporation. His work involved "looking beneath the tent" as he called it of large organizations. Mark also explained how he implements financial strategic planning for institutions, determining how one company fits with another. My face twisted. My head swam. He must have noticed.

"It's all right. Even my insurance friends don't get what I do," Mark said.

While I did not possess the wherewithal to understand all the flora and fauna which inhabited his domain, I could tell that he carried years of experience in institutional finance and an ability to take apart the intricate mechanics of an operation while deciding what worked and what didn't. He also carried a fair amount of military training, having gone into the Army just 16 days after graduating Saint Joe.

"Ever seen one of these?" Mark asked.

He took a glossy 8x10 photo from his case and flopped it on the table before me. It showed a twin engine, turbo-prop airplane, somewhat odd in its configuration but unmistakable to military aviation buffs like me.

"That's a Mohawk," I said.

"Hey Mark, this guy knows a Mohawk," Bob said.

Mark flew as a right-seater, Technical Observation Specialist on an OV-1 Mohawk flying out of Alaska and not all that far from Soviet airspace.

"If you slept well in Rensselaer as a kid, it's because of Mark," Bob said.

As for Bob, he started his own business as well. As head of the Neville Group, Bob took his years of experience in marketing and provided strategic communication guidance for successful companies of all sizes. Through this work, Bob knew exactly what an organization needed to say, when they needed to say it, and how it needed to be said.

“We should have joined up and made more money,” Mark said to Bob.

“We would’ve made less because we’d be drinking chardonnay all the time,” Bob replied.

Mark grunted and shrugged.

“I’m not saying it wouldn’t have been fun,” Bob said.

In addition to Bob and Mark, their friends (and 1971 classmates) Doug Monforton and Paul Muller brought their own talents and experience to the table. Doug was the owner and CEO of a chemical company, while Paul was the founder and CEO of a financial services and leasing company. Like Bob and Mark, they had run companies, met payrolls, balanced budgets, and executed strategic plans for their own companies and those of their clients. and, as Bob put it, "we knew a lot of alumni who were a lot smarter than we were." Each of these alums possessed expert levels of skill, experience, and connections that should have been invaluable to the College in its situation.

Together, they seemed like a businessman's "Justice League of America."

I asked how everything got started for Bob, Mark, and the others in terms of working with the Saint Joe Board and attempting to save the College. The genesis of the effort occurred in June of 2014, right after the mass exodus of President Dennis Reigelnegg and three of his vice presidents. While we faculty saw that moment as a chance for a refreshing new start, minds outside of the situation saw something far more turbulent. Like all alumni, Bob and Mark received a June 2014 letter from Board of Trustees Chairman Ben Sponseller, informing the community of the executive level departures.

"We read the letter and started to wonder what was going up there," Bob said.

"Any time I see someone is resigning to 'pursue new opportunities', red flags go up!" Mark said.

The “communications weather system,” as Bob described it, of how Saint Joe, like any organization, generates its own swirl of factoids and rumors, each with varying degrees of attachment to the truth, added to the confusion. Among this morass came talk of long term-debt for the College, but the exact figure remained uncertain at the time. Bob, Mark, and their friends heard $5 million, $23 million, and $28 million. Which was it? Bob heard that in June 2013, the College had refinanced $27 million of debt with Farm Credit of Rensselaer.

“I remember thinking that sounded like a lot of money at the time,” Bob said. “But keep in mind that we didn’t know what cash flow was, what other income there might be besides tuition, etc.”

Paul Muller listed a few other obvious questions in regards to how the College operated in 2014. Was the number of full-time students trending up or down? How much financial assistance did students receive and what funding source backed it? What had been the total contributions from alumni over the previous ten-year period? One would not expect to find full answers to these questions in the alumni newsletter. Bob did, however, see an obvious need for alumni to have timely, transparent, and meaningful communication about Saint Joe's finances.

Sponseller closed the June 2014 announcement letter with "Let us not forget how important you, our alumni, are to the College."[4] Both Bob and Mark took that as an offer. They knew Ben Sponseller was a fellow alum, and believed all could meet to discuss their mutual investment in Saint Joe. Bob and many of his classmates became Fellows of Saint Joe, served numerous terms on the Alumni Board, organized seminars for the College, and served as guest lecturers. Bob spent two years organizing the 2012 First Annual SJC Alternative Energy & Sustainability Forum, trying to help the College capitalize on its unique position with the Waugh wind farm.

Along with Paul, Bob and Mark brought Doug Monforton into the fold and founded the Gang of Four, the name being a humorous and even ironic riff on a political faction of communist leaders in China of the late 1960s. The Puma Gang of Four decided to collaborate on a letter to Sponseller, requesting an accurate financial picture while extending an earnest invitation to provide any and all assistance to their College. This letter went to Sponseller in August of 2014.

Reception was positive. All parties planned a conference call for that August between the Gang of Four (GOF), Ben Sponseller, and Steve Ruff.[5] The GOF sent the two Board members a lengthy set of questions, including requests for information on 10-year trend data in admissions, donations, and the like. Sponseller expressed admiration for the breadth and depth of the questions, but would need a few extra days to have detailed responses. Fine, for as Bob saw it, no meaningful dialogue and planning could transpire unless the financial and higher educational equivalent of a topographical map could be drawn.

"I told him that they had absolute zero chance of engaging alumni without timely, accurate and ongoing communication," Bob said. "In today's world, transparency is the name of the game. Nobody I know is going to start laying money on them without having the facts."

During the conversation, Bob and the others learned that much of the College's debt came from major capital expenditures back in the 1990s, namely the construction of the Core Building and the student apartments. The debt and the rate of repayment in 2014, meant it would take 20 years to retire. In fact, the principal stood at $27 million and the interest at $15 million over the period of 20 years, adding to a total $42 million in obligation with annual payments of $2,100,000. And tuition discount rates? In the high 50% range.

"I about fell off my chair," Mark said.

"It all took my breath away," Bob said. "I thought they were kidding me."

The GOF ended the conversation by asking if Sponseller and the Board would have any interest in meeting with them in Rensselaer to hear ideas about what the GOF could do in service to the Board and the College to get this financial situation resolved. Or if not resolved, then at least a stoppage of the bleeding so the College could be stabilized and placed on a path to recovery. The Chair and Vice Chair of the Board pointed out that Saint Joseph's College in August of 2014 was an institution in great flux with interim leadership at the presidential level as well as in three vice presidential offices. Sponseller did, however, say he viewed the GOF as a catalyst for alumni involvement and that a limited number of alumni could be allowed to be "in on" the financial situation with the hopes of currying a few donations. In fact, could the GOF donate \$100,000 by June 30th, 2015? Saint Joe just started transitioning from coal to natural gas power and a few unforeseen hitches came up in the process. The \$100k could help fix the problem.

By the time the conversation ended, Ben Sponseller agreed to and eventually did send documentation regarding the \$42 million amortization schedule and the timeline for the presidential search. Still, so much more remained in doubt. For example, with such enormous challenges with finances, enrollment, and infrastructure, why concentrate efforts on

$100,000 for a new gas boiler? Doug Monforton expressed particular perturbation with the outcome of the call, calling himself "unfulfilled." He saw no long-term thinking, no admissions strategy, and no energizing spark for the future.

"We are awash in red ink, with no leader (president) on campus, yet the BOT is perfectly willing to let the process play its way out until a candidate is found," Doug said at the time. "I remain 'involved for life', which is why this is such a painful thing to see unfold."

Despite these misgivings, they formulated the outline of an initial plan they christened 'Fight for St. Joe,' which took its name from the first lines of the St. Joe fight song, which, as they pointed out in their accompanying letter, was 75 years old that year, an anniversary year that it shared with the College itself, which was celebrating its 125th anniversary in 2014. It was designed to serve as an outline for recruiting others to pitch in and begin to change the financial situation at Saint Joseph's College."

The step-by-step outline called first for the crafting of a message to alumni that would be urgent in nature, but not conveying panic. Once the call went out, and an Alumni Leadership Group could be identified, most likely consisting of former athletic team captains, former members of student government, and the like. The ad-hoc Alumni Leadership Group would organize task groups to serve on the presidential and vice-presidential searches, consult and assist in admissions and recruiting, and aid in financial management and fundraising, with debt reduction being the primary goal. The ultimate outcome would be a sustainable framework of alumni involvement and a symbiosis of transparent and ongoing communication with the Board of Trustees.

They also believed the academic curriculum at Saint Joe needed revision. At that time, there were too many majors. Under-enrolled majors should be cut while new, innovative, marketable skills should be added. Business ranked as the second biggest major at Saint Joe. Every college has a business degree. Why not have one that focuses on entrepreneurship? Every college has a computer science degree. In fact, someone could go to Purdue University, just half an hour south of Saint Joe, and get the same IT degree for less money. But what if Saint Joe offered a degree in cybersecurity? All of this would have to be examined in tandem with the fundraising aspect as a means of increasing enrollment and therefore income.

Between the four of them, the GOF saw they could amass a database of perhaps as many as 1,000 alumni email addresses. It would mean hard work and time away from both careers and families, but for Saint Joe, the GOF stood willing and able to march down the road ahead. They just needed approval from the Board and they'd hit the launch button. So the plan went to Sponseller.

As Bob and Mark described their work process to me, I couldn't help but lean back and smile. The energy, the synergy between the four, the sense of being an unstoppable force moving in a common direction, I've felt it seldom in my life: once with fellow Saint Joe students in undergrad who later became my best friends, and then with my fellow professors in

December of 2016, just before the bottom fell out. Since I knew the end of this story, I also knew that the bottom must have, indeed, fallen out from underneath the GOF at one point or another.

During September of 2014, the GOF corresponded with each other via a series of emails amounting to the financial version of Oprah's Book Club when Bob acquired and distributed a copy of Saint Joe's 2009-2014 Strategic Plan. Mark noted the importance of attaining this document as applied to the "Fight" plan.

"When I take on a new client, the first thing I want to know is what their business culture is," Mark said. "How do they get things done?"

Reading the 2009-2014 Strategic Plan for Saint Joseph's College came to be, well, an underwhelming experience for these four men.

"I read it. That's 30 minutes of my life I'll never get back," Doug said.

"It's two paragraphs of fiscal analysis and the rest is flippin' fluff," Mark said.

"It bears no resemblance to any strategic plan I've ever seen," Bob characterized it. "There is essentially no mention of debt reduction, nor even any acknowledgment that they have significant debt. This is, at best, a crucial oversight."

The GOF puzzled over how such plan, if one could indeed call it that to hear these gentlemen say it, could have been authored in the first place. Then came more news to jilt their once energized spirits. An email arrived in response to the GOF's proposed plan.

"Out of the entire email, the most telling thing to me was the fact that, by the *second sentence*, they once again asked for the $100,000 from 'you and your fellow alums'," Bob said.

"This is what could very well be the most critical juncture in the history of the College," Mark said.

Mark's comment came not so much as statement of fact, but disbelief at the proceedings. Or lack thereof. All communication with the Board up until that point caused the GOF to conclude that the Board intended to "kick the can down the road" so to speak. Bob, "with a very heavy heart" as he put it, raised the serious question of how much longer they could continue on with the Board in this manner.

"I cannot be involved with asking other people for money that will be managed by the same people who spawned this mess," he said.

"I believe very few people know or are even aware that a huge debt exists with the College," Mark said in an email in the exchange. "Gents, I do not like the way this is playing out—like a dying company—with minimal options for possible success."

Given the brick walls they faced, given their love for Saint Joseph's College, and given the sheer exigency of the matter of the College's debt, stagnant enrollment, and myriad other matters, Mark proposed an unforeseen change in tactics.

Do they turn whistleblowers and spread what they know to the Saint Joe alumni community?

Paul Muller opposed the idea. He feared stirring hundreds of alums into a frenzy who would then, without clear information, distort the facts and spread stories of a debt far greater than $27 million. Who would send their child to an institution that might not even be around when it's time for them to graduate? Such talk could do irreparable harm to a recruitment effort which already appeared stymied in previous years. In fact, Paul's rationale gave a glimpse into what may have been the thinking of the Board in the years leading up to February 2017.

How does an organization like a college admit with all transparency that it is multiple millions of dollars in debt and *still* attract all the students it needs? Students are of course essential for the future of a college, yet if there is a debt of such magnitude that it must be reconciled through means far greater than that of tuition, there can be no future without calling for a massive influx of donations. I admitted I could formulate no answer to this Scylla and Charybdis dilemma. In that moment, for the first time, I actually felt a sense of empathy for the Board's challenges.

Doug agreed with Paul, saying that going public with what they knew about the financial woes might fracture the alumni. Too much precious time might be expended explaining and convincing. They agreed to continue to work with the Board and to hope that a new president would be more workable and that he or she would agree to immediate action and turn things around in time.

That new president turned out to be, of course, Dr. Robert Pastoor. Bob Neville met Pastoor in May of 2015 in Indianapolis on a stop of the alumni "meet and greet" tour for the President. Bob gave Pastoor copies of the GOF outline along with the group's correspondence with Sponseller. In the weeks that followed, Bob sent several emails to Pastoor, asking him to meet with the GOF. Bob told Pastoor that the GOF felt that their plan deserved meaningful discussion after submission to Sponseller and Ruff.

"This did not happen," Bob wrote. "After a brief exchange of emails, we essentially ceased communicating with Ben and Steve."

After many unanswered emails, Pastoor at last invited the GOF to a conversation in his office in McHale Hall in Rensselaer on July 15th, 2015. Not much came from it.

"Well, he did relate to us that he had commissioned a survey that had identified at least $35 million of deferred maintenance. I asked him if the BOT had leveled with him during the interview process about the amount of the debt and the financial challenges he would face, he hedged on that," Bob said.

"We really wanted to like him, to give him a chance to succeed," Mark said of Pastoor. "But when he spent more time planning his coronation tour than the financial health of the College…Bob and I have met dozens of CEOs during our careers. You get a quick sense of whether they're a doer or a talker."

“And a lot of what he talked about was his formal investiture the following October,” Bob said. “It appeared to us that he was more fixated on planning for his inauguration than he was on planning for the HLC audit and strategizing to fight the debt. A real leader would have eschewed the inauguration and rolled up his sleeves and gotten to work.”

These suspicions and the overall “I’ve got a bad feeling about this” vibrations intensified when Bob acquired a copy of the President’s monthly update to the Board of Trustees from June of 2015.[7] There is a subsection in the report marked “Personal Note” where President Pastoor writes of his family settling into their new house and that he had “hired the fourteen year-old neighbor to cut the lawn for me—my attempt at building good relations with my community.”

“Are you kidding me?” Bob wrote in the margins of the report. “He takes time in the President’s Report to let everybody know he hired a 14-year-old kid to cut his grass?”

What happened next is what Bob and Mark refer to as "the lost year." Not much of anything happened, but contacts on the Board assured the GOF that hard work was already underway on the problem.

In late spring of 2016, the GOF accepted an invitation to be a part of Saint Joe's new Strategic Planning process. This process would include many members of the alumni community, drawing on their professional experience to construct the means to revitalize Saint Joseph's College and help it thrive in the 21st century higher education marketplace. The planning would be divided into four areas: 1) Manifesting Catholic identity, 2) Enhancing academic quality, 3) Improving fiscal strength, and 4) Heightening the quality of campus life. Bob and the others of the GOF wasted no time grabbing seats on the subcommittee for finance.

The powers that be, however, believed that the strategic planning needed an extra boost, a steroidal injection of brainpower that could spring only from the waters of that Ponce de Leon fountain so revered by corporate America.

Consultants.

For the Saint Joe Strategic Planning team, those consultants came from the Pelican Group, an organization based out of Virginia. They would be the guiding hands of the long-range strategic planning process.

As of this writing in 2021, getting any solid information on the Pelican Group is a spotty endeavor. The Pelican Group's website is no longer responsive. As would follow, email addresses of its members linked to this domain are no longer valid. In the digital world, which in the 21st Century might as well be the whole world in business terms, The Pelican Group appears to be dead and buried, thus making it most difficult to find and contact its former membership for any kind of comment.

But in 2017, the group was a financial and professional services firm that provided strategic, managerial, financial, and developmental counsel and support to Catholic dioceses, colleges, universities, and other Catholic-based organizations.[8] The CEO was Jack Whelan. Whelan also brought with him to the

Pelican Group at least a few members from his previous outfit, O'Meara, Ferguson, Whelan, and Conway, a firm likewise devoted to a mission of "Catholic organizations with advice and counsel on the best possible use of their temporal resources as they work to further their missions" according to a 2012 press release.[9] The financial consulting firm had also done work to strategize Wall Street investment and fundraising for the Archdiocese of Chicago.[10] In 2014, they even partnered with the University of Mary, a small, Catholic college in North Dakota, in a move that would have allowed the college to perhaps buy a for-profit financial firm thereby "helping its professors do more outside consulting."[11]

"We're talking about building the kingdom of God, serving the mission, and making a reasonable living," O'Meara was quoted as saying.[12]

To what degree did O'Meara, Ferguson, Whelan, and Conway, again the Pelican Group's previous incarnation, understand the challenges of Catholic higher education? In an editorial run in *The Criterion*, a publication of the Archdiocese of

Indianapolis, Daniel Conway of the firm cited sobering research painting a dismal future for Catholic education if nothing changed:

"Since 1970, more than 4,000 Catholic schools have closed, including more than 1,400 since 2000."[13]

It would not be hard to correlate that steep dive post 2000 with the wide publicity of the sex abuse scandals in the Catholic Church. These figures and trends mirrored what I found that cold night back in January 2017. The citations of such research would indicate that The Pelican Group would be an organization well-versed in the unique financial struggles facing Saint Joseph's College. Yet in the first meeting of the long-range Strategic Planning Group, Doug Monforton did not believe the most pressing matters received swift enough attention.

"Hey when are we going to talk about the debt?" he asked in the first ten minutes of the meeting.

They told Doug to "trust the process" and assured him the matter of institutional debt would soon be addressed in the

SWOT…Strengths, Weaknesses, Opportunities, Threats…analysis. Indeed, the crushing $27 million debt and the $4-5 million operating deficit found their way into the "Weaknesses" column. Why, Bob wondered, did the debt not get placed in "Threat" column as well? This omission might have been indicative of much else. As Bob and Mark recounted in depth the strategic planning process and its five or more "planned meetings" under the Pelican Group, I could only envision a metaphor. A massive whale…perhaps Moby Dick himself in keeping with previous literary comparisons…has washed ashore on a beach. It flounders on said beach, making languid and lurching movements back towards the sea. Bereft of hands, feet, or paws, it can never gain any real traction or speed. At its weight and its pace, it certainly cannot make it to the water in time before dehydration takes its toll and the cetacean "drowns in air." Such was the process of the strategic plan according to Bob, Mark, and Doug.

"Nobody associated with the enterprise had any remote sense of urgency," Bob said. "The place [Saint Joseph's College] was literally on fire and, rather than bringing in a fire hose, these guys were engaged in the process of how to design a new hose. Worst strategic plan group I've ever seen. If it was free it would've been too expensive."

Mr. Monforton rendered a bit more succinct appraisal.

"The Pelican Group was a fucking joke," he said.

In 2016, the men brought their concerns to the attention of the Pelican Group. The three members of the Gang of Four wanted a firm understanding of what form of involvement they would have ahead in the process and equally as important, at what level they would be involved. Such desires were, after all, understandable. The Gang of Four already devoted years and a few hundred hours of effort to the matter and at that point in 2016, they just did not feel that could continue on by engaging with a "subcommittee." In short, the men wondered if continued efforts and or donations would, in fact, be "throwing good time/money after bad." Another log on the fire of concern was Doug Monforton learning that the Pelican Group's fee ranged somewhere in mid to high six figures, and rather than being paid upon completion of the strategic plan, they received payment for each visit to campus.[14] In response to all of these issues, the three men were again told "trust the process." In fact, The Pelican Group distributed a two-page list of "Suggested Prayers", including the Prayer of Saint Joseph, for all involved in the strategic planning process.[15]

"Can you believe this shit?" Bob said to Mark and Doug. "The freaking place is burning down and they devote two pages to suggested prayers?"

Somewhere amidst this morass of 2016 came word of HLC's ruling of "probation" for Saint Joe's accreditation. Like anyone else paying attention, Doug Monforton took the news with grim seriousness, the "Doomsday Clock" for Saint Joe ticked louder than ever. He wasted no time reaching out via email to a contact of his on the Board of Trustees.

"You realize this is the official beginning of the end," Doug wrote. "There is no fuckin' way we are ever going to climb out of this $28mm hole you and your BOT buddies let us slide into."

Though the light seemed to be fading, a bright spot for the GOF was Saint Joe Vice President of Business Affairs, Spencer Conroy. In both email exchanges and face-to-face meetings, the GOF described Conroy as nothing less than cooperative and forthcoming with institutional data regarding the debt, cash flow, student demographic and enrollment decline data, and the upper administration's views of "strategic planning" and "transformational planning." In September of 2016, the GOF asked Conroy about the HLC decision of probationary status and how much "breathing room" the College retained. Conroy responded that the upper administration of Saint Joe did not perceive the probation as a "death sentence" and by executing strategies already underway, the College could secure three to five years of liquidity.

However, as strategic planning meetings plodded on through October, November, and December, the attitude of the

GOF towards the planning process and the Board of Trustees continued to sour.

"If they [the BOT] can blow it off, I'm out of here," Mark said.

One additional appeal, a tormented experiment of sorts, came from the GOF in November of 2016. Bob and other members of the GOF, as people with 20-40 years of business experience, performed their own SWOT analysis of Saint Joe's situation and presented it to the Strategic Planning Committee. The proposal called for the College to "develop a system of governance and, secondarily, to develop a management system for St Joseph's College" that would allow it to move forward in a fiscally sound manner while avoiding the mistakes of the past that precipitated the crisis. In accordance with "developing a system of governance," they called for a re-engineering of the Board of Trustees "with all deliberate speed," including a clear mission statement defining the scope of responsibility for the Board, term limits for its members to optimize the right combination of experience and new ideas, and guidelines for

Board members of how to interact with Saint Joe alumni, faculty, students, administrators, staff, and other stakeholders “in a climate of enhanced transparency.”

Bob reported that after completing his presentation, a Board of Trustees member grew demonstrably irate, stood up, and came around the table towards him.

“Good luck finding a Board that will contribute as much money as we did,” they said.

Calm and composed, Bob thanked this Board member for their contributions and service over the years, but also pointed out that it was also part of the problem. The Board of Trustees of 2016 took a “far too parochial” approach to fundraising, and that they could never raise enough funds *within* the Board to correct the deficit.

Nothing came of either the meeting or the proposal. More meetings continued in December and then into January of 2017, even after Pastoor sent out his letter of “Presidential Discourse,” informing all of the College’s “dire” situation.

I dropped my pen, played with my coffee cup, and took a look around the hotel's breakfast nook.

"Did you know?" I asked Bob and Mark. "Did you know on February 3rd that the College was finished?"

Bob took a breath and thought for a moment.

"The key to your question is 'on February 3rd,'" he at last said. "There were many things that could have been done up until that point. There were great ideas. But *on* February 3rd? It was just too late. Yes. We knew."

Both of them went on to explain how in October 2016, during their 45th Homecoming reunion for the class of 1971, ironically and somewhat symbolically, the last Homecoming that they would ever attend, because it was also the last Homecoming that the College would ever hold, Spencer Conroy told them that St. Joseph's College had, at most, six months' worth of cash left. To them, the end was clear. But who listened?

"We tried to use what learned at Saint Joe to save the College," Mark said. "The morals we picked up from our education were 'Don't burn it down. Work within the infrastructure and make it better.' That held us back. I did four resurrections of financially struggling institutions. Had we led the charge, the College would be alive today."

He turned and looked out the window and into the distance. I asked them for their overall summation of the collapse. What were the causal factors? Where did the fault lie?

"I had an ex-business associate tell me in the 80s—'Do not let the perfume of your position hide the stink of your results'," Mark said as he looked at the cars rolling past on Indiana Route 30. "Our College closed because of incompetent buffoons—who were turned on by their own perfume and could not smell the stink."

"There is a saying that success has many fathers while failure is an orphan," Bob said. "Here, the failure has many fathers, going back ten or more years at least."

What about John Groppe's contention as published in his "A History of Subsidies" op-ed in the Saint Joe *Observer*? What about the effect of the transition of so many clergy retiring from teaching and the need to hire new faculty from secular pools, thus increasing the amount being paid in salaries?

"Groppe is an apologist for the Board," Bob said. "Subsidies are not why things fell apart. Every Catholic college has had to deal with the same challenge and many of them are doing just fine right now. No, Winston Churchill once called World War II 'The Unnecessary War.' Well, this college closing was 'The Unnecessary Tragedy.'"

As for Mark Nestor, he referred me to his own piece of writing, "Lessons Learned." *The Rensselaer Republican* published it as an op-ed in April of 2017, just days before the formal May 12th sealing off of the campus:

"Is there a lesson to be learned here? Certainly. The lesson learned is that if something is a major problem, time will not resolve the problem; it will only exacerbate it. Would aggressive action have helped, had such action been undertaken in the summer or fall of 2014 – or preferably before? We'd all like to think so, but the truth is that we'll never really know, because it wasn't tried.

"For current students, the lesson might be this: If, in your future professional or civic life, you find yourself in a position where you feel in your heart and mind that a catastrophe might occur, don't hesitate to seek the truth, speak up, and do the right thing. Inaction is hardly ever the right course.

"For alumni, the lesson might be that, had more alumni questioned what was happening at the BOT level, it might have made a difference."[16]

As for going forward with my research, each offered his own advice.

"This problem with the debt, it was just downplayed and kicked down the road for years by the Board of Trustees," Mark said. "Follow the money."

Bob's advice, with which Mark agreed, came with a bitter pill to swallow.

"I don't mean this as a way to flatter you because I don't know you that well and I don't much care about your reaction," Bob told me. "Your father is a world-class academic. But he was on the Board for about 15 years. Where was he during all this? Why did he not stand up, pound the table, and ask 'What the hell are we doing? The emperor has no clothes'? How do you not see that budget line item for millions of dollars of debt service and not ask what's going on? And it's great that 12 Board members voted to keep the College open, but where were they five years ago?"

Bob, Mark, and I made a commitment to continue working together and sharing information as we came across it. I thanked them for their efforts, bid them safe journeys to their respective homes, and left the hotel with the uncomfortable perceptions of a newly sober man. Later, I asked former Board Chairman Ben Sponseller by email about his side of the whole Gang of Four saga:

"We also had inquiries and suggestions from multiple interested parties who said they could help. To the best of my knowledge each suggestion was scrutinized, none was ignored," was all Sponseller said on this matter.

What then did happen at the Board level? With Sponseller, with my father, with all the others? Questions of Board governance intermingled with questions I recalled from an article in the *Rensselaer Republican* of March, 2017[17]:

"But why didn't the college adapt to the times? Why the unbalanced budget?" the writer asked.

"It's killing me to go through what we are going through now," Sponseller was quoted in the article.

My next step was clear: find out as much as I could about the Board of Trustees.

NOTES

1. I interviewed Mark Nestor several times starting in 2017 through 2020. Notes with author.
2. I interviewed Paul Muller on 21 Apr. 2018. Notes with author.
3. I interviewed Doug Monforton several times starting in 2018 through 2020. Notes with author.
4. Letter in author's possession.
5. Agenda and notes for this call in author's possession.
6. Document in author's possession.
7. Document in author's possession.
8. "The Pelican Group"
9. O'Meara Ferguson Whelan and Conway
10. Brachear
11. Rivard
12. Ibid.
13. Conway
14. Board minutes
15. Documents in author's possession.
16. Mark Nestor provided the text of his op-ed. Text in author's possession.
17. Dimitrova

CHAPTER TEN: Command and Control

"I walked in and saw this room full of old white men."

Thus, Kris Sakelaris described her initial reaction on her first day as a member of the Saint Joseph's College Board of Trustees. She told that to me in May 2018 as we sat in an RV camper with a bunch of other alums at the Rensselaer fairgrounds. Though campus remained blocked off and "quarantined" so to speak, the Saint Joe Alumni Association undertook efforts to keep the Puma spirit alive and held a gathering of alums for two days of cold beer, grilled brats, and salty, delectable Wagonmasters. Many brought campers and RVs and stayed the night at the fairgrounds. As a member of the Alumni Board, Sakelaris played a key role in putting the event together.

She is a ball of positive energy, always exuding a bright and sweet smile and eager to talk about most any subject. Like me, Sakelaris also comes from a Puma family. Not only did she graduate from Saint Joe, but her husband, her sisters, and her brother-in-law did as well. Her own daughter even became a member of the final graduating class of the College. What did Sakelaris do with her own Saint Joe education? A lot. She became an accountant, a lawyer, and even a judge. For a time in 2016, she also taught Sports Law in the MBA program at our beloved alma mater. Long before that however, she was Board of Trustees member.

"Steve Ligda [then the Chairman of the Board] came over to my house in 2009 with a bottle of wine for the formal ask," Sakelaris recalled. "He thought the Board needed more women."

Perceptive. As pointed out by Sakelaris' thoughts on her first day on the Board, the Board of 31 members had fewer than ten female members at the time of the "suspension of operations" vote and very few people of color. General thinking in 21st century is that greater diversity brings greater variety of experiences, thus multiple perspectives, and thereby better results. That would seem to be a good rule of practice anywhere, however my reflecting on the issue caused me to ask: "What exactly are best practices for a college board of trustees?"

Should they be from the geographic community of the college? Should they all be alums? Should there be people unconnected to the college who can grant objective opinions? Should they know higher education or finance? Should they govern and give direction, or should they instead advise and oversee, allowing administration to set the course?

Then again, could the complete opposite of the spirit of all those questions be true? From the viewpoint of faculty members and perhaps even administration, is there an inherently adversarial role boards play in a higher education ecosystem? I ask not only because of the Saint Joe experience circa winter/spring 2017, but because of the case studies of Sweet Briar College and Antioch College where faculty, alumni, students, and staff, mounted active and combative counteroffensives against their respective boards in order to take back their college communities. Even in the case of Dowling

College, stakeholders regarded the board with suspicious eyes given the suddenness of the closure announcement.

College boards: friend or foe?

Might the answer to every question just asked be, "yes"?

I figured a sensible starting point would be finding literature and research studies regarding the benchmarks of a "good" college board of trustees and by just what rubric they may be assessed, while also examining best practices in institutional finance. I took to this research like a child to cold peas, but I knew a baseline understanding to be an absolute necessity in any post mortem of the Board of Trustees of Saint Joseph's College.

"Leading the University: The Role of Trustees, Presidents, and Faculty" is a collection of narrative perspectives by current and former board members and college presidents published in the journal, *Change*. In his piece "The Effective Board", Richard Legon, then president of the Association of Governing Boards of Universities and Colleges and a board member at Virginia State University and the University of Charleston, outlined a series of bullet points describing Legon's selected characteristics of a good board. These points are numerous, but I believe every one of them apply to what transpired with the Board of Trustees of Saint Joseph's College and the eventual downfall of the institution. Legon's characteristics of a "good board" include:

"Recruiting and appointing board members who are familiar with higher education and the institution on whose board they are being asked to serve. For public institution boards, merit prevails over politics.

"Appointing or selecting board members who are committed to their voluntary role and aware of the responsibilities of an independent board.

"Appointing members who include men and women from sufficiently diverse areas of expertise—corporate, professional, and academic. Institution and policy leaders also determine the appropriate number of board members required to meet their policy responsibilities."[1]

Legon is not alone in that final point of criteria of an effective college board. Dr. Cindra Smith[2], a nationally-recognized expert in developing trustee and board governance while serving for several years as director of education services for the Community College League of California, wrote "Assessing Board Effectiveness: Resources for Board of Trustees Self-Evaluation." While it is true community colleges have differences from four-year institutions in terms of mission and connection to home-base communities, the essential mission of a board of trustees in each case is the same: serve the students and sustain the institution. Like Legon, Dr. Smith argues for boards to develop a robust means of self-evaluation policies and processes examining strengths and areas needing work, and to carry out these processes regularly.[3]

"Governing boards that engage in the self-evaluation process and thoughtfully consider and use the results to improve their performance provide excellent leadership for their communities and colleges. They are embracing their responsibilities and ensuring that board members have the skills and knowledge to lead and govern," Smith writes.[4]

In "Governance over the Years: A Trustee's Perspective," Potter and Phelan argue that "the board is principally involved in deciding ends. Ends are the board's desired outcomes for the college, as opposed to means, the operations needed to achieve those goals. Thus, the creation of institutional goals, both short- and long-term, is a critical board responsibility." How does a board arrive at these goals? By acting through policies.[5]

Construction and execution of these goals requires a committed, engaged, and cohesive board. However, a weather system of factors can often impede such an entity from ever coming together. As Cowen illustrates, "The majority of trustees at both private and public institutions come from the business world, and often only a single-digit percentage has a background in academia."[6] This means boards made of a majority of individuals who have considerable responsibilities and commitments to their businesses, employees/employers, and overall their means of income. In “The Career President,” John Lombardi reminds that, “Most trustees are unpaid volunteers who find it challenging to provide the time for official meetings. Few care to engage in dialogues with each other or with other university constituencies in open meetings, for when they read the headlines the next day they find themselves represented in ways they had not intended.”[7]

Add in the understandable need to give attention to one’s family, this situation can and does naturally lead to a detachment or even outright absence of certain board members from college governance. Barringer and Riffe found signs of this absence in their own research on boards: “While these trustees were in no way shirking their duties, it was nevertheless noteworthy that not all trustees engaged with these institutions in the same ways and to the same extent.”[8] What does this lead to? As Lombardi describes:

“Consequently, they [detached board members] often operate on inadequate information, sometimes mediated by gossip, backroom conversations, influential associates, or high-level opinion pieces in national publications. Translating these sources of information into effective policy for the university is difficult without expert guidance and especially without the advantage of data-driven budgets linked to performance criteria for their institution."[9]

Not only does a board made up of mostly business professionals present challenges with engagement and attendance, there can also be misunderstandings regarding the purpose and mission of higher education. For example, colleges will sometimes make decisions that a for-profit product-seller would not because the decision was in the best interest of students and the idea of a university. Conversely, most if not all small, private colleges are classified as nonprofit entities, and this might lead to misconceptions where someone could look at a budget deficit, shrug, and say, "Well it's not supposed to make a profit."

Dr. Michael K. Townsley, the former president of The Pennsylvania Institute of Technology and a consultant with many years of experience with the financial systems of colleges and universities, describes this very phenomenon in his book, *The Small College Guide to Financial Health: Beating the Odds*, and what happens when it intermixes with the volunteer aspect of being a board member:

"Many boards make the mistake of granting the board a charity assumption, assuming that since the operation is a charity and not a real business the college does not have to be held to rigorous standards. Board members who see their role as an honorary, community-service function abdicate oversight of the college to administration."[10]

This may speak to an inherent confusion over how board members see their roles in terms of serving the institution. There are those who seem unaware of their role in governance, and instead see themselves as promoters, cheerleaders, and glad-handers for their college. Gary Rhoades, director of the Center for the Study of Higher Education at the University of Arizona, wrote in "Shared Governance for Enduring Change" about this very misconception of boards and how it leads to mishandling of situations. As a case example he points to the sexual abuse crisis at Penn State, including a lack of transparency, a series of payouts, and a complete reluctance to act.[11]

"The role once played by most boards is exemplified by the Penn State board—a booster group that raises support, that loyally and vigorously promotes the institution, but that does not actively consider its work to be safeguarding a broader public interest. That booster role entails a corporate-style deference to the CEO and a corporate-like view that what is good for the university is good for the state."[12]

Lest I be accused of painting all college boards as being comprised solely of out-of-touch corporatists interested only in doing a little charity work, let us for a moment consider what James Martin, author of "Trustees: Allies in Integrity" has to say. In that article, Martin cautions college faculty against dismissive attitudes towards board members. "Professors, with fantasies of a medieval community of scholars, sometimes like to say, 'We are the university.' But, from a legal point of view, trustees are the university; professors are the hired help."[13] Martin goes on to establish that this is not merely a matter of authority, but that often board members have their roles because they do know what they're doing. As he describes in his own experience:

"We [faculty who met with trustees] had an unarticulated assumption that all the really smart people were professors (the contrapositive equivalent is more pointed: no non-professors are really smart). We learned that some trustees were, in fact, not only smart, but quite knowledgeable about the university. Indeed, they had a much more comprehensive understanding than we did (about students, staff, budget, the physical plant, faculty turnover, etc.) and were often quite shrewd about how to get things done. While they did not always know the correct vocabulary for articulating their points, their instincts were often sound. They cared about the students, about the quality of education, about whether the university had the right priorities, and whether it used resources as effectively as possible."[14]

I stopped and considered Martin's point for it could not be ignored. I really did not have an idea of what it meant to be a board member. If I did, I wouldn't have been doing all this research. We faculty bemoaned that they didn't know what we did. At the same time, I had no idea what trustees did.

But in all of this, is there any one single, overriding designation of a board's role? The more I researched, the more I kept finding the same exact two-word phrase: "fiduciary responsibility."

From the Teachers College at Columbia University: "Trustees and their boards uphold their fiduciary responsibility by working with the president and top administrators to approve major policies, make long range plans, and oversee the budget."[15]

Perhaps most succinct of all, Harvard sociologist David Reisman said, the role of boards is to "protect the future from the present."[16]

For as Saint Joe found out, "What seemed far-fetched yesterday arrives tomorrow."[17]

As he told Justin Hays during that night in the Shen Auditorium on February 6th, 2017, Ben Sponseller's time on the Board amounted to 13 years with four years of that tenure as Chairman. Saint Joseph's College was an institution stretching back over 100 years, and history demands that the previous incarnations of the Board be examined in order to find how things came to be. For example, Saint Joseph's College came to an end with just under 1,000 students, 600 or so of those being residential, but with a Board of Trustees standing at 31 members. To many eyes this would be interpreted as disproportionate. How did the Board become so…bloated?

"You have to go back to the Chip Banet days, probably," Mark Nestor said, referring to Fr. Charles Banet, Saint Joseph's College president for all of my formative years. "The Board was a 'good ol' boys' club."

What this means is it appears that Fr. Banet recognized even as far back as the 1980s that the College's financial picture was shaky and revenue was a dire need. He used the Board as a fundraising arm, just as many colleges sometimes do. Make a generous, sizeable donation and you too can have a seat on the Board. A shiny plaque comes with it, suitable for display in your corporate office. This is not to say at all that every trustee added during the expansion was in it for vanity. Take Larry Laudick for example.[18]

Laudick is a 1969 graduate of Saint Joseph's College with a degree in accounting. When asked to remark on that time, he says "My memories recede with my hairline." Despite his self-deprecating humor, he is rich with detailed anecdotes and an understanding of institutional finance that he maintains came straight from Saint Joseph's College. In the first semester of his freshmen year, Laudick earned a 1.5 GPA.

"The professors and the priests, they gave me a second chance," he said. "They helped me, and they showed me what I could do if I worked."

As evidence, he offers his experience in his first job out of college at Ernst & Ernst, later to become Ernst & Young.

"They sat me at a desk next to a guy from Harvard," Laudick recalled. "I thought 'Oh shit, what chance do I have next to this guy?' Well he eventually got fired because he thought he had it on Easy Street because he was from Harvard, while I knew I had to work."

And work he did, all the way to becoming Senior Vice President of Accounting of Wendy's International until retiring from the company in 2005 after 30 years. In 1989 he was invited to become a member of the Saint Joseph's College Board of Trustees and remained on the Board until the day of the closing, with part of his tenure as Chairman of the Board and for much more of the time as the head of the Finance Committee.

"He's a quiet guy, but with a sharp mind," my mother told me before I interviewed Laudick. "I'd see him at functions and I could tell he was sizing things up. I always wondered what he was thinking."

Given all this experience I thought he would be among the best to answer the question, “When did you first think Saint Joe was in trouble?”

“At my first Board meeting,” Laudick replied, much to my surprise.

He went on to explain that in that first meeting at the dawn of the 1990s, Fr. Banet announced an error in the financial audit and that the College possessed less money than thought…to the tune of $2 million less.

“We were never well financially,” Laudick said. “We were always playing catch up. Our facilities were so out of date. Keep in mind, most kids coming to college came from having their own rooms and their own bathrooms sometimes. Then we ask them to live in barracks with a communal bathroom down the hall. Most university students don’t live like that. I remember mothers would be crying after seeing where they were leaving their kids.”

Truer words were never spoken. There is in fact also evidence to suggest the presence of a laissez-faire attitude among Saint Joe's "old guard" of faculty and administration towards physical improvement of the campus at the time of Laudick's joining the Board. In his Centennial Pictorial History of Saint Joseph's College, Fr. Dominic Gerlach published a photo of students in a typical dorm room from 1989. I know it was 1989 because I know the people in the photograph. The caption to the photo reads "Essentials for the 1980s" and there is accompanying text arguing:

"Whereas formerly students were brought to the College by their parents (or train) with only a few creature comforts, and even willing to live in a barrack-type dorm to save a few dollars, now many students come with their own automobiles and rearrange their rooms with sofas, TV sets, stereos, refrigerators, microwaves, etc."[19]

Austerity once came as part and parcel of the Catholic educational experience. That and remembrance of this "willingness to live in a barrack-type dorm" of the 1950s and prior may have fostered a notion among the ruling "old guard" that anything that did not directly contribute to the academic experience was a mere frivolity. Indeed, it does not take all that much close-reading of Gerlach's words to pick up on the "spoiled kids" rhetorical subtext. I saw this stance reflected many places in the Saint Joe community during my undergrad years, including in a few dinner table conversations.

Before the beginning of a new academic year, I once expressed woe at the notion of enduring the heat and humidity of another Indiana August as my dorm, just like all the other dorms on campus save one, did not have air conditioning. To get air circulating, we would all run fans and prop the doors of the dorm open all day and night. The downside to this tactic meant we would be overrun by flies, adding insects to an already hot, sweaty, sticky mess, lasting until sometime in at least mid-September and that merciful first frost.

"Then go read in the library," my father said.

I could go to the air-conditioned library, I said, but they didn't allow sleeping overnight, and adequate and comfortable sleep without flies buzzing about my face was my primary need, hence the desire for air conditioning.

"You really need that, huh?" my mother asked with equal parts skepticism and "try to see things reasonably."

No one *needs* an air conditioner in the "hunter-gatherer" sense of survival, but that did not prevent the appliance from becoming something of a staple of modern living by that point in the late 20th century. Going without it though did build a sense of comradery and those who attended Saint Joe all four years did so for the quality of the education and the deep ties of community, not for any real structural amenities. We even came to see buildings steeped in antiquity as part of the "Saint Joe charm." Perhaps this fed into the "old guard's" sense that physical improvements to the campus could wait. Facilities are not why one goes to college, right?

That is something of a tough sell to prospective students visiting campus with their parents, particularly if they have no prior connection to or knowledge of Saint Joe. Academic gems such as the Core program are abstractions while the absence of basics such as air conditioning and the sight of decades-old dorms and academic buildings that sometimes looked like East Berlin after the Soviets pulled out are concrete realities, vividly visible to the consumer. Does one pay more for the promise of quality education, or do they drive half an hour south to Purdue and pay less while getting comfort and better facilities in return?

A new presidential administration in the mid-1990s at last recognized the severity of this situation, and started to drag the campus into the 20th century. That decade saw the construction of new athletic facilities, a row of modern student apartments and suites for upper classmen, and the modern two-story Core Building where I would one day have my office and hold my classes.

All of these structures blessedly came with air conditioning.

The necessity of these new buildings could not be questioned. The financing of their construction, however, gives pause for scrutiny. Often, colleges and universities will hold fundraisers to pay the tab for bold new initiatives. In this case, Saint Joseph's College financed the campus makeover with bank loans. A high amount of debt just got higher.[20]

It is important to note that none of these construction projects could have come to pass without the approval of the Board of Trustees at that time.

Board and administration no doubt hoped to cover the costs of these new loans with increased enrollment. Townsley underscores the dangers of such a gambit by pointing to the case study of Bradford College, who followed steps similar to Saint Joseph's College at about the same time. In 1998, the president of the Boston, Massachusetts-area college borrowed $17.9 million to build a new, state-of-the-art dorm to attract new students and push overall enrollment over the 700 mark and reduce unfunded student discounts. One of Bradford's trustees resigned over the decision while the rest of the board endorsed the endeavor. In the years that followed, the college's budget deficit ballooned to $6.1 million and its enrollment dropped to 497 while unfunded tuition discount went to 60%. The class of 2000 was Bradford's final graduating class.[21]

Like Bradford College, Saint Joseph's College seemed to share a similar mindset of "if you build it, they will come." Saint Joe was spared the precipitate fall after two years that Bradford experienced and was thus afforded more time to correct any possible ill-considered decisions as a new administration came into power in the early 2000s. It may come as a surprise, however, to learn that the new administration chose not to rectify anything, but to make a decision that may have been the turning point resulting in the collapse of Saint Joseph's College.

At a February 10th, 2006 meeting of the Board of Trustees, Frank Ferguson made a proposition. Yes, this is the same Frank Ferguson of the Pelican Group, but in 2006 he worked for OFK Capital Advisors. Ferguson presented an alternate approach to paying for campus construction and facelifting projects, such as new roofs. As stated in the meeting minutes:

"Instead of waiting for pledges to be paid and then doing relevant construction, he outlined a strategy that would get construction done immediately and still generate increased endowment for the College. Basically it involved issuing long-term tax-exempt bonds to do the construction, putting all payments on pledges as they appear into the endowment, and using the difference ("arbitrage") between the interest rate on tax-exempt bonds and the earnings from the increases in endowment to pay off the bonds and to compound into even further increases in the endowment."[22]

One of the trustees would serve as an expert adviser on the matter as his company engaged in this form of asset management work all the time. This trustee was Jack Whelan and his company was, you guessed it, The Pelican Group. As to the 2006 decisions of the bonds, it is made quite clear in the minutes that Whelan would not be involved in the selection of a firm to work with the College on the matter and that any conflict of interest would be avoided.[23]

On May 19th, 2006, the Board met again and a three-page statement of resolution was presented in regard to a bond issue in the amount of $7 million. The motion passed.[24]

By a Board meeting the following year on February 9th, 2007, an obstacle to this chosen method of long-term financing of projects arose. The College at that time was involved in a $750,000 fundraising challenge from The Kresge Foundation, the philanthropic organization founded by Sebastian Kresge, the same man who long ago founded Kmart. Kresge grants, the Board learned, do not permit using arbitrage to bolster endowment. How this bit of "missed homework" happened is left only to conjecture. Board members argued back and forth about alternative methods to finance and complete construction projects by the end of 2007, and decided accepting the Kresge challenge to be the best course of action, while seeking short-term financing of projects.[25]

To magnify matters, the October 27th, 2007 meeting saw a call for a new bond issue of $8 million to pay for the construction and renovation projects.

"It really made sense," Carol Wood testified to the proposition.

She was the Board member I met that tear and alcohol-soaked night in the bar on February 3rd, 2017. Wood served as a Board of Trustees member for many years. A Rensselaer native and a 1974 graduate of Saint Joe herself, Wood spent her career working in computer technology for various companies, with nearly 30 years as Computer Services Manager at Purdue University. She knew higher education, she knew Saint Joe, and she knew the practicalities of working in the private sector as well.

"If people saw it working and saw the progress, then they would be excited about giving [to the capital campaign]," she said.

When the proposal was on the floor for the Board, Bill White was the faculty representative.

"I spoke out against the arbitrage," he said. "I was then told by other Board members at the time that I 'didn't understand business and finance.' I can't remember my vote, but I was the only Board member to either vote no or to abstain."

The arbitrage passed. What went wrong?

"The problem is we double dipped," Wood said.

What did that mean, "double dipped?" It meant that money gathered by the capital campaign fundraiser never went to pay off the bonds and instead got spent on projects elsewhere, in essence being spent twice. Bonds issued earlier then got folded into the College's overall debt.

"They should have restricted the funds," Kris Sakelaris said. "They didn't."

“The 2008 recession hit SJC hard, but harder still was the hit from forgetting the plan to pay off bonds with the pledge payments from the capital campaign,” Dad told me.

Why did this happen?

“Amnesia,” my father called it.

As he explained it, the Board would review options and plans and then decide upon a course of action. Several months would elapse before the next meeting. At the next meeting, something bizarre, inexplicable even, would transpire despite the presence of minutes and other documentation.

“The Board would completely forget what was decided at the previous meeting,” Dad said.

This may be due to several factors outlined at the outset. Just as with so many other college boards, the Saint Joe Board was all volunteer. No one got paid. In fact as previously mentioned, most of, if not all, members contributed considerable sums of money to the College. They also had their own careers, families, and lives, creating varying levels of participation in Board deliberation. There is, however, an alternative view as to why the bond payoff did not happen.

"In the Finance Committee, we set aside $7 million to pay it [bond debt] off," Larry Laudick said. "We were celebrating about it. Then the fall's incoming freshmen class enrollment only came in at 200. We didn't have the tuition revenue, so we just couldn't do it."[26]

And the result? Well, I can perhaps paint a picture with a personal analogy involving questionable financial decisions. Not long after moving out on my own and working my first job, I came upon the need for a printer. As a birthday gift, Dad gave me the money for one. I bought a decent Canon printer with my credit card. I did not, however, pay off the purchase with the money Dad gave me. What did I do with funds? I can't exactly remember, but I think a Batmobile may have been involved. Regardless, I spent that money the way young, privileged, inexperienced men sometimes do. Meanwhile, the printer purchase sat on my credit card accruing interest…and I did not have the original funds earmarked to pay it off. Things like that tend to snowball.

It may also be that a few trustees held different concepts of the Board's role. Did they act as advisers or did they create policy as suggested by earlier-explored best-practice studies?

I asked this question of Carol Wood and she gave me a glimpse into the Board mindset.

"We made policy, but we weren't into the nitty-gritty," she said. "We were told by the Board Chairman to let the administration handle that."

Whatever the cause, debt, as it tends to do if left unattended, went on festering with interest just as surely as the campus properties continued suffering from deferred maintenance. Tiles fell from ceilings and physical plant staff spent more of their days working to just keep the place from falling to the ground.

As mentioned before, 2008 dealt a considerable blow. Lehman Brothers collapsed in September of that year and America was forced to come to grips with what is now known as The Great Recession. Home foreclosures and unemployment skyrocketed as federal interest rates dove. The full effect of this considerable economic downturn on higher education would not be fully seen for another ten years, but sufficient to claim it was not good for small colleges. I can remember in the dawn of the 21st century how my father would tell me about the massive influx of college students on the way. Higher education would need to have enough faculty on hand to meet the demand.

The tidal wave of students never appeared. Parents, many having lost their jobs or homes in the economic recession, could not be sources of tuition, if they ever really were in the first place. Colleges began competing for students by issuing tuition discounts. A 2017 report from the National Association of College and University Business Officers found that by 2009, a student applying to a college with a $26,980 sticker price could expect, on average, an $11,249 discount. By 2017, tuition discounts at many private colleges and universities reached 50%.[27]

Thinking also shifted among college presidents and boards. Governing members found themselves forced to transition from long-term visions to short-term steps for survival. One of these steps was to move away from the humanities as majors as incoming students in turbulent economic times sought fields of study perceived as safer in terms of getting "a good job." In other words, the world encouraged young people to study business and medicine and the like out of financial survival if nothing else. A tremendous effect rolled through liberal arts colleges as the number of history majors dropped by 44% after 2008, while political science and sociology plummeted 20%. Saint Joseph's College got slapped by this wave as well, but due in part to misperception.[28]

"One thing I could never get across to people at the College was that we *weren't* a liberal arts college," my father said. "We were liberal education. A student can major in business, pre-med, computer science, or something like that, but along with the major they also get a solid education in humanities through the Core program."

That, however, is a complex and nuanced distinction to make to working parents as they make decisions with their children on a college, especially if the child is a first-generation student and the family is new to higher education. Even with successful alumni touting Core and praising the curriculum for what it did for them, it remains most difficult to get an understanding of it across in the world of marketing, where 30 second soundbites and "elevator pitches" rule the day. This grew even more complicated in tumultuous economic times of the Great Recession when students took to a growing trend: take all general education requirements at a community college for a fraction of the cost at other institutions, then transfer those credits over to a college where the student will complete their major course of study.

In other words, colleges are no longer "hotels," but "airports." Core at Saint Joseph's does not fit this schema all that well. Implemented at a college that spent a significant stretch of its history as a seminary, and created in an era where students often attended one college, freshman through senior year, Core did not have much flexibility due to its linear coursework, not anticipating a world where students might have high school credits that could allow them to skip Cores, or students who might pop in and out of different colleges.

"Core is a boutique product for a niche market," a new Saint Joe professor told me after their first year on faculty.

This comment perplexed me, maybe even put me off a bit when I heard it. Now, I confess, I get it. As explained earlier, the lion's share of the Core program depended upon small groups of students together in a room. While many small colleges moved online to drew new students and revenue, Saint Joe faced that 21st century prospect with great difficulty, not only because of needs in IT infrastructure, but in how we taught our courses. In its own way, Core became antiquated.

"I have deep appreciation for Core, especially after your Dad explained it to me," Larry Laudick told me. "But I had a few discussions with other Board members away from your Dad, asking if Core was holding us back. We needed to be able to compete and I wondered if we should drop it. The other Board members countered and ultimately we decided that we couldn't give up Core as it was our identity."

And so it went…into the second decade of the 21st century. Despite the economy's rocky road to recovery post Great Recession, the 2011 Institutional Self-Study of Saint Joseph's College reported fundraising successes and that the College had "an alumni donor participation rate that hovers at or above the national average of 22%, whereas many ICI [Independent Colleges of Indiana] institutions have a rate of less than 20%."[29] There was also the matter of a farm.

Juanita K. Waugh was a proud farmer and one the largest landowners in the state of Indiana. She died in 2010.[30] Both of these facts would have significant consequences for Saint Joseph's College in the form of several hundred acres of farmland. Dave Bechman is an attorney for FarmFirst, LLC, providing farm management services for Rensselaer and the surrounding counties of Indiana, and one of his clients was Juanita Waugh.[31]

"The property was deeded to Saint Joseph's College following Juanita's death according to her Trust Agreement, which I was a Co-Trustee for," said Bechman. "There is also a Conservation Easement on the property."

For those like me who are challenged in the discourse of legalese, FarmFirst, LLC explains the phrase:

"A Conservation Easement is a voluntary legal agreement between a landowner and a legal entity (or government) that limits, restricts, or dictates how land can be used. It typically prohibits development of the property for commercial or residential use. Granting of a Conservation Easement may have tax benefits. The main purpose is to control the future use of the property."[32]

The development of this easement and the donation of the land itself all stemmed from the close friendship Waugh shared with Fr. Charles Banet, former president of Saint Joseph's

College. She met him at a dinner party and casual conversation turned to years of friendly debates about religion. Be that as it may, what vested interest would this farmer have in giving to a Catholic College? Recall that in the insipient stages of its history, Saint Joseph's College farmed to live. Through her deepening friendship with Banet, Waugh learned the history of the College and how the original priests, brothers, and students worked the land. The College also remained committed to local agriculture by renting many acres of land to farmers. This convinced Waugh of where her family legacy would go upon the day she shrugged off this mortal coil.[33]

Yet she was uneasy. Waugh was a devout and outspoken atheist. If she gave her land to Saint Joe, what might happen if the Catholic Church one day tried to nullify any concordance and sell the land off for cash? In 2009, as Waugh prepared her bequest of 7,634 acres of farmland to Saint Joe, she made certain all documentation contained a conservation easement stipulating that the land could never be sold by Saint Joe or the Church. In fact, it could not be sold at all and the land must always be used either for farming or for energy production in the form of a long line of windmills. How then would Saint Joe benefit from this arrangement? The College would collect the "fruit of the land" in the form of a $1.5 million annually.[34]

What if by chance, just by chance, Saint Joseph's College should go belly up? In that case, the land reverted to Waugh's other philanthropic cause, The Mayo Clinic. In any event, Juanita Waugh's legacy would remain farmland forever.[35]

The dedicated annual income of approximately two million dollars of revenue came without question as a welcome benefit for Saint Joseph's College in 2011. However, it would not be panacea. Even as I arrived in 2012, all bright-eyed and bushy-tailed to begin teaching, Saint Joe's financial picture stood in stark contrast to my own demeanor. By that point, the total debt stood at well over $27 million with annual debt service due of just over $1 million. By way of comparison, the market value of the endowment was just shy of $24 million. There were, however, approximately $78 million in permanent, restricted assets. At the same time, the tuition discount rate was

59%...more or less the same rate as the aforementioned and closed Bradford College…with over $11 million in unfunded scholarships awarded.[36]

Which brings us up to my first faculty meeting in September of 2012 when then-President Riegelnegg described contentious discussions between his office and the Royal Bank of Scotland, the financial institution that grabbed the College's debt. The Business Affairs Assessment Report announced an operational loss in FY 2011-2012 of $2,031,438. In FY2010-2011, the operational loss was $788,400. The College also failed to meet two bond covenants and a bond from 2007 was coming due on June 1st, 2013. Refinancing would not be possible.[37]

Then the Vice President of Business saw an opportunity. Since Saint Joe owned and rented out farmland, this opened the door for the College to refinance its long-term debt of $27 million for a fixed interest rate of 20 years through partnerships with Farm Credit Mid-America (FCMA) and DeMotte State Bank of nearby DeMotte, Indiana. The latter bank would service the loan on behalf of FCMA. The arrangement was publicized in local newspapers and the alumni newsletter.[38]

"That's why it's true to say that the amount of debt was never kept secret," Bob Neville said. "Of course, it was also long a matter of public record, but who looks at that?"

While President Riegelnegg expressed to faculty with a broad smile that he no longer bore the Royal Bank of Scotland's full weight on his back, not everyone in the world professed excitement at the news.

Bert Ely is a consultant and expert on banking issues who writes Farm Credit Watch for the American Banking Association's Banking Journal. In a January 2015 post, Ely called the transaction an "egregious lending abuse." "Clearly the FCS [Farm Credit System] is not authorized to lend to educational institutions," Ely wrote. "Which raises the question: How could FCMA make this loan to the college?" The logical answer to Ely's question would be the Waugh land plus the other farmland owned by Saint Joe. Ely, however, countered that the language of the Farm Credit Act states that such loans are to go to "bona fide" farmers, meaning those actually engaged in the act of farming, and not a college "who merely owns the farmland and leases that land to actual farmers." He also raised the question of the Waugh land easement. "Can FCMA place a valid first lien on the farmland given that the college is barred from selling the land under any circumstance?"[39]

Ely's queries on the matter to Michael Stokke, the FCA's Director of Congressional and Public Affairs, were answered with, according to Ely's writing, the statement that the loan "does not involve a loan for which you [Ely] are obligated."[40]

Despite this legal murkiness, the load did indeed go through and Saint Joe's considerable debt changed hands. What did Board members think? Kris Sakelaris, an accountant herself, recalls being shocked at the overall amount of the figures.

"When this was presented, I raised my hand and asked how we got in such debt. I was told it was from building the Core

Building and the apartments," she said. "'We thought we'd have it [paying off the debt] figured out by now' they told me."

President Riegelnegg resigned in June of 2014.[45] This came only months after the resignations of the Vice President for Business and the Vice President for Academic Affairs. In truth, many faculty saw this as a positive development as we did not hold the administration in high regard, most especially in the case of Academic Affairs. One professor described the situation by quoting Leo Amery, who in turn quoted Oliver Cromwell, in the House of Commons upon the departure of Neville Chamberlain: "You have sat too long here for any good you have been doing. Depart, I say, and let us have done with you. In the name of God, go!"

Meanwhile, Saint Joe needed a president and a search began. This would be a process involving most every sector of the community and would last perhaps a year. Interim leadership would be needed in the office of the president until a new one could be found, so leadership…what was left of it…contacted the Registry for College and University Presidents.

In response, Dr. Steve Hulbert came to Saint Joe's as temporary president while under contract to the Registry. Though originally from the Northeast, Dr. Hulbert retired after serving for several years as President of Nicholls State University in Thibodaux, Louisiana. He could be seen walking Saint Joe campus with his tiny dog, getting the lay of the land, the pulse of the community, and confronting an immediate and somewhat surprising challenge.

"Saint Joseph's College was under threat of lawsuit from the EPA [Environmental Protection Agency]," Dr. Hulbert told me.

As mentioned before, in particular regarding a request from Ben Sponseller to the Gang of Four, Saint Joe got its heat from a coal burning plant. Federal regulations demanded a switchover to a more environmentally sustainable source. In one of his first faculty meetings, Hulbert reported a few Board members did not know about the coal plant.

“You see that big smokestack in the middle of campus?” Hulbert said he answered them while pointing at the red brick pillar.

What would it take to “update a grossly outdated heating system?” as Dr. Hulbert called it?

“$800,000,” Hulbert said.

A switchover needed to be done and it needed to be done soon, otherwise the College would be subject, as stated before, to a lawsuit and steep fines.

“You had wonderful, skilled, hardworking people in central administration,” Hulbert said. “But with little understanding of physical plant. The change from coal to natural gas could have been done a decade earlier and for cheaper. The Board and the administration just needed to act.”

Hulbert made this longstanding weakness in levels of administration known in his August 2014 report to the Board of Trustees.

“I came to this interim assignment with an expectation of certain standards of administrative practice and institutional sophistication,” Hulbert wrote. “Those expectations were based on forty-plus years of experience in small to medium sized colleges and universities. Almost immediately after my arrival, I had to adjust my frame of reference and I will probably continue to do so.

“I doubt that I am saying anything that is not known in some part by members of the Board of Trustees, but I have found a lack of seasoned administrative leadership, structured administrative process and what might well be referred to as strategic decision making.”[42]

A close reading of the August 2014 report reveals the addressing or correcting of institutional problems that did not, in reality, have to become problems. One example would be the former bar in basement of Halleck Center, Core XI. My eyes went to that section of the document as having been a bartender in the establishment my senior year of undergrad, it remained somewhat near and dear to my heart. Despite being closed, the bar resulted in "an issue with the State of Indiana that involved the long-standing failure to pay taxes on revenues from liquor sales in Core XI." Since the bar no longer operated, Saint Joe did not renew its liquor license and then negotiated a deal with the State of Indiana to pay a penalty plus a reduced figure of back taxes amounting to $8,262. This is not a bank-breaking figure by any means when looking at a budget on an institutional level, but it is head-scratching as to how this came about at all.[43]

The boiler project stands as an even more puzzling case given its integral importance. The switchover Hulbert initiated wouldn't even be complete until October 2015, long after his departure. When analyzed, I would posit the entire matter of the boiler may be seen as something of a microcosm of the "Saint Joseph's College Way." As further evidence, Rensselaer is the provider of all gas and electric utilities to the town's residents and businesses. If Saint Joe needed a gas line for its new boiler, then it needed to contact Steve Wood, Mayor of Rensselaer. Mayor Wood gave an account of that conversation to Dave Bangert at the *Lafayette Journal & Courier*:[44]

"They called and said, 'We need a gas line right away,'" Mayor Wood said. "I said, 'That's fine. When do you need it?' They said, 'Well, we need it tomorrow.' I said, 'Tomorrow?' They said they were bringing in a gas boiler, on a flatbed truck. I mean, we're talking they wanted it done right then."

Bangert writes that the city hired a company to run a 4-inch line to the new boiler.

"This was in October and it was getting cold and they didn't have heat," Mayor Wood said. "They just had no planning. They knew they were going to have to shut down that coal-fired boiler at some point. … There was no planning. They were more reactive than proactive. If a building had a leak in the roof, they fixed it. I think that's how they've been doing it for a while."

As stated before, however, Dr. Hulbert did not see the end of the boiler saga. During his time, Hulbert needed to keep the institution in a "steady as she goes" mode. I asked Hulbert for his assessment of Saint Joe's Board, the fiscal situation, and if he could see the ugly storm on the horizon.

"I had a good, open relationship with Ben Sponseller," Hulbert said.

The feeling was mutual according to Sponseller.

"Steve Hulbert was a great help to us while he was interim president," he said.

I asked Hulbert if he saw any indication of an impending closure of the College.

"I talked with him [Sponseller] about things that *might* happen as it became clear to me in a short amount of time that there was a significant amount of debt and deferred maintenance, failure to spend on physical plant. You could tell there were cases of putting a finger in the dike here and there, but that was it."

Did the Board get that? An equally fair question might be, did faculty and staff get the Board? Doug Monforton undertook his own survey of those populations to explore the perceptions of the Board. The unscientific, soft poll yielded the following results:[45]

"Nice people that like to drink."

"The Board is invisible."

"More of a reunion than a management meeting."

"Good old boys" got mentioned twice.

Kris Sakelaris agrees with that very phrase as an assessment.

"You had to be a male," she said. "How does that fit with a Christian Humanist institution?"

By far though, the most common answer to the survey was "None."[46] In other words, no perception because many reported "no interaction" with any of the Board's members. One cannot form a solid, informed perception without interactivity. This tracks with my own experience. Recall those cold, bitter nights of January 2017 when I started researching just who composed our Board.

Even the institutional/community study completed by the vaunted Pelican Group consultants painted a less-than-flattering portrait of the Board of Trustees and a financial situation upon which respondents claimed they could only speculate. The following findings are responses regarding willingness to participate in a capital campaign:[47]

-"Interview participants regard the Board of Trustees as less than transparent and effective. They believe that over the years Board members have lacked the requisite skills and abilities to provide effective administrative guidance."

-"Numerous participants mention their concern about the College's lack of financial transparency and the perception of poor fiscal management."

Kris Sakelaris, at least, argues on her own behalf that she maintained continued personal connection to the campus. She would attend College events, eat with faculty and students in caf, and overall make herself a presence on campus. I can attest to this fact, having met and spoken with Sakelaris in several such instances. It also helped that her daughter, B.K. Sakelaris, attended Saint Joe and lived on campus.

"I engaged!" Kris Sakelaris said. "A Board member once said to me, 'I hear we have an MBA program now.' Well, I *knew* there was because I was on campus! There was no engagement. They had no idea what was going on. There was just no heart in that Board Room. If we could have taken the enthusiasm of the Alumni Board and combined it with the Board of Trustees, it would have been powerful. But…how can you know what's going on if you only meet two times a year?"

"I've never been on a board where that happened," said Carol Wood of the disconnect. "We were able to talk to people and people wanted to talk to us. We could raise money doing that and we proved that."

But how this money came in gave Larry Laudick cause for concern.

“Someone would die now and then, leave a couple hundred thou to SJC, and that’s what we would use to balance the budget. We were using too much soft money,” he said.

This leads to examination of another issue. There were claims by Board members that the full financial picture of the College was not presented to entire Board. Rather, according to Dad, only the operational budget was distributed. The difference being that an operational budget only shows income, expenses, and net loss or gain. The entire fiscal picture, on the other hand, includes physical plant, the endowment, and debt.

“We were never given enough information,” Carol Wood said and cited the February 2nd-3rd meeting to close as case in point. “We didn’t get documentation until five seconds before talking.”

Ben Sponseller and Larry Laudick present an alternate view.

“In order to stay abreast of and clarify questions around financial information, most Boards and certainly the SJC Board, expect and receive regular financial reports from the Administration as well as copies of the complete annual audits," Sponseller said. "In fact, the SJC Board must annually approve the outside auditors' report. While the outside auditors spend most of their reporting time with Board's audit committee, the entire Board receives copies of the full audit report. The chairman of the audit committee spends time reviewing the auditors' findings during full Board sessions, making observations about the meaning of its results, and encouraging all Board members to read and understand the audit."

As Chairman of the Finance Committee, Larry Laudick corroborates this statement.

"I personally handed them [audit reports] out after Stu Miller, our auditor, came and reported the audit to Finance Committee," Laudick said. "Every audit, after my first, was a clean audit. I would explain it line by line. And I could tell a few members had just opened their packet of information upon arriving at the meeting, since there wasn't a crease on any page. I would end my presentations with 'Any questions?' Anybody who said they didn't get enough information…that's bullshit."

Terra Maienbrook,[48] an Associate Professor of Accounting at Saint Joe, also served as the faculty representative to the Board of Trustees in the final years of the College.

"Audited financial statements—we had access to them," she told me. "We did get summary reports…we never went over them with a fine-tooth comb, but they were there if you wanted to look at them."

"There were 50-page documents, I think they had six copies of them you could look over if you were interested," Wood said.

"One word of caution," Maienbrook stressed, lending her professional expertise. "Audits are historical. They give you very little information about the future plans of the College. We were given lots of projections from the Business Office—all of them failed to have us with a balanced budget."

How much concern or sense of urgency did these projections generate? Well, if you've ever seen the film *Rashomon*, then you might already realize that any group of people can hear and see the same event and have multiple and contradictory recollections of it. Perception and very human personalities contribute in large parts to what constitutes "reality," and it can sometimes give one a creeping sense of unease as to how multiple people can live through the exact same experience, yet have entirely different understandings of it.

Dr. Ed Habrowski[49] is an alum of Saint Joseph's College and at one point in the late 1980s served as its Registrar before going on to become the Superintendent of the Rensselaer Central School Corporation. Like many in the Saint Joe community, I had known Habrowski in one capacity or another for several years and knew he possessed a commitment to and reverence for education and Saint Joseph's College that equaled that of my father's. Already a member of the Alumni Board, he came to serve as a Trustee in 2012, right around the same time I came back to campus.

"There was some sense of urgency and the adage "we can't kick the can…meaning debt…down the road anymore" emerged," Habrowski said of his first meeting in October 2012. "But, in my view, there was no sense of immediate urgency."

Larry Laudick came to a different appraisal of the situation.

"In 2012 I said, 'We've got five years left.'" Laudick argued. "Then it became we got four years left. Then three and so on. I said, 'Guys! Something's got to change!' We could never figure out what to do."

For his part, Laudick lobbied for offering online courses just like many colleges both large and small. Many of the Saint Joe faculty dragged their feet on the proposition. I can confirm this as I sat at the table of many discussions of the matter both formal and informal. Several of my colleagues could not see how the Core program could be successfully moved online when so much depended upon face-to-face, small group discussion and interaction. In this regard, our operating position was rather unique among higher education and that, in its own way, may have been a considerable stumbling block as more and more institutions moved online effectively.

On the subject of fundraising, what role did the Board have? Larry Laudick reports that many, if not most, Board members contributed multiple thousands of their own dollars to Saint Joe. This corresponds to the vehement response Bob Neville received from another member of the Board, saying "Good luck finding a Board who gives as much as we do." At the same time, Laudick asked about the status of fundraising efforts.

"The priests told me, 'God will provide,'" Laudick said. "Then I asked them what we were doing to increase enrollment of new students. The priests again said, 'God will provide.'"

Laudick launched into a well-known joke about a man warned to leave his house due to an oncoming flood. Rescuers in a jeep, boat, and at last a helicopter are all turned away as the man stood with faith and said, "God will save me." After drowning, the man came to face God and asked why he was not granted salvation. God responded, "I sent a jeep, a boat, and a helicopter."

"It was deathly quiet after I told that joke," Laudick said with a slight laugh. "The priests were hard working men, but they didn't understand finances. They eventually asked me, 'Is this serious?' And said, 'Yes! It's serious!'"

"I recall Larry Laudick being very clear at every meeting I was at—we need to do something…we were running out of time," Maienbrook said. "I just never felt like anyone else in the room took him very seriously. I think people thought the money would somehow come or we would turn the ship in time. We never had any serious discussion about building an online college or merging."

Larry Laudick did indeed propose maybe merging with a financially stronger college or university. The suggestion, it is said, generated skepticism. Did any institutions in that moment in higher education want to take on Saint Joe? Would the Saint Joe alumni continue giving if the College were to no longer exactly be “their Saint Joe”? If a merger was indeed the way forward, then would it not be prudent to wait until the College hired a full-time, permanent president to oversee such a massive change?

Laudick proposed another tactic. After applying all the high discounts and sale prices, the cost of tuition at Saint Joe came down to about $18,000 in real terms.

“Why not advertise that as the price?” he asked. “I know other small colleges who were doing that and they attracted a lot more students that way.”

According to Laudick, other members of the Board felt that such a price would devalue the true worth of a Saint Joe education and make the College look cheap. Once again, alumni might not like the “actual price” either. Offered as case in point was the reaction that followed Saint Joe’s announcement that SAT or ACT scores would be strictly optional in a student’s application.[50] This was not an especially radical step as more and more academics and admissions departments began to see such standardized tests as blunt, ineffective tools in determining a student's academic aptitude. Instead, the test scores merely measure one's ability to take the SAT or the ACT. Worse yet, the tests carried racist and classist complications. A few Saint Joe alumni cried foul over the abandoning of the test scores, making such comments on social media as, "Thanks for devaluing my degree."

On the matter of raising funds via alumni donations, the Board split. Kris Sakelaris urged the Board to inform alumni of the deteriorating fiscal situation.

"We're family," she said. "Who do you go to when you need help? Your family. We have mortgaged the College to an inch and we have to do something. We need to have a 'burn the mortgage' campaign to retire the debt."

Others on the Board professed similar concerns as Doug Monforton and Paul Muller of the Gang of Four. Could telling the alumni cause a greater crisis? Could the debt figure get distorted through "grapevine" communication, and eventually make the amount sound insurmountable?

“In the fall of 2014 a subset of the Board reviewed potential correspondence to alumni that elevated the urgency for financial support to a much higher level than in the past,” Ben Sponseller said. “It was never sent out, due to concerns that it would be perceived as more of a reason NOT to give than to give. Some thought that people would not be inclined to give if we made it sound too much like a request to maintain the status quo, a plea for survival funds, or if it was about operating expenses rather than a more exciting cause, such as a major campus improvement.”

Fundraising, enrollment, and retention already presented challenges. What would sounding an emergency alarm do to those challenges? Can an institution of higher education turn to its left and cry out to its alumni for emergency funds while turning to its right to smile at high school seniors and their parents, cooing, “Hey, we’re still taking applications for fall,” plus somehow reassuring current students, “Sure, you’ll graduate from here”? Additionally, misperceptions among alumni already harmed Saint Joe as Larry Laudick saw it.

"I think alumni saw the Waugh land grant and thought we were in good shape and so they didn't donate much anymore," he said. "The problem was that because of the easement, we couldn't sell any of the land if we needed to."

Ed Habrowski also pointed out another unique aspect of the Saint Joe alumni as a whole. True, many of the Puma Board members did well for themselves in business just like others in the greater alumni population. However, the Catholic mission of the College meant that even more graduates went on to service professions. After all, the number one major at Saint Joseph's College for many years had been nursing, and education ranked not far behind. In other words, we turned out a lot of nurses and teachers who wanted to make the world a better place, and in America that does not tend to come with a great deal of monetary reward. Many alums might not be able to give as much as would be needed to even begin to offset the financial crisis. Conversations and questioning continued while a clear path forward never seemed to materialize from the talks.

“It is during these discussions, as well as during the financial reporting section of each Board meeting, that the entire Board had been repeatedly and transparently told that without increased profitable enrollment and increased giving, the model at hand cannot survive,” Sponseller said.

When Robert Pastoor came on as the permanent president in 2015, the Board and administration hoped that someone new would be able to help provide administrative leadership to set a course out of the morass.

“I thought it was good to get somebody from the outside to come in here with fresh eyes and do what has to be done,” Sakelaris said of the hire.

Any analysis of the situation would likely concur with Sakelaris. While a college board of trustees is, according to best practices, the entity primarily charged with creating policy, it is the office of the president that must execute and guide all action. As Townsley writes:

"The president's leadership underpins everything as he or she prepares the college community for the strategic revolution and the future of the college. Resistance to the new approach will undoubtedly surface, with influential members of the institution working at cross purposes with the leadership. But the president—invested with the confidence of the board, key members of the administration, and the college community—must authoritatively push the strategic plan ahead, noting, rather than entertaining, dissension."[51]

Whether it would be new programs such as online classes, a massive appeal to alumni, or even a merger with a stronger college, it would be the new president who would carry out the action. In September of 2015, Pastoor did engage the alumni with a one-page message carrying the large headline of "The President's Call to Action." The third paragraph contains the following sentence printed in bold: "The challenges that we face at Saint Joseph's College are real, and we must join together now to address these challenges." The paragraph goes on to describe a "significant" need to improve on campus infrastructure, increase enrollment, and "address debt." The final sentence is also bolded, reading: "But by failing to address these critical needs for our campus and our students, Saint Joseph's College can easily slide into irrelevancy with 21st century students of tomorrow."[52]

Odd vocabulary choices aside (we were already 15 years into the 21st century and thus our students at the time were already "21st century students"), this communication does technically support Ben Sponseller's and President Pastoor's claim of having announced the problem. The alumni were indeed notified of the Saint Joe's situation in 2015 and it cannot be claimed otherwise. Ben Sponseller points to this very message when asked why alumni were not notified sooner of Saint Joe's financial condition.

"If you look, you'll see things started to get more urgent," he said. "There was one [communication] that said it was a call to action. The school of thought says stay in touch with alumni which we did, but there's a point when alumni don't want to support efforts they don't believe are backed by financial pictures that are stable. We have some very generous alumni. But we never said if you don't give money, we'll close, but that is not the way to get a return from alumni."

There are, however, two issues to consider with the "call to action" notification.

For one, there are no numbers given as to the size of the $28 million debt plus interest over time, the amount needed to correct the issue of deferred maintenance, the amount of tuition discounts backed by nothing, and the annual budget shortfalls. In other words, the full context was not declared and thus the extent of the emergency wasn't either.

The second issue is one of graphic design. My copy of Pastoor's message came by email and it looks like most any other college e-fundraising appeal. It's possible I also received a hardcopy in the mail, but I have no recollection. That is because, like just about every other college graduate in the United States, I receive frequent mailings from every institution where I've earned a degree. I take newsletters or donation packets from the mailbox when I get home at the end of the day, I glance over them, and then I toss them in a pile before going to see if there's any salsa in the fridge. I do this because one mailing looks very much like all the others, and I daresay most other alums nationwide carry out a similar practice.

If, on the other hand, I saw communication designed and printed in blood red to reflect a "dire" situation at, say, DePaul University, announcing that closure was imminent (which would never happen to DePaul), I would sit down right away and read it to understand the situation. What's more, the 2015 "President's Call to Action" message carries the visual of a form letter. As mentioned earlier, the bolded sentences are buried in the third paragraph of a seven-paragraph letter that carries an overall positive and "we can do this" tone.

As analogy, imagine if you received the following "Christmas update" from a family member:

"Timmy is getting his braces off soon. Hannah just made the honor roll. Grandpa might not find a liver donor in time. Hey we're going to Busch Gardens next summer!"

The 2015 message carried neither context for the magnitude of the situation, nor any sense of the crisis. This seemed to indicate that the Board and the upper administration did not have a clear sense of how to communicate with alumni.

As 2015 turned into 2016, Carol Wood encountered the first indication for her that the College might be on the brink of financial exigency. She undertook a fundraising effort for specific improvements to the Chapel, including tuckpointing and the addition of a wheelchair access ramp. Wood claims Chairman Sponseller contacted her in May 2016 and asked who gave her permission to go through with the Chapel fundraising drive.

"He said 'If you go through with this we'll be the first closed campus with the best Chapel,'" Wood told me. "It's the first indication I had we were in trouble."

Later in 2016, results of the HLC site visit arrived and along with them a judgment of "probation." If you recall from the fall of that academic year, Saint Joe planned something of a three-pronged attack going forward. Faculty assumed responsibility to revitalize and reinvent majors and academic programs, while also looking at how to create "revenue positive" courses with no fewer than seven students in any class at any time. Thirdly, a recapitalization plan would buy three to five years of breathing room, but remained dependent on an offer from the Mayo Clinic for the Waugh farmland.

Saint Joe extended an offer to Mayo Clinic in a letter dated January 6th, 2017 from President Pastoor. "We have concluded that an outright sale of the Waugh Farm Land from SJC to the Mayo Clinic would be in SJC's best long-term interests," Pastoor wrote. "As a result, SJC now offers to sell the Waugh Farm Land to the Mayo Clinic for the cash sum of $25,000,000." The text also included that "monetization of the Waugh Farm Land is of great Importance [sic] to the continued financial viability of SJC and the furtherance of its educational mission."[53]

At the now-infamous January 2017 faculty meeting, Pastoor broke the news that the offer from Mayo came in much too low and that he "didn't have much runway to land this thing." Later, a written report from Pastoor provided to the Board of Trustees dated February 2nd, 2017 states, "The Mayo Clinic, while willing to participate in a transaction to purchase the land outright, has stated resolutely that their offer price would be in the neighborhood of $15 million. After significant pressure was applied during preliminary negotiations they indicated that the most they could possible imagine paying would be $25 million." The likelihood of the settled amount, however, was stated as being between $15-20 million, causing doubts as to whether even that amount would "provide us sufficient time to address our systemic and pervasive financial challenges and to address the HLC's concerns."[54]

There is, however, another school of thought on this statement from Dave Bechman.

“To my knowledge Mayo Clinic Foundation never made any type of offer to St Joe regarding the property,” he said. “I was told that someone approached Mayo on the College’s behalf, but based on my information that was not done as an official request from the College and Mayo did not make an offer.”

It must be noted though that Bechman stressed this is “purely secondhand information.” The only other possible corroboration comes from Kris Sakelaris, who said, “The Mayo Clinic never wanted the land.” This all joins that series of anomalies and contradictory claims floating in the ether during those foggy days of January 2017. It is difficult to ascertain a truly accurate picture vis-à-vis an offer to Mayo.

“And January was when they went to Hemmelgarn,” Kris Sakelaris told me. “Sponseller and Pastoor traveled to Ohio and met with him. That’s when they made the decision to close the College.”

According to Ed Habrowski, this meeting took place at the C.PP.S. Saint Charles Center in Carthagena, Ohio[55] on Monday, January 16th, 2017.

"I knew about this meeting date and called Sponseller and asked if I could also attend the meeting as well as visit some of the C.PP.S. at St. Charles," Habrowski said. "Sponseller told me that there was no need of me to attend the meeting. In my opinion, I think it was at that meeting where it was decided to close SJC between these three men and possibly the other C.PP.S. members who were on the Board. I have no evidence of this and I don't know if there were any minutes taken."

What was the significance of taking a meeting with the Provincial, Larry Hemmelgarn?

"Hemmelgarn once said, 'Everything has a life and maybe Saint Joe's life is over,'" Larry Laudick reported to me. "I thought 'Hey! You're giving up too soon.'"

Kris Sakelaris recalls the very same comment from Hemmelgarn.

" 'Things run their course,'" she reported him saying. "It struck me as odd at the time, but now…"

I did come into possession of text copied from an email between Hemmelgarn and Pastoor confirming a meeting did occur on or around January 16th, 2017 in Carthagena.[56] What all they discussed that day, however, remains unknown but to the parties present. But the faculty meeting where we learned of the College's "dire" situation occurred on Wednesday the 18th. In the minutes of that meeting, Pastoor is recorded as saying, "I went to Carthagena and spoke with the C.PP.S. They look at it differently than I do." The minutes make no mention of the date of that admitted meeting, nor do they clarify just how Pastoor and the clergy "saw things differently." If Pastoor elucidated on the matter during the meeting, my swirling brain caught none of it that night. What can be confirmed though is leadership at Saint Joseph's College examined two different merger possibilities.

In a document dated January 9th, 2017 and listed as being created by Spencer Conroy, Vice President for Business Affairs, a plan was put forth called "Marian Merger Conceptualization."

The plan presented three possible paths “forward for Saint Joseph’s College (SJC). It will illustrate the likelihood of success for several possibilities being considered and demonstrate why the Marian Merger option has the best possibility of future success and provides an opportunity for SJC to be a leader in higher education, serving as a model of partnership and innovation for other small colleges.”[57]

A neat, rubric-like graphic laid out the pros and cons of merging with Marian University, merging with Calumet College of Saint Joseph, or remaining an independent college. Each scenario was evaluated against several criteria, including continued C.PP.S. presence, retaining the Waugh income, and the strongest step towards removing HLC probation. Only a merger with Marian University earned checkmarks in every row, save for “no change to alumni support.” The plan post-merger called to “Completely re-invent SJC.” This meant eliminating all athletics and music, cutting the academic offerings down to somewhere between five and ten majors, and shuttering all buildings except for Halleck, Core, the Science Building, Justin, the Chapel and Schwietermann. Employees, both faculty and support staff, would likewise be scaled back in order to provide "just the bare minimum resources to support remaining students." Additionally, the Core program "would be changed significantly."

In other words, it showed a scenario not unlike the kind Bill White once imagined where "the axe really starts swinging" and perhaps as much as 75% of the Saint Joe faculty are laid off. Indeed, the plan called for the Board of Trustees to declare financial exigency on May 14th, 2017. What would be in it for Marian University? They would gain "a subsidiary College to serve the underserved and to advance mission throughout Northwest Indiana." Students successful on this campus might then transfer to the main Marian campus in Indianapolis and go on to complete other degree programs. The plan also offered speculation that such a merger would offer Marian an "opportunity to be a trend setter in higher education as well as to be a model for partnership that other small, private colleges could follow."

There is one other notable aspect to this merger plan.

"None of this was ever discussed with the Executive members of the Board," my father said.

A meeting of the Executive Board did take place, much prior to the date on the merger document, according to Ed Habrowski in December of 2016. Another meeting in late January 2017 followed.

"I was on the Executive Council as I was appointed Chair of the College's Mission Committee and attended both of those meetings along with Dr. John Nichols and Carol Wood. A sense of urgency, on the part of the Trustees, came to the fore," Habrowski said. "It was at these two meetings when the alarm sounded that SJC was running out of money."

Yet the proposed merger plan did not receive consideration. Thus, it may be speculated that the composers and negotiators of this proposal could have been acting on their own in an effort to somehow salvage parts of Saint Joe. But for whom?

“They did a lot of things without telling us,” said Carol Wood.

Obviously, this merger didn’t happen, although Marian does enter the picture a bit later. Why it didn’t happen is open to conjecture as none of the principal players involved wish to speak on the matter. One immediate possible reason for a rejection on Marian’s part is that the university’s leadership got a clear assessment of Saint Joe’s true financial state and then opted to decline. While there is a good deal of uncertainty which envelopes and obfuscates the events of January 2017, it is clear that a number of meetings were held and at least a few different plans germinated in secrecy with no involvement from Saint Joe faculty. It is therefore not unreasonable to ask the following question:

Was there any pre-planning of the closure? Chairman Sponseller’s response is as follows:

“In the days leading up to February 3rd and 4th [sic], I had no idea what would happen at the Board meeting in terms of a vote, or even if there would be a vote. I was in almost constant contact with certain members of the Administration to be sure as much data were available as possible. I will say the data was voluminous, and it clearly, very clearly, gave guidance as to what must be done if student and faculty were to be treated fairly. I wanted each and every Board member to have the opportunity to talk, reminisce, persuade, and opine at the Board meeting. They did."

Which brings us to the infamous days of February 2nd and 3rd of 2017, days of bright sun, but matched with a bitter cold that scythed across campus.

NOTES

1. Legon, et al. 26
2. Smith, Cindra J. ACCT Searches
3. Smith, Cindra J. 6
4. Smith, Cindra J. 14
5. Potter and Phelan 17-20
6. Cowen
7. Legon, et al. 27
8. Barringer and Riffe 166

9. Legon, et al. 29
10. Townsley 91
11. Roebuck and Snyder
12. Legon, et al. 31
13. Martin 80
14. Martin 79
15. "What Do Trustees Do?"
16. Trower and Eckel
17. Outka
18. I interviewed Larry Laudick on July 14th, 2020. Notes in author's possession.
19. Gerlach 195
20. Kenley
21. Townsley 92-94, and Van Der Werf "The Death of a Small College"
22. 2/10/2006 Board minutes in author's possession.
23. Ibid.
24. 5/9/2006 Board minutes in author's possession.
25. 2/9/2007 Board minutes in author's possession.
26. THIS MUST BE CONFIRMED
27. 2017 NACUBO Tuition Discounting Study
28. Selingo
29. 2011 Institutional Self-Study
30. "Obituary."
31. I interviewed Dave Bechman by email on 6/18/2020. Notes in author's possession.
32. "A View from the Windmills"
33. DiMento
34. Ibid.
35. "Saint Joseph's College Waugh Farmland Liquidation October 1, 2016"
    Document in author's possession.
36. Saint Joseph's College Fact Book 2014-2015, p. 4-5
37. Business Affairs Assessment, September 19th, 2012 in author's possession.
38. 5/13/2013 Board resolution in author's possession.
39. Ely

40. Ibid.
41. Dixon-Fitzwater
42. Dr. Stephen Hulbert's report to the Board of Trustees, August 28th, 2014, notes in author's possession.
43. Ibid.
44. Bangert, "Bangert: Saint Joseph's closing no surprise?"
45. Copy of survey results in author's possession.
46. Ibid.
47. Page 34 of report compiled by the Pelican Group in author's possession.
48. I interviewed Terra Maienbrook by email on 11/6/2018. Notes in author's possession.
49. I interviewed Dr. Ed Habrowski by email on 7/3/2020. Notes in author's possession.
50. Decision to go test optional was made by unanimous vote on September 16th, 2016 in an Executive Session of the Board of Trustees. Minutes in author's possession.
51. Townsley 122
52. Copy of email letter in author's possession.
53. Letter in author's possession.
54. President's Consolidated Report to the Board Trustees, February 2nd, 2017. Document in author's possession.
55. "Saint Charles Center, A Beacon of Faith."
56. Text from email in author's possession. Information listed in the DOC file reads that it was created by Robert Pastoor on 1/3/2017 and last edited by Sheila Hanewich, Pastoor's personal secretary.
57. Document in author's possession.

CHAPTER ELEVEN: "All honorable men"

Members of the Board of Trustees descended upon the campus on the afternoon of the 2nd from all ends of the nation for the most critical meeting in the history of the College. Nine of their number would be attending the meetings by phone. Those who made the effort to be there in person might have been met by Jackie Bradway. She positioned herself outside the Board Room, so she could greet each Board member as they arrived in the Chapel basement that morning of the 2nd.

"I stood there with my Alumni Association nametag on and a clipboard in my hand," Jackie said. "I had a list of all the Board members' names. Turns out I didn't recognize most of them, these businessmen, and I didn't know just how they got on the Board. So, I wasn't about to let them make ill-researched decisions about my College."

Like a Wal-Mart greeter, Jackie remained by the glass door to the walkway between the Board Room and Schweiterman Hall, the dormitory reserved for priests and adult students, and where several Board members would be spending the night. She stopped each Board member as they came in, introduced herself and her executive role with the Alumni Association, and encouraged the Board to work towards a solution to the current problem and not do something drastic. Her flesh-pressing did not go unnoticed. The head of campus security arrived and asked what she was doing. Jackie told him she remained polite and respectful, making mere introductions between herself and the Board members.

The security guard stayed and watched Jackie, and then must have been convinced of her good intentions because he walked away. Her encounters slowed to a trickle and then disappeared altogether. Late arrivals of Board members seemed to find an alternative door to enter.

"I think they were tipped off by the others that I was standing there," Jackie said. "So I moved over to the seating by the bathrooms by the Board Room. Those are the only bathrooms on the entire floor. I knew the trustees eventually had to go there."

Inside the Board Room, Kris Sakelaris took a seat next a long-time friend, one of the C.PP.S. priests who also happened to be an alum.

"He looks at me and says, 'This is so sudden. I can't believe we're going to close the College. I can't vote to close the College. What's going on?''" Sakelaris said. "It was the first time anybody had said anything to me about 'closing.' And he's asking me what's going on?"

To wit, Sakelaris held in mind the previous Board meeting on October 21st, 2016. Not only was said meeting a central component of the presentation she would make that night, it was also where Spencer Conroy, along with the Vice Presidents for Enrollment and for Institutional Advancement, gave a PowerPoint presentation for strategic goals and benchmarks for both enrollment and fundraising that would be met in 2017-2018. These included a fundraising contribution revenue goal of $3 million and a sharp decrease in the ratio of athletic to non-athletic students, thus sparing the 71% average discount rate granted to athletes. This presentation indicated forward thinking, not "dire need."[1]

Still in disbelief, Sakelaris' typical bright and extroverted demeanor turned subdued. She took a look around the mahogany-paneled room, listening to the dull rumble of meet-and-greet chitchat as the Trustees filtered in and found seats.

During my entire lifetime in the Saint Joe community, I think I might have been in that Board Room only once. We held a faculty committee meeting there, only because of a bizarre confluence of events and room availability. I recall thinking that if anyone ever needed a stereotypical set for a board room in a movie about a college or a deal made in a smokey chamber, this would be the place. Portraits hung on the wood panel walls of the Board Chairman, in this case Sponseller, of the President, in this case Pastoor, and the Pope, who I guess was Francis by that point. The chairs provided a hefty amount of cushiness, and a bar at the back offered libations.

The most significant aspect of the room, to my thinking anyway, is that it sat beneath the Chapel, the most historic building at the College and the centerpiece of the campus. Right in this iconic locality, the future, if any, of College would be decided. Did the locale inspire any Board members to save Saint Joe? Did they even notice the room and its place in Saint Joe history, or was it just a place to meet? What, if anything, would the space mean to those Trustees who phoned in their votes? Much of this may have weighed on Sakelaris' as she commenced what she would call "the most physically and emotionally draining two days of my life."

"We were locked in that room. Only reason we could leave was to use the bathroom," she said.

But word came of more alumni congregating in the lounge chairs near the bathrooms, right where Jackie took up station.

"I think there were about 30-40 students, faculty and alumni [who] were outside the Board Room," Habrowski said.

Yes, I in fact, I would later be one of those very faculty and alumni sitting with Jackie and the others in "the hospital waiting room" later in the evening. Leadership reminded Board members that all discussions were confidential and then instructed, in no uncertain terms, to speak to no one while on their way to and from the bathroom. Board leadership enacted a few extra steps to fortify this "cone of silence."

"Head of Security made sure no one entered the meeting except Board members and he accompanied Board members to the restrooms," Habrowski said.

Additionally, Habrowski, like several in the extended Saint Joe community, recalled the melancholic coincidence of the date.

"The meeting date is ominous as it was also the 44th anniversary of the Administration Building fire and in which some thought SJC would have to close back in 1973!" he said. "But Pumas at different levels rallied behind SJC and kept it going!"

That same spirit remained present in the Board Room…but not among all. That much became apparent as the meeting unfolded.

At 4:00pm the meeting came to order. Fr. Hemmelgarn led the opening prayer. Ed Habrowski read the College's Mission Statement. Sponseller reminded attendees of the importance of the meeting and throughout everything the students of the College must be the number one priority.[2] In that spirit, Jared Smith[3] took the floor first. Jared was a senior philosophy student at Saint Joe. The previous semester students elected him President of the Student Association, and as such afforded a voting position on the Board of Trustees. It was his very first Board meeting.

"I walked over to that meeting with my head held high," Jared said. "We were going to fix this. We had to fix this. Pastoor had told me we had time to fix it, and from my impression he seemed like a good dude."

Upon his arrival, the social temperature of room felt cold to Jared.

"The majority of the Board members avoided me like the plague," he said.

That is except for a few members.

"I remember Carol Wood welcoming me in and telling me we would do this right," Jared said. "Terra Maienbrook was of course hugely helpful in keeping me sane as she was the only other "outsider" as the faculty rep. Fr. Larry Hemmelgarn welcomed me warmly and assured me that we would do everything possible for SJC…"

As he rose to speak, Jared distributed letters to the Board. Each letter came from the hand of a current Saint Joe student and responded to the prompt, "What SJC means to me."

Kris Sakelaris spoke next and asked that her prepared remarks be added to the minutes.[4]

"The last two years have been particularly painful, with the last 2 months being nothing short of heartbreaking," she said. "As board members we all share the same fiduciary duty to the college. I, for one, am going on the record to say that I am not at all comfortable with the way things have transpired the last two months."

She went on to reference a Board meeting three years prior where she claimed to have been part of a break-out group tasked with wordsmithing a letter to alumni that would, with no ambiguity, lay out the true financial difficulties of the small college and to plea for help. The letter was never approved let alone sent "because this Board was afraid of the 'panic' that might ensue" if alumni knew such information. In addition, she referenced the October 2016 meeting where the Board voted to give the Executive Committee the authority to explore a transaction with the Mayo Clinic regarding the Waugh farmland, however no authority was extended from the Board as a whole for the administration or anyone else to investigate mergers with other colleges or make any major announcements to the community.

"The proper course of action, in my opinion, was to have called an emergency full board meeting, vetted all our options and then TOGETHER voted on a course of action," Sakelaris said. "Ironic that the panic we so wanted to avoid 3 years has now ensued. But be assured that that panic, is not alone, it is peppered with great anger."

Before sitting down, she distributed her own collection of letters. This time they came from alumni and other concerned constituents of the Saint Joe community, but they responded to the same prompt: "What SJC means to me."

A break for dinner followed, but not before President Pastoor passed out a document containing the financial situation and visions of possible futures. He asked Board members to review the information as they ate in order to have a baseline with which to engage later.

Such a simple act of taking a break to eat together can reveal so much about human beings and allegiances. These are obvious in any high school cafeteria, and so it often goes with adults in the professional world. Upon examination, a picture begins to emerge of a board divided into four distinct camps. Each camp ate in their own grouping that night.

First, the loyalists wanted to keep Saint Joe open and its mission alive by any means necessary. They also believed they never received adequate information as to anything going on. Second, the pragmatists, people a bit more "in the know" about the financial situation, possessed grim outlooks for the College. They also maintained that any and all information was always available. Third…and I don't know what else to call them…you had the detached. These Board members fall into the category of "nice people who like to drink" as mentioned on the Doug Monforton survey, and their interests leaned towards the social aspects of being on the Board, and they may not have possessed an understanding of the situation one way or the other. As Kris

Sakelaris said, "How do you know what's happening if you only meet two times a year?"

Finally, the four members of the C.PP.S. dined together in seclusion that night and their discussion is known only to them.

Shake and serve, and you've got one volatile cocktail poured into a board room-shaped decanter.

"It [the Board] was divided," Carol Wood said.

"Very fractured," Laudick agreed.

Dinner ended and Pastoor made his presentation along with two of his vice presidents. He began by extoling the virtues and "C.PP.S. mission" of the College.[5]

"Therefore, it is with a heavy heart that I present a report to the Board of Trustees which includes options for the future which are particularly difficult," he said.

The Board learned that Saint Joe would run out of cash by "mid-year 2017." A $5 million shortfall was expected and even if that amount were somehow fall into the institution's lap by May, another $15 million would be needed "soon thereafter."

"We were told the gravity of the situation, just how much debt we were in," Jared Smith said. "And yet to hear the VPs and Pastoor tell it, this was a seeming act of God, one that could not be foreseen and one that could not be pinned on anything except damn kids not wanting to go to college."

Conroy presented a few options, such as cutting costs, renegotiating the debt, and generating revenue. Debt renegotiation would be unlikely due to issues with suitable collateral and most of the revenue generation methods had already been tried or would need significant capital of their own to even get off the ground. For cutting costs, though, the College faced a few options.

Like cutting all athletic and music programs.

I asked Bill Massoels, then the Athletic Director for Saint Joe, if anyone on the Board or in the Administration ever discussed this scenario with him.[6]

"I had one conversation with Pastoor for about five minutes," Massoels said. "He pulled me out of practice the day of the [January] faculty meeting when he told the faculty that the Board was going to discuss things at their February meeting…So no, NOTHING was discussed with me prior…I do find it odd that they thought they could stay open without those two groups [of students], look at how many students were in those two groups. Without them, you don't have many students."

Perplexing indeed that such a scenario could even be considered as viable. Despite its questionability, inclusion of the option did perhaps serve a rhetorical purpose.

"It was intended to look terrible, so that their real proposal would appear the most attractive," my father said.

And the "real" proposal? According to meeting minutes, Conroy argued: "The recommended course of action is to suspend all academic activities on the Rensselaer Campus."[7] The nursing program would continue to be offered at St. Elizabeth's Hospital. The presentation shifted to covering layoffs, severances according to handbook, and Dr. Pulver outlined a "Teach-Out" plan of various universities where students could transfer and complete their education on time. "The 'Teach-Out' will be submitted to the HLC for approval."[8] This "suspension of operations" would, in theory, allow for pause in order for the College to pay down the debt and to reinvent itself for the future. In what way exactly? According to the President's Consolidated Report to the Board of that night:

"We can create the antidote to the problems within the educational system. The problems begin at the first levels of our children's lives. The formidable years are stoked with experiences that tell our students to, 'Sit in rows. Be quiet. Quit moving. Just answer my question.' Students matriculate through a system that is focused more on data than development. Data (test scores, feedback, education plans) are supposed to drive innovation, not create stagnation. Children of all ages learn to resent school, schedules, routines, and instruction. Those that continue on to higher education are often the individuals who learned to conform and work within the broken system. Education is meant to spur the spirit, enrapture the soul, and produce passion."[9]

The "Cardinal and Purple would break the traditional, higher education mold," it would "reach out to those who need it most – students forgotten by the broken system," and educate with "Gospel Values."[10]

How any of that would come to pass or precisely what concrete curriculum or pedagogy would be executed was not provided, though. I showed this proposed plan to Bill White to get his rhetorical analysis.

"This has Tom Ryan's fingerprints all over it," Bill said.

My own rhetorical analysis resulted in the same conclusion given other written and conversational expressions from Ryan, where he extolled education steeped in "Gospel values," and spent a lifetime expressing bitter venom towards classrooms arranged in rows. While this is by no means a "smoking gun" of authorial identity, the presence of this "vision of the future" in President Pastoor's report to the Board suggests in rather strong terms that academic leadership already began a pivot towards a "new Saint Joe" before the vote, and did so by consulting very few…if any…faculty.

As the evening wound down, a member of the Board's Finance Committee argued that deciding on the matter by the following day would allow students more time to find new colleges and for professors to seek new jobs. Larry Laudick found himself thinking similar thoughts.

"My biggest fear sinking in was that we would run out of money halfway through the 2017-2018 academic year," Laudick said. "That wouldn't be fair to the students. That wouldn't be fair to the faculty."

The thoughts of other Trustees tended towards the spiritual. After all, the Chapel was one floor above their Board Room where a mass and prayer vigil took place.

"I thought of the alumni sitting there in the Chapel," Carol Wood said. "People who were genuinely concerned. Not Board, not faculty, but regular people."

"I felt for the students, faculty, and staff," Ben Sponseller said. "I often thought of Jesus on Holy Thursday when he asked His Father to let this cup pass. I wanted this cup to pass for me."

If someone told me I shared the exact same thought as Ben Sponseller on the night of February 2nd, 2017, well, I would have responded with incredulity…an incredulity I now see as unfounded and misguided.

The Board adjourned. Night fell away and morning came. The second day.

Jared woke up that morning and went to grab his shower kit.

"I realized I was out of shampoo and conditioner," he said.

Quite a predicament due to Jared's long hair. He needed to go across the street in the freezing cold to Wal-Mart. Upon reaching the store, he found it yet to open for the morning. That meant going further down the street to Walgreens and crossing his fingers to get back to the apartment with time to shower and not be tardy to the Board meeting.

"I guess it ended up be a shitty omen for the morning I should have paid attention to," he said.

At the same time, Carol Wood hosted several members of the Board at her house that morning for breakfast, including Kris Sakelaris, Ed Habrowski, and my father.

"We needed to get our game plan together," Sakelaris said. "Clearly they [pro suspension Trustees] had their game plan."

As they discussed the situation though, reviewing the reports and recommendations of the night before as well as gauging the reactions of other Trustees, a sobering reality settled upon the twelve.

“We knew we were on the short end of the vote,” Wood said.

“I wasn’t letting any of the Board out without a fight,” Sakelaris said despite the assessment. “It was worth it.”

Together, the “Keep Saint Joe Open” coalition of the Board of Trustees determined to make their stand for the College that day.

Just how Alamo-like that action would be was underscored by the very first agenda item for the meeting: a presentation on how to close a college. Dr. Jean Scott spoke to the Board.[11] Dr. Scott was once President of Bradford College, which as shown before, was one of the very colleges Townsley examines as a case study of closed colleges in his book. On that day, Dr. Scott was President of Marietta College.[12] Before Saint Joe, President Pastoor served as a member of her cabinet in the form of Vice President for Student Affairs.[13] No doubt Pastoor personally asked her to present given her experience with a closing college.

“Closing or ‘suspending operations’ was the only option we considered that day,” my father said.

After explaining Bradford College’s particular circumstances that led to its closure, Dr. Scott said it was “extremely important for all members of the Board to present a united front in public.” They debated in private, but always presented as unified in public. This would of course. be in keeping with best practice research for college boards.[14]

One of the Saint Joe Trustees at one point during the discourse asked about how faculty members would fare on the job market. The questioner said they presumed the older and experienced tenured professors would have no trouble securing a new faculty position at another college. Professor Maienbrook explained that in academics, the opposite is the case. As for how the unemployed of Bradford College landed, Dr. Scott reported the following:

“Approximately one-third of the faculty found it easy to get a new job. Another third eventually found faculty jobs, but it was not so easy. The remaining third were unsuccessful in finding jobs in higher education."[15]

That described the academic job market for Bradford College professors in 2000. The prospects for Saint Joe faculty in 2017 promised to be several shades more dismal. Dr. Scott then spoke of possible emotional reactions from the community. What course of action did she recommend for aiding students in need of new schools and employees in need of new jobs and facing immediate financial uncertainty?

"If operations are suspended on the Rensselaer Campus, take time to recognize accomplishments and celebrate events. Remember the good things," Scott said according to the minutes.[16]

Once Dr. Scott concluded her presentation, Fr. Larry Hemmelgarn made a statement on behalf of the Missionaries of the Precious Blood. He stood before the assembled Board in his black, Roman-style cassock with a massive crucifix attached by a gold chain.

“Change is a constant,” Hemmelgarn said. “It is important to read the times and respond in an appropriate way.”[17]

He also argued that the best path forward would be to suspend operations then collaborate with another Catholic institution of higher learning. What’s more, he asserted that the C.PP.S. did not have a mission focused on education. Dr. Ed Habrowski counters this claim as being “not entirely correct.”

“He needs to do some research, vis-a-vis, the C.PP.S. archives and the archives of the Fort Wayne Diocese when the College was suggested by Bishop Joseph Dwenger, C.PP.S., second Bishop of Fort Wayne,” Habrowski said. “It was Dwenger who purchased land in the greater Rensselaer area to establish a COLLEGE.”

Indeed, all of Dr. Habrowki’s comments are reflected in Fr. Gerlach’s history of Saint Joseph’s College.[18]

The Board broke for lunch at approximately noon.

Jackie Bradway sat in the tense "waiting room" during this lunch, in the same seat where she spent all morning as well as the previous night. She noticed two polished-looking women in business suits seated a few tables away. Jackie, having worked in public relations, knew "the style" of various firms. Her estimation was that the women came from the Borshoff firm in Indianapolis.[19] During the lunch break, Bradway reports Hemmelgarn emerged from the Board Room and brought an older woman over to the two ladies seated at the table.

"They all patted each other on the back about a decision letter from Hemmelgarn," Jackie said. "He was saying, 'Isn't this a good letter? Didn't I do a good job?' This was three hours before any vote."

After lunch, the Board went into Executive Session.

"It was not fun," Larry Laudick said, and then paused a moment to contemplate. "Vicious isn't the right word…contentious. It was the most contentious meeting I've ever been in."

“Emotionally contentious,” Habrowski concurred then added, “But civil.”

Jared Smith recalls the conversation as being but an extension of Dr. Scott’s presentation.

“Rather than really debate whether or not the College should close, we spent the majority of the time talking about who would work with the bank and if the PR firm’s press release sounded okay,” he said.

He knew he needed to do something. Jared spoke up. He asked the Board if the College could remain open for the next year while students and alumni worked to raise money necessary to try to keep the College afloat. He then watched Fr. Hemmelgarn “laugh in my face as though I did not belong there and suggested ‘we simply print more money.’”

One more pro-Saint Joe voice stood to be heard, one most practiced in rhetoric.

"I made an impassioned speech as to why we needed to keep the College open," my father said.

He argued, as corroborated by Dr. Ed Habrowski and Professor Terra Maienbrook, that Saint Joe should remain open as the College had a mission to serve for the good of the Church and that the Core program was the avenue of keeping SJC alive and open. By supporting Core, the C.PP.S. spirituality was a witness to the growth of the College and the improvement of the human condition.

Would that plea, along with contributions from Sakelaris, Habrowski, and Wood, be enough to sway any of the possible fence-sitters that day in the Board Room?

Outside in the "waiting room," Jackie Bradway received a startling notice in her email. A friend sent her a screen capture from Marian University's website inviting Saint Joe students to transfer to Marian. A slate of welcome sessions had already been scheduled on the Marian campus. It was the same announcement

Bill White showed me that day as I walked Eric Mills around campus. Jackie bit her lip for a moment, then looked over at the women she suspected as being PR reps.

"I decided to make a loud comment," Jackie said. "I started passing my phone around to the other alumni, saying 'Look at this! Look at what's on Marian's website!"

In Jackie's telling of the account, one of the women in business suits whipped her phone from her pocket and held it to the side of her face. After that, she started screaming.

"That's not supposed to be out there yet! What the fuck is it doing out there? Take it the fuck down!"

Back in the Board Room…the voted commenced.

At first, it would be by anonymous ballot. Kris Sakelaris moved fast to change that. In her view, everyone needed to take responsibility for their vote.

“I was the conscience of the goddam Board,” she said.

The motion seconded to the floor by Fr. Larry Hemmelgarn was simple. “Suspend all academic operations at Saint Joseph’s College, Yes or No?”

One at a time, around the table and the telephones, each Board member cast their vote.

“It was tense,” Wood recalled. “Everybody was keeping track of the vote with their own pen and paper.”

She voted “No” but said, “I knew we were going to close.”

“I sat there keeping score on my notes packet,” Jared said. “I allowed myself to hope as we were in the lead at one point, all for it to be quickly dashed by the string C.PP.S. of votes.”

Hemmelgarn voted “Yes.” When it came a priest’s turn to vote, Sakelaris reported that Hemmelgarn would look over at each of them as they spoke “Yes” and he nodded his head. What of her friend in the C.PP.S.? The one bewildered the previous day that closure or "suspension" was even on the agenda?

"He looked down at the table in front of him and said 'Yes,'" Sakelaris said. "He wouldn't even look at me."

Sakelaris, Habrowski, Maienbrook, Jared Smith, and of course Dad, all voted "No."

Sponseller voted "Yes."

"I knew I was the chairman and that ultimately it was me who would be at the other end of the pointing fingers," he said of his vote. "And I was willing to do my duty, primarily out of love for and in thanksgiving for all the sacrifices the Precious Blood have made for me."

It came to be Larry Laudick's turn. He drew in a slow breath, choked a bit, and then voted "Yes."

"It was the hardest thing I've had to do," Laudick said. "But there just wasn't a way forward."

The motion carried 18-12 with seven of the 18 "Yes" votes coming via telephone or otherwise in absentia.

"I was naïve to think we had a fighting chance going in that day," Sakelaris said.

"Enemies were made that day," Wood added.

The Board members gathered their things at the end of the most somber moment in Saint Joe history. Tears rolled down cheeks, but not every cheek.

"Some of the 'Yes' votes were laughing and joking," Jared said. "Like they hadn't just stolen my home away from me. Like they hadn't just forbidden my fiancée and I from getting married in the Chapel…they were fucking laughing, Jon."

Many of those who voted "No" prepared to accompany Ben Sponseller over to the Shen Auditorium for the official announcement. What of those who voted "Yes?"

"They high-tailed it out of there," Sakelaris said.

“They got out of Dodge,” Wood agreed. “That bothered me more than the actual vote. No running away. You made this decision, now own it.”

“I remember the scared looks on the Board members as they saw the students and alums amassed in the Chapel basement,” Jared said. “I heard their requests that security escort them out.”

Jared came out of the room and found Jackie Bradway. Without speaking, he took her in his arms and gripped tight, tears flowing down his face, as he “apologized for failing.”

“What’s scarred into my mind though is what happened after the meeting ended,” Jared said.

He walked out of the Chapel basement and headed for the Core building and the Shen. His mind raced, trying to process what just happened, but not having much success. He lifted his phone to his mouth and called his fiancée, asking her to meet him in front of the Core building before going into the Shen. They found each other.

“Then I broke down in her arms bawling,” Jared said. “I couldn’t help but feel that I had failed every person in that room [the Shen] and I felt fucking guilty in spite of my vote to keep the place open.”

The announcement in the Shen kicked off an awful night for Kris Sakelaris. She spent it with her daughter B.K. in the student apartments, crying with the students.

“They [the Board members who voted “Yes”] made a liar out of me,” she said. “There were seven students I personally recruited. They weren’t going to graduate. I personally called their parents and said I was sorry. It was horrific.”

For Trustees such as Wood and Sakelaris, the drama would drag on for another two full months as the Board continued to meet each week by phone to oversee the “wind down” operation. Rather than acting on a decision in unity after a vote as best practice research prescribes, those final weeks served only to underscore the reality of deep rifts in the Board’s composition.

“The 12 who voted to keep the College open were cut out of the process,” Sakelaris said. “I’d ask a question. Dead silence for something like 30 seconds. Then Ben would say, ‘Okay, next item on the agenda.’”

In a further departure from best-practice research, Sakelaris and others commented open and often with others in the community as to how they saw the meeting of February 3rd unfold. Others of the Board, particularly C.PP.S. members it is said, chastened the opposition for violating confidentiality rules of the Board. Such rules, according to Sakelaris, exist nowhere in the Board’s by-laws.

“I got yelled and screamed at for violations,” she said. “You talk about confidentiality, what about fiduciary responsibility? You’ve devastated a town, you’ve taken away people’s livelihood. You might have thought we were going to be one voice, but I never agreed to that.”

This tension in the organization intensified as Habrowski, Wood, and Sakelaris, each of them members of the Alumni

Board, hustled to meet the challenge of fundraising $23 million before May, sending what one might interpret as yet another signal of a splintered Board. One of the "Yes" voters told Sakelaris "Well, I can tell you haven't gotten your head around the decision."

"Well yeah!" Sakelaris said she responded. "Because you made the decision for us!"

As faculty and students went through the horror of those weeks, Board members went through a tumult of their own. In the President and VPs presentation of February 2nd, they portrayed a scenario where Saint Joe would hold on to its nursing program while suspending all other operations. They believed this would be a pathway to retain both accreditation and Waugh property income for said income was dependent upon Saint Joe remaining an educational institution. They could not hold on to the nursing program. They surrendered accreditation. As rumors percolated that the campus might be turned into a Catholic prep high school, there likewise came rumors that no one seemed to realize just how long it takes to become an accredited high school in Indiana and the plan, whether substantial or not, sank into the same sand as the nursing program and the College's accreditation, despite any claims of "we know how this will work."

"They were lying to us the same as they were lying to you guys," Carol Wood told me.

While flailing and spit-balling went on for the future, the "wind down" operation continued to unfold on campus. Administration issued an order of stewardship and retention of all campus assets. This order, seen earlier taped to a faculty member's door, came from the office of the Vice President for Business Affairs, and thus presumably from presidential order. Athletic Director Bill Massoels told me he was "treated like shit" by administrators despite having been a member of Puma athletics for 27 years. He was informed, in no uncertain terms, that should any single item of athletic equipment end up missing or not returned they would turn him in to "the authorities," presumably suggesting Rensselaer police. As revealed in August of 2017, this draconian effort regarding assets was undertaken in order to get the maximum cash value from the auction sale.

"I did not like the way we closed the place," Larry Laudick said. "I was not impressed by how Larry Hemmelgarn and the C.PP.S. seemed to take control."

Once the weeks wore away and the final ever Saint Joe commencement came and went, every member of the Board resigned and the dust at last settled. There remain a few key figures and mysteries though to examine. One figure is Vice Chairman Steve Ruff. He told me the following:

"I am content with the Board's efforts to find new colleges for its students to attend and I am content with the Board's efforts to make the financial landings for each faculty member and for each hourly staff worker post cessation of academic activities to be as soft as financially feasible.

"Jon, this chapter in the College's life is now over. The page needs to be turned."

Another figure is Congressman Todd Rokita, the House Representative for Indiana District 4. That is Rensselaer's district. What's more, he served as a member of the House Committee on Education and the Workforce.[20] His motivations, as logic would dictate anyway, would have been to protect the economic well-being of his district and to find ways to continue to provide education and work skills development for the people of Indiana. Rep. Rokita did not respond to press requests for an interview in the aftermath of February 3rd, 2017.[21] What is known is that as per Board meeting minutes, he voted to "suspend operations" and he did so by phone.[22] Motivation for his vote is known only to him.[23] Rokita later went on to run for Senate, but lost.

Yet one other untold aspect of the saga that I wanted to know was what was it like for Ben Sponseller? He is after all a human being and he became in those final months the most public face of the collapse of Saint Joseph's College. As such, he bore the brunt of all backlash and was subjected to vituperative and vitriolic attacks both in the digital domain and in real life.

Not one, not two, but three votes of no confidence passed against him. There must have been deleterious effects. What got him through it?

Steve Ruff.

“I was miserable for weeks and months,” Sponseller said. “Thank God for Ruff, my good friend and sacred confidant. But I knew then and I know now that the Board made the correct decision, one that allowed the students, faculty and staff time to transition in a timely fashion.”

“I still wake up at night and wonder ‘what if?’” Sakelaris said. “Had we gone to the alumni, we might still be in the same place, but there wouldn’t be all this anger.”

Though boisterous throughout our conversation, Sakelaris turned quiet and solemn.

“I failed,” she said after a beat. “The whole Board failed.”

“It was the whole Board. The result of a fractured Board,” Wood said in her own verdict.

"Yes! The whole fucking Board!" my father said and shook his head. "That decision to take out more bonds but then never pay them off…that's what sunk us."

That phrase. "The whole Board." Or even just "the Board." It encompassed many people over many years who involved themselves in institutional decision-making with varying degrees of energy. "The whole board" also carried a truth inside it. This truth grew throughout my research like a worrisome, then ominous embryo. During the process it evolved and began to creep and crawl, revealing itself just a bit at a time. In tackling the clunking and out-synch-motor and machinery that was the Board of Trustees, the slithering thing at last broke through the surface to sit full up to stare me in the eyes. Its tail coiled about its haunches while a strident hiss escaped its mouth. This truth would no longer be ignored.

Dad was a Board member. He served as a Trustee for many years in fact. Board minutes reflected a number of unanimous votes, including the vote to take out those additional bonds and add them on to the debt, and granting alienation protection to the C.PP.S. This of course means Dad endorsed the measures. With those votes, he, in effect, bore a share of culpability in undoing his own life's work. "Hoisted on his own petard."

He also kept a ringside seat for Board affairs all those years and like so many others, did not recognize the reality of the situation. He attended the December 2016 meeting of the Executive Board, yet appeared sucker-punched in January 2017 when I came to him after the faculty meeting and reported we'd been told that the College teetered "at a precipice." If he sat in on the Executive Board meeting, shouldn't he have already been aware? Shouldn't he have warned his sons? When I set out on my journey to find "the truth," this was a "truth" I did not foresee. Then again, there are never guarantees that you'll like the truth when you find it.

I did not know how to approach this matter. I did not even want to approach this matter. Yet anyone with any amount of intellectual honesty would rightly demand that it is exactly the matter I must approach. I asked a friend for help.

"I think he thought that if you just believe enough in the institution, and you work hard enough, and you pray hard enough, then everything will be all right," Brian Capouch said to me. "I've noticed that among members of Catholic organizations."

Dad also has tendency to cling to any glimmer of positivity. As example: Right after undergrad, I applied to a graduate program in the most half-assed way anyone could, for as I said before, I did not yet have any kind of real bearing on who I was or what I wanted to do. Only much later in the admissions process did I find out that the program accepted a mere two applicants per year.

"I knew that," Dad told me later. "But I thought you might be one of the two!"

Of course I wasn't.

My best guess is that Dad must have heard something at the Executive Committee meeting similar to the patter thrown at the community in late January, something along the lines of “there are still a few things we can try,” and he locked on to the phrase.

I confess, I spent days, months even, not sure at all as to how I would discuss this with Dad. We both lost something. Now, ruminating in the dark of night once more, I felt like I was losing something else, only “something else” eluded identification. I only knew I didn’t like it. Sitting in his study one December morning, I at last asked him. When I finished speaking, he went quiet and looked out his window at the snow for a moment, his face frozen still.

“I understand institutional finance on a sophomore level,” Dad said. “I can read a balance sheet, I can manage an academic budget. For anything beyond that I relied on the advice of the Board’s Finance Committee. I’ll take full credit for the academic quality of the College. That was my focus. I see now that a Trustee’s duty includes far more than that. I recognized that too late and I’ve been chastising myself for it.”

I was this many years old when I fully learned my parents don't know everything, and that they are as flawed and human as anyone else. A solemn end came to a childish notion.

If we take the deliberations and actions of the Board of Trustees of Saint Joseph's College and view them through the lens of research in best practices presented at the beginning of this chapter, what conclusions might we draw?

Legon argued for board members with knowledge of business and finance, but also for members well-versed in the mission and the workings of higher education. Going through the roster of the Saint Joe Board, I counted maybe six people out of 30 who might qualify as "experienced" with colleges. Legon also warned of varying degrees of trustee commitment. This is most evident in the third of the Board I would classify as "detached." These being the "nice people who like to drink," the ones Jared Smith saw joking at the end of the vote to close (or "suspend"), and the ones who more and more regularly attended by phone, especially during inarguably the most critical Board meeting in the history of the College. The influence of this element may also be evident in the vote tally. Knowing my penchant for science fiction, Bob Neville used a metaphor to explain it.

"Say you were an alien who dropped down from space for that February Board meeting," Bob said. "You know nothing about the College, but you look at the documentation provided that day, you listen to the Vice President for Business Affairs, and first thing in the morning on the 3rd, you see a presentation on how to close a college. Afterward you'd say, 'Well of course we have to close.' If someone hadn't been paying attention through the years, it would look like something out of the Board's control reared up and there was no other choice."

Placing myself in the position of a Board member on the afternoon of February 3rd, I conceded that indeed I would have voted to close.

Best practices also call for assessment and self-evaluation of the functionality of a board. According to my father, the Board did undergo periodic assessments. The rubric for this procedure came from the Association of Governing Boards and examined academics and general oversight of the Board. It is uncertain just how useful this assessment process was. Given the ultimate result, the outcome of the assessment was either inaccurate or misunderstood, or perhaps the process of measurement was flawed.

There were also tests administered by the Department of Education to determine the financial health of an educational institution through ratio analysis involving income, assets, liabilities, and debt service. I was somewhat familiar with this concept after speaking with Mark Nestor and hearing about how he determines the fiscal health of a client. In 2014, Saint Joe "passed" this ratio test.[24] But these ratios can be deceptive.

"They can show you that you're really sick, but they don't predict death…until you're dead," Dad said.

Looking at things through another perspective, Martin gave his own cautionary tale of how faculty can often be unaware of the depths to which board members selflessly give of their own time and finances. I can without doubt testify to my own opaque view of the Board. That view should be evident by this point. In reality, many of the Board were Saint Joe alums who, from what I can now see, kept the best interests of the College and its extended community in their sight even when they voted to suspend operations. My conversation with Larry Laudick is evidence enough of that truth. As Shakespeare wrote in Julius Caesar: "—for Brutus is an honorable man; they are all honorable men," even if that day they felt forced to thrust a dagger into the heart of Saint Joe.

At the same time however, Cowen called for "principled decisions responsive to the particular realities you confront." It's hard to see what responsive actions and decisions came as answer to mounting debt, declining enrollment, and decaying infrastructure. Sponseller said both at his meeting with employees on February 6th, 2017 and in several interviews that the Board "looked at many" options. Somehow though, that led to only one being presented to the Board on the morning of

February 3rd, 2017, that being a former university president giving guidance on how to close a college. Likewise, it is difficult to understand why there came no open-arms embrace of the proposal and offer from the Gang of Four. When speaking to Trustees, I always asked if the proposal ever made it in front of the Board. The answer was always "no."

"First I heard of it was when the op-ed appeared in the *Republican*," Carol Wood said.

"Mystifying" is the word I would choose to describe rejecting discussion of the plan at the Board level or at the very least the presidential, and thereby making a decision to "go it alone." There may be one explanation, though. As I have said before, just how does a college cry out for financial help while trying to recruit enough students to reverse course on a downward trend in enrollment? This kind of precarious Catch-22 can lead to a sort of psychological paralysis where one feels stuck, unsure which way to move, or if they should even move at all. And "stuck" is indeed an apt descriptor of the Board I came to know. A cloud of dense fog sat between where they were and where they wanted to be, but there seemed to no way whatever to remove the fog and to once more see things in the clear.

But a final question remained for which I needed satisfaction. The thought's germination began back in 2018 as I sat sullen in the booth of the pizza place during the RPI. I had just overheard someone chastise us for our inability to recognize Saint Joe's imminent collapse. It was a dreadful revelation that led to equally dreadful speculations. The possible explanation of a sort of subconscious "willful ignorance" on the part of large swaths of the community moved from being a possible reason to being one of the primary reasons. As Ben Sponseller told me:

"The love people have for the institution, and their desire to keep the doors open for the sake of the students, blinded so many of us. It silently urged us to continue at all costs and obfuscated our view of the facts in favor of taking on more debt, delaying key maintenance, and increasing tuition discount rates well above the market." He closed his correspondence with "Forever a Puma."

There it was. “Too loved to fail.” The “College that would not die” would always find a way to come back.

Not on February 3rd, 2017.

Of any of Sponseller’s statements either to the community at large, or to me in interview, I find this confession to be the most telling, forthright, and human of them all. As he said in his opening remarks at the student forum on February 6th, 2017, “We didn’t want to change this place we love.”

Jackie Bradway told me that after she went into full PR/journalist dynamo mode to save Saint Joe in 2017, the TV and radio reporters she met with often offered the same response to her story: “Where is this mythical Camelot people keep talking about? We’ve never heard people talk with such love about their college.”

Indeed, so many of us did love Saint Joe and saw it as such a special place in the world. While unquestionably true for us, that point of view came accompanied by a myopia, a sense that we would shield it from any true harm, despite at least a basic awareness of the considerable challenges we faced. This self-perpetuating psychology was endemic in Saint Joseph's College, much as it often is in collaborative human systems. In the last two remaining years, I can attest to a definite sense among faculty that we knew there was a problem and we knew we needed to change Saint Joseph's College. At the same time, however, many did not want to change things to the point where we would stop being Saint Joe, even if that would have been exactly what we needed to do. We would instead be the scofflaws of the academic set.

Well, I see now this as a sort of "magical thinking," particularly at the upper levels. No, more like "magical groupthinking." For so long, the idea of complete and utter collapse was unfathomable to many in the Puma community and the thought was seldom entertained, save for a few such as Bill White, and Bob Neville and the rest of the Gang of Four. Someway, somehow, someone would come through with the money. Anything else was unthinkable.

In June of 2017, just one month after the doors of Saint Joe closed, Chad Raymond wrote a piece for *Inside Higher Ed* called, “Here There is Danger.” Raymond, chair of the Department of Cultural, Environmental and Global studies at Salve Regina University, offered his own list of warning signs that a college is approaching failure. In the process of doing so, Raymond called us out a few times, particularly on our shock and surprise at our demise. “They had not given sufficient attention to evidence that their employer was in imminent danger of shutting down.”[25]

Though perturbed by Raymond’s flippancy at the time and by what reads like a callous disregard for those who lost jobs not only at Saint Joe but at other small colleges, I can no longer disagree with him. So many people beyond Ben Sponseller, beyond the Executive Board members, beyond the Board itself, either did not see fiscal realities or our minds simply could not entertain the idea of collapse until it was too late. These denizens of the Saint Joe community fell prey to one of the deadliest forms of magical thinking any human being could hold: “It won’t happen to us." I count my father in that number. I count myself in that number.

You don't recognize the signs when you don't want to see them.

The more I learned, the more my list of "villains" in the saga dwindled. No Saurons. No Darkseids. I now feel sympathy for my devils, and see love as a kind of blindness.

NOTES

1. "Division Goals" presentation in author's possession. It should be noted that the presentation indicates many of the goals outlined are predicated upon liquidity from a deal for the Waugh farmland.
2. Minutes of the 2/2-3/2017 Board Meeting. Document in author's possession.
3. I interviewed Jared Smith by email on August 13th, 2020. Email in author's possession.
4. Document in author's possession.
5. Quotes and details from the presentation come from President's Consolidated Report to the Board of Trustees, February 2nd, 2017. Document in author's possession.

6. I interviewed Bill Massoels by email on 8/6/2020. Notes in author's possession.
7. Minutes of the 2/2-3/2017 Board Meeting.
8. Ibid.
9. From President's Consolidated Report to Board of Trustees, February 2nd, 2017.
10. Ibid.
11. Minutes of the 2/2-3/2017 Board Meeting.
12. "President Jean Scott"
13. "Marietta College VP named President at Indiana college"
14. Minutes of the 2/2-3/2017 Board meeting.
15. Ibid.
16. Ibid.
17. Written statement from Fr. Larry Hemmelgarn. Document in author's possession.
18. Gerlach 8
19. I contacted Linda Jackson, formerly from Borshoff, on Twitter. She confirmed that she had worked for Saint Joseph's College, but could not participate in any interviews.
20. "Kline, Rokita Statements on Student Success Act."
21. Holden, "Rokita stays silent"
22. Minutes of the 2/2-3/2017 Board Meeting.
23. I contacted Todd Rokita's Attorney General campaign for an interview. There was no reply.
24. Saint Joseph's College 2014-2015 Fact Book 4-5
25. Raymond

CHAPTER TWELVE: The Summation

"The old man admitted to being a retired English professor who had been thrown out upon the world forty years ago when the last liberal arts college shut for lack of students and patronage."

-Ray Bradbury, *Fahrenheit 451*

We might have been screwed from the start.

Fr. Gerlach's history of Saint Joseph's College shows just how the Church came into possession of the land that would become Saint Joe. A man named George Spitler came to Rensselaer in the 1830s and built a house on the very land the Chapel would one day occupy. In 1866 it is said that Spitler was struck dead by a bolt of lightning while standing outside on that exact property. The family then wanted sell their land and move, so a Catholic priest acquired the land for the purpose of building orphanages. There are, of course, a number of quasi-spiritual interpretations, both benign and malevolent, one might make of a religious college built on land purchased after the owner fell dead, struck by a bolt from the heavens.[1]

In 2018, there came another cruel, symbolic bookend to the saga of Saint Joseph's College. On January 22nd of that year, the Center for Biological Diversity issued a press release announcing that the eastern puma was extinct. "The agency cited [eastern puma] habitat in the Adirondacks, New England, the Great Lakes region and elsewhere in the Midwest." Two years after Saint Joe closed, all signs of the species vanished.[2]

Bookends aside, I guess this is where you pin me down. I suppose this is the part where I present to you what killed Saint Joseph's College.

Saint Joseph's College came to an end in 2017 due to decades of financial deterioration overseen by a fractured, dysfunctional, and at times paralyzed, Board of Trustees. This is evident in the wholly different perspectives that remain to this day in separate sectors of the fractures. The Board of Trustees, as an entity, stopped functioning. Three separate bodies of the Saint Joe community passed votes of no confidence against Sponseller and Ruff, but this was something of an injustice.

The vote should have been against the whole Board of Trustees.

There was no cabal working to bring about Saint Joe's demise. No devious plot existed to take the College out of the hands of the community. There is no one person to blame. There aren't even just ten people to blame. Dozens upon dozens are culpable in the eventual demise of Saint Joe, including multiple incarnations of the Board over many years, overseeing a financial crisis with a genesis stretching back as far as perhaps three decades. Honestly, I'm surprised we lasted until 2017.

It would be an understatement to say I feel silly now as I look back now on all my hellfire-fueled calls to battle and "last stands." In February 2017, there was nothing left fighting for. I could not see it at the time, mind clouded with emotion and the fog of war, but everything was already gone. I screamed to avenge wrongs and settle grudges that were in large parts imaginary or misconstrued. This revelation shocked me, humbled me, and yet somehow, I found it all the more saddening. Research and a reasoned, objective analysis changed my perception of many trustees in what seemed like the twinkling of an eye, for the moral barriers I once imagined between us were tenuous...if they existed at all.

Most everyone in these multiple rosters of the Board was well-meaning, but that was not enough, for a key component in this breakdown was an utter lack of decisive action. A change of course never came. This is inconsistent with other crucial points in the history of Saint Joseph's College.

During the Great Depression, as enrollment numbers plummeted, Father Kenkel made the steadfast decision to turn Saint Joe into a four-year college as he saw a market for such Catholic education. Though it took shepherding and austerity, it worked. In the early 1970s as times changed, Saint Joe made the decision to go co-ed and thus increased enrollment. Later, Fr.

Charles Banet made a bold choice and supported the Core program in response to Vatican II and a changing, oftentimes turbulent, world. It worked. Core brought more attention and funding to Saint Joseph's College than most any other academic of aspect of the school. In 1973 when the Administration Building burned to the ground, many thought Saint Joe would never recover from the physical and financial blow. Decisive action and collaboration and engagement with the community of Rensselaer made certain that didn't happen, earning Saint Joe the moniker of "The College that would not die."

Sadly, I could find no similar, authoritative actions taken by the Board or the administration to face the long deteriorating financial situation until February 2017, when the College was all but out of money and the majority of the Board made the active decision to "suspend operations." In speaking with my friend Chad Turner about what he and I went through, he gave a concise and accurate answer as to what happened, but not before looking down and offering a sheepish laugh.

"Asking me about Saint Joe is like asking me about a woman who dumped me," he said.

I returned the laugh and then we both got quiet as he seemed to sit and think for a time.

"They failed us," he said. "The whole board failed us."

Indeed, it is difficult to dispute that conclusion. If the board of a college has fiduciary responsibility, if it is entrusted…note the relationship of "entrusted" to the word "trustee"…with what Kant would call a "categorical imperative" consisting of a moral as well as legal obligation to sustain the institution's existence, then by virtue of the pure fact that Saint Joe closed, the Board of Saint Joseph's College did, in fact, fail.

During the course of my research, I have become something of an armchair "disaster scholar." I read books about the Johnstown Flood by David McCullough and Al Roker (yes, *that* Al Roker). I read *Midnight in Chernobyl* by Adam Higginbotham, and also a few articles and thinkpieces about New Orleans in the aftermath of Hurricane Katrina. While Saint

Joe is, without question, unlike all of those scenarios in terms of the loss of life, limb, and property, I did see commonalities in terms how human systems respond, or don't respond, to threat.

First, someone always sees the disaster coming. There were design flaws in the Chernobyl RBMK reactor. Many worried that levies and pumps would not hold if New Orleans was hit by a hurricane of sufficient magnitude. Many voiced concerns that modifications to the dam and the removal of "costly" drainage pipes as well as years of "deferred maintenance" to infrastructure could lead to disaster in Johnstown. The Gang of Four could see the financial downward spiral of Saint Joe, as could Larry Laudick. A phrase that keeps coming up in many of these accounts I examined is "It was inevitable, but it didn't have to be."

Second, many who see the potential for catastrophe are overwhelmed as to how to change things, or are reluctant to engage in such an undertaking over something that "might" happen. If one RBMK reactor has a flaw, then all 14 of them have to be taken offline and remodeled, and systems vital to the progress of society go without power. If the dam or the levy needs changing, it will require considerable time, expense, and inconvenience. "How long can we kick this down the road? Could we tackle this next month, maybe?"

Third, there is the fatal flaw of human hubris. They modified the dam in Johnstown in order to create a recreational lake for the wealthy. It was unable to withstand the torrential downpour of rain on the last day of May in 1889. Among the many reasons for the Chernobyl disaster was an authority who pressed forward with a technical test despite unfavorable conditions because he "knew what he was doing." Also, after the identification of reactor design flaws, the senior nuclear scientists shut down criticisms. After all, they built careers on the reactor designs, and a Soviet system that could not dare appear the least bit weak to the West. At Saint Joe, a collective sense of "we know what we're doing and it will all work out somehow" manifested among Board members, administrators, and C.PP.S. alike for years. How do business and finance administrators "suddenly" realize an institution will be out of money within mere months?

Fourth, as things get truly dangerous, there is the steady broadcasting of "Everything is under control and just fine." In April of 1986, scientists in Sweden detected abnormal levels of radiation in their country. They called the Soviets to ask what the hell was going on. The reply was, paraphrasing, "Everything is fine, situation normal. How are you?" The Soviet people received a happy and reassuring message of "there's no problem, pay no attention to the man behind the curtain" for many days via state-run media. Post-Katrina, then President George W. Bush made his now infamous "You're doing a heckuva job, Brownie" comment to Mike Brown the director of FEMA while the people of New Orleans begged on rooftops for rescue.

In November of 2016, President Pastoor told students there was plenty of time to fix the financial situation and there would be no need to transfer. On the eve and morning of Saint Joseph's College's closure announcement, a priest told us, "God's got this!"

Most of all, it's never just one person responsible. The breakdown happens from multiple moving parts and numerous miscommunications. Together, the implications of people's actions…or again, the inactions…get stitched together to create a Frankenstein's monster of catastrophe. Certainly in the case of Saint Joe, one gets the sense from reading documents such as the HLC's notice of probation and a comparison of Board minutes between October 2016 and February 2nd-3rd, 2017 that few breathing the Saint Joe air harbored any real idea of the mess the College faced. In many of the disasters I studied, one's immediate reaction to the aftermath might be, "Who would ever make decisions like these?"

Humans.

Humans who are scared. Humans who don't know what else to do. Humans overwhelmed by such a massive problem. Humans who must project and maintain an appearance of competency during a situation that is well out of hand. In such a flawed system, even the well-intentioned may falter. In another most human reaction, you will see people in the wake of disaster form a circular firing squad. "There's someone to blame, but it sure is heck isn't me. Maybe there's really no one to blame."

"Nobody *wanted* this," came the administrative cry of protest to rumors of conspiracy theories after Saint Joe's closing.

That's missing the point. No one ever "wants" it. No one wanted to flood Johnstown. No one wanted Chernobyl to melt down. No one wanted *Challenger* to explode. But they all happened just the same. By no coincidence, all of them, like Saint Joe, happened due to a complex breakdown of multiple human systems at once.

On the other hand, did anyone pre-plan Saint Joe's closure…or "suspension of operations"…in the months leading up to February 3rd, 2017 and what would happen following the shutdown? I could find absolutely no concrete, documented evidence of any such conspiracy.

This, however, is not an exoneration. As happens in astronomy, sometimes the presence of celestial bodies may be suspected not by direct sighting, but by the gravitational tugs they have on other stars and planets. Such was the case with the discovery of Neptune. In the case of Saint Joe's closing, enough "odd ripples in the gravitational field" suggest the presence of an unseen "something else" moving and shifting in the ether.

Consider Tom Ryan's two comments to me, one after the announcement on February 3rd ("We're just taking a break") and his reaction on February 6th, 2017 when a student asked Ben Sponseller what was being done to assist faculty who lost their jobs ("Are we going to buy them a car? Are we going to get them a blanket?")

Consider Justin Hays' account of asking Dr. Pulver if anyone would take seriously any suggestions from students on what a "new Saint Joe" would look like, and Pulver's alleged response of "That's up to the C.PP.S."

Consider the plans…if you can call them that…for "a new Saint Joe" presented in private to the Board the evening of February 2nd, 2017. How these proposed plans came together and who exactly composed them is unknown to faculty, athletics, and any directors of the student activities proposed to be cut. No one consulted any of us on the matter.

Consider the C.PP.S. priests who were Board members on February 3rd, 2017 and then carried over onto the "new" Board of the "new" Saint Joe.

Consider the online transfer offer announcement from Marian University, doubtless created *at least* a day in advance, posted to the university's website well before the Board's vote. Likewise, there is the account of Jackie Bradway witnessing Fr. Hemmelgarn with possible representatives of a PR firm in a congratulatory round-robin over a letter, possibly the same closing letter Hemmelgarn would issue later that day.

"You can't tell me there wasn't a conspiracy," Jackie Bradway said as her voice choked and tears fell from her eyes to her jeans. "I sat there and I watched it happen."

"The Church mushrooms people," Dad said. "Do you know what that means?"

I told him that indeed I understood it meant to be kept in the dark and covered in manure. Such behavior prompts the question, “Is making secret decisions about someone else’s life an act of true Christian Humanism?”

The element of secrecy and the heavy presence of the Catholic Church’s role prompted more than a few of my interviewees to draw comparisons between Saint Joe’s closing and the sex abuse scandal that has rocked the Catholic Church for decades. While I can see parallels in terms of decisions made with little or no transparency and the imperious tone of “We will decide what is best, for we know best, and no one shall question,” two important distinctions must be made. First and foremost, no one in the Saint Joe debacle suffered in the way that the victims of the sexual abuse scandal suffered throughout their lives, nor was there the sheer magnitude of victims as in the sexual abuse scandal, with 1,000 children abused by priests in Pennsylvania alone.[3]

Also critical to point out is that the Society of the Precious Blood encompasses many hundreds of priests, brothers, and sisters. So many of these people are committed to doing God's work to better humanity in so many places across the globe right now. As just one example, I can personally vouch for the outstanding work going on right now on the South Side of Chicago with the Reconciliation Ministry, which aims to reduce gang violence and give disadvantaged young people hope for a brighter future. What happened at the end of Saint Joseph's College involved only four C.PP.S. priests and one of their lay acolytes. They are by no means representative of the C.PP.S. or even the Church as a whole.

But Saint Joseph's College is representative of something else and it is grim. As evidenced by institutions such as Dowling, Dana, and St. Catharine's, and others leading up to 2017, we were not the first small college to fall. Sadly, we have been far from the last. As predicted, a wave of small college closures has crossed the nation in a bloody wash.

Just three months after Saint Joe, Marygrove College in Michigan announced it would halt all undergraduate programs.[4] One adult-returning student at Marygrove, a music major one year shy of graduation, conveyed the feelings of what would become an all-too common student: “I worked hard, so hard. And then, all in one moment, it was gone.”[5] The following November, St. Gregory’s University of Oklahoma announced it would “suspend operations” midway through the academic year.[6] In May of 2018, Marylhurst University of Oregon announced it would close due to low enrollment and a dim financial future.[7] However, just as in the case of Saint Joe and Sweet Briar, a few Marylhurst faculty did contest their board’s decision, claiming that the board did not exhaust all possible options for a path forward.[8] Just before the fall of Marylhurst came the announcement that Mount Ida College in Massachusetts would close at the end of that academic year.[9] Like Marylhurst, Mount Ida’s situation likewise held parallels with Saint Joe.

Numerous students and faculty felt blindsided by the Mount Ida announcement. Faculty pointed to 2018-19 contracts that they came to believe were signed in bad faith. As a Mount Ida professor told *Inside Higher Ed*: “‘Not only did they not tell us this was coming, we didn’t even a have a chance for last-minute applications' elsewhere, said a full-time professor of design who did not want to be identified by name, for fear of compromising a promised severance package." Like Saint Joe, the aftermath brought cries of betrayal and an unswerving distrust of administration from the whole Mount Ida community.[10]

Even so, there may be few students and staff of closed colleges informed of the decision in quite the way that Cincinnati Christian University chose to make their announcement. "We hope this finds you well!" the opening sentence read.[11]

For three years I tracked each time a college closed and added its name to a list. This proved an exhausting effort as I could not keep up with the closure announcements. By August 2019, there were predictions that 25% of small colleges would close over a period of 20 years.[12] So commonplace were these closure announcements that industry publications such as the *Chronicle of Higher Education* ran thinkpieces with headlines such as "Will Your College Close?"[13] The cases of abrupt closures produced calls for accreditors and regulatory agencies to more closely monitor the finances of the colleges in their charge and to, since there appears to be a need, develop a rigid checklist of procedure for any college that decides it must close, particularly in regard to teach-out plans for students.[14]

How and why do stories like Saint Joe's keep happening and how and why are they expected to continue happening for decades to come?

Ghidorah.

That's what I call it, anyway.

I've already shared how I spent much of my youth in front of the TV watching b-movies. The Japanese Godzilla series is a special favorite of mine. Grown men in rubbery monster suits would engage in choreographed wrestling over model cities made of cardboard and balsa wood. It's said that foreign film is inaccessible to American audiences, but whoever said that never gave the portfolio of Toho Pictures a serious viewing. Anyway, Godzilla fought a mortal enemy named Ghidorah, a giant monster with three, dragon-like heads. A similar three-headed monster has consistently stalked and consumed small colleges for decades and, sadly, will continue to do so in the future.

The first head is declining enrollment. There are many reasons for this decline and most of them are readily found by a simple search. Many small colleges are located in rural communities with sparse populations. Just take a look at the ones examined thus far and their localities. Such geography is not a draw for many young people, and relatedly the lack of quality facilities at a small college as compared to a large university is a further detriment. Economics is another factor. As states invest less in education, even tuition at a public university is out of reach for many working-class families.[15] What does that mean for small, private colleges that traditionally have higher tuitions? It means the second ugly head rears full up: Unsustainable tuition discounts.

In an August 2019 report for *CBS This Morning*, Brook Silva-Braga spoke with Robert Allen, President of Green Mountain College in Vermont. Green Mountain closed the previous spring, and Silva-Braga asked why colleges are closing if tuition is so high. They should be making plenty of money. Allen responded that that would be so if anybody really paid tuition. “At Green Mountain College this past year, we didn’t have one full-pay student.”[16] In order to remain competitive and to offset flagging enrollment, a great many small colleges keep discounting their tuition.

Both of those two previous heads help create and perpetuate the third head of Ghidorah: crippling debt. When tuition discounts are not backed by either grant funding or a sizeable endowment, logic dictates that the college then heads into deficit spending, taking on more debt just as Saint Joseph’s College did with bonds and other obligations. Saint Joe year after year went into deficit spending. Physical maintenance gets deferred again and again, and when a critical structural problem can no longer be deferred, the institution must go further into debt to correct the problem. Saint Joe learned this the hard way in its transition to a natural gas power plant.

All of this is interconnected. Each head of Ghidorah feeds the others while consuming small colleges whole. If a college does not have leadership at the board and administrative level that can see these threats and take sound, resolute action, then it is sunk.

Then in 2020 another monster arrived on the scene. As of this writing, the coronavirus pandemic is playing havoc with higher education as a whole, but particularly with small colleges that were already on shaky financial ground. Smaller institutions, ones with greater dependency on tuition plus room and board, took the hardest hits as campuses across the nation went online while students sheltered in place at home. In a doubly tragic blow, even small colleges executing action plans to turn their situations around were undone by the sudden attack of the virus. MacMurray College in Illinois announced that it would close at the end of the 2020 spring semester.[17]

“Despite our best efforts, we were unable to secure the capital to fund a viable path forward,” Charles O'Connell, Board of Trustees chair at MacMurray, said in a statement.[18]

Damn, if that doesn't sound familiar. There is a strong likelihood that even if the "Fight for Saint Joe" plan constructed by the Gang of Four or some such other emergency fundraising operation went into action in 2014, Saint Joe still would have closed as it would not have survived COVID-19. This point is not lost on Gang of Four member Paul Muller, who called Saint Joseph's College "ahead of its time in its closing."

"We knew the big problem was the Board being asleep at the wheel," he said. "However…I don't believe our efforts or that of any multi-millionaire could have saved Saint Joe's. The coronavirus would have killed it dead with no chance of survival. I believe the problem will be magnified at smaller Catholic institutions. I'm sure our own Board would have pointed to the virus, but not recognized years of mismanagement."

There is at present across the nation a tug-of-war between faculty and administration over what constitutes "safe opening" in the time of coronavirus. Faculty tend to side with caution and call for online courses, while administrators at residential colleges feel other pressures to have face-to-face classes no matter what. One of my former Saint Joe colleagues went on to teach at a mid-sized Catholic university. When grappling with the pandemic, he appealed to the institution's stated mission of preserving the sanctity and well-being of all human life in arguing for remote coursework.

"Mission is one thing," an administrator told him. "This is about politics and finance."

The financial end of that statement stems in large part from how much essential revenue a small college or university receives from residential students. In February of 2021, *The Detroit Free Press* did a study of small, midwestern colleges, focusing primarily on Albion College in Michigan:

> "If students aren't on campus, Albion's budget can take a massive hit. The college pulled in $16.3 million from residential halls in the 2018-19 school year, according to audited financial statements obtained by the *Free Press*. That was 22.9% of the school's total $71.1 million in revenue."[19]

In 2019, Albion's tuition discount rate was 71.7%.[20]

I have watched many inside and outside of higher education greet this prospect for small colleges with a shrug. "That's how the free market goes when something's just not needed anymore." While I have an obvious bias, I still must ask if we have given full examination to what the loss of small colleges means to the nation. I asked many of the people I spoke to during the course of my research what may result if small colleges continue to disappear.

"If small colleges are gone, then you take away choice for a student," said Hassan Rahmanian from Antioch. "At Antioch we have a large population of diverse, first generation students."

Expanding on what that means, Carol Wood offered her own experience as reason for why small colleges are critical for such populations.

"I grew up in Rensselaer and was a first-generation college student," she said. "I couldn't make it at Purdue or Notre Dame. I could make it at Saint Joe, and I went on to be successful. If we lose small colleges then we lose the marginal student."

Consider for a moment two types of student who often found their way to Saint Joe and other small colleges. One grew up in a rural area and graduated from high school in a senior class of 100, or perhaps even fewer. They go to a large state university such as Purdue because it is the closest and most economical option. Whiplash and shock sets in as they sit down in their first auditorium-sized class of 300 and end up dropping out saying, "college isn't for me." Another student may come from the Chicago Public School system or Indianapolis public schools. They may have a tenuous academic record due to social, economic, and psychological factors in addition to the strained resources of a large school system. At a small college such as Saint Joe, this student will find comfortable classes and specialized attention from professors. In both cases, each student may come to realize, "Yes, college *is* for me and deserve to be here" and become contributors to both economy and society.

As just indicated, small colleges afford special opportunities for professors as well as students. Milt Heinrich gave me clear and succinct elucidation of just what this means.

"No matter what level you teach, you teach more about who you are than what you know," Heinrich said. "That's harder to do in very large university classes. Students also don't easily acquire mentors. At a small school, they see the same faculty every year and that builds personal and professional relationships."

That sums up my Saint Joe experience as both student and professor. One might call it an updated version of the old private college approach of "in loco parentis" or "In the place of a parent." While we did not have bed checks and no one monitored student dietary habits, we often did share tables together. We often knew one another as real people. As a student, these relationships brought comfort to me as I knew where to go for career, and sometimes personal, advise. As a professor, I was in a unique position to gain a real understanding of what individual students needed in order to learn.

In the September following the demise of Saint Joe, a former student contacted me for help. He just transferred to a large university in Indiana as a sophomore, and found himself in a general education class with about 100 other students. He had forgotten how to write a thesis statement. He asked his professor, but was told "it's in the syllabus." I knew the student and his "language," and could talk him through the construction of a thesis for his paper.

"Thank you. You were a lot more help than my professor," he said to me.

Large colleges and large classes can create large problems for certain populations of students. Not everyone learns well in an auditorium of 300 students.

"Our small classes provide students with the fora to actually engage in material presented," said John Ashbrook of Sweet Briar class sizes. "It offers the chance to become better, heterodox thinkers. The small classes offer them more and better opportunities to improve their persuasive and writing skills."

“Higher education would become more and more mass produced, its graduates alarmingly similar to each other in their skill sets and beliefs,” Camilla Smith-Barnes said when asked what will happen if small colleges continue to disappear. “The nation would thereby lose some of its vitality and versatility.”

“We lose the human part of education,” Milt Heinrich said.

Additionally, there is the troubling issue of the perceived low value of the humanities. It is a thread that runs through almost all of the small college closings thus far examined. That thread continues to trend as news stories of more closures roll out, stories with opening sentences often reading, “(Institution name here), a small liberal arts college, will close its doors after graduation in May.” When I would read the comments sections of these reports, respondents would be digitally dancing with glee. Many justifiably pointed to the cost of student debt as a reason to eschew college altogether, but just as many others demeaned the courses taught in college curricula, particularly those dealing with anything human, and encouraged teens to "go into the trades." Among my favorite comments:

> "Humanities. Yeah, thatll [sic] hook up the water mane."

The comment is symptomatic of what is now the prevailing thought in higher education: bolster any discipline the market deems as employable at the moment, and pitch to the trash heap any class that does not visibly lead to a job. This knee-jerk reaction is understandable as both students and parents are demanding a return on what is a quite costly investment. This line of thinking is short-sighted though and is essentially an example of the "either/or" logical fallacy. At Saint Joe, the approach was "both/and."

"Even future mechanics and firefighters can appreciate Homer or the origins and meaning of historical events," wrote Willard Dix in *Forbes* magazine. "Surely, to study the history of race relations in the U.S. can help anyone become more conscious of today's social and cultural needs, for example."[21]

Dix raises a crucial point in examining the value of the humanities. Is it not in fact “elitist” to presume a person doesn’t need to know how to write and speak well, and to have an understanding of the society they work and live in because they’re going to be a mechanic or a welder? Dix further underscores the need for humanities education by arguing such coursework:

> “…may not have "value" according to strict economic rules, but the liberal arts do have a leavening value that helps make every student more than just a future drone, narrowly confined to his or her job without an awareness, let's say, of cultural context or an appreciation for art and literature. Applying strict cost/benefit analyses to academic fields may seem like a short-term cure, but in the long run, eliminating the humanities and other ‘unprofitable’ fields does more harm than good.”[22]

Not everyone is convinced a common education in humanities is even necessary for college students to develop communication and critical thinking skills. When I spoke to John Groppe, the former Saint Joe English professor now in the comfort of retirement, he heaved a sigh and argued "we already do that" at the high school level, and that his own discipline may no longer be necessary.

"A college should be a place of ideas, and if a college can still be a place of ideas without an English department…" he said. "How much impact does an English department have on a university? I'm not sure you'll notice much of a change."

Others see this continued morphing in higher ed as a sign of even more dire things to come.

"I fear that the US will go down the road the USSR did in overspecialization in education that nearly destroyed the Soviet Union's engineering field," Dr. John Ashbrook said.

For further reading he recommended *Ghost of the Executed Engineer: Technology and the Fall of the Soviet Union* by Loren Graham.

"If liberal arts fails, the world will be at the mercy of people that know quite a lot about a single subject, but very little about other things," Ashbrook said. "Or more worrisome, how to ethically apply their knowledge in ways beneficial to their country and society. They will also be unable to express their ideas in cogent, written form. Just as problematic, they will not have the tools to think critically."

Dr. Stephen Hulbert concurs, sharing concerns about a populace of highly skilled workers with little ability to express themselves or to ask "why?"

"I'm old school, and humanities shouldn't just survive, but thrive," he said. "Boards and administrations should be committed to them. You can produce business people, you can produce nurses, and you can produce engineers, but if they don't know how to communicate in oral and written forms, then they won't succeed. You get a job with a degree, but it's your depth of skills and your understanding of the world that are critical to building a career."

"Someone with liberal arts plus experiential education is someone who has tolerance, and an understanding of diversity, complexity, and ambiguity," Dr. Hassan Rahmanian said. "Without humanities, you limit the complexity of the world."

There is yet one more distinctly American strand tangled up in the forces devaluing both small colleges and the humanities, and that is anti-intellectualism. Knowledge is for nerds and in America nerds get punched.

In 2018, I met Dr. Aaron Lawler.[23] He would become both a colleague and a close friend. Dr. Lawler's PhD is in Educational Philosophy, and his dissertation is titled, "The Cult of Ignorance: A Visual Inquiry into Anti-Intellectualism in American Culture."

"Pragmatically, the biggest issue is the humanities are how we communicate," he said. "We use the humanities to persuade, argue, and conceptualize anything. We stand on the shoulders of giants, we steal fire from the gods, and we venture into the cosmos because each generation better knows what it means to be human, better knows our place in the universe, and better understands morality and life. Without philosophy or history, we cannot build on the generations past, and we will find ourselves reinventing the wheel each generation."

How could then the humanities thrive once again? According to Aaron Lawler, the answer is small colleges. So what does America lose if small colleges continue to close?

"Everything," he said simply.

He described his own undergraduate experience at a small college as one with access to mentors, opportunities for deep discussion and debate.

"We aren't meant to learn as a huge group," he said. "[Education] is meaning-making and semiotics, but it's also self-growth and transformation. Like Joseph Campbell says, we are the heroes of our own journey, and must enter the belly of the beast and come out different. The quest changes us. Small colleges are perfectly suited for this. You cannot quest with 50 questers."

As an analogy, Dr. Lawler offered Gandalf's limiting of the number of questers in Tolkien's *The Fellowship of the Ring*. For similar reasons, that's why small colleges work. While I'm all for hobbits, I felt the need to ask about the financial realities of sustaining a college with low enrollment.

"[Schools] aren't just pinnacles of capitalism," Dr. Lawler said. "Screw Nixon. Screw Reagan. Screw the industrialization of education. The project of education should cost money, not make money. It's a service for the good of humanity. We need teachers as mentors, not factory foremen. Make it holy. Make it a quest. Make it Merlin coaching Arthur, and Plato guiding Aristotle."

Lawler's not alone in these thoughts. Christian Smith, professor of sociology at the University of Notre Dame, wrote a contentious and controversial piece for *The Chronicle* in January of 2018 titled, "Higher Education is Drowning in BS."[24] Smith pointed to a number of charges that may indeed be seen as corrosive realities in the higher educational system.

One is the corporate model of education that says education should be similar to manufacturing product or "enormous universities processing hordes of students as if they were livestock, numbers waiting in line, and shopping consumers."[25] In such a "corporatized" system, adjuncts make an even more efficient and economic choice for administrations. Smith holds faculty to account for this resultant system as many professors shrug the teaching of first-year or intro-level classes onto the growing sea of adjuncts. Why?

"Snobbery" might be one reason. And higher ed is steeped in snobbery. As vaunted as the humanities may be to their faculty, there is often great reluctance to take on the challenge of teaching first-year learners along with the accompanying 21st century struggles these students face. Dr. Elaine Maimon, former president of Governors State University, gave an interview to the *Chronicle* wherein she beseeched, "We have to change the snobbism. We have to make it so that we're preparing Ph.D. students in English and the humanities to have jobs inside the academy, where they take the teaching and the scholarship of first-year learning and English composition seriously."[26]

That might make for big strides in how both administrations and faculty view the value of first-year and "Intro to" courses in terms of the critical role they play for the freshman student, however it may do little to combat the endemic snobbery from which the repulsion towards teaching lower-level courses stems. Namely, there can be a strong strand "I'm better than you" running throughout higher education faculty and administration that is sometimes communicated to the rest of the world. To wit, the very first Vice President of Academic Affairs I worked for believed there were basically two types of people in the world. You are either "Ph.D." or "P.o.S." and you are treated accordingly. I am sad to report that while such experiences have been rare, this administrator was not the last time I encountered the attitude from both administration and professors in higher education. It is not difficult to see why colleges large and small have garnered a stereotype as "shelters" for arrogant eggheads.

How can we expect others to see higher education, let alone small colleges, as something worth saving from collapse when this is the image projected? Is it any wonder that I've seen the comments sections of closed college articles crammed full of rejoicing, and taunting of "the revenge of trade school?" If that many people are celebrating the burning of your house, it might do one good to pause and ask "where does that feeling come from?" What incentive does someone have to go into debt and learn in such an environment, or to go to work in it for the humiliatingly low wages of an adjunct? This arrogant and cancerous attitude is in and of itself born of a kind of ignorance, and I am ashamed to have projected it myself at times. I believe whole-heartedly that erasing these attitudes will be an essential step in revitalizing higher education into a more sustainable model for all. Arrogance, condescension, and ignorance make poor attractors for potential students who want to learn, and for faculty who are trying to teach.

In anticipation of any questions/objections, no. I don't have a solution to the college closure problem. If I knew how to overhaul higher ed and particularly how to help small colleges survive, I would be disseminating such information by peddling it on the lecture circuit and no doubt making a fair amount of cash as one of those venerable "consultants." However, the onslaught of COVID-19 has made any kind of revitalizations of small colleges beyond difficult, but there are methods still being tried.

Tim Pedrotty[27] is a Saint Joe grad and a former employee of the University of Akron and St. Michael's College. He has worked in a variety of roles, such as Manager of Custodial Services and Manager of Skilled Trades. His experience in these positions has afforded him a few unique insights for small colleges.

"There are things that have to be competitively outsourced. You can't afford to have it on campus," Pedrotty said.

He suggests that regional, small colleges band together as a purchasing consortium. This would help provide leverage in contracting for custodial and food services. It also helps these small colleges to somewhat ameliorate an omnipresent predicament.

"Technology costs kill these colleges," Pedrotty said. "Trying to keep up with it is insane."

In a purchasing consortium, a collective of small colleges could bargain with tech companies and IT service providers in hopes of driving down costs. I also asked him if he might know of a current small college success story. He pointed me to one right in his home area: Champlain College of Vermont.

"They're growing left and right," he said. "New, up-to-date buildings."

Upon visiting Champlain's website, I noticed something interesting right away. They touted an "Upside Down"[28] curriculum focused on gaining immediate job skills in fields such as criminal justice and technology, and the option to earn a degree entirely online. At the same time though, students take courses in something called a "Core Program"[29]...a liberal arts-centered curriculum which looked awfully familiar to me.

As an aside, Tim Pedrotty remarked to me, "Most of the business managers I've known have been liberal arts grads."

There are those who argue that small, rural colleges need to draw more upon the students in their own backyards. Robert F. Fried, director of the New Baccalaureate Project, and Eli Kramer, director of research for the project and an affiliated researcher at the Institute of Philosophy of the University of Warsaw, argued for "A Rescue Plan for America's Small Colleges" in *Inside Higher Ed*.[30] This plan would recruit students with "overlooked potential" and place them in small class settings with the best liberal education has to offer, paired with internships at local businesses, underwritten in part by philanthropists and foundations.

> "These small colleges create a new baccalaureate option for every self-motivated and independent-thinking student, one that is based on assessed performance of

projects, portfolios and internship reports, rather than exam-based grades and that combines the best of traditional liberal arts with skills required by the best area employers. What cannot be overstated is that we must empower students themselves to participate and co-lead the transformational process."[31]

In such a model, the issue of enrollment would still be foundational, but it would be tempered by a critical understanding of the economic needs of the college's surrounding community.

Another method of survival for the small college might be mergers, or other forms of partnerships with larger institutions that have more stable financial footing. One example of this just happened in Indiana. On August 28th, 2020, Marian University announced it was entering into "a strategic partnership" with Ancilla College of Donaldson, Indiana. Ancilla is in a rural location where 11% of the population attains a Bachelor's degree or higher. There is then opportunity for Ancilla to not only strengthen its financial situation, but to provide greater availability of education to its residents, and more skilled workers for regional businesses and industries. Ancilla and Marian, both being Catholic colleges, came together as a natural fit for one another. Other mergers and partnerships between colleges might not be as simpatico, and as with the merger of any two entities, there is the risk of duplication and therefore jobs eliminated.[32]

Despite the coal-black tide looming over small colleges, there may yet be even a few more causes for hope. Adrian College in Michigan planned to decimate its humanities program by eliminating the departments of history, theater, and philosophy and religion. Eleven professors would lose their jobs. This prompted a backlash from several thousand Adrian alumni who undertook a #SaveHCHumanities social media campaign that amounted to steady bombardment of the administration with demands to reinstitute those disciplines. In September of 2020, President Jeffrey Docking announced that he would "pause to reconsider my decision" and the termination notices sent to faculty were rescinded.[33]

"It's not enough to conserve," my Dad said of the state of small colleges. "But that does not mean do not conserve. Perhaps Pope Leo XIII struck the right balance in '*Rerum Novarum*,' his encyclical on the new ideas in the world at the beginning of the 20th Century. *Vetra novis augere et perficere*."

"Enhance and perfect the old things by means of the new."

What may be most symbolic of all? Sweet Briar College and Antioch College remain open today.

"I am quite optimistic about where we're headed," Hassan Rahmanian said of Antioch.

On a completely different note, it must be considered what the loss of small colleges does to their host communities. Many small colleges such as Saint Joe are in rural areas and the economies of local towns are dependent in many regards upon the colleges' students and staff. Communities in Vermont have been especially hard hit because of this wave of closures, affecting everything from the tax base to small businesses.[34] We have yet to examine what affect the "suspension of operations" had on the town of Rensselaer, Indiana and I believe it is about time that happened.

To find out what the loss of Saint Joe meant, I went to Janet's Kitchen, a diner just down from courthouse square in the center of Rensselaer. It's a small, homey place. The silver metal milk dispenser has a red, white, and blue USA magnet, plus a yellowed, full-page ad from a newspaper thanking Peyton Manning after his leaving the Indianapolis Colts. It's not a bad nutshell representation of Rensselaer.

A placard warns patrons that "This isn't Burger King. You don't get it your way. You take it my way, or you don't get a damn thing." I stared at the sign for a bit after walking through the door.

"They remembered the comma before the conjunction," I thought. "So many these days don't."

There was a table reserved for “Farmers, Fishermen, and other liars.” I thought I might sit there and consider where I fit in that triad as I awaited my interviewee.

“Hey Jon!” a voice said.

He was already there and seated.

I sat down with Greg Whaley for coffee. Whaley[35] moved to Rensselaer in seventh grade. He remained in town to raise two kids and run a successful real estate firm. In 2016, he was one of a few members of the Rensselaer community who attended an open forum with President Pastoor as Pastoor discussed committees for a “20-year plan” for Saint Joseph’s College. The closure of Saint Joe came as a shock to Whaley as much as it did anyone else.

“He wasted three months when he could have had people in town helping to work the problem,” Whaley said of Pastoor.

After downing our first cups of coffee and gabbing a bit, I asked him what the loss of the College meant for Rensselaer. As there aren't a whole lot of jobs for college professors in the area, many speculated that real estate value in Rensselaer would plummet as the exodus occurred. Not so in reality. Whaley said that even though many former Saint Joe employees would pick up and go, the housing market would not be the biggest hit to the community.

"The houses up for sale are selling," he said. "The real loss will come over the coming years. We had alumni come here for Homecoming and Little 5. Many weekends we had parents of student athletes come to watch their kids play sports. Then there were the all families for move-in day and graduation. All those people stayed overnight in our hotels. They ate at our local restaurants. They fueled up at our service stations. Saint Joe brought in money from outside the community, and we can't replace that. The real pressure is on the Jasper County Tourism Board. You have to create four or five events a year to replace that revenue."

Whaley pointed out that the loss of the College might not only be felt in fiscal matters, but also as a "brain drain."

Agriculture remains the area's driving economic force. Saint Joe afforded local farmers an advantage other area towns did not have. If farmers ran into trouble with growing crops or another environmental challenge, there were professors in chemistry and biology living right in town and available for free consultation.

"Professors moved here and contributed to the community," Whaley said. "We've lost that. We don't have those minds anymore. Rensselaer had a package unlike any other community for many miles."

Brienne Hooker voiced similar concerns.[36] She is a lifelong resident of Rensselaer. Her family roots in the area go back nearly 100 years. She is a 2003 graduate of Saint Joseph's College, living at home during her collegiate years and working for her father's trucking company in town. Now, she is the Executive Director of the Jasper-Newton Foundation, a nonprofit organization that connects residents and businesses of the two-county area through coordinated investments and strategic grantmaking in order to solve local challenges.

Like Whaley, Hooker underscored that the costliest damage to the Rensselaer community is not best expressed in monetary terms.

“We’ve lost humans,” she said.

Rensselaer schoolchildren would visit the Saint Joe campus and meet professors while seeing science labs and a hoop house full of vegetables grown through sustainable farming. In the opposite direction, Saint Joe education majors would student teach in the Rensselaer schools and if they made a strong enough impression, would be hired on full-time. Not only did these new teachers come with a solid education, but also an understanding of both the community and its children gained through firsthand experience.

“The idea that higher education is possible and available was visible right here in our own backyard. It gave the community glimpses of a bigger world, of things that aren’t here, but could be here,” Hooker said.

She recalled bringing her daughter to see a group of Buddhist monks who visited Saint Joe and stayed on campus in 2016. Together they watched the living representatives of a different culture painstakingly create a resplendent and chromatic mandala out of colored sand. Fittingly, a mandala's intent is to transform ordinary minds into enlightened ones and to assist with healing.

"We have zero of those experiences anymore," Hooker said. "We experienced other cultures and that could have made a big difference in the past 12 months."

The mentioned timespan was a reference to the Black Lives Matter protests throughout 2020 in the wake of George Floyd, Breonna Taylor, and others killed during interactions with police officers. A Black Lives Matter vigil took place that summer in Rensselaer. In response, members of a motorcycle gang known as the Invaders guarded storefronts, and the vigil stopped early due to chants of "all lives matter."[37] If still in operation, Saint Joe and its professors would no doubt have hosted and facilitated community discussions on race, culture, and social issues. For Hooker, this speaks to the larger issue of the nature of higher education.

"That education was what made a difference for me," she said. "I found a world larger than where I was raised. I learned about other cultures, charity, kindness, and just how to be a good human being. We aren't just a thing meant to learn job skills and produce a product. That's what higher education can do, and I wanted other people in my community to have it. The whole idea of that is gone now."

The physical structure of Saint Joseph's College still sits there where it always has.

I have not set foot on the campus since that day in May of 2017. I couldn't tell you what the buildings are like now, but in 2018 the campus was placed on a list of "Indiana's Most Endangered Landmarks."[38] At present, the current incarnation of the Board of Trustees has rented out classroom space in the Core Building to other institutions such as Ivy Tech, and to certification programs. It is thought the College may be brought back by "diversifying revenue streams" and turning the campus into a "university center" where a student may take classes offered by various institutions all under one roof. In one classroom, you may have students taking a business certification class from Ivy Tech. Right next door, you may have a Certified Nursing Assistant's class offered through another college or educational entity.

It's like an educational shopping mall, minus the Sbarro's.

I get a newsletter from the Board every now and then. Most of the content touts "notions of glory and bull market gain" to quote R.E.M., but I hope they forgive me for not sharing their enthusiasm.

Looking at the campus now, allowed to get only as close as the Wal-Mart parking lot, the same place I made all those furtive calls to Jackie Bradway, I can no longer see any indication of the power the place once held. Today it's simply a collection of sealed, red brick buildings containing only the faintest whiffs of what once was joy and what once was pain. I think of lines towards the end of *Beowulf* about empty halls, and helmets no one will wear again, about being the last person left of your culture. I have zero desire to return to the campus…but I do miss the people.

Professor Chad Turner and his wife Jessica moved to Reed City, Michigan, where he teaches humanities and history at Ferris State University. Specters haunt him from time to time. They say things like "shared governance is a sham" and "administration is the enemy," and it's understandable why they would. Chad, being the consummate academic that he is, shunts them aside goes on teaching and writing.

Dr. April Toadvine is still an English professor, but now teaches at Southern University in Baton Rouge, Louisiana. I asked her what she believes the world should know about the end of Saint Joseph's College. She grew thoughtful for a moment before responding.

"I'd hate to think we're just another small college that closed," she said. "There's no easy answer for what happened. Such a history of people who didn't know what they were doing, our inability to select qualified presidents. Other schools should look at their decision-making processes for hiring leadership."

Professor Jordan Leising headed to Tyler, Texas, and taught political science for a time while enjoying quality barbecue. He returned to the Midwest and now works with a team of instructional designers at the University of Illinois. When I asked for his reflection, he referred to a quote from Fr. Charles Banet that used to be printed at the top of every Saint Joe meeting agenda. It reads, "Colleges do not grow by themselves. They are built by people who believe in them."

"Somewhere we lost sight of who we are," he said. "We lost sight of Saint Joe. We stopped believing in this place, our identity. Was the Saint Joe I knew a figment? A façade that let me ignore the worst parts about it? When you run a college there are two things I ask. Be transparent in a way that lets everyone know what the situation is, and take care of your people, the people who have placed their trust in you."

Dr. Bill White is at Purdue University. In 2018, Purdue University launched its Cornerstone Integrated Liberal Arts program to give engineers a grounding in humanities. It became a sort of "ark" that floated northward to Rensselaer and rescued three former Saint Joe professors from the floodwaters and Bill was one of them.

"They should teach what happened at Harvard Business School," Bill said of Saint Joe. "It resembles what happened at Chrysler and GM long ago."

He recommend I read the book *Crash Course* by Paul Ingrassia about the American auto industry's descent into bankruptcy and "how GM's board took a hands-off approach that led to the government bailout," he said. Bill also made comparisons to "board paralysis" as response to the sexual abuse scandal involving USA Gymnastics and Michigan State University. All, he argued, mirrored factors leading to the collapse of Saint Joe. I asked him what/who he thought the primary culprit was.

"I'm willing to go with incompetence. Leadership didn't get it," Bill said. "I should have called for a vote of no confidence against the entire Board back in 2014. Spread the word far and wide no matter how little that might have achieved."

The brutal battle of the faculty lawsuit still lingers about in his mind all these years later. He draws comparisons to the marathon court case at the heart of *Bleak House* by Charles Dickens, which featured contested and conflicting wills, and procedures once thought settled in amity.

Brian Capouch bought and restored a house he calls Sunnycrest. He is committed to making each of his meals from scratch as much as possible with vegetables grown from his bountiful garden. He even still uses a few non-stick pans from the kitchen in the Saint Joe Chapel basement. He keeps an eye on them, though.

"I don't trust that they won't flake off," he said.

Though retired at the time, the closure of Saint Joe hit him hard. The College was his social center. Once a week he could count on going to the cafeteria and having dinner with students. That disappeared. Now it can be a while before Brian even sees another person.

"Well, the final chapter is not yet writ," Brian said when I asked him about Saint Joe. "Their plan is still kept secret hush-hush. The best we can hope for is that one of them one day slips up or has an attack of conscience, and we get to find out what really happened. I'm sure we'll find out it was all about the Waugh farm. They only wanted the income from the farm, and probably found a way to get it without the burden of running a college. What I'll never forget though is the cold, heartless way they closed down the place. Just the empty looks on their faces…"

Jose Arteaga earned a Masters in Communication, and now teaches undergraduates at Purdue University Northwest.

"Time has been beneficial to me," he said. "Every once in a while I think of Saint Joe and the great people that I met there and I begin to feel less angry and more empowered."

Stephen Nickel works in the Sherwinn-Williams management program in Madison, Wisconsin.

"I feel like the whole experience bonded all of us who fell on that short end of the stick for life," he said. "Like soldiers in the trenches, the experience definitely brought me closer with my SJC family. The thing that really sticks with me though is that, in hindsight, we almost should have seen it coming. Everyone knew the College had issues that were not being dealt with properly."

Nate Wade has similar thoughts. He lives in Dallas where he works as a recruitment consultant at Nigel Frank International.

"There was just a common theme of people dropping the ball," Nate said, looking back at the closure. "It changed all of us. I'm more cynical now. I question authority more."

Both Alex McCormick and Justin Hays graduated law school at Indiana University in 2020. I asked them for their thoughts.

"Too many questions. Too few answers," Alex said of the Saint Joe saga. "And if they wanted us to keep our heads down and not ask any questions, then they never should have had us in the Core program."

As I might've expected, Justin offered a precis of the experience of many Saint Joe students that attended that final semester of the College:

"A community of passionate, involved people were completely let down by the very people who were supposed to have our best interests in mind. Like Nate said, this has left us all a bit cynical."

What of the other Saint Joe students? Many went on to graduate from Marian University or other colleges, but other students were forced to discontinue their education. Alexis Skinner was one of them.[39]

Skinner earned extra money by working shifts on student security while at Saint Joe. She was even asked to help protect members of the Board of Trustees as they exited the boardroom on February 3rd, 2017. One small, Indiana college accepted her transfer, but after a year of study, the institution's financial aid office took away her scholarships and "didn't offer the financial services [after] they promised to honor the scholarships we received at SJC." Skinner left that college and went to another, but half of her credits from Saint Joe came up as "invalid." Since she could no longer afford to pursue her social work degree, she dropped out of college. Her story, I am saddened to report, mirrored too many others.

"The teach out programs were a joke," Skinner said. "It was just a disaster."

Katie Albanese's[40] personal experience with the closing was unique to say the least. She had attended an all-girls private school for high school. During her junior year, the administration announced that the school would close and that Albanese would be forced to finish high school somewhere else. Then on

February 3rd, 2017, she found herself in the Shen Auditorium, learning that the college of her choice would close and she would need to complete her degree elsewhere.

"I was crying, pissed off, angry, every negative feeling you could think of," she said. "I just wanted to go to one school for four years. Is that so much to ask for?"

Though it meandered and careened, her schooling did at last come to an end when she earned a B.S. in Elementary Education. Albanese still keeps in close contact with the friends she made at Saint Joe with weekend meet-ups to keep the Puma spirit alive.

The Phoenix Team, formed at the end of May in 2017 to keep Saint Joe alive, atrophied and later disbanded altogether. Dr. Pulver left to coach basketball at Rensselaer's high school. This left Dr. Tom Ryan in the VPAA role. Not long after assuming that title, Ryan entered retirement, ending his teaching career as a vice president of a college with no students and no faculty. My brother Michael went to Marian University to serve as the assistant dean of a two-year program meant to emulate Core for marginalized students. Two years later, he departed Marian to eventually teach at Purdue University. He lives with his wife and two sons in the Indianapolis area.

Mark Nestor and Bob Neville are still doing well in their respective careers. On one occasion I did remark on how it remains most difficult to find a way to contact any member of the (former?) Pelican Group, the consulting firm hired by leadership at Saint Joe during the waning days. Mark Nestor did however send me a 50-page complaint he found that was filed in September of 2020 against the Pelican Group by Aqua Acceptance in the United States District Court of Maryland Baltimore Division.[41] The lawsuit is lengthy and twisty, but it argues that the Pelican Group was hired to raise money for the University of Mary, invested its fee in a land deal, later borrows $700,000 from Aqua to make payments on the land deal, and then failed to pay back Aqua. As it goes with such weighty legal claims, the case will no doubt be argued back forth for quite a while.

Me? I survived. That might be a little surprising despite the fact I'm the one writing. To tell you the truth, I didn't know if I'd make it either. But though Troy burned, it lit the way to Rome. Today, I'm a full-time English professor once again, this time at Waubonsee Community College in Sugar Grove, Illinois. I live with my wife and family again, I have a better salary than ever, and I once again have amazing students and colleagues. It's a joy to go to work every day. What's more, this college is a financially sound institution with a board of seven members plus a student representative. They all live in the area and they meet once a month. The phrases "fiduciary responsibility," "sound fiscal management," and "transparency" are immediately visible in their policy manual.

To say the entire experience of Saint Joseph's College changed me would be an understatement. I changed in a number of ways, including how I view college administrations. For my colleagues in higher education I would recommend this: know your board. Know the background of every member. Know what they bring to the table when decisions are made. I spent most of my time at Saint Joe uninformed. You can't afford to be. If you're not a professor at a public institution where financial data is available to all, then together with other fellow faculty and employees, demand…yes *demand…* as a unified whole, fully transparent disclosure of the college's financial health. There isn't a small college or university in this nation, regardless of the deep loyalty of its alumni base, that is "too loved to fail."

Also, any miniscule vestige that might have remained in me of the Puritan-Yankee equation of virtue with well-being is erased for good. It won't be coming back. I learned that most of us are just one bad day away from disaster. One good shove in just the right place and all the dominoes fall. The homeless, the working poor, those among us who struggle the most are never far from my mind when I hear of an employer closing, or in the large-scale upheaval we face in the Covid-19 pandemic at the time of this writing. I now do and give what I can, but it just doesn't seem enough.

The financial crisis of job loss is, sadly, familiar to many. What is less understood is the devastation of when one's identity is so intertwined with the lost vocation. That is what happened to so much of the faculty and staff of Saint Joseph's College. Could anyone else understand it?

In December of 2020, the Arecibo Telescope in Puerto Rico collapsed. In May of 2021, I read the account of astronomer Dr. Marcel Agueros. He wrote that the "observatory was like family," and that "it raised me, and I helped control its fate. Could I have done more to protect it before its sudden collapse?"[42] Those words echoed in my brain and chest. Somewhere, someone I didn't know knew my story in his own way.

I have read of owners of small, family farms dying of suicide so their families could receive a payout.

"I'd sacrifice my life so my family could keep the farm," one such farmer said of his suicidal ideation in *The New York Times*.[43]

There is grim familiarity in those words. How arrogant I was to think it couldn't happen to us for no better reason than "we're a college"? "How can a college just close?" a professor from another institution said to me after first learning of Saint Joe. The answer to that as we've seen by now is, "all too easily." Despite all its know-how, higher education is afforded no special immunity to the forces of change, just as others are not. For example, I am terrified of the effects of climate change, and I believe it is imperative we change how we, among other activities, generate energy. At the same time, what will that do to coal mining communities? Where will a 50-year-old coal miner and their family go after their mine is shut down? What happens to people who get cast aside in order for others to move forward? Those on the receiving end of change deserve a voice in what happens to them, and I hope someone smarter than me is working on this dilemma.

For it is soul-crushing to lose everything. I believe I have made that most abundantly clear by this point. I am also aware that there may be those who responded to expressions of my inner thoughts with “Get yourself together” or “Suck it up and just get a new job.” Those are both tall orders for someone with a depressed mind, as depression magnifies an already demanding task into what feels like a mission to Mars. That is why I wanted to be open and honest about what I thought. Seldom, if ever, during the final months of Saint Joe did I say what was really on my mind. Instead I got up and did what I needed to do. I say that not to beg for kudos, but for you to stop and consider who in your immediate circle might be doing the same.

So often we ascribe a moral weight to sadness. So often we set a digital timer on someone’s period of mourning, and apply a rubric to discern what really counts as “loss.” We don’t get to decide the magnitude of a loss for someone else. Likewise, we don’t get to limit how long they may grieve for the answer is invariably “however long it takes.” To paraphrase what James Baldwin wrote, my hope is that in relating all of this my suffering will be my bridge to others, and that they may know they’re not alone if they have such thoughts and there can be a way out. If, at the end of it all, you cannot relate to what I've said, then I suggest you be grateful you've never felt that way.

Similarly, many ask me if I'm still as angry as I described myself in earlier chapters. "No, thank God," I tell them. I look back at what I wrote about those weeks following February 3, 2017 and the words just feel…old. They aren't what I would write today. When one is hurt, the mind wants simple answers. The Board of Trustees vote suggested there were "good guys" and "bad guys." This was not the case as seldom is life so neatly divided into heroes and villains. Additionally, so many of our wounds were self-imposed.

We were "too loved to fail." So deep ran the love for Saint Joseph's College that so many could not conceive of a universe without it, therefore no one would ever let it vanish. We saw "deferred maintenance" as "Saint Joe charm." We saw the successes and the unique academic depth of the Core program, but through a sort of survivorship bias, we did not see the ways it created severe marketplace challenges. We reveled in the common bond of the College…while it all rotted out beneath us.

Despite these realizations, anger still does percolate at times.

When someone affiliated with the husk that's left of Saint Joe still insists on calling what happened "a suspension of operations," it stokes a white-hot glow in my gut once more. Those who most utter the saying seem to have a rudimentary knowledge of Foucault, and of language as a system of control over meaning and control over others. "If we present it this way and say it enough times, then it will become reality, and it will shape exactly how others should think of us."

The reality is that for every student and professor, Saint Joseph's College *closed.* It closed with all of the weight and resonance of a reinforced steel door slamming shut. Saint Joe is closed to us and we can never go back to what we had. That may be why the anger surfaces at certain times of the year, such as February and May, and focuses on select individuals who played roles not in just the fiduciary oversight of Saint Joe, but much more so in the manipulations that occurred in the murky shadows following the announcement.

"After such knowledge, what forgiveness?"

I deal with those thoughts by reminding myself I'm not an especially good person. I am as broken and unclean as anyone else. Throughout my life I have failed. I have hurt others either with intent or out of sheer thoughtless neglect. Whatever good I have done is not enough to make up for these acts, and instead I am reliant upon mercy and grace to be truly forgiven. If I wish to receive those gifts, then I must be willing to extend them to others.

And I'm trying. I'm trying real hard.

Last of all, I learned a hard lesson about the nature of human existence. I think my brother Michael put it best: "Life is just one tornado touching down after another." Loss is a constant. A little over one year after I began my new faculty position and life came back together again, we lost our sweet Butterscotch. At age 14 and a half, her little arthritis-racked body and her dementia-addled brain could no longer contain her bright and loving spirit. There was nothing I could do to stop what happened. Six months later, Chewie died of bladder cancer at age 15. His daily explosion of life, smiley vibrance, and heavy metal energy, turned to a limping and languid existence. Again, there was nothing I could do to stop the losses. On a long enough timeline, everything comes apart and all chances of survivability drop to zero. All anyone can control in the face of despair is how they show up and give love to those in need. I hope that is what I did at the end of Saint Joe.

For in a way, I was lucky. I got to be there at the end. How fitting that the tiny child in the arms of his grandmother in front of the Saint Joe reflecting pond so many years ago would also be one of the last out when the place closed? Where else, really, would I have wanted to be? I could be there for my parents, I could stand shoulder to shoulder with wonderful faculty to help support them and share in their fate, and I could let my students know that whatever darkness they were in at the time, they were never in it alone, for I was with them. In doing so, I gained a unique form of friendship hitherto unknown to me.

It's the kind of bond where despite…or perhaps because…of everything we went through, we're always laughing when we reunite. The same jokes come back, the same fun stories are retold, and we now meld them with accounts of what we've accomplished since. Though once knocked to the ground and kicked in the gut by faceless men with hands wrung, we still stand.

I think that might be called "survival."

We remain there for each other to this day. Later I would learn of the Iranian festival of Yalda, which takes place on the winter solstice. "It is a beautiful way of assuring you that you have lived through long nights before," Omid Safi, professor of Iranian studies at Duke University said to the *New York Times*. "It is precisely at the point that the night is longest and darkest that you've actually turned a corner."[44] I very much appreciate that sentiment. My hope is that the student and faculty survivors of Saint Joseph's College go on reminding one another, as needed, that we have indeed lived through long nights before.

My parents still live in Rensselaer. Of course, I go visit them sometimes. The green, directional signs for Saint Joseph's College are gone from I-65 now, but the "HELL IS REAL" billboard is still there facing southbound traffic outside of Hebron. Whenever I see it I make the same placid remark.

"Yes. I know."

NOTES

1. Gerlach 5-6
2. "Eastern Puma Officially Declared Extinct, Taken Off Endangered Species List."
3. Goodstein and Otterman
4. Kozlowski
5. Einhorn
6. KFOR Digital Desk
7. "Marylhurst Board of Trustees Votes to Close University by End of 2018"
8. Manning
9. Krantz
10. Flaherty, "Collateral Damage"
11. Kelderman and Bauman
12. "Expert predicts 25% of colleges will fail in the next 20 years"
13. Zemsky, et al.

14. Whitford, "A Checklist for Colleges That Must Close" and "Background on College Closures"
15. "IHEP Analysis Finds the Majority of State Flagship Universities Fall Short of Their"
16. "Expert predicts 25% of colleges will fail in the next 20 years"
17. Korn, et al.
18. Whitford, "How Much Did Coronavirus Disruptions Affect 2 Closing Colleges?"
19. Jesse
20. Ibid.
21. Dix
22. Ibid.
23. I interviewed Dr. Aaron Lawler on May 28th, 2021. Notes in author's possession.
24. Smith, Christian
25. Ibid.
26. Brown
27. I Interviewed Tim Pedrotty on March 7th, 2018. Notes in author's possession.
28. "Upside-Down Curriculum"
29. "Core Curriculum"
30. Fried and Kramer
31. Ibid.
32. "Marian University and Ancilla College Announce Strategic Partnership"
33. Flaherty, "Alumni Blitz for the Liberal Arts"
34. Hewitt
35. I interviewed Greg Whaley on May 24th, 2017. Notes in author's possession.
36. I interviewed Brienne Hooker on April 8th. Notes in author's possession.
37. Tomlinson
38. "Indiana's 'most Endangered' landmark list released"
39. I interviewed Alexis Skinner on February 4th, 2021. Notes in author's possession
40. I interviewed Katie Albanese on February 4th, 2021. Notes in author's possession.
41. Copy of lawsuit in author's possession.
42. Agueros
43. Kilgannon
44. Dias

Works Cited

"A Statement from St. Joseph's College (Rensselaer, IN) Alumni: We Demand Transparency after Board Votes to Close Campus." Saint Joseph's College Alumni press release, 9 Feb. 2017 https://www.prnewswire.com/news-releases/a-statement-from-st- josephs-college-rensselaer-in-alumni-we-demand-transparency-after- board-votes-to-close-campus-300404972.html Accessed 23 Dec. 2019

"A View from the Windmill." Farm First, LLC. Dec. 2017. https://static1.squarespace.com/static/54a2cd22e4b037c1971b0427/t/5 a43ce4b24a694671fe1bd13/1514393171706/Fourth+Quarter+Newsletter.pdf . Accessed 08 Oct. 2020

Abourezk, Kevin. "Dana College in Blair to Close." *Lincoln Journal Star*, 30 June 2010. http://journalstar.com/news/state-and-regional/nebraska/dana-college-in-blair-to-close/article_d83eb3e0- 847b-11df-9040-001cc4c03286.html. Accessed 23 Apr. 2019.

Albanese, Katie. Facebook Messenger interview. Received by Jonathan Nichols. 04 Feb. 2021.

Agueros, Marcel. "The Arecibo Observatory Was Like Family. I Couldn't Save It." *Wired*. 05 May 2021. https://www.wired.com/story/arecibo- observatory-family-collapse/ Accessed 26 May 2021.

Aqua v. Pelican Group Consulting, Inc. et al.

"Antioch College Alumni Association Creates Framework for Plan to Open an Independent Antioch College with Support from Antioch University Board of Trustees," Great Lakes Colleges Association press release, https://web.archive.org/web/20081029120753/http://intranet.glca.org/F CKeditor/UserFiles/File/Antioch%20final.pdf Accessed 23 Dec. 2019.

Ashbrook, John. "Interview request". Received by Jonathan Nichols. 10 Aug. 2017.

"Background on College Closures." *New America*. n.d. https://www.newamerica.org/education-policy/reports/anticipating-and-managing-precipitous-college- closures/background-on- college-closures/. Accessed 08 Oct. 2020.

Bangert, Dave "Bangert: After St. Joe's: Where are they now?" Lafayette Journal & Courier, 1 Sept. 2017. https://www.jconline.com/story/opinion/columnists/dave-bangert/2017/09/01/bangert-st-joes-liquidation-where-they- now/618683001/. Accessed 27 Dec. 2019.

--- "Bangert: Saint Joseph's closing no surprise?" *Lafayette Journal & Courier*, 10 Feb. 2017 https://www.jconline.com/story/opinion/columnists/dave-bangert/2017/02/10/bangert-saint-josephs-closing-no-surprise/97709458/ Accessed 26 Dec. 2019.

--- "Bangert: Shuttered St. Joseph's College apologizes selling hall fame plaques." *Lafayette Journal & Courier*, 12 Oct. 2017. https://www.jconline.com/story/opinion/columnists/dave-bangert/2017/10/12/bangert-shuttered-st-josephs-college-apologizes- selling-hall-fame-plaques/758771001/ Accessed 27 Dec. 2019.

Barnes, Camilla Smith. "Interview request." Received by Jonathan Nichols. 01 Aug. 2017.

Barringer, Sondra N. and Riffe, Karley A. "Not Just Figureheads: Trustees as Microfoundations of Higher Education Institutions." *Innovative Higher Education*. Jun. 2018, Vol 43 Issue 3, pp.155-170.

Bechman, David. "Interview request." Received by Jonathan Nichols. 18 Jun. 2020.

Bennett, William J. "To Reclaim a Legacy: A Report on the Humanities in Higher Education." National Endowment for the Humanities, Nov. 1984. https://files.eric.ed.gov/fulltext/ED247880.pdf. Accessed 09 Oct. 2020.

Bidwell, Allie. "Two Private Liberal Arts Colleges Will Shut Down." *U.S. News and World Report*, 3 March 2015, www.usnews.com/news/articles/2015/03/03/declining-enrollments-financial-pressure-force-two-liberal-arts-colleges-to-close. Accessed 23 Apr. 2019.

Blackford, Linda. "St. Catharine College closing because of financial challenges." *Lexington Herald Leader*, 3 June 2016, www.kentucky.com/news/local/education/article81098527.html. Accessed 23 Apr. 2019.

Booth, Olivia and Bolger, Timothy. "Dowling College Abruptly Closing, Sparking Sadness, Anger." *Long Island Press*, 3 June 2010, www.longislandpress.com/2016/06/03/dowling-college-abruptly- closing-sparking-sadness-anger/. Accessed 23 Apr. 2019.

Brachear, Manya A. "George looking to Wall Street to shore up archdiocese finances." *Chicago Tribune*, 29 Jan. 2012. https://www.chicagotribune.com/news/ct-xpm-2012-01-29-ct- met-archdiocese-finances-20120129-story.html. Accessed 1 Feb. 2020.

Bradway, Jackie. Personal interview. 18 May. 2018.

Brown, Sarah. "A Veteran College President Calls on Colleges to Stop the Snobbery." *The Chronicle of Higher Education*, 12 Aug. 2018. https://www.chronicle.com/article/a- veteran-president-calls-on- colleges-to-stop-the-snobbery/. Accessed 09 Oct. 2020

"Bureau of Study Counsel Founder Dies." *The Harvard Crimson*, 28 Jan. 1998, https://www.thecrimson.com/article/1998/1/28/bureau-of-study-counsel-founder-dies/. Accessed 24 Apr. 2019.

Carlson, Justin. Personal interview. 6 July 2017.

Carlson, Scott. "A House Divided." *The Chronicle of Higher Education*, 7 Jun. 2007. https://www.chronicle.com/article/A-House-Divided/2991. Accessed 23 Dec. 2019.

Capouch, Brian. Personal interview. 4 Apr 2017.

Chiddister, Diane. "Faculty vote determines 'no confidence' in Murdock." *Yellow Springs News*, 6 Sept. 2007. https://ysnews.com/old/stories/2007/09/090607_noconfidence.html Accessed 23 Dec. 2019.

--- "Mix of big dreams, hard reality." *Yellow Springs News*, 28 Jun. 2012. https://ysnews.com/news/2012/06/mix-of-big-dreams-hard- reality#comment-5130 Accessed 23 Dec. 2019.

Chronis, Kasey. "Parents of Saint Joseph's College students speak out." WNDU, 10 Feb. 2017. https://www.wndu.com/content/news/Parents- of-Saint-Josephs-College-students-speaking-out--413415973.html. Accessed 26 Dec. 2019.

Commonwealth of Virginia v. Sweet Briar Institute, Paul G. Rice, and James F. Jones Jr. Case number 15009373. Filed in Circuit Court of Amherst County, Virginia, 30 Mar. 2015. Accessed 23 Apr. 2019.

Conway, Daniel. "Revitalizing Catholic Schools." *The Criterion*, Archdiocese of Indianapolis, 10 Feb. 2012, https://www.archindy.org/criterion/local/2012/02-10/editorial.html Accessed 1 Feb. 2020

"Core Curriculum." Champlain College, n.d. https://www.champlain.edu/academics/undergraduate-academics/core- curriculum. Accessed 09 Oct. 2020.

Cowen, Scott. "Want to Be a Really Effective Trustee?" *Higher Education Today*. 11 Jul. 2018. https://www.higheredtoday.org/2018/07/11/want-really-effective- trustee/. Accessed 07 Oct. 2020.

Davich, Jerry. "Soft-Spoken Couple, Farmhand for the Lord behind Soul- Saving Sign." *Chicago Tribune*, 26 Sep. 2015, https://www.chicagotribune.com/suburbs/post-tribune/opinion/ct- ptb-davich-hell-is-real-sign-st-0927-20150925-story.html. Accessed 23 Apr. 2019.

Dias, Elizabeth. "How We Survive Winter." *New York Times*, 20 Dec. 2020, https://www.nytimes.com/interactive/2020/12/20/us/how-to-survive-winter.html. Accessed 03 Feb. 2021.

Didion, Joan. *The Year of Magical Thinking*. Knopf, 2005.

DiMento, Maria. "No. 13: Juanita Kious Waugh." *The Chronicle of Philanthropy*, 6 Feb. 2011, https://www.philanthropy.com/article/No- 13-Juanita-Kious-Waugh/159143. Accessed 24 Apr. 2019.

Dimitrova, Anelia K. "Sponseller: Lessons learned from SJC—Face the facts and figures." *Rensselaer Republican*, 02 Mar. 2017.

Dimitrova, Anelia K. and Sievers, Caitlin. "St. Joe, RNI mull potential partnership." *Rensselaer Republican*, 20 Mar.

2017. http://www.newsbug.info/rensselaer_republican/st-joe-rni- mull- potential-partnership/article_a53d6d5a-0dd7-11e7-ba21- ebc229b5f98f.html. Accessed 26 Dec. 2019.

Dix, Willard. "It's Time To Worry When Colleges Erase Humanities Departments." Forbes, 13 Mar. 2018. https://www.forbes.com/sites/willarddix/2018/03/13/its-time-to-worry-when- colleges-erase-humanities-departments/#4092c072461a. 09 Accessed Oct. 2020.

Dixon-Fitzwater, Janice. "Dr. F. Dennis Riegelnegg Resigns From SJC." *Northwest Indiana Business Magazine*. 05 Jun. 2014. https://nwindianabusiness.com/community/business-news-bits/dr-f-dennis-riegelnegg-resigns-sjc/. Accessed 08 Oct. 2020.

Donahue, Bill. "Can Antioch College Return From the Dead Again?" *New York Times*, 16 Sept. 2011, https://www.nytimes.com/2011/09/18/magazine/can-antioch-college- return-from-the-dead-again.html. Accessed 23 Apr. 2019.

Douglas-Gabriel, Danielle. "The Catholic college that claimed the Education Dept. pushed it to the brink of closing — is closing." *Washington Post*, 1 June 2016.

"Eastern Puma Officially Declared Extinct, Taken Off Endangered Species List." Center for Biological Diversity, 22 Jan. 2018. https://www.biologicaldiversity.org/news/press_releases/2018/eastern- puma-01-22-2018.php. Accessed 6 Oct. 2020.

Editorial Board. "Our view: Sweet Briar board should resign." *The Roanoke Times*, 14 Mar. 2015, www.roanoke.com/opinion/editorials/our-view- sweet-briar-board-should-resign/article_e4b317e4-200a-5081-b41f-4139f5e3969a.html#facebook-comments. Accessed 23 Apr. 2019.

Einhorn, Erin. "Getting a college degree was their dream. Then their school suddenly closed for good." NBC News. 04 Aug. 2020. https://www.nbcnews.com/news/education/getting-college-degree- was-their-dream-then-their-school-suddenly-n1235512. Accessed 08 Oct. 2020.

Electron. "Electron/Electron." GitHub, 23 Apr. 2019, github.com/electron/electron. Accessed 23 April 2019.

Ely, Bert. "Farm Credit Watch: CoBank Does Big Financing Deals With AT&T, U.S. Cellular." *Reform Farm Credit*. n.d. http://reformfarmcredit.org/farm-credit-watch-shedding-light-on- americas-least-known-gse-2/. Accessed 08 Oct. 2020.

"Expert predicts 25% of colleges will fail in the next 20 years." *CBS News This Morning*. 31 Aug. 2019. https://www.youtube.com/watch?v=joTFddr3wFk&feature=youtu.be. Accessed 08 Oct. 2020.

Ferrette, Canidce and Schwartz, David M. "Dowling Grants Last Degrees, Loses Accreditation Wednesday." *Newsday*, 31 Aug. 2016, https://www.newsday.com/long-island/education/dowling-grants-last-degrees-loses-accreditation-wednesday-1.12244873?pts=453198 Accessed 17 Dec. 2019

Field, Kelly. "Senators Vow to Crack Down on 'Bad Actors' in the For-Profit Sector." *The Chronicle of Higher Education*, 24 Jun. 2010, https://www.chronicle.com/article/senators-vow-to-crack-down- on/66058 Accessed 17 Dec. 2019.

Flaherty, Colleen. "Alumni Blitz for the Liberal Arts." *Inside Higher Ed*, 22 Sep. 2020. https://www.insidehighered.com/news/2020/09/22/when-adrian-college-threatened-cut-history-and-more-alumni-organized?utm_source=Inside+Higher+Ed&utm_campaign=cfaf6f79e 8DNU_2020_COPY_02&utm_medium=email&utm_term=0_1fcbc04 421-cfaf6f79e8 223160837&mc_cid=cfaf6f79e8&mc_eid=20b4c56f24. Accessed 09 Oct. 2020.

--- "Collateral Damage." *Inside Higher Ed*. 23 Apr. 2018. ______https://www.insidehighered.com/news/2018/04/23/when-college-goes- under-everyone-suffers-mount-idas-faculty-feels-particular- sense?utm_source=Inside+Higher+Ed&utm_campaign=e 057cf8bf5- DNU20180111&utm_medium=email&utm_term=0_1fcb c04421- e057cf8bf5- 223160837&mc_cid=e057cf8bf5&mc_eid=20b4c56f24. Accessed 08 Oct. 2020.

"Food services company sues closed St. Joseph's College." *Chicago Tribune*, 02 Aug. 2018. https://www.chicagotribune.com/suburbs/post-tribune/ct-ptb-st-joe-college-sued-st-0803-story.html. Accessed 26 Dec. 2019.

"Founder – Missionaries of the Precious Blood." Missionaries of the Precious Blood, cpps-23 April 2019.preciousblood.org/about/founder/. Accessed 23 Apr. 2019.

Fried, Robert L. and Kramer, Eli O. "A Rescue Plan for America's Small Colleges." *Inside Higher Ed.* 21 Jan. 2020, https://www.insidehighered.com/views/2020/01/21/rescue-plan- america%E2%80%99s-small-colleges-and-perhaps-our-democracy- well-opinion Accessed 15 Mar. 2021.

Friedenberger, Amy. "Sweet Briar College faculty passes resolution opposing closure." *The Roanoke Times*, 16 Mar. 2015, https://www.roanoke.com/news/education/higher_education/sweet- briar-college-faculty-passes-resolution-opposing-closure/article_dec8426a-e75e-585a-970f-aabc0fc96774.html#.VQevtoUC-fI.twitter. Accessed 17 Dec. 2019.

Fuoco, Linda Wilson. "Ohio college approves Mark Roosevelt as its new leader." *Pittsburgh Post-Gazette*, 17 Oct. 2010. http://old.post- gazette.com/pg/10290/1096061-100.stm#ixzz12eJLf75N Accessed 23 Dec. 2019.

Gerlach, Dominic B. *Saint Joseph's College Rensselaer, Indiana: A Centennial Pictorial History from Its Beginnings to 1990*. 1990.

Gibbs, Jessica. "News revives painful memories for those connected to Dana College." *Pilot-Tribune and Enterprise*, 22 Mar. 2016. http://www.enterprisepub.com/news/local_news/news-revives-painful- memories-for- those-connected-to-dana-college/article_930e404a- efac-11e5-8f76-d7be9881ea71.html Accessed 17 Dec. 2019.

Goodsetin, Laurie and Otterman, Sharon. "Catholic Priests Abused 1,000 Children in Pennsylvania, Report Says." *The New York Times*, 14 Aug. 2018.

https://www.nytimes.com/2018/08/14/us/catholic-church-sex-abuse-pennsylvania.html. Accessed 6 Oct. 2020.

Gore, Sherese. "The enslaved founders: Letters from 1800s reveal life on 'Sweetbrier' plantation." *The News & Advance*, 08 Apr. 2015. https://www.newsadvance.com/new_era_progress/news/the-enslaved- founders-letters-from-s-reveal-life-on-sweetbrier/article_f675b944- de21-11e4-b1ef-23f622d62746.html. Accessed 17 Dec. 2019.

Gottlieb, Daniel. "Why close this college? Sweet Briar was in better- than-average financial shape." *The Washington Post*, 29 May. 2015. https://www.washingtonpost.com/news/grade-point/wp/2015/05/29/why-close-this- college-sweet-briar-was-in-better-than-average-financial-shape/. Accessed 17 Dec. 2019.

Groppe, John. Personal interview. 10 Mar. 2018.

--- "SJC: A History of Subsidies." *The Observer*, 23 Feb. 2017.

Gull, Anne. Personal interview. Apr. 2017.

Habrowski, Ed. "Interview request." Received by Jonathan Nichols. 03 Jul. 2020.

Hays, Justin. Personal interview. 20 Mar. 2017.

Hemmelgarn, Larry. "A Full Day's Work." *C.PP.S. Today*. Summer 2009, https://www.scribd.com/document/28171704/CPPS-Today- Summer09. Accessed 24 Apr. 2019.

Heinrich, Milt. Phone interview. 30 July 2017.

"Here's How Much You'll Pay to Attend Sweet Briar College." US News and World Report. https://www.usnews.com/best-colleges/sweet-briar- college-3742/paying Accessed 17 Dec. 2019.

Hewitt, Elizabeth. "The other victims when colleges decline or close: their hometowns." *The Hechinger Report*, 12 Feb. 2019. https://hechingerreport.org/the-other-victims-when-colleges-decline- or-close-their-hometowns/. Accessed 09 Oct. 2020.

"History." Sweet Briar College. 2019. http://sbc.edu/about/history/ Accessed 17 Dec. 2019.

Holden, Meghan. "Campaign to save St. Joe's raises $2.5M." *Lafayette Journal & Courier*, 3 Apr. 2017. https://www.jconline.com/story/news/college/2017/04/03/alumni- campaign-save-st-joes-raises-25m/99872848/. Accessed 26 Dec. 2019.

--- "Can Saint Joseph's College keep its accreditation?" *Lafayette Journal & Courier*, 17 Feb. 2017. URL Accessed 26 Dec. 2019.

--- "The fall and rise of a college." *Lafayette Journal & Courier*, 14 Apr. 2017. https://www.jconline.com/story/news/college/2017/04/14/fall-and-rise-college/99968338/ Accessed 23 Dec. 2019.

--- "Memorabilia, cars for sale at St. Joe's asset sale." *Lafayette Journal & Courier*, 11 Aug. 2017. https://www.jconline.com/story/news/local/2017/08/11/st-josephs- college-selling-its-assets/556103001/. Accessed 27, Dec. 2019.

--- "Rokita stays silent about role on St. Joe's Board." *Lafayette Journal & Courier*, 2 Mar. 2017.

--- "Saint Joseph's College leaders discuss school's fate." *Lafayette Journal & Courier*, 2 Feb. 2017, https://www.jconline.com/story/news/college/2017/02/02/saint- josephs-college-leaders-discuss-schools-fate/97396076/. Accessed 25 Apr. 2019.

--- "St. Joseph's holds a tearful final graduation." *Lafayette Journal & Courier*, 6 May 2017, https://www.jconline.com/story/news/college/2017/05/06/st-josephs- holds-its-final-graduation/101025902/. Accessed 27 Dec. 2019.

Huckabee, Charles. "Dana College Announces It Will Close, Blaming Accreditor's Decision Against New Owners." *The Chronicle of Higher Education*, 01 Jul. 2010. https://www.chronicle.com/article/Dana- College-Announces-It-Will/66110 Accessed 17 Dec. 2019.

Hooker, Brienne. Zoom interview. 08 Apr. 2021.

Hulbert, Steve. Phone interview. 24 Apr. 2019.

"IHEP Analysis Finds the Majority of State Flagship Universities Fall Short of Their Promise of an Affordable Education for Students." Institute for Higher Education Policy. Sept. 2019.

http://www.ihep.org/press/news-releases/ihep-analysis-finds-majority- state-flagship- universities-fall-short-their. Accessed 09 Oct. 2020

Indiana Election Results. 08 Nov. 2016. indianaenr.blob.core.usgovcloudapi.net/archive/2016General/index.html#%20https://www.in.gov/sos/elections/2400.htm. Accessed 24 Apr. 2019.

"Indiana's 'most Endangered' landmark list released." *South Bend Tribune*, 30 Apr. 2018. https://www.southbendtribune.com/news/local/indiana-landmarks-releases-most-endangered-list-for/article_790e6194-54a3- 5264-9b1d-fd903c4fd397.html. Accessed 09 Oct. 2020.

Jahn, Mike. "A Troubled Landmark Reborn." *The New York Times*, 20 Nov. 1977. https://www.nytimes.com/1977/11/20/archives/long-island-weekly-a-troubled-landmark- reborn-a-landmarks-past.html. Accessed 26 Nov. 2019.

Jesse, David. "Michigan's small liberal arts colleges are in fight for survival." *The Detroit Free Press*, 11 Feb. 2021. https://www.freep.com/in-depth/news/education/2021/02/11/michigan-liberal-arts-college- tuition-discount/6310395002/. Accessed 11 Feb. 2021.

Kauffman, Steve. "Interview request." Received by Jonathan Nichols. 8 Aug. 2017.

Kay, Jeanne. "Editorial." *The Record*. 25 Oct. 2007. https://recordonline.org/wp-content/uploads/2007/10/record-vol63- issue10-10-26-07.pdf Accessed 23 Dec. 2019.

---"Nonstop." Received by Jonathan Nichols. 28 Sep. 2017.

--- E-mail interview. 28 Sep. 2017.

Kapsidelis, Karin. "Sweet Briar College's decision to close stuns students." *The Richmond Times-Dispatch*, 03 Mar. 2015. https://www.richmond.com/news/virginia/article_105c880d-25d1- 5305-be18-8d5f08c50776.html. Accessed 17 Dec. 2019.

Kean, Thomas H. et al. "The 9/11 Commission Report." National Commission on Terrorist Attacks Upon the United States, 22 Jul. 2004. https://www.9-11commission.gov/report/911Report.pdf. Accessed 09 Oct. 2020.

Kelderman, Eric and Bauman, Dan. "Cincinnati Christian U. Will Shut Its Doors." *Chronicle of Higher Education*. 28 Oct. 2019. https://www.chronicle.com/article/cincinnati-christian-u-will- shut-its-doors/#:~:text=Cincinnati%20Christian%20U.%2C%20besieged%20b y,end%20of%20th-e%20fall%20semester. Accessed 08 Oct. 2020.

Kenley, Casey. "A Eulogy for Saint Joseph's College." *Indianapolis Magazine*, 21 Jul. 2017, https://www.indianapolismonthly.com/lifestyle/travel/eulogy-st- josephs-college Accessed 06 Jun. 2020

"Kentucky's St. Catharine College warns in lawsuit it is at 'brink of extinction'." WDRB, 22 Feb. 2016. https://www.wdrb.com/news/education/kentucky-s-st-catharine- college-warns-in-lawsuit-it-is/article_da8ed3eb-16f3-5035-b931- 4b81aab87dd3.html Accessed 17 Dec. 2019.

KFOR Digital Desk. "St. Gregory's University suspending operations at end of semester." KFOR. 08 Nov. 2017.https://kfor.com/news/st- gregorys-university-suspending-operations-at-end-of-semester/. Accessed 08 Oct. 2020.

Kilgannon, Corey. "When the Death of a Family Farm Leads to Suicide." *The New York Times*, 19 Mar. 2018. https://www.nytimes.com/2018/03/19/nyregion/farmer-suicides-mark-tough-times-for-new-york-dairy-industry.html. 09 Oct. 2020.

"Kline, Rokita Statements on Student Success Act." *Committee on Education, Labor Republicans*. 27 Feb. 2015. https://republicans-edlabor.house.gov/news/documentsingle.aspx?DocumentID=398499. Accessed 08 Oct. 2020.

Korn, Melissa, et al. "Coronavirus Pushes Colleges to the Breaking Point, Forcing 'Hard Choices' About

Education." *The Wall Street Journal.* 30 Apr. 2020. https://www.wsj.com/articles/coronavirus-pushes-colleges-to-the-breaking-point-forcing-hard-choices-about-education-11588256157?shareToken=st41736fd507904955a7b2cd8b9be9ea01&reflink=share_mobilewebshare. 09 Oct. 2020

Kozlowski, Kim. "Marygrove College halting undergrad programs." *The Detroit News*, 09 Aug. 2017. https://www.detroitnews.com/story/news/local/detroit-city/2017/08/09/marygrove-college-stops-undergraduate-programs/104433912/. Accessed 6 Oct. 2020.

Krantz, Laura. "Baker criticizes Mount Ida leadership after college's sudden closure." *The Boston Globe*. 10 Apr. 2018. https://www.bostonglobe.com/metro/2018/04/10/baker-criticizes-mount-ida-leadership/Gak7qGQae5mZ2Nes62KuGM/story.html. Accessed 08 Oct. 2020.

Laudick, Larry. Phone interview. 14 Jul. 2020.

Lawler, Aaron. Personal interview.

Legon, Richard, et al. "Leading the University: The Roles of Trustees, Presidents, and Faculty." *Change*. Jan/Feb 2013, Vol. 45, Issue 1, p24- 32.

Leising, Jordan. Personal interview. 28 Mar. 2017.

"Lenny Bruce - The Meaning Of Obscenity." YouTube, 15 Feb. 2010, www.youtube.com/watch?v=gDkoCtMOFOg. Accessed 24 Apr. 2019

MacGregor, Carol Ann. "Why the Decline of Catholic Schools Matters." Scholars Strategy Network, 1 Mar. 2013, scholars.org/brief/why-decline-catholic-schools-matters. Accessed 24 Apr. 2019.

Maidenberg, Tony. "Interview request." Received by Jonathan Nichols on 18 Jun. 2020.

Maienbrook, Terra. "Some claims to assess." Received by Jonathan Nichols on 06 Nov. 2018.

Manning, Rob. "Marylhurst Faculty Challenge Decision To Close University." OPB. 18 May 2018. https://www.opb.org/news/article/marylhurst-university-close-faculty-challenge-board-letter/. Accessed 08 Oct. 2020.

Marcus, Jon. "Once invisible, college boards of trustees are suddenly in the spotlight." *The Hechinger Report*, 30 Apr. 2015, https://www.hechingerreport.org/once-invisible-college-boards-of- trustees-are-suddenly-in-the-spotlight/. Accessed 24 Apr. 2019.

"Marian University and Ancilla College Announce Strategic Partnership." Marian University, 28 Aug. 2020. https://www.marian.edu/newsroom/newsitem/2020/08/28 /marian- university-and-ancilla-college-announce-strategic-partnership. Accessed 09 Oct. 2020.

"Marietta College VP named President at Indiana college." Marietta College. 29 Jan. 2015. https://www.marietta.edu/article/marietta-college-vp-named-president-indiana-college. Accessed 08 Oct. 2020.

Martin, Jerry L. "Trustees: Allies in Academic Integrity." *Academic Questions*. Winter 2003/2004, Issue 1, pp. 79-82.

"Marylhurst Board of Trustees Votes to Close University by End of 2018." Marylhurst University. May 2018. https://www.marylhurst.edu/closure/. Accessed 08 Oct. 2020.

McGowan, Dan. "Saint Joseph's College: Situation 'Dire'." *Inside Indiana Business with Gerry Dick*, 27 Jan. 2017, www.insideindianabusiness.com/story/34362160/saint-josephs- college-situation-dire. Accessed 24 Apr. 2019.

McKenna, Laura. "The Unfortunate Fate of Sweet Briar's Professors." *The Atlantic*, 10 Mar. 2015. https://www.theatlantic.com/education/archive/2015/03/t he- unfortunate-fate-of-sweet-briars-professors/387376/. Accessed 17 Dec. 2019.

Melville, Herman. *Moby-Dick*. Fall River Press, 2015.

"Mission and Vision." *Antioch College*. antiochcollege.edu/about/mission- and-vision. Accessed 24 Apr. 2019.

"Mission and Vision." *Dana College*, web.archive.org/web/20090106063837/http://www.dana. edu/about/mi ssion/. Accessed 24 Apr. 2019.

Monforton, Doug. Personal interview. Numerous dates starting 21 Apr. 2018 through 2020.

Muller, Paul. Personal interview. 21 Apr. 2018.

Mytelka, Andrew. "Antioch College Will Close Its Main Campus." *The Chronicle of Higher Education*, 12 June 2007, www.chronicle.com/article/Antioch-College-Will-Close-Its/39028. Accessed 23 Apr. 2019.

Nestor, Mark. "Lessons Learned—Lost Opportunities." *Rensselaer Republican*. Apr. 2017.

--- Personal interview. Numerous dates beginning in September 2017 through 2022.

Neville, Bob. Personal interview. Numerous dates beginning in September 2017 through 2022.

O'Meara Ferguson Whelan and Conway. "O'Meara Ferguson Releases Groundbreaking Analysis of Catholic Education." *Cision PRNewswire Press Release*, 17 Jan. 2012. https://www.prnewswire.com/news- releases/omeara-ferguson-releases-groundbreaking-analysis-of- catholic-education-137510138.html. Accessed 2 Feb. 2020.

Pastoor, Robert. "Presidential Discourse." Received by Jonathan Nichols. 25 Jan. 2017.

Potter, George E., and Phelan, Daniel J. "Governance over the Years: A trustee's perspective." *New Directions for Community Colleges*. Spring 2008. Vol. 2008 Issue 141. pp 15-24.

Pounds, Jessie. "Judge issues 60-day injunction against using solicited funds to close Sweet Briar." The News & Advance, 15 Apr. 2015. https://www.newsadvance.com/news/local/judge-issues--day- injunction-against-using-solicited-funds-to/article_ec0d0506-e3b3- 11e4-8230-6b1ac07a1906.html Accessed 17 Dec. 2019.

--- "Students, parents join with alumnae on Sweet Briar College legal action." *News & Advance*, 22 Apr. 2015, www.newsadvance.com/new_era_progress/news/students - parents- join-with-alumnae-on-sweet-briar-legal-action/article_29cde2b0-e7bb- 11e4-9993-43b5849e30ef.html. Accessed 23 Apr. 2019.

---"Sweet Briar faculty file complaint seeking more than $40 million in damages." *The News & Advance*, 24 Apr. 2015. https://www.newsadvance.com/news/local/sweet-briar-faculty- file-complaint-seeing-more-than-million-in/article_21799a78-eacc- 11e4-a8f8-0fae364fcdf6.html?mode=jqm. Accessed 17 Dec. 2019.

---"Transfer of power complete at Sweet Briar College." *The Roanoke Times*, 02 Jul. 2015. https://www.roanoke.com/news/education/higher_education/transfer- of-power-complete-at-sweet-briar-college/article_bf55f125-f8c3-532f- 9793-4c7ad2a88f5a.html Accessed 17 Dec. 2019.

Pounds, Jessica and Petska, Alicia. "Faculty of Sweet Briar College votes no confidence in board, president." *The News & Advance*, 30 Mar. 2015. https://www.newsadvance.com/news/local/faculty-of-sweet-briar- college-votes-no-confidence-in-board/article_8809eddc-d74a-11e4- 844a-a39cfb5fbb71.html. Accessed 17 Dec. 2019.

Puzzanghera, Jim and White, Ronald D. "Closing of ITT Tech and other for- profit schools leaves thousands of students in limbo." *Los Angeles Times*. 12 Sept. 2016, www.latimes.com/business/la-fi-for-profit- schools-20160912-snap-story.html. Accessed 23 Apr. 2019.

"Obituary." Legacy.com. https://www.legacy.com/obituaries/thehj-info/obituary.aspx?n=juanita- waugh&pid=139547111. Accessed 08 Oct. 2020. Juanita Waugh, died 06 Feb. 2010.

"Our view: Sweet Briar board should resign." *The Roanoke Times*, 14 Mar. 2015. https://www.roanoke.com/opinion/editorials/our-view-sweet-briar-board-should-resign/article_e4b317e4-200a-5081-b41f- 4139f5e3969a.html#facebook-comments. Accessed 17 Dec. 2019.

Outka, Elizabeth. "How Pandemics Seep into Literature." *The Paris Review*. 08 Apr. 2020. https://www.theparisreview.org/blog/2020/04/08/how-pandemics-seep-into-literature/. Accessed 08 Oct. 2020.

"President Jean Scott." Marietta College. n.d. https://www.marietta.edu/president-jean-scott. Accessed 08 Oct. 2020.

Rahmanian, Hassan. Phone interview. 18 July 2017.

Raymond, Chad. "Here There Is Danger." *Inside Higher Ed.* 06 Jun. 2017. https://www.insidehighered.com/views/2017/06/06/signs-institution- path-toward-unrecoverable-failure-essay#.WTjGrXn8w4d.facebook. Accessed 08 Oct. 2020.

Rivard, Ry. "Unusual Collaboration." *Inside Higher Ed*, 4 Aug. 2014. https://www.insidehighered.com/news/2014/08/04/north-dakota-university-looks-partner-and-maybe-buy-profit-consulting-firm. Accessed 1 Feb. 2020.

Robinson, Jessica. Interview by Facebook Messenger. 04 Feb. 2021.

Roebuck, Jeremy and Snyder, Susan. "Some Penn State trustees again questioning Sandusky payouts." *The Philadelphia Inquirer.* 14 Jul. 2016. https://www.inquirer.com/philly/news/20160715_Some_Penn_State_tr ustees_questioning_Sandusky_payouts.html. Accessed 08 Oct. 2020.

Rohman, Katie. "Renewable Nations Institute seeks city support." *Pilot- Tribune & Enterprise*, 29 Mar. 2016. http://www.enterprisepub.com/news/local_news/renewab le-nations- institute-seeks-city-support/article_1374d788-f5f4-11e5-b62c- 43543618d511.html. Accessed 17 Dec. 2019.

Roy, Yancey and Ferrette. Candice. "Dowling College scraping by day-to- day, official says." *Newsday*, 23 May 2016, https://www.newsday.com/long-island/suffolk/official-debt- ridden-dowling-college-scraping-by-day-to-day-1.11832329?timestamp=1506284630197. Accessed 17 Dec. 2019

Ruff, Stephen. User Profile, www.linkedin.com/in/stephen-ruff-73332420/. Accessed 24 Apr. 2019.

"Saint Charles Center, A Beacon of Faith." Missionaries of the Precious Blood Cincinnati Province. n.d. http://cpps-preciousblood.org/where- we-serve/st-charles-center-a-beacon- of-faith/. Accessed 08 Oct. 2020.

"Saint Gaspar del Bufalo." Visions of Paradise. www.therealpresence.org/eucharst/misc/PHP/par_sgd_bu falo.pdf. Accessed 23 Apr. 2019.

Saint Joseph's College Alumni. "A Statement from St. Joseph's College (Rensselaer, IN) Alumni: We Demand Transparency after Board Votes to Close Campus." Saint Joseph's College Alumni, 09 Feb. 2017, www.prnewswire.com/news-releases/a-statement-from-st-josephs- college-rensselaer-in-alumni-we-demand-transparency-after-board- votes-to-close-campus-300404972.html. Accessed 24 Apr. 2019.

"Saint Joseph's College say financial woes led to suspension." *The Daily Herald*, 7 Feb. 2017. https://www.dailyherald.com/article/20170207/news/302079903 Accessed 23 Dec. 2019.

Sakelaris, Kris. Personal interview. 18 May 2018.

Schanzer, Olivia. "Professor Precarious." Believer, 23 Jul. 2020. https://believermag.com/logger/professor-precarious/. Accessed 09 Oct. 2020.

Selingo, Jeffrey J. "How the Great Recession Changed Higher Education Forever." *The Washington Post*. 21 Sept. 2018. https://www.washingtonpost.com/education/2018/09/21/how-great- recession-changed-higher-education-forever/ Accessed 30 Jun. 2020

Seltzer, Rick. "A Cash Crisis and Collapse." *Inside Higher Ed*, 10 Feb. 2017. https://www.insidehighered.com/news/2017/02/10/saint-josephs-plan- suspend-operations-prompts-questions-looking-ahead-and-behind. Accessed 26 Dec. 2019.

Skinner, Alexis. Facebook message interview. 04 Feb. 2021.

"Small US Colleges Feeling the Squeeze from 'Soft' Tuition Revenues." ICEF Monitor - Market Intelligence for International Student Recruitment, 19 Feb. 2016, monitor.icef.com/2015/12/small- us-colleges-feeling-the-squeeze-from-soft-tuition- revenues. Accessed 23 Apr. 2019.

Smith, Christian. "Higher Education is Drowning in BS." *The Chronicle of Higher Education*, 09 Jan. 2018. https://www.chronicle.com/article/higher-education-is-drowning-in- bs/. Accessed 09 Oct. 2020.

Smith, Cindra. ACCT Searches. 06 Jun. 2018.

--- "Assessing Board Effectiveness: Resources for Board of Trustees Self- Evaluation." *Community College League of California*. 2009. https://files.eric.ed.gov/fulltext/ED509091.pdf. Accessed 07 Oct. 2020.

Smith, Jared. Email interview. Received by Jonathan Nichols 13 Aug. 2020.

Smith, Kate. "Here's What Happens to Endowments When Colleges Close." *Bloomberg*. 6 Mar. 2017. https://www.bloomberg.com/news/articles/2017-03-06/orphan- endowments-of-dead-schools-bedevil-states-across-america. Accessed 26 Nov. 2019.

Sponseller, Benedict. "Your Book." Received by Jonathan Nichols. 22 July 2018.

--- *User Profile*, www.linkedin.com/in/benedict-sponseller-9a04757/. Accessed 24 Apr. 2019

Steinhour, Michael. Personal interview. Apr. 2017

Stratford, Michael. "U.S. Keeps Scrutiny of Risky Colleges Secret." *Inside Higher Ed*, 26 Mar. 2015. https://www.insidehighered.com/news/2015/03/26/education-dept- keeps-secret-names-colleges-found-be-risky-students-taxpayers Accessed 17 Dec. 2019.

Stephen L. Ruff Jr. | Ruff, Freud, Breems & Nelson Ltd., www.rfbnlaw.com/attorney/stephen-l-ruff-jr/. Accessed 24 Apr. 2019

"The Pelican Group." *The Official Catholic Directory*. n.d. http://digital_sample.officialcatholicdirectory.com/publication/?m=45 390&i=393206&p=18&pp=1. Accessed 08 Oct. 2020.

"The Story of Cold Dark Matter." Tate. https://www.tate.org.uk/art/artworks/parker-cold-dark-matter-an- exploded-view-t06949/story-cold-dark-matter Accessed 26 Dec. 2019.

"Sweet Briar College Faculty Salaries." Chronicle Data. https://data.chronicle.com/233718/Sweet-Briar-College/faculty- salaries/. Accessed 17 Dec. 2019.

"Todd Rokita." CongressWeb. http://www.congressweb.com/scham/voterinformation/candidateprofil

e/referredby/IN/electionid/3519/candidateid/34167/. Accessed 24 Apr. 2019.

Tomlinson, Harley. "'Black Lives Matter' rally at Jasper County Courthouse peaceful, informative." The Rensselaer Republican. 11 Jun. 2020. https://www.newsbug.info/rensselaer_republican/news/black-lives- matter-rally-at-jasper- county-courthouse-peaceful- informative/article_5d711fd9-fb43-5407-9b8e-1727fc19f4cb.html. Accessed 09 Apr. 2021.

Townsley, Michael K. *The Small College Guide to Financial Health: Beating the Odds*. National Association of College & University Business Officers Press, 2002.

Trower, Cathy and Eckle, Peter. "Damned if You Do, Damned if You Don't." *Inside Higher Ed*. 04 Mar. 2016. https://www.insidehighered.com/views/2016/03/04/challenges-and- tensions-being-board-member-difficult-times-essay. 08 Oct. 2020.

2017 NACUBO Tuition Discounting Study, National Association of College and University Business Officers, 30 Apr. 2018, https://www.nacubo.org/News/2018/4/NACUBO-Releases-the- 2017-NACUBO-Tuition-Discounting-Study Accessed 29 Jun. 2020

Turner, Chad. Personal interview. 28 Mar. 2017.

"Upside-down Curriculum." Champlain College, n.d. https://www.champlain.edu/academics/undergraduate-academics/upside-down-curriculum. Accessed 09 Oct. 2020.

van der Werf, Martin. "More Colleges are Seeing the Virtues of Merging." *The Chronicle of Higher Education*, 23 Mar. 2001, ______https://www.chronicle.com/article/More-Colleges-Are-Seeing- the/20069. Accessed 26 Nov. 2019.

---"The Death of a Small College." *The Chronicle of Higher Education*, 12 May 2000, https://www.chronicle.com/article/The-Death-of-a-Small-College/18748. Accessed 12 Jun. 2020

Vizza, Chris Morrisse. "Wake-Up Call: Professor Says Tension High As Saint Joseph's College Shutdown Looms." WBAA, 18 Apr. 2017. https://www.wbaa.org/post/wake-call-professor-says-tension-high- saint-josephs-college-shutdown-looms#stream/0. Accessed 26 Dec. 2019.

Whaley, Greg. Personal interview. 24 May 2017.

"What Do Trustees Do?" Teachers College Columbia University. 10 Mar. 2019. https://www.tc.columbia.edu/articles/2009/march/what-do-trustees-do/. 08 Oct. 2020.

Whitford, Emma. "A Checklist for Colleges That Must Close." *Inside Higher Ed*, 31 Mar. 2020. https://www.insidehighered.com/news/2020/03/31/being-honest-students-can-help-prevent-abrupt-college-closures-report-says?utm_source=Inside+Higher+Ed&utm_campaign=42108796fd-DNU_2019_COPY_02&utm_medium=email&utm_term=0_1fcbc044 21-42108796fd-223160837&mc_cid=42108796fd&mc_eid=20b4c56f24. Accessed 08 Oct. 2020.

--- "How Much Did Coronavirus Disruptions Affect 2 Closing Colleges?" *Inside Higher Ed*, 02 Apr. 2020. https://www.insidehighered.com/news/2020/04/02/two-small- colleges-winding-down-operations-coronavirus-impact-looms-over- higher-ed. 09 Oct. 2020.

White et al. v. Saint Joseph's College

Wilkins, Ron. "Faculty sues St. Joe's College." *Lafayette Journal & Courier*, 12 Apr. 2017. https://www.jconline.com/story/news/college/2017/04/12/faculty-sues- st-joes-college/100356650/. Accessed 26 Dec. 2019.

Wood, Carol. Phone interview. 24 Jun. 2020.

Woodhouse, Kelly. "Moody's Predicts College Closures to Triple by 2017." *Inside Higher Ed*, 28 Sept. 2015, www.insidehighered.com/news/2015/09/28/moodys-predicts-college- closures-triple-2017. Accessed 23 Apr. 2019.

Zemsky, Robert, et al. "Will Your College Close?" Chronicle of Higher Education. 07 Feb. 2020. https://www.chronicle.com/article/will-your-college-close/. Accessed 08 Oct. 2020.

Made in United States
Orlando, FL
30 May 2022

18312047R00409